University of London Historical Studies

XXVIII

UNIVERSITY OF LONDON HISTORICAL STUDIES

SIR HENRY VANE
THE YOUNGER

This volume is published with the help of
a grant from the late Miss Isobel Thornley's
Bequest to the University of London

SIR HENRY VANE THE YOUNGER

portrait by Lely (c.1645–50)

Sir Henry Vane
the Younger

A Study in Political and Administrative History

by

VIOLET A. ROWE

with a Foreword by
Dame Veronica Wedgwood O.M.

UNIVERSITY OF LONDON
THE ATHLONE PRESS
1970

Published by
THE ATHLONE PRESS
UNIVERSITY OF LONDON
at 2 Gower Street London WC1

Distributed by Tiptree Book Services Ltd
Tiptree, Essex

Australia and New Zealand
Melbourne University Press

U.S.A.
Oxford University Press Inc
New York

ISBN 0 485 13128 5

Printed in Great Britain by
WESTERN PRINTING SERVICES LTD
Bristol

FOREWORD

SIR HENRY VANE the younger played a vital part in the English Revolution. 'The Independents', writes Dr Rowe, 'perhaps owed their victory in the Civil War more to Vane than to any other single man except Cromwell.' She is right about this. As a Parliamentary tactician Vane was brilliant, if unscrupulous, in securing advantages for the Independents. As an administrator he did much to build up the Navy which, under the Commonwealth, astounded Europe by successfully challenging the Dutch. Although he had refused, for private reasons, to take any part in the trial of Charles I he was executed soon after the Restoration because he was regarded as too dangerous to live.

Yet his part in the seventeenth-century crisis has been very little written about in England and has never been studied in any detail. He is better known in America where his outspoken Republicanism found many eighteenth-century admirers and his political thought has been the object of recent study.

Dr Rowe has done a real service to all students of the seventeenth century by her careful enquiry into Vane's activities as a Parliament man and administrator. Political theories and general ideals are all very well, but it was the in-fighting in the House of Commons and the Committee of Both Kingdoms that shaped the outcome of the Civil War no less than the victories in battle. Reading this book we at last begin to understand how the Vane-Cromwell partnership worked in practice during the critical years from 1644 to 1649. Dr Rowe also provides valuable details about Vane's activities as a practical administrator in naval affairs, traces his career during the Commonwealth before the elevation of Cromwell to supreme power shattered his hopes of a true Republic, and investigates the sources of his income and the extent of his personal enrichment during the period of his power. Like most other statesmen of his time he came under criticism for this, and like most other statesmen of his time he had indeed enriched himself, though perhaps not excessively by the standards of the day.

This dispassionate and factual study is a valuable addition to our knowledge of a significant and interesting man and throws light on the political mechanics of the English Revolution.

C. V. WEDGWOOD

ACKNOWLEDGEMENTS

The author's thanks are due to

Mr R. C. Latham, M.A., who first suggested the subject of this study, and who read through several versions of the book with unexampled patience. I owe much to his perceptive and penetrating advice.

Dame Veronica Wedgwood, O.M., whose kindness in writing the Foreword I acknowledge gratefully. Her generous interest when I began the research was a source of encouragement and her help in preparing the work for publication has been of great assistance.

Mr R. E. Maddison, M.A., for so courteously responding, out of his wide knowledge of the Press in the 1640s and 1650s, to my many queries on this subject.

Mr B. H. G. Wormald, M.A., for his help and encouragement.

Lord Barnard of Raby Castle, Durham, for permission to quote from the Vane family deeds in his possession and for kindly allowing the reproduction of a portrait of Sir Henry Vane by Lely.

The Corporation of the City and County of Kingston upon Hull, for permission to quote from the records of the city.

The Hon. Lady Salmond and the Hertfordshire County Record Office for permission to quote from the Panshanger MSS.

Miss Jean Jackson, particularly for helpful information on Vane House, Hampstead.

CONTENTS

ABBREVIATIONS

AHR	*American Historical Review*
A.O.I.	C. H. Firth and C. S. Rait, *Acts and Ordinances of the Interregnum, 1642–1660* (Oxford, 1906)
Baillie	*The Letters and Journals of R. Baillie*, ed. D. Laing (Edinburgh, 1841–2)
Burton	*The Diary of Thomas Burton*, ed. J. T. Rutt, 4 vols. (London, 1828)
CJ.	*Journals of the House of Commons*
Clarendon, *Rebellion*	Edward, earl of Clarendon, *The History of the Rebellion and the Civil Wars in England*, ed. W. D. Macray (Oxford, 1888)
Clarendon, *S.P.*	*State Papers collected by Edward, earl of Clarendon*, ed. R. Scrope and T. Monkhouse (Oxford, 1767–86)
Clarke Papers	*Selections from the Papers of William Clarke*, ed. C. H. Firth, Camden Soc. (London, 1891–1901)
Coates, *D'Ewes*	*The Journal of Sir Simonds D'Ewes*, ed. W. H. Coates (New Haven, Connecticut, 1942)
CSPD.	*Calendar of State Papers, Domestic Series*
CSPV.	*Calendar of State Papers in the Archives of Venice*, ed. H. F. Brown and A. B. Hind (London, 1900–25)
Davies, *Elections*	G. Davies, 'Elections for Richard Cromwell's Parliament', *EHR.*, lxiii, 493
Davies, *Restoration*	G. Davies, *The Restoration of Charles II* (San Marino, California, 1955)
EHR.	*English Historical Review*
Gardiner, *Const. Docs.*	S. R. Gardiner, *The Constitutional Documents of the Puritan Revolution, 1625–60* (Oxford, 1906)
Gardiner, *CW.*	S. R. Gardiner, *History of the Great Civil War, 1642–49* (London, 1893)
Gardiner, *CP.*	S. R. Gardiner, *History of the Commonwealth and Protectorate* (London, 1894–1901)
HMC.	Historical Manuscripts Commission
Holles, *Memoirs*	*Memoirs of D. Holles*, reprinted in *Select Tracts*, ed. F. Maseres (London, 1815)
Hutchinson	T. Hutchinson, *History of the Colony of Massachusetts Bay* (Boston, Massachusetts, 1765–8)

JCC. London	Journal of Common Council, London City MSS, Guildhall, London
LJ.	*Journals of the House of Lords*
Ludlow	*Memoirs of E. Ludlow*, ed. C. H. Firth (Oxford, 1894)
Mordaunt	*The Letter-Book of John, Viscount Mordaunt 1658–1660*, Camden Soc. (London, 1945)
Notestein, D'Ewes	*The Journal of Sir Simonds D'Ewes*, ed. W. Notestein (New Haven, Connecticut, 1923)
Peyton	Parliamentary Diary of Sir Thomas Peyton, Bodleian Library, Oxford
Somers Tracts	*A collection of tracts from libraries, particularly that of the late Lord Somers* (London, 1748–52)
Thurloe S.P.	*A Collection of the State Papers of John Thurloe, Esq.*, ed. T. Birch, 7 vols. (London, 1742)
Tryal	Anon., *The Tryal of Sir Henry Vane at the King's Bench, Westminster* (London, 1662)
Whitelocke	Bulstrode Whitelocke, *Memorials of English Affairs* (Oxford, 1853)
Whittaker	L. Whittaker, Diary of Proceedings in the House of Commons, BM. Add. 31, 116
Willcock	J. Willcock, *The Life of Sir Henry Vane the Younger* (London, 1913)

NOTE: MSS referred to in this volume are in the Public Record Office, London, unless otherwise indicated.

Introduction

As a constructive statesman Sir Henry Vane the Younger[1] was a figure of considerable stature. It is remarkable how many of the decisive measures of the 1640s and early 1650s were either initiated by him, carried out by him, or both. In fact the Independents perhaps owed their victory in the Civil War more to Vane than to any other single man except Cromwell. The re-introduction of impressment in the navy was largely due to his efforts; with one other M.P. he drafted the ordinance by which the Court of Wards was finally abolished[2]; he negotiated the Solemn League and Covenant with the Scots. With St John he was responsible for the establishment and the renewal of the Committee of Both Kingdoms, and the Self-Denying Ordinance, proposed by Tate, was seconded by Vane. Vane was associated in one way or another with the bold and imaginative schemes of union with Holland in 1651 and with Scotland in 1652; he may even have toyed with the idea of union between Parliamentarians and *Frondeurs*. In foreign affairs he played an important part from the establishment of the republic to the dissolution of the Rump, and again when he returned to political activity in 1659.

He was an outstanding protagonist of religious toleration, on which he spoke and wrote with passionate conviction. The struggling colony of Rhode Island was twice protected from the clutches of intolerant Massachusetts by Vane's efforts. It is important to notice that his method of securing religious toleration was to omit all reference in the relevant documents to the State's coercive power in religion. He was correspondingly opposed to clerical control by bishops or by Presbyterian ministers. Except for the Solemn League and Covenant episode, he consistently supported religious toleration, and the

[1] In this book referred to as 'Vane' whenever possible.   [2] *CJ.* iv, 452.

determination with which he fought for this novel principle, against opponents of all kinds, compels admiration, as do the logical and sincere arguments on which he based his policy.

On the other hand it may be said that he also contributed substantially to the ultimate downfall of his cause. His support for continuing the civil war, his ruthlessness, the rumours of his financial gains, which had a considerable basis in fact, must have cost him and his cause much unpopularity. He spoke and wrote of the freedom of the people, but it was the freedom of the 'good party', not of those who differed from him in politics. Vane was to pay dearly for his faults of character, but he met death with a courage and loyalty to principle of which his Protestant forebears would have approved.

He came of a family which had played a part in the public life of England at least since the fourteenth century. His great-grandfather had taken part in Wyatt's rebellion, and had narrowly escaped death for treason,[1] but had lived to be a a member of Elizabeth's first two Parliaments.[2] His grandfather had died in the English forces at Rouen, fighting for Henry IV of France, in 1596.[3] His father's part in English diplomatic, political and administrative history would require a volume to itself. The family were early converts to the Reformed religion,[4] and their Protestant tradition was strong. His father, the elder Vane, had risen in the world. According to his own account[5] the land he inherited in Kent (where the family had been settled at least since Henry VI's reign) was worth only £460 a year, of which £160 was his mother's dowry. But his marriage to a wealthy heiress and his good fortune at court enabled him to buy Fairlawn in Kent, for £4000,[6] and in 1629 he purchased estates in Durham at Raby, Barnard Castle and Long Newton for £18,000.[7] Frances Wray, the bride of young Sir Henry, brought with her a dowry of £5500,[8] £3000 of which was used to purchase a farm and other lands in Staindrop,[9] the village which adjoins Raby Castle. At the same time the elder Vane purchased Cockfield, a colliery in the Durham coalfield, for

---

[1] A. Collins, *Peerage of England* (London, 1812), iii, 284–95; iv, 500–3.
[2] *Return of M.P.s*, i, 402, 407.   [3] Collins, op. cit.   [4] Ibid.
[5] Dalton, *History of the Wrays of Glentworth*, ii, 112. His wife's dowry was £3000.
[6] Ibid., 114.   [7] Ibid.   [8] Raby deeds, indenture, 30 June 1640.
[9] Ibid., indenture, 15 June 1640.

£900.[1] In the 1640s and 1650s he bought yet more property in Durham and Kent. He had also acquired by 1623 a house in the Strand next to the earl of Northumberland's.[2] Writing in 1649[3] Sir Henry Vane senior asserted that his estates were well worth £3000 a year, and 'when my leases expire, which will not be long' they would be worth nearer £5000 than £4000 a year. (Both he and his eldest son were well aware of the possibility of 'improving' rents.[4])

The younger Vane was sent to Westminster school,[5] where he was a contemporary of his future colleagues the republican politicians Sir Arthur Hesilrige and Thomas Scot. In later life he retained some connexion with the school, for its well-known puritan ex-master, Lambert Osbaldeston, appealed to Vane in 1649 to assist the brilliant and impecunious Henry Stubbe.[6] Vane's biographers have failed to notice that it was while Vane was at school that he experienced his religious 'conversion'.[7] After only a short time at Magdalen Hall, a puritan college at Oxford, Vane travelled abroad. Viscount Conway's correspondent, Garrard, wrote that the elder Vane's sons were 'all bred up at Leyden',[8] while Clarendon asserted that Vane had spent 'some little time in France and more in Geneva'.[9] His father tells us only that he had brought up his eldest son and six others 'beyond seas'.[10] It is interesting that Charles Vane, a

[1] Ibid., indenture, 28 May 1640.

[2] He writes for the first time from Charing Cross in 1623. (*CSPD. 1619-23*, 550.)

[3] Dalton, op. cit., 115.

[4] Vane wrote to his father on 9 May 1640, 'If you shall please to make £600 per annum joynture and present maintenance and to let the demeanes of Barnard Castle be part thereof; which in present doe yeild but £230 per annum or thereabout, but some five or six yeares hence will improve £100 or £120 per annum and some nine or tenne yeares hence will improve another £100 or thereabouts.' (S.P. 16/452/92. See also *CSPD. 1650*, 242.)

[5] Wood, *Athenae*, iii, 578. (Vane's name is not in J. Welch, *List of scholars of St. Peter's College, Westminster* (London, 1788), but the list is obviously incomplete for this early period.)

[6] See below, p. 72.

[7] Though Wood, who had read Sikes's biography, hints at this, Vane's 'conversion' took place when he was 14 or 15 ([G. Sikes], *The Life and Death of Sir Henry Vane* (London, 1662), 7-8) and he went up to Oxford at about 16 years of age. (Wood, *Athenae*, loc. cit. Wood's information about Vane at Oxford was obtained from Stubbe, and is therefore reliable.)

[8] *CSPD. 1635*, 385.   [9] *Rebellion*, iii, 35.

[10] Dalton, op. cit., 114.

younger brother, is recorded as Master of Arts of Saumur.[1] This academy was the intellectual centre of French protestantism until the revocation of the Edict of Nantes; it is very possible that Vane studied here, like his brother, and this would explain his excellent French.[2] In 1631 he was in the train of the English ambassador in Vienna.[3] On his return to England he was disappointed in his hopes of a place in the king's privy chamber.[4] (A military career was distasteful to him.[5]) By 1635 he was friendly with Pym and Pym's friend, Sir Nathaniel Rich,[6] and he left in that year for Massachusetts.

He sailed for Boston in September, carrying with him a commission, issued to Hugh Peters, the younger Winthrop and himself, to negotiate with the settlers in Connecticut who had recently come from Massachusetts. This is a pretty clear indication of his close relations with the Saybrook patentees, Lords Say and Brooke, Pym, Nathaniel Rich and others. Pym, Hampden, Hesilrige and Cromwell, according to a letter which Governor Hutchinson, the eighteenth-century historian of Massachusetts, had seen, intended to emigrate to America themselves,[7] and a reference in Whittaker's parliamentary diary confirms that this was indeed Pym's intention.[8] The colonists warmly welcomed Vane, and within six months, at the age of only 23, he was elected governor of Massachusetts. He kept unusual state as governor; whenever he went to church or the Court of magistrates, four halberdiers walked before him.[9] At first all went well; he reconciled John Winthrop and Thomas Dudley, who had been leading rival parties, he secured an agreement with masters of ships in Boston harbour, to enable the authorities to prevent disorderly conduct by sailors on shore, and concluded a treaty with the Narragansett Indians, who might otherwise have joined the Pecquot Indians in a war against the colony. In this last, the good offices of

---

[1] Wood, *Fasti*, ii, 504.   [2] Harl. 164, f. 94v.   [3] S.P. 80/8/19.

[4] S.P. 16/211/18. 5 February 1632.

[5] 'Je suis si peu penchant au faict de la guerre.' Vane to his father, who had suggested a military career, 20 August 1631. See above, n. 3.

[6] *The Earl of Strafforde's Letters and Despatches*, ed. W. Knowler (London, 1739), i, 463.

[7] Hutchinson, i, 41, 42.   [8] Whittaker, f. 99v.

[9] Hutchinson, 53.

Roger Williams had been enlisted,[1] and the key to Vane's failure in Massachusetts lies in his association with those who, like Williams, had the temerity to claim the right to think for themselves on religious matters.

He had become friendly with a remarkable woman, respected by many in Boston, who dared to preach herself and to hold theological views different from those of most of the leading ministers. This was Mrs Anne Hutchinson, the mother of eleven children, and with a son nearly as old as Vane himself. She held that the faithful Christian was in personal union with the Holy Spirit, but her opponents believed that though the Holy Spirit indwelt a Christian, there was no 'communication of personal properties'.[2] Behind this hair-splitting theological dispute, however, lurked the more serious question of a Christian's right to his own religious interpretation of Scripture. The town of Boston supported Mrs Hutchinson, most of the other settlements opposed her. Her sister-in-law had married a minister, John Wheelwright, who played a prominent part in the controversy. Winthrop and Hugh Peters were Mrs Hutchinson's leading antagonists; Vane was her champion, to his cost.

So bitter were the divisions among the colonists that Vane, only nine months after becoming governor, secured the permission of the Court of Massachusetts to return to England. There was a scene in which he upbraided those who put the blame for the dissensions on him and he burst into tears. The church at Boston, however, persuaded him to stay. Three months later his opponents moved that the annual elections should be held not at Boston as usual, but at Newtown, one of the towns where Winthrop's party was strong. Vane, understandably indignant at this manœuvre, refused to put the question to the Court; it was carried nevertheless. Shortly after, the Court censured Wheelwright for sedition, and on the election day, Vane presented a petition on the minister's behalf, he and his supporters protesting they would not allow the election of the governor to proceed unless the petition was

---

[1] J. Winthrop, *History of New England*, ed. J. K. Hosmer (New York, 1959), i, 169–70, 180.

[2] Hutchinson, 56.

read. The crowd at Newtown however, roused by one of the ministers, shouted, 'Election, election!' and Vane had to give way. Winthrop was elected as governor, and Vane and all his supporters were routed in the contests for the other offices.[1] Vane's apprenticeship to politics was served in a hard school.

The Massachusetts Court, to prevent future disputes, now made an order that no one could settle in the colony unless approved of by the Court. Winthrop wrote a defence of the order, and Vane's first political treatise was a *Brief Answer*[2] to Winthrop, a most telling and penetrating polemic. He assailed Winthrop and the intolerant Massachusetts Court on all sides, legal, political and scriptural. The magistrates were claiming the right to refuse to admit to the colony 'those whose Society they knew would be harmful to them'. Vane pointed out that the royal grant had allowed *any* of the king's subjects to settle in the lands granted. He reminded the magistrates of how Ahab had accused Elijah of troubling the Commonwealth, and of how the Greeks had complained that Paul and Silas had 'turned the world upside down'. In what must have been to the Court an infuriating passage, he pointed to their own position in Massachusetts, where the Indians thought that the co-habitation of the English tended to the utter ruin of the Indians, yet Winthrop and his friends would not say that the Indians might lawfully keep out the English on that account. He had realized that no general rules for the admission of settlers were laid down—the decision would depend on the whim of the magistrates. Even the Egyptians and Philistines, he contended, allowed God's people to settle among them, and, with a characteristic touch of irony, he declared, 'Christ bids us not to forget to entertain strangers, Heb. 13.2. But here by this law we must not entertaine, for any continuance of time, such stranger as the magistrates like not, though they be never so gracious.' He made a powerful plea for religious toleration: 'Scribes and Pharisees, and such as are confirmed in any way of error, all such are not to be denied co-habitation, but are to be pitied

[1] Ibid., 61.
[2] Printed in *The Hutchinson Papers*, ed. T. Hutchinson (Albany, N.Y., 1865), i, 84–96.

and reformed.' Years later he was to make a similar plea in the House of Commons.[1]

The *Brief Answer* was written just before he left for England. He had been humiliated by the electors who had not even made him an Assistant (Director of the Massachusetts Company), and who had made an order, sensible in itself, that no one should be governor in future unless he had been in the Colony for at least a year.[2] In August 1637, he left Massachusetts, accompanied by Mrs Hutchinson's brother-in-law, Richard, one day to be Vane's deputy, and later his successor, as Navy Treasurer.[3] In 1645, with remarkable magnanimity, Vane responded to an appeal by Winthrop, to assist Massachusetts merchants whose ships had been seized by the Admiralty Court. He showed himself, wrote Winthrop, 'a true friend to New England, and a man of noble and generous mind'.[4]

According to Clarendon, Vane was much reformed in his 'extravagancies', that is, his puritan convictions, after his return from New England,[5] but very little is known of his life between August 1637 and the opening of the Long Parliament. At some point during the 1630s he was attending the meetings held by a puritan of Barnard Castle, Matthew Stoddart, on his private days of fasting and humiliation,[6] but this could have been either before or after Vane's visit to Massachusetts.

He embarked however on what was to prove a long career in naval administration, when in January 1639 he became joint-Treasurer of the Navy with Sir William Russell. The earl of Northumberland, the elder Vane's friend and neighbour, had sought the post for young Vane, but failed. The king however granted it at the suit of Vane's father. The half-share of the office was certainly obtained by purchase. The value of the office is difficult to establish. Professor Aylmer accepted £800 per annum as its worth to a single Treasurer,[7] but from the

---

[1] See below, p. 197. [2] Hutchinson, 64.
[3] The town of Boston itself was loyal to him to the last.
[4] Winthrop, op. cit., ii, 256. [5] Clarendon, *Rebellion*, iii, 35.
[6] W. H. D. Longstaff, *The Acts of the High Commission Court within the Diocese of Durham*, Surtees Soc. vol. xxxiv (Durham, 1858), 193, note a. Vane was at Raby, a few miles away, in 1638.
[7] G. Aylmer, *The King's Servants* (London, 1961), 207.

letter whence this figure was originally derived[1] it is clear that the £800 would be Vane's share alone. Even this sum seems inadequate for an office which contemporaries agreed was a very profitable one,[2] and according to the warrant for monthly payment in January 1639, the value of the poundage, if navy expenditure continued at the same rate, would have been over £4000 a year[3] to a single holder of the office. The officially admitted poundage bears no relation to this figure. In 1638 Sir William Russell, according to his account for that year, drew £275 5s 6d as poundage.[4] When he and Vane presented their joint account for 1639 their poundage (to be divided equally between them according to the terms of Vane's appointment), amounted to £728 14s 0d.[5] The Navy Treasurer had sources of income however outside his official fees and allowances, and probably £800 can be accepted as the minimum figure which a joint-Treasurer might be expected to derive from the post. It is interesting that as joint-Treasurer, Vane was responsible, with Russell, for the ship-money accounts.

In his new post he soon showed the energy and efficiency which were to mark all his career. 'The new treasurer of the navy', wrote Secretary of State Sir Edward Nicholas in July 1640, 'takes very much upon him, and has already, as I hear, wearied all the officers of the navy'[6] (i.e. the Principal Officers of the Navy Board). The officials may well have been 'wearied' by one change introduced into Navy administration two months after Vane's appointment, and probably therefore due to him; instead of charging the service accounts with payments for lodging, firing and dinners when they were in London for their meetings, a fixed sum each year was allowed the officials for

---

[1] 'The office whereof Mr. Vane now standeth possessed of is worth £800 p. ann. and if Sir William Russell dy will be worth as much more . . . If Mr. Vane dispose of the office, then if Sir Henry Vane rescieve the whole benefit hee to make up £800 p. an. maintenance.' (S.P. 16/452/92.I.) (Sir Christopher Wray or his representative to Sir Henry Vane the elder.)

[2] Clarendon called it an office of great trust and profit (*Rebellion*, iii, 34), and Hollond (*Discourses*, 308) declared it to be a 'warm thing'.

[3] *CSPD. 1638–9*, 307. 11 January 1639. The expenditure on the navy was over £26,000 a month, and the treasurer was entitled to 3d for every pound spent.

[4] A.O.I./1704/81.   [5] A.O.I./1704/83.

[6] *CSPD. 1639*, 383. 10 July 1639.

these expenses. The king saved over £300 a year by the new arrangement.[1]

There is some evidence that at the end of 1639 Vane was regarded as a reliable 'court' candidate for Parliament, for this seems the only reasonable interpretation of the king's extraordinary action in ordering the withdrawal of an Exchequer Court case against the corporation of Hull.

The corporation had been charged in the Exchequer Court with failure to maintain their castle and block-houses as they were bound to do under their 1552 charter. The case had dragged on for nearly six years when the elections for the Short Parliament were announced. The earl of Northumberland requested the corporation to elect Vane as one of the city's M.P.s, but the corporation refused. They denied the right which the earl had claimed, as Lord Admiral, to nominate one of the town's members, and of Vane they wrote with some asperity, 'nor was the gentleman known who he was'. The elder Vane however offered a powerful inducement—he would secure the withdrawal of the vexatious and expensive Exchequer case. The city corporation Bench Book records the outcome—'in respect of divers favours this Towne hath lately received from the said Sir Henry Vaine concerning a suite in the Exchequer by his Majesties Attorney against this Towne, touching the Castle and Blockhouses there', young Vane was to be elected. To qualify for election, he had hastily to be made a burgess, but without the inconvenience of travelling to Hull to take the oath. He represented the town for thirteen years, and seems to have served its interests conscientiously.[2]

But Vane was very busy at the time of the Short Parliament with business affairs connected with his marriage to Frances

---

[1] Privy Seal Docket, Index, IND 6789, March 1639. There are other indications of Vane's official activity at this time, e.g. *CSPD. 1638–39*, 568; *1640*, 137. I have found no indication that Vane advanced money to the government in the same way that his fellow-Treasurer had done, except on one occasion, to be described below. For Russell see R. Ashton, 'The disbursing official under the early Stuarts; the cases of Sir William Russell and Philip Burlamachi', *Bulletin of the Institute of Historical Research*, xxx (1957), 162–74. For the later value of the Navy Treasurer's office to Vane, see below, pp. 172, 270.

[2] V. A. Rowe, 'Sir Henry Vane the Younger as M.P. for Hull', *Notes and Queries*, New Series, vol. vi, no. 1 (January 1959).

Wray,[1] daughter of Sir Christopher Wray, the member for
Grimsby, and perhaps this caused him to absent himself from
the Commons during the session.[2] His marriage took place on
1 July 1640,[3] and in view of the well-known puritan sympathies
of his bride's family,[4] it would seem that the elder Vane must
have shared the Wrays' views. But even if he had not been
inclined to puritanism, the action of the earl of Strafford, who
took the barony of Raby as one of his titles in February 1640,
though the elder Vane had owned Raby Castle for seven years,
was well-calculated to drive the Vanes into the camp of those
who hated the earl.

It would appear from the letters concerning the marriage
settlement of the younger Vane and Frances Wray, and from
the family deeds,[5] that he was to enjoy the £800 a year which
it was reckoned that his share of the Navy Treasurer's office
would be worth, and that his bride would have £600 a year
from the lands settled upon her at her marriage. The elder
Vane also settled on his son the third part of the *sub-poena* office
in Chancery, which he had bought some years before.[6] The
marriage took place at St Mary's, Lambeth, though the Vane
house in the Strand was just opposite St Martin-in-the-Fields;
probably St Martin's was not puritan enough for Vane and his
father. The younger Vane had been knighted eight days before.[7]
He did not take part in the Scots War, notwithstanding assertions to the contrary by his detractors and biographers.[8]

His friendship with Pym continued, and when Pym came
to see him in September 1640,[9] Vane disclosed a document
which was later to become famous. It was a transcript that Vane
had made of his father's notes of a Privy Council committee
meeting, and it was used with great effect by Pym in the
impeachment of Strafford. One of the charges against the earl

---

[1] A large number of deeds in connexion with the marriage settlement are
recorded at Raby.

[2] He was not nominated to a single committee. *CJ.* ii, 4–14, *passim.*

[3] Dalton, op. cit., ii, 101.   [4] Ibid., i, 154.

[5] Raby deeds; 'The settlement of the inheritance in the North', 30 June 1640,
and S.P. 16/452/92.

[6] Dalton, op. cit., ii, 115.

[7] W. A. Shaw, *The Knights of England* (London, 1906), ii, 207.   [8] See below, p. 22.

[9] Vane had an ague, Clarendon (*Rebellion*, iii, 131) says. If Vane had contracted
malaria abroad, it would go far to explain his later ill-health.

was that he had raised a regiment of Irish Roman Catholics, which he threatened to use against England in April 1640. The elder Vane gave evidence that Strafford had declared at the Privy Council committee that the Irish Army could be used to reduce 'this kingdom'. Four Privy Councillors asserted they had never heard Strafford propose to bring the Irish army to England, Strafford pointed out that a single witness was insufficient to prove treason, and it looked as though the impeachment was going to fail, since the Lords would dismiss the charge. It was at this point that Pym produced the notes that he had made of young Vane's transcript. They corroborated the elder Vane's testimony, greatly increased the distrust of Strafford which many peers and members of the Commons felt, and seriously weakened the earl's case. How had the younger Vane obtained the notes? He explained that he had been searching through his father's black velvet cabinet (or red, so Clarendon thought), for papers in connexion with his own marriage settlement in September 1640, when he saw the Council notes. Out of concern for the public interest, he made his copy. The story is very odd, for his father's secretary had not seen the letter which authorized Vane to open the cabinet, nor the key (which the secretary presumably normally kept in his own possession when his master was away), which Vane had used. And the marriage settlement, so far as the estates in the North were concerned, and these comprised the greater part of the property involved in the marriage settlement, is dated 30 June 1640. Of course some question in connexion with the settlement could have come up three months later, but how could Vane confuse Privy Council meeting notes and the property deeds for which he was looking? This is the first of many baffling incidents in Vane's career.[1]

Pym is the one friend Vane is known to have had in England when the Long Parliament met, and only some half-dozen members were at all closely related to him. The Vane 'connexion' in Parliament, in so far as it depended on consanguinity, was remarkably small, smaller indeed probably than

[1] This brief discussion of a complex episode is based chiefly on J. Rushworth, *Tryal of the earl of Strafforde* (London, 1721), 51–2, 556–65: R. Verney, *Notes on the Long Parliament*, Camden Soc. (1854), 37.

that of most M.P.s. Young Vane's father-in-law, Sir Christopher Wray, was a prominent member of the Lower House, and Wray's half-brother, Sir John Wray,[1] and brother-in-law, Sir Edward Ayscough,[2] were also members. Vane's name figures largely in the Wray family deeds of the period;[3] his ties with his wife's family were close. (They did not prevent Sir Christopher Wray from being a leading member of Holles's group.) Sir Thomas Pelham, member for Sussex county, was a brother-in-law of Vane;[4] among Sir Thomas's friends were Henry and Peregrine Pelham and Antony Stapley.[5] But Vane's family connexions in Parliament seem to have extended no farther than this.

He or his father however had friendly relations or business ties with a number of other M.P.s and peers. The elder Vane sat for Wilton in 1640,[6] which would indicate that he counted the earl of Pembroke among his well-wishers, but a common antipathy to the earl of Strafford may explain this. Cornelius Holland, the member for Windsor, and later to be one of the regicides, was said to have been a 'link-boy' taken into the elder Vane's service after his father had died in prison for debt;[7] he was certainly one of the parties to the 1640 marriage settlement and also one of the overseers of the elder Vane's will,[8] so that the connexion between the two men lasted until the end of the older man's life. Through his friendship with Pym Vane was linked with the extensive Warwick-Barrington-St John group. There is no sign however that he showed Warwick any friendship in politics, such evidence as there is indicates rather hostility between the two men.[9] St John and Vane were

---

[1] Maddison, *Lincolnshire Pedigrees*, Harleian Soc. (1906), iv, 1323. Sir Antony Irby was another brother-in-law of Sir Christopher.

[2] 'My brother, Sir Edward Ayscough' was a trustee with Vane under Sir Christopher's will. (P.C.C. 36 Twisse. 4 October 1645.)

[3] Wray's will, loc. cit.; Dalton, op. cit. ii, App. 24; will of Sir Christopher's widow, Lady Albinia, P.C.C. Reg. 174 Bath.

[4] Willcock, 352.

[5] Keeler, 302; *Return of M.P.s*, 483. Peregrine Pelham was Vane's fellow M.P. for Hull.

[6] *Return of M.P.s*, i, 484.

[7] *The Second Centurie*, E 465(13); *Chipps of the Old Block*, 669 f. 23, f. 14.

[8] P.C.C. Aylett 159. D'Ewes called Holland the elder Vane's servant, e.g. Harl. 164, f. 334v.

[9] See below, pp. 43–124.

probably close friends, and certainly close political associates.[1] The earl of Northumberland and the elder Vane were friends as well as neighbours,[2] but the earl was also a reforming Lord High Admiral,[3] and his official duties brought him into close contact with the younger Vane before the Long Parliament began.[4] The elder Vane was a close friend of the queen of Bohemia, and one of his daughters married her steward, Sir Robert Honeywood, in 1642;[5] this would be a link with the many M.P.s who were interested in the fortunes of the Winter Queen. William Say, a 'Recruiter' M.P., and a regicide, was a friend of the elder Vane by the time the latter's will was drawn up in 1654.[6] He also had a distant connexion with the much-respected Northern M.P., Sir Thomas Widdrington; a colourful Newcastle character, Mark Shafto ('six bottle Mark'), who was acting as steward at Sir Henry Vane senior's courts baron and courts leet in 1645,[7] was Widdrington's father-in-law. Shafto was a close friend of the elder Vane's solicitor in legal matters, Henry Dingley.[8] Incidentally, when Sir Henry Vane senior became the leading member of the important committee of the King's Revenue, its secretary was Edward Cousins,[9] who had been in his employ before 1640, dealing with estate matters,[10] and Cornelius Holland was one of the committee.[11]

Vane's links in 1640 with those who afterwards took the royalist side were few—perhaps this partly accounts for his somewhat uncompromising attitude towards 'malignants'. Lilburne accused Vane's next brother, Sir George, who managed the family collieries[12] in Durham and lived at Long Newton, of being a royalist at first, but this, though probable,

---

[1] See below, p. 27.   [2] HMC. *3rd Rep.* App. 82; *CSPD. 1645–47*, 215.

[3] Hollond, *Discourses*, 25.

[4] 'My Lord Admirall hath sent for mee to attend his Lordship with all possible speed.' (S.P. 16/452/92.)

[5] Willcock, 352.   [6] Loc. cit.

[7] *Records of the Committees for Compounding . . . in Durham and Northumberland*, ed. R. Welford, 337.

[8] Ibid.   [9] *CSPD. 1644*, 235.

[10] *CSPD. 1639–40*, 530. Clement Walker stated that the elder Vane's 'man' Cozens, 'is clearke to the Committee, and gets £2,000 p.a. by it' (*The Second Centurie*). Note also *CSPD. 1645–47*, 58.

[11] See e.g. BM. Add. 19,398 (Letter from the committee to the corporation of Norwich, signed by Vane, Holland and others.)

[12] *CSPD. 1644–45*, 96–7.

is not certain.[1] Sir George Vane's father-in-law, Sir Lionel Maddison, a royalist at the beginning of the Civil War, changed sides just before the storming of Newcastle. The elder Vane's fourth son, Sir Walter, was certainly a royalist.[2]

Vane's preparation for his public career in England had thus included a period of Continental travel likely to reinforce the interest in foreign affairs that his father's diplomatic experience would have given him. He had had experience as governor of Massachusetts, and nearly two years of active work in naval administration. He came of stout protestant stock, who had suffered for their faith, and his education and marriage were calculated to strengthen this factor in his inheritance. He and his wife probably enjoyed a joint income of some £1400 a year, but with the prospect of much more when old Sir Henry Vane should die. His varied experience before 1640 gave him an advantage over almost all his contemporaries, and foreshadowed the major interests of his career, religion, the navy, and foreign policy. In the two latter subjects no-one who supported the Parliamentary cause in 1642, except his own father, possessed Vane's expert knowledge.

[1] See below, p. 90.
[2] His knighthood is not listed in Shaw's *Knights*, but his father refers to him as Sir Walter Vane in his will of 1654. He must therefore have been knighted during the Civil War, and this would accord with the fact that Charles II appointed him in 1664, only two years after Sir Henry's execution, as envoy to the Elector of Brandenburg. (H. R. F. Bourne, *Life of John Locke* (London, 1876), i, 100.) It was probably Sir Walter who saved Vane in 1662 from the loathsome tortures associated with a traitor's death.

CHAPTER I

The Rise to Leadership,
November 1640 to December 1643

IN THE early weeks of the Long Parliament, Vane's part, as became a new and young member, was a minor one; the records of the debates confirm Clarendon's statement that at the beginning of the Long Parliament some eight or nine men managed the 'designs', that is, the political planning, and Vane was one of the 'stout seconders' who were trusted only upon occasion.[1]

In January 1641 however the House began to appoint him to important committees,[2] and in May he managed a conference with the Lords for the first time; it seems that his part was to deal with naval topics.[3] The Commons' growing respect for him was shown in the same month when his name replaced Kirton's in the Subsidies committee, Kirton having disgraced himself in the eyes of the House by declaring that Strafford's trial was unjust.[4] All through the summer of 1641 he was coming to the fore as a member of important organizing committees.[5]

Vane however cannot be reckoned one of the half-dozen foremost men in the Commons until the time of Pym's illness in October of 1643.[6] As late as June 1643, when the king speaks

---

[1] Clarendon, *Rebellion*, iii, 55.

[2] *CJ.* ii, 67. 12 January. This committee was to consider how money could be obtained for the Army. It later obtained responsibility for the relief of the Northern counties, and the Navy, and Vane, though already a member, was added to it; a not infrequent occurrence. (Ibid., 82, 83.) There was a multiplicity of committees at this time—for Vane's membership of two committees which were to meet at the same time, see ibid., 139.

[3] *CJ.* ii, 140. 8 May.   [4] Ibid., 137. 6 May.

[5] Ibid., 180, 188, 190, 207–8, 210.

[6] The Puritan writer who lists 'the best' of the king's subjects in October 1642 names 15 M.P.s or peers, but does not include Vane. (*A Speedy Post from Heaven to the King of England*, E 121(6).)

of the House of Commons as being overawed by a powerful faction, Vane was not one of the members of Parliament excepted from the royal offer of pardon.[1] When in this same month Edmund Waller and his fellow-conspirators planned to arrest Say, Wharton, Pym, Stapleton, Hampden and Strode, there was no mention of Vane.[2] Nevertheless, by the beginning of 1642 the Commons had become aware that he was extremely skilful in drafting documents, and in this and the following year he was frequently entrusted with this kind of duty.[3] When an answer to a petition had to be framed, or a reply to a message from the Scottish commissioners or the king had to be composed, he was very likely to be one of the committee.

Meanwhile already, in 1642, Vane was a critic of the Lords. When on 8 February 1642 the Lords made amendments to a Commons' declaration concerning the forts and militia of the kingdom, Vane suggested 'wee may send upp to the Lords in our message that wee should consent to ther amendments upon condition that they would consent to our additions'. D'Ewes, evidently scandalized at Vane's attitude, spoke against 'such a conditionall message'.[4] In May 1643 when the Commons were discussing the provision of a new Great Seal, Vane wanted the bill so phrased that the two Houses *or either of them* should provide a remedy,[5] clearly indicating that he considered that legislative power lay in the hands of the Commons alone. Certainly it would be difficult to believe that the peers who were then at Westminster could claim any legislative power when in that summer their numbers at divisions totalled only

---

[1] Harl. 164, f. 278v. 27 June 1643.   [2] Ibid., f. 396v.

[3] See e.g. *CJ.* ii, 388, 439, 449, 478, 513. After the dismissal of the Vanes from their official posts in December 1641 it is more often difficult to decide which of the two is indicated when only the name 'Sir Henry Vane' is written, for the elder Vane was no longer 'Mr. Treasurer' after that date. Moreover between 4 August and December 1641 he had accompanied Charles to Scotland (*CJ.* ii, 236). Occasionally D'Ewes establishes the identity which the *Journals* leave undecided (e.g. *CJ.* ii, 625. 15 June 1642, and Harl. 163, f. 162), and less often the *Journals* themselves clarify the point later (*CJ.* ii, 665), or identify the Vane to whom D'Ewes refers (Harl. 164, f. 46 and *CJ.* ii, 266), but there are many occasions on which it is impossible to say whether Vane junior or his father is being referred to. On rare occasions only the surname is given, in which case George Vane, M.P. for Callington, Cornwall, is also a candidate for recognition.

[4] Harl. 164, f. 237.

[5] Ibid., f. 388. 11 May 1643. The italics are mine.

sixteen.[1] He was anxious that the making of a new Great Seal should go through; when the Lords sent messages desiring a conference with the Commons which would put an end to the discussion in the Lower House for that day, it was he who moved that the House should take up the matter of the Seal on the following morning.[2] But he derided the idea that the members should consult their constituents on important matters. When Killigrew argued in April 1642 that before the House concluded matters of 'great moment' it should send some M.P.s into each county to have the county's consent for 'it was not the enacting of a Law that made it in force but the willing obedience to it', Vane and others took 'great exceptions' to Killigrew's words, though unfortunately D'Ewes does not tell us what Vane said in the 'hot debate' that followed.[3]

His attitude both to the Upper House and to peace with the king was evinced in the negotiations which Mazarin's special envoy, the Comte d'Harcourt, hoped to initiate in November 1643. The Commons had 'especially recommended' the consideration of Harcourt's overtures to Vane, and he was one of the managers of the conference with the Lords on the reply to be made to the French envoy.[4] He was at least partly responsible for the reply which the Commons formulated,[5] which differed markedly from the answer that the Lords had already drafted. The Commons deleted the Lords' expression of thankfulness to the French king and queen, and for the 'most affectionate desire' of the French king to procure peace in England, but included a reference to the liberties of the three kingdoms, which the Lords had not mentioned, and to the Solemn League and Covenant. The Lords' answer had promised that when Harcourt approached Parliament, the two Houses would reply in such a way as to make it evident that nothing was more desired by them than peace. The Commons' committee's draft

---

[1] Harl. 165, f. 125. 11 July 1643. For Pym's declaration to the Lords as early as November 1641 that the Commons were the representative body see Gardiner, *History of England from the Accession of James I to the outbreak of the Civil War*, x, 94.

[2] Harl. 164, f. 389. 12 May 1643.

[3] Harl. 162, f. 58v. 1 April 1642.

[4] *CJ*. iii, 316, 317.

[5] The quorum for the drafting committee was four, of whom Vane would have to be one, as the matter had been 'especially recommended' to him.

does not promise an answer at all, only that Parliament would do 'that which shall be fit', and all reference to the desire for peace was omitted.[1] The total effect is of a very chilly welcome indeed to the French mediation proposals.

Certain incidents in 1643 lend support to contemporary allegations of Vane's duplicity.[2] In March the Commons instructed five of their members, including Marten and Gurdon, to destroy the 'superstitious monuments' in the chapel of Somerset House, Henrietta Maria's private residence, which was served by Capuchin friars. The members carried out their duties with zeal, and arrested five of the friars.[3] A fortnight later a protest was despatched from the French king; the French *chargé d'affaires*, Monsieur de Bures, wished to present it to the House. Vane opposed the reception of the letter; he argued that the House did not know whether Monsieur de Bures was indeed the French king's agent, but, as D'Ewes pointed out, the House had given passes to travel to Monsieur de Bures's servants, thus implicitly accepting his credentials, only two or three days before.[4] Vane's specious argument was undoubtedly being used to protect Marten, Gurdon and the others from attack, and it cannot have strengthened his reputation for honesty. He was also implicitly defending the rights of the Commons as against the Lords—the peers had refused to support the Lower House in this matter, and the Commons alone had authorized Marten's action.[5] A disingenuous attitude on Vane's part is reflected also during the investigations into the Waller plot in May 1643. When the Lord Mayor had been thanked for his 'care and pains' in discovering the plot, it was Vane who moved, as the Mayor was going out, that he might be: 'desired to conceale this business of the new conspiracy until it should be published into

---

[1] *CJ.* iii, 318.

[2] Clarendon, *Rebellion*, iii, 34. 'Of great natural parts and of very profound dissimulation.'

[3] *CJ.* ii, 843, 1001. 13 March 1643; Harl. 164, ff. 348v, 368v. D'Ewes considered that Marten had obtained the order as a means of delaying peace talks, ibid., f. 361. Marten was not noted for religious zeal, and D'Ewes was probably right.

[4] Harl. 164, f. 366. 13 April 1643. The House had actually done so on 5 April, ibid., f. 356.

[5] Marten's speech in 1646. (Harrington, BM. Add. 10,114, f. 22.)

the city by order of the house'.[1] There was no obvious reason for concealment.

At times he showed that there was a ruthless side to his character. When details of Waller's plot had been laid before the House, John Glyn moved that the earl of Manchester might name M.P.s who held command in the Army to try Edmund Waller the poet and his fellow-conspirators by martial law. Some members began to excuse themselves from this duty, and Denzil Holles moved: 'that wee might bee very wary how wee proceeded in taking away the lives of men, and to goe upon sure ground'. Vane however supported Glyn in arguing that Manchester possessed the necessary power to try the accused by court martial, though this must seem to any modern reader a most unjust proceeding.[2]

Again, in October 1643, when reporting to the House on the negotiations which led to the Solemn League and Covenant, Vane informed the House that the Scots had announced that all who refused the Covenant were to be declared enemies to the king and state and the true religion, incapable of bearing any office in the commonwealth; their lands and goods were to be confiscated.[3] Some days later, the House discussed what punishment should be inflicted on M.P.s who had refused to take the Covenant. The English version had no penal clause attached. The parliamentary diarist, Whittaker, implies that Vane again repeated the Scots' penalties.[4]

On a very large number of committees Vane was a fellow-member with Pym. Pym's language was more diplomatic,[5] and

---

[1] Harl. 164, f. 398v. 6 June 1643.

[2] Harl. 165, f. 103. 29 June 1643. Two of Waller's accomplices were tried in one day and executed two days later. Waller himself escaped with a fine. (*DNB*, Art. *sub* Edmund Waller.) A royalist pamphleteer (E 554(14)) writing in 1649, remembered that Dorislaus had 'made a shift to hang Tomkins and Challoner in broken Dutchified English'. BM. 669, f. 10 (55) has one or two details of the plot not mentioned in Gardiner.

[3] Whittaker, f. 86v. 26 October 1643.

[4] Ibid., f. 90. On the following day Vane took care to inform the Commons, apropos of another matter, that the masters, captains and crews of ships would not be permitted to go to sea without taking the Covenant. (BM. Add. 18,778, f. 84.)

[5] 'It will be a disadvantage to us and draw a partie against us if we treate not before soe the forts may be putt into indifferent hands; the forts are for the protection of the kingdom' (i.e. Pym wants the question of the forts, magazines, etc., settled before the negotiations for a peace treaty proper, but the use of the word

he was much more aware of the importance of public opinion than Vane,[1] but his conclusions were the same. The vow and covenant which Pym pleaded for so 'vehemently' in October 1642, and the impeachment of the queen, were measures intended to widen the rift between the Parliament and the king. Neither can be defended as constructive war measures, and both were pre-eminently Pym's work.[2]

That Vane himself vigorously opposed peace negotiations in a forthright way which evinced his impatience with the whole idea of 'treating' with the king is not open to doubt. As early as April 1642, when he opposed Killigrew on what might be called a 'referendum'[3] he was incidentally attacking the peace party, for it is surely hardly possible to doubt that the country would have been in favour of continued negotiations, even a compromise, rather than war. Again, in November 1642, when Holles and others wanted peace propositions to be sent to the king, Vane vehemently opposed the plan, 'leaste we send propositions which will be returned us again to our scorne'. 'If we send propositions', he concluded, 'to send them when we are in good case.'[4] Similarly in February 1643 he declared that he would have no treaty before the disbandment of troops. 'We are to have no mediators between us and the king . . . our purpose will be accomplished without a treaty, because the disbanding . . . will carry us on in our ancient way of parliament.'[5] A few days later, when the Lords were objecting to the demand for the disbanding of troops before peace talks were begun, he showed his impatience to prosecute the war by saying '[let us] propose we desire an ordinance for money. [This would demonstrate Parliament's intention to continue the war.] The Lords will not agree. The disagreement is on their side. We must not recede our votes els the Lords will not agree with us, and therefore would have the question putt

'treat' here has a soothing effect). The speech ends, however, 'If the king yeeld not to a disbandinge we shall have no hope of peace.' (Add. 18,777, f. 151. 11 February.) D'Ewes lists Vane, Marten, Pym, Strode and Wentworth in that order, as the 'hot spirits' opposing peace. (Harl. 164, f. 301v.)

[1] 'If we change our debate and treate, we should treate upon those points as may induce the kingdom to joyne with us.' (Ibid., f. 157.)

[2] J. F. Hexter, The Reign of King Pym, 29–30.

[3] See above, p. 17.   [4] Add. 18,777, f. 64,

[5] Ibid., f. 151, 11 February.

whether we should adhere to our former votes.'[1] In his usual
politer language Pym had just said that the Lords would
eventually give way. 'The Lords will not adhere to their votes
absolutely, but with limitations . . . before, they voted a treaty
before disbanding and a cessation from hostilities without
limitation of tyme, now they would have a resolution for twenty
dayes for the cessation'[2]—i.e. the Lords had already given way
on the duration of the armistice. Pym may have had to restrain
his youthful colleague's exuberance, but there was no real
difference of policy between them. Probably both knew that
the king would not disband his forces before entering into
negotiations—the royalists had been winning. On 18 March
1643, when the second Oxford proposals actually passed the
Commons, Vane was one of those who absented themselves,[3]
since they saw they would not be able to persuade the House to
vote for their policy: this withdrawal from Parliament when he
was in a minority has parallels in Vane's later career.

It should be noted that Vane did not join in the attacks that
were made by Henry Marten, Alexander Rigby and Sir Henry
Mildmay on the Committee of Safety, Pym's committee.[4]
Certainly the elder Vane was often its chairman, but Vane did
not scruple to oppose his father on occasion, and he would not
have kept silent out of loyalty to him. Vane's policy on this, as
on so much else, was in line with Pym's. But if the two men
were in substantial agreement on policy it would seem on a
superficial reading of the sources that they did differ in their
attitude to two people, the earl of Essex and Henry Marten.

After the failure of the March 1643 peace propositions
suggestions for an accommodation were not renewed until
July, when the earl of Essex, discouraged by Parliament's
military reverses, took the initiative. In a letter to the Commons he suggested that: 'If the House should thinke it fitt to
desire peace of his Majestie hee wished that some propositions
to that end might speedilie be sent unto him.' William Strode,
Sir Peter Wentworth and other 'violent spirits' were observed
to 'pluck their hatts over ther eyes', presumably to express their
impatience with the earl's attitude, and during the debate Vane

---

[1] Ibid., f. 157.   [2] Ibid.   [3] Harl. 164, f. 334.
[4] For their attacks see Hexter, op. cit., 58.

made a sarcastic speech. Seeing the Commons had neglected, he said, 'upon the severall messages of the Lords to entertain the consideration of sending propositions to the king', Essex had 'done well to stirre us upp to it, although our fatherlie care of the kingdome should have preceded his Lordship's care'. He added that he observed Essex's letters to mean 'that if wee would send propositions of peace to his Majestie and they did not take effect, that then hee would doe his dutie'. Vane's criticism brought a vigorous defence of Essex by his partisans; Stapleton and Goodwin objected to Vane's words, and he had twice to apologize.[1]

On 13 July Essex replied, also in sarcastic vein, to the attack of two days before. He 'desired that Sir Henry Vane the younger might bee sent to him, of whom the House of Commons had a very good opinion, that soe he might advise with him touching the great affairs of the Kingdome, and that if the said Sir Henry Vane should advise him to march up to the walls of Oxford hee would goe with him'.[2] Clarendon later noted that it was Vane whom of all men Essex 'hated and looked upon as an enemy'.[3] It is significant that Vane's provocative remarks of 11 July, after the reception of the letter from Essex, followed a very critical speech from Pym, who rose and declared that Parliament could not make overtures again to the king, as the earl was suggesting, because all Parliament's offers of peace had been rejected by Charles.[4] Vane as usual

---

[1] Harl. 165, f. 123v. 11 July.

[2] Ibid., f. 126. Vane's biographers have assumed that Essex was slyly referring to the inglorious part which a royalist lampoon (*Somers Tracts*, vii, 92) alleged Vane had played at the battle of Newburn in 1640. The contemporary accounts of this skirmish (HMC. *10th Rep.* App. part iv, 393, *Percy MSS*, and *CSPD. 1640*, 645) refer to 'Captain Vane', but this cannot have been Sir Henry. Firstly because he had been knighted in June, and could not be referred to in August as 'Captain Vane', secondly, because he had been busy all that summer with ship-money accounts, by virtue of his position as joint Navy Treasurer. (*CSPD. 1640*, 272, 305, 485, 566.) One ship-money account is actually dated 28 November 1640, the very day of Newburn, (ibid., 644). Captain George Vane, Sir Henry's brother, was near Newcastle with his troop on 9 July (ibid., 460), and is probably the officer mentioned in the Newburn Heath accounts, for he was knighted in November 1640. (Shaw, *The Knights of England*, ii, 208.) Another brother, William, is mentioned as raising a troop in March. (*CSPD. 1640*, 545.) Essex may have been emphasizing Vane's inexperience, but not his cowardice.

[3] Clarendon, *Rebellion*, viii, 92. (Writing of 1644.)

[4] Harl. 165, f. 123v.

spoke in a more intemperate way but he was following Pym's lead.

Indeed there is nothing to show until his speech of 11 July that he was among the critics of Essex. In April he had moved that one subject of conference with the Lords should be the sequestration of Sir Arthur Capel's estate, which should be assigned to Essex to compensate him for the loss of his own.[1] If Vane had found this motion uncongenial he could no doubt have found someone else to sponsor it. He had taken no part in a debate in June on the earl's conduct of the war.[2] In short, in this as on other major issues, Vane's attitude and Pym's were similar.

The Solemn League and Covenant is an important episode in connexion with the development of Vane's religious views. When in the summer of 1643 Parliament's fortunes were at a low ebb, and it was decided to invite the help of the Scots, it was natural that Vane, as the friend of Pym, should be sent[3] for the Scots alliance was Pym's policy.[4] The House no doubt also remembered that Vane was skilled in finding the right phrase or word, and the members must have realized that in this negotiation many discordant interests would have to be reconciled. According to Clarendon it was Vane who was chiefly responsible for the negotiations with the Scots, though three others were joined with him,[5] and it was he who altered many expressions in the Covenant, until he 'made them doubtful enough to bear many interpretations'.[6] Ludlow and Burnet also asserted that Vane was responsible for inserting the phrases which enabled the English Parliament to avoid introducing the full Presbyterian system.[7] The English Church would be reformed not only according to the example of the best Reformed Churches, a term always taken at the time to mean

---

[1] Harl. 164, f. 380.   [2] Ibid., f. 233v. 2 June.

[3] *CJ*. iii, 132. There is no satisfactory account of the Solemn League and Covenant, its genesis and importance.

[4] Harl. 164, f. 381. 1 May 1643. The suggestion may well have been made before —a pamphlet of 28 April urged the Scots to help the Parliamentarians. (E 99(31).) The Venetian ambassador had written in March that the king's opponents counted on help from Scotland. (*CSPV. 1641-42*, 257.)

[5] Clarendon, *Rebellion*, vii, 266, 274. (For Colonel Birch's assumption in 1659 that Vane was responsible for the Covenant, see Burton, iv, 331.)

[6] Ibid., vii, 266, 274.   [7] Ludlow, i, 65.

the Calvinists, but also 'according to the word of God',[1] on
which there might be infinite differences of opinion.

Though there is no direct proof that Vane dominated the
negotiations, he probably did; none of the other emissaries of
Parliament who accompanied him were so prominent, and
Clarendon very likely heard what was being said in London—
there was a great deal of coming and going between Oxford
and the capital.[2] In a contemporary pamphlet which included
various documents concerning the Solemn League and Covenant, one account of the negotiations mentioned Vane alone
among the English delegates,[3] and he was said to have brought
up to London the figures concerning the Scots Army.[4] The same
pamphlet printed a letter from Edinburgh in which 'the truly
worthie and right worshippful Sir Henry Vane' was the only
lay commissioner mentioned.[5]

His responsibility, however, for the words which could
relieve Parliament from the necessity of introducing Presbyterianism cannot be proved. The Solemn League and Covenant
met with strenuous opposition in England—this is evident
from the pains taken by numerous preachers to answer the
many cogent objections.[6] A royalist writer at once noted that
the oath to the Covenant was 'capable of a million of interpretations, as when they swear to promote the reformation of
the Church of England, according to the word of God, and the
best Reformed Churches'.[7] He also commented upon the gulf
between swearing to maintain the Presbyterian discipline in
Scotland, and the words used concerning a religious reformation in England.[8] 'But here', he wrote, 'you may see the crafty
dealing of these men, that had the framing and contriving of
this covenant. They knew well enough with whom they had
to do . . . the Scots on the one side, much wooed and courted
by them . . . the various sectaries and disagreeing humorists on

---

[1] Gardiner, *Const. Docs.*, 267–71.

[2] See e.g. *A royal declaration repealing all licences for bringing goods from London*,
BM. 669, f. 7 (59).

[3] E 74(5), p. 23.   [4] Ibid., p. 26.

[5] Ibid. Marshall is only 'truly zealous'.

[6] E 78(4), E 72(12), E 71(13), 1208(1). Marshall's was by far the best sermon.

[7] E 73(1) (Thomason's date 26 October 1643), p. 11.

[8] Ibid., p. 12. '. . . if they do like it [the Scottish Discipline] why durst they
not sweare to introduce it here?'

the other side. These must both be pleased.'[1] The writer however had only the internal evidence of the Solemn League and Covenant to work upon and there is no indication that he had other reasons to suspect the English negotiators of double-dealing. Clarendon believed that Vane was already, in the late summer and autumn of 1643, an enemy of Presbyterianism. On the other hand, his one reported speech of any length on religious matters, that of June 1641,[2] would not be incompatible with Presbyterian sympathies, and the information which he gave the House in October 1643 of the Scottish penalties imposed on those who would not accept the Covenant, facts which he surely could have withheld had he not wished England to follow the Scottish example, supports that view.

But there are serious objections to it. In the 1630s as governor of Massachusetts he had, as we have seen, pleaded eloquently for the admission to the colony of men whose religious views differed from those of the ruling religious group. In the spring of 1644 he secured toleration for Rhode Island, and by the autumn of that year Baillie was writing angrily that Vane was one of the leaders of the toleration party.[3] It is unlikely that he veered to religious intolerance and Presbyterianism during the intervening period. No doubt the parlous situation of the Roundhead armies in 1643 which is reflected in the contemporary sermons[4] justified in his mind the concessions which had been made to Presbyterianism.

In November 1643, with the Scots alliance safely settled, and Pym too ill to take part in politics, the situation had changed. When Stapleton, the defender of the earl of Essex and possibly his spokesman, declared that Essex lacked regular pay for his troops it was Vane who rose and declared that the committee of the Navy had met the day before with another committee, and that he thought £20,000 was already provided for Essex's immediate use; the committee were to meet next day to

---

[1] Ibid., p. 13. The whole pamphlet is able and penetrating. See e.g. p. 15, 'not a word of the Law in the whole oath. You may see by that how they meane to governe', and the extraordinary prophecy, 'Tis too cleare the purpose is to leave the people at liberty, to kill the King's person, and to trample on his authority', ibid.

[2] See below, p. 192.   [3] Baillie, ii, 235-6.

[4] E.g. E 80(1); (2).

consider the question of arranging for regular payment.[1] It
sounds as though he was trying to silence Essex's protest, and
if so, he succeeded, for the House was satisfied with his assurance
for the time being. In December D'Ewes, in conversation with
Sir Walter Earle's son after a desultory debate on recruiting
for Essex's army, heard an interesting account of the party
divisions in the House. Young Earle told D'Ewes that there
were now 'sparkes' or factions in the House. The first was
'Those that desired all [money] that might possibly bee spared
for the satisfying of the Scotts, and were therefore loath that
the Lord Generall's [the earl of Essex] army should either bee
too numerous or require too much money, and the cheife
leader of this party was young Sir Henry Vane, with whom
joyned most of the Northern gentlemen whose estates were
seized by the Earl of Newcastle.'[2] The second consisted of 'such
as desired to further Sir William Waller's expedition into the
West . . . the cheife leaders were Mr. Trenchard and Mr.
Prideaux, being Western men'. The third party consisted of
'Sir Philip Stapleton and others that had command in the
Lord General's army, and of all those who were not compre-
hended in the associations, who as appeared . . . did almost
equall the number of the other two'.[3] Like other political
explanations which D'Ewes accepted,[4] the analysis was probably an over-simplification of the situation, but it does confirm
the impression that diaries give of Vane as leader of the pro-
Scottish and anti-Essex party at this time. On 12 December
1643, Vane evidently attempted to divert the House from
proceeding with the discussion of recruiting for the earl's
forces, by delivering a letter from Parliament's commissioners
in Scotland, 'alleging that there was great necessity for the
reading thereof', but on this occasion Vane was unsuccessful,
and the House, after dealing with the letter, went back to the
subject of Essex's army.[5]

[1] Harl. 165, f. 226. 10 November 1643.
[2] The Vane family estates in the North suffered crippling losses during the Civil
War. See CJ. iii, 690; CSPD. 1644-45, 162, 310.
[3] Harl. 165, f. 233. 6 December 1643.
[4] D'Ewes held that it was men of 'mean estates' who supported the war party—
they were not so aware of the ruin of the country, and were silly enough to follow
Pym and some others, whichever way they went. (Harl. 164, f. 346. 28 March 1643.)
[5] Harl. 165, f. 242.

As far as Henry Marten is concerned, there are one or two indications that he and Vane gave support to one another in Parliament at this time.[1] This would be natural—in their undisguised hostility to the Lords and to peace negotiations the two men had much in common. But Marten had wittily attacked Pym, and it was Pym who had Marten expelled from the House. This would indicate some difference of opinion between Pym and his young friend; but Vane was not there to object, for in fact Marten was expelled while Vane was in Scotland.[2] In considering Vane's attitude to Pym, one must bear in mind however that parties as we know them today did not exist, and that in the changing war situation M.P.s modified their policies. Vane and Pym could openly differ on occasion, on minor matters.[3]

Pym's friend Oliver St John was a close associate of Vane—a contemporary diurnal refers to the two as 'intimate friends'[4] —and the parliamentary diaries give a strong impression that the two men were co-operating in Parliament. On many occasions St John is found taking exactly the same line as Vane,[5] seconding[6] or immediately following up a suggestion he had made.[7] Both men, with Pym and Glyn, formed the committee set up to investigate Edmund Waller's plot, and carried out their duties with great energy.[8] With St John, however, as with Pym, Vane could disagree on occasion, and in January 1642 they differed on an important point. St John had just brought in a bill of tunnage and poundage which was to be in force for the king's lifetime. Vane rose to move that a short bill, authorizing the levy for two months only, should be brought in.[9] St John, in the cause of financial stability, was trying to get

---

[1] See p. 18, and n. 3 below.

[2] Hexter, op. cit., 148. Vane left for Scotland on 20 July.   [3] Harl. 162, f. 54v.

[4] *Anti-Aulicus*, E 31(17), p. 6. 3 February 1644. There is much other evidence pointing in the same direction.

[5] E.g. Harl. 164, f. 275. 26 December 1642 (peace proposals).

[6] Ibid., 876v, Harl. 165, ff. 213v, 254.

[7] Whittaker, 86v. 26 October 1643. Vane said, on his return from Scotland, that the Scots were discouraged because they had heard nothing about money for the forces they were to levy for the English Parliament. St John at once brought in the ordinance providing for the money to be raised.

[8] Harl. 164, ff. 210, 397v *et seq.* Harl. 165, f. 103.

[9] Harl. 162, f. 351v. 26 January 1642.

tunnage and poundage put on a permanent basis. He probably expected opposition—he had brought the bill in early in the day, and the House ordered that it should be brought in between 11 a.m. and 4 p.m. in a fuller house. D'Ewes noted that: 'divers . . . who were the intimate friends of Mr. Saint John the king's sollicitor [Vane was almost certainly one] spake against the bill',[1] and the House took Vane's advice.[2] No doubt his objection was not so much to the impracticability of the bill, but to the power which it would give the king *vis-à-vis* Parliament. On the following day St John brought in a new act[3] which was to be in force for some two months only.[4]

There are indications that Vane's circle in the early days of the Long Parliament included some prominent Londoners. Clarendon wrote of the end of 1644 that the war party prevailed among the mayor and aldermen of the City, for Vane had 'diligently provided that men of his own principles and inclinations should be brought into the government of the city, of which he saw they should always have great need'.[5] As early as March 1641 Alderman Pennington reported to the Commons that Vane was one of the M.P.s of whom the City had a good opinion, and he was accordingly sent with five other M.P.s to make a request to the City for a loan of £100,000.[6] At the beginning of November 1641 when the Irish rebellion had broken out and Parliament wished for another loan from the City, to deal with this emergency, Vane was one of the committee of twenty-four M.P.s who, with representatives of the Lords, were sent to the City to negotiate the loan.[7] When the Recorder of London declared to this committee that the protections allowed to M.P.s' servants hindered the lending of money and stopped trade it was Vane who replied that the House was taking steps to deal with this question of protections.[8]

---

[1] Ibid., f. 353.
[2] Pym also spoke against the bill, on the grounds that subsidy bills should only be brought in by order of the Lower House. (Peyton, 26 January 1641-2.)
[3] Harl. 163, f. 354v.   [4] *Statutes of the Realm*, v. 140.
[5] Clarendon, *Rebellion*, viii, 188.
[6] Notestein, *D'Ewes*, 421. 1 March 1641.   [7] *CJ.* ii, 302.
[8] Ibid., 303. 3 November 1641. Vane is the only M.P. mentioned by name in the Commons report. The names of the delegates from Parliament are not given in the Journal of the Common Council, nor any except the briefest account of what was said. (JCC., London, vol. 39, f. 240.)

In June 1642, when war was imminent, six peers and twelve M.P.s were sent to the City to request another substantial loan; Vane was not among them.[1] But when the Lord Mayor had issued his precept to the several Companies to meet and decide what they would raise, the House decided to send several M.P.s who were to go into the City and be present at the Companies' meetings, to 'advance' the loan, and Vane was one.[2]

He was not an inevitable member of the committees on London;[3] but when on 25 October the House decided that able-bodied Londoners should be exempt from the fast fixed for the following day, so that preparations for defending the City should not be impeded, he was one of the four M.P.s appointed to draft the necessary order.[4] This again was probably due to his ability to frame suitable phrases (it would not be altogether easy to convince the godly that material considerations should be put before religious ones). On 8 November 1642 Vane and five others were sent to a Common Hall to report what endeavours Parliament had made for peace,[5] perhaps because he could argue convincingly, or because the City respected him. He informed the City at this meeting of the king's refusal to accept Sir John Evelyn as one of Parliament's envoys in negotiating for peace, and that it was Parliament's determination to remain loyal to their impugned member, and not any unwillingness to make peace, that had made it impossible for the negotiations to continue.

By February 1643, when the Oxford negotiations were still continuing, D'Ewes was convinced that the 'fierie spirits' in the City were working with Hampden, Pym, Rous and 'others of the same minds', though he does not name Vane among these.[6] But on 27 April D'Ewes again suspected collusion between certain M.P.s and some of the City leaders, and on

---

[1] *CJ.* ii, 598.

[2] Ibid., 605. 4 June. The Livery Companies were not impressed, and comparatively little money was forthcoming. (Pearl, *London and the Outbreak of the Puritan Revolution*, 208–9.) Dr Pearl does not mention the M.P.s' personal appeal.

[3] E.g. *CJ.* ii, 684.   [4] Ibid., 823.

[5] Ibid., 840, E 126(44). Vane made one of the three speeches to the Common Hall, and Lord Brooke made the other two. It is puzzling that this meeting is not reported in any of the London records, and hence finds no place in Dr Pearl's book, nor in R. R. Sharpe, *London and the Kingdom* (London, 1894–5).

[6] Harl. 164, f. 303. 20 February 1643.

this occasion Vane was involved. On that day D'Ewes came into the House to find him talking of a conference with the Lords, who were to be asked to join the Commons in sending a delegation to the Common Council of London. He proposed that the parliamentary delegates should have certain curiously vague powers. 'When we should move them', said Vane, 'that the City might advance more money for the payment of the army . . . if there should be anything objected against the said advancing of money . . . that then the said committee might have power to remove the said obstructions.' D'Ewes was suspicious of Vane's proposal—'I did at this verie instant suspect that one of the obstructions which would be made by the fierie spirits in the cittie of London would be that we should enter into a new oath or covenant, and that this business was before plotted betweene themselves and those of the same leaven in the House, which proved so in the issue.'[1]

The Court of Common Council had put forward the demand for a covenant twice before, in February and March,[2] and again in April.[3] The sting of the covenant plan lay in clause 2 —'That the rents, revenews, goods, monies and estates of such as shall refuse to joyne in the association and Covenant aforesaid shall be imployed in such maner and proporcion as the howses shall thinke fitt for the good of the kingdom, and their persons be secured.'[4] This was a monstrous proposal whose severe penalties would have been more appropriate for active royalism. Once more Vane was taking a harsh attitude towards his opponents, and it is certainly difficult to believe that he was not acting in collaboration with a party in the City. He did not carry the Commons with him however—the House let the matter of the London covenant drop.[5]

He was in Scotland while Marten's project for raising a volunteer regiment of Londoners under Sir William Waller's command was being attempted in July and August 1643, though it is unlikely that this impractical project would ever have commended itself to Vane. His Scottish visit also precludes

[1] Harl. 164, ff. 380–380v.   [2] Pearl, op. cit., 258–61.   [3] *CJ*. iii, 37. 10 April.
[4] JCC. London, 40, ff. 47v, 48. 18 February; f. 49. 21 February.
[5] Ibid., f. 50v. (Parliament promised only to *consider* Common Council's proposal.)
Harl. 164, ff. 381, 381v; Whittaker, f. 46v.

any possibility that he had a hand in organizing the London mob who arrived at the Houses of Parliament on 6 August, to denounce the peace party. He may well have been connected however with the audacious and successful attempt to 'rig' the London Common Council elections in December 1643. The elections were always held on 21 December, and St John, on the day before they were to take place, rose in the Commons to present an ordinance excluding, both from voting and from standing as candidates for the Common Council, all those who had been questioned for 'malignancy', or who had not taken the religious Covenant the Scots had insisted upon. D'Ewes urged the omission of the 'malignancy' clause, asserting with truth that many might have been unjustly suspected.[1] But the House was informed that there was a plot in the City to 'put out' from the Common Council 'divers well-affected men', and St John's ordinance passed. There was no time to organize any counter-pressure on the House—the stratagem had been well-planned. There is no record that Vane spoke in the debate. He was in the House two days later, when he and St John spoke on the same side.[2] It seems highly likely that it was to this incident that Clarendon was referring when he wrote of Vane's securing men of his own principles in the government of London.[3] If Vane was widely blamed for the manœuvre this also would strengthen his reputation for being dishonest in political matters.

There are indications that the hostility between Vane and John Maynard, the prominent lawyer and politician, which can be clearly seen in Burton's diary for the 1659 Parliament, and which culminated in Maynard's leading the prosecution at Vane's trial for treason, dates at least from 1643. In February of that year, when Vane was arguing that disbandment of the two opposing armies must precede a peace treaty, Maynard made a very telling reply, pointing out that the House had

---

[1] Harl. 165, f. 249v. Dr Pearl (op. cit., 274) says that there was a shift in power in the City when in October Pennington gave up the mayoralty to Wollaston, a moderate. If so, St John's ordinance was a counter-move. Whittaker, f. 102v, has 'convinced of malignancy'.

[2] Harl. 165, f. 254. 22 December 1643.

[3] Clarendon did not blame St John for the London ordinance; either he did not know of his part, or treated more kindly one who afterwards welcomed Charles II's return.

voted disbanding to mean that the king would disband all his armies, whereas Parliament would keep the garrisons and the navy. Besides, Parliament could reassemble its army quickly whereas the king could not, for Parliament's army came mostly from London and adjacent counties.[1] Later in the same year the two men crossed swords on the making of a new Great Seal, which Maynard strenuously opposed.[2]

The period 1640-3 shows Vane co-operating with Pym and St John, and to a much lesser extent and only on occasions for specific purposes, with Marten and Glyn. His association with Cromwell and Sir Arthur Hesilrige at the time of the Root and Branch bill in the summer of 1641 is probably significant, though it has left few other traces.[3] Sir Philip Stapleton, before the rift between Sir William Waller and the earl of Essex, may well have been another of Vane's collaborators. Vane vigorously supported the Scottish alliance, and his hostility to Essex is related to this. There are some tenuous but interesting hints of his connexions with the City. These early years of the Long Parliament shed much light on Vane's character. Possessed of a subtle mind, and a power of sarcasm which may well have made him enemies, Vane stands out in the diaries as a very individual member of Parliament.[4] His ruthlessness is marked, and though there is no evidence of republicanism in him, there are hints that he was working with Marten in other ways. The diaries and *Commons Journals* give a strong impression of a politician essentially radical in attitude, both towards the king and the Lords, with an intelligence and an adroitness in manœuvre which already marked him out from his fellow-members.

---

[1] Harl. 164, ff. 301v. 17 February 1643.

[2] Ibid., f. 389. 12 May 1643. For examples of Maynard's rising in the Commons to reply to Vane, see Yonge, BM. Add. 18,777, ff. 148v, 149, 151.

[3] Cromwell moved that Vane should be added to a committee on Kent. (Harl. 162, f. 56v.) Hesilrige frequently took the same attitude as Vane, and developed his ideas (e.g. BM. Add. 18, 777, f. 64).

[4] It was Vane who raised the question of the care of manuscripts seized from royalists and stored at Camden House. This led to the appointment of a committee, including Selden and D'Ewes, to see that such manuscripts should be safely 'laid up'. (Harl. 165, f. 202. 2 November 1643.)

CHAPTER II

The Struggle with Holles, 1644

BY JANUARY 1644 the king himself was referring to Vane as the leader of a party in the House,[1] and the diaries bear this out, though St John was probably equally important, and Strode hardly less so. It is also clear that by January 1644 Denzil Holles and Sir John Clotworthy were the most usual opponents of Vane and St John. Holles had begun to support peace negotiations in November 1642,[2] but the formation of a cohesive political group with Holles as its leader seems to have been a very gradual process. Stapleton was persuaded by Pym in the summer of 1643 not to give his support to the peace party, as he had been inclined to do,[3] and was probably not in general accord with Holles until December of that year.[4] Even in 1645 he was once a teller against Holles.[5] It seems that Holles emerged as a leader, with others such as Sir John Maynard, in the spring of 1643, during the debates on the peace negotiations, that he led the opposition to the Scottish alliance (which of course was related to the continuation of war) later in 1643, and that throughout 1643 and 1644 the key questions were political ones.[6] The terms 'Presbyterian' and 'Independent' will not be used here therefore for the 1644 period, but only for 1645 and later, when religious issues had more clearly emerged, (though their importance has often been exaggerated), and

[1] See below, p. 42.
[2] According to D'Ewes, Harl. 164, f. 302.
[3] He had spoken strongly in favour of a peace treaty the day before, says D'Ewes, but it was thought he and others had been 'taken off' by Pym, Say and some others. (Harl. 165, f. 123v.)
[4] D'Ewes names him as a leader of the earl of Essex's group in December, ibid., f. 233v.
[5] CJ. iv, 471.
[6] As Professor Hexter saw. 'The problem of the Presbyterian Independents', Re-appraisals in History (London, 1961), 177.

when the terms have the justification of common contemporary usage.

Vane's collaborators in 1644 again included St John, and their names were coupled on innumerable occasions. Both wanted the Committee of Both Kingdoms, not Parliament, to control peace negotiations,[1] and to direct the earl of Essex's army;[2] later the two friends tried to weaken that army by giving more authority to Skippon and Waller.[3] There are many other instances of their co-operation. Hesilrige often supported them,[4] and Zouch Tate belonged to this group.[5] Strode took the same line on referring peace negotiations to the Committee of Both Kingdoms,[6] and on other matters too,[7] though he was an important and independent-minded member, and Samuel Browne, whose part in Parliament has not been sufficiently valued, sometimes at least co-operated with Vane and St John.[8] Cromwell of course was associated with them, and D'Ewes suspected, probably with reason,[9] that John Lisle, the member for Winchester, was willing to act as their agent in the Commons. One must remember that leading M.P.s might vote sometimes with a group and sometimes against it; nevertheless it is still true to say that Vane and St John in some sort led a 'war-party', or at least a group opposed to peace negotiations. And though Vane and St John could not always carry the House with them in 1644, they used adroit parliamentary tactics in their endeavours to do so.

Undoubtedly their most important instrument for the control of the Commons was the Committee of Both Kingdoms,[10] the executive committee which S. R. Gardiner saw as the forerunner of the modern cabinet, in its powers of independent action. This committee, like so many of the constructive

---

[1] Harl. 166, f. 33.   [2] Ibid., f. 36.

[3] Ibid., f. 128v. For other examples of their co-operation, see ibid., ff. 48, 53v, 61v, 128, et al.

[4] Ibid., ff. 36, 37, 46.

[5] Ibid., f. 33. 'Tate, set on by yong Fane, Sollicitor, and others.' See also ff. 38v, 40.

[6] Ibid., f. 41   [7] Ibid., f. 128.   [8] See below, pp. 42, 48, 66n.

[9] Ibid., f. 149. 'Mr. Lisle by a pre-arrangement doubtless of some the violent moved very earnestly that writts might be issued out for new elections.' 16 October 1644. See also f. 36.

[10] W. Notestein, 'The establishment of the Committee of Both Kingdoms', 477–95.

measures of 1643–5, was evidently Vane's brain-child, and there are important aspects of its establishment and work in which Vane was concerned.

Its predecessor as a council of war was the Committee for the Safety of the Kingdom, established in July 1642. This was set up to direct the war,[1] and was pre-eminently Pym's committee.[2] A royal proclamation speaks of 'the whole power of parliament, and more, being resolved into a committee of a few men, contrary to all law, custom and precedent',[3] and for fourteen months the Committee of Safety was a very powerful committee. When Sir John Hotham, the governor of Hull, was approached by Lord Savile, the Yorkshire landowner, with the offer of the surrender of York on condition that Hotham made Savile's peace with Parliament, Hotham consulted the Committee of Safety, and not Parliament. D'Ewes asserts that some M.P.s were indignant on hearing this.[4] One diurnal declared that when the establishment of the Committee of Both Kingdoms was being considered, the Commons held that the new committee would in no way detract from the power of the Lord General, the earl of Essex, 'for the Committee of the Safetie had the same power formerlie'.[5] But in October 1643 Pym fell ill, and the Committee of Safety lost all its drive. On 17 October Whittaker reported that: 'the Committee of the Safety not now sitting, Mr. Pym being sick', a committee was named to 'consider of a Council of War'.[6] It should be noted that Whittaker evidently equated the Committee of Safety with a council of war. It seems however to have acquired a reputation for dilatoriness even before Pym's death.[7]

The committee set up in October to consider the nomination

---

[1] *CJ.* iii, 314, 316, 318, 323, *et al.*

[2] For Pym's reports of its activities see ibid., ii, 659, 668, 696, 714. The Committee's secretary was Henry Parker, the political pamphleteer. (Harl. 165, f. 210v.)

[3] Clarendon, *Rebellion*, vii, 141.   [4] Harl. 165, f. 133v. 2 August 1643.

[5] *The Kingdomes Weekly Intelligencer*, pp. 330–1. 7–14 February 1644. E 33(6). For D'Ewes's view of the committee as an extremely powerful committee which 'communicated as much to us as they thought it fitting for us to know', see Harl. 164, f. 818v.

[6] Whittaker, f. 84v.

[7] In March 1643 Rigby asked for gunpowder to be supplied to Lancashire from the magazine at Hull. When some M.P.s moved to refer the matter to the Committee of Safety Rigby said he would rather be refused. Pym protested vigorously,

of a council of war made no report. The nominating committee's membership is odd: it included Pym, St John and one of the Vanes, but with the exception of Hesilrige and Sir William Waller (then probably supported by Vane's group), no M.P. with actual experience in the field; the friends of the earl of Essex, such as Stapleton, were pointedly excluded.[1] One wonders why the committee never reported. It was probably because the council of war was intended by the opponents of Essex to take the direction of military operations out of the hands of the earl, but they realized that the House would not tolerate a council of war from which both Stapleton and Clotworthy were excluded, as the nominating committee would have liked.

The Committee of Safety therefore continued to exist; on 18 October it was instructed to recruit men for the army of the earl of Essex.[2] On 22 October Hesilrige was actually added to it,[3] and it was ordered to meet in the afternoon, and at Pym's home, Derby House, just as the Committee of Both Kingdoms was to do in the following years. It looks as though a determined attempt to secure government by committees was made on 13 November 1643—the Committee of Safety, followed by other committees, was to sit on three days a week, and the Commons were to sit only on the other weekdays.[4] But perhaps the House did not want a directing committee at this juncture, for the Commons were soon sitting on the days reserved for the committees,[5] and it looks as though the Commons merely wanted a body that would do some preparatory and follow-up work, and not a 'cabinet'.[6] Moreover, the Committee of Safety seems to have lacked some essential energy. On 12 December it was ordered to sit every day at 3 p.m. but evidently it did not, for six days later it was ordered to meet 'peremptorily' at 3 p.m. at latest, an unnecessary instruction if the previous order had been obeyed.[7]

---

but Rigby said he had waited on the Committee endlessly and fruitlessly, and according to D'Ewes the House rested very 'well satisfied' of Rigby's complaint. (Harl. 164, f. 338. 22 March 1643.)

[1] *CJ.* iii, 278.   [2] Ibid., 280.   [3] Ibid., 299.   [4] Ibid., 309.   [5] Ibid., 322, 324.

[6] The Committee of Safety did not, as the Committee of Both Kingdoms afterwards did, prepare drafts for the House to ratify, unless the House instructed it to do so.   [7] *CJ.* iii, 339, 344.

The first open move foreshadowing the Committee of Both Kingdoms was made in November 1643; this was probably due to Vane, St John and Lord Say, for Pym was already ill.[1] Vane had arrived from Scotland, probably on 25 October.[2] But there is nothing to indicate that even yet there was any intention to supersede the Committee of Safety; the obvious method of constituting a Committee for Both Kingdoms was to join the Committee of Safety with some of the Scots commissioners who had been sent to London to sign the Solemn League and Covenant, and supervise the carrying out of its terms. On 30 January 1644, very shortly after the arrival of the Scots commissioners, the ordinance establishing the Committee of Both Kingdoms was drafted by Vane and St John[3] and by this Holles's group were excluded from the new committee. Presumably the Scots acquiesced in the exclusion of Holles and his supporters because they were the peace party and the friends of the earl of Essex, if indeed the Scots understood the political situation in England at all.[4]

It should be noted that those prominent M.P.s who generally supported Holles and who were excluded from the Committee[5] were those who had particularly crossed swords with Vane. Holles himself, though he was one of the most respected M.P.s[6] and had had military experience, was not nominated. About this time Holles was more than once in opposition to Vane in the House, and Vane was defeated, for Holles's following was considerable. In this same month of January 1644, for instance, Vane and Hesilrige were in favour of impeaching the earl of Holland who had deserted to the king at Oxford, but had later returned to Parliament; they were

---

[1] Notestein, op. cit., 480.

[2] Harl. 165, f. 202. It was intended that Vane should return to Scotland 'shortly' but he did not. (Ibid., f. 200. 31 October 1643.)

[3] Baillie, ii, 141.

[4] For Holles's view, that the earl of Essex was obnoxious both as a monarchist and peace-lover, see his *Memoirs*, 195.

[5] Stapleton was the only supporter of Holles who was a member of the new committee. (He wanted to be sent to the Scottish army, according to Baillie—this may explain his inclusion.)

[6] For the respect in which he was held see for instance Sabran, 'Mm. Holis et Vanes fort accrédités dans la Chambre des Communes . . .' (BM. Add. 5460, f. 50. 23 May 1644.)

tellers in the division, against Holles and Stapleton, and were in the minority.[1] Clotworthy's exclusion from the new committee is also remarkable for he too had had military experience. But Vane had clashed with him several times. Clotworthy had argued vigorously in favour of appointing an English nobleman to command the English troops in Ireland, rather than allowing General Leslie to control the troops of both nations,[2] and Vane had also accused Clotworthy of complicity in the Brooke Plot in January, though he did not persist with the charge.[3]

Another aspect of the original ordinance of 30 January is important.[4] If this ordinance had passed, the Committee of Both Kingdoms would have had authority over the vital issue of peace or war. This was a bold attempt to take peace negotiations out of Parliament's control, and the circumstances of the time show why. The royalist Parliament at Oxford had met on 22 January 1644.[5] Within five days it had sent peace overtures to the earl of Essex.[6] The 'war party' in London must have been well aware how strong was the demand for peace,[7] and Vane's trials of strength with Holles had shown him that in the House he might lose the day. Hence the attempt to give the new committee a power the Committee of Safety had never had, that of negotiating peace terms. The attempt was unsuccessful, and the ordinance of 30 January did not pass, though months later the coveted authority was obtained, after a struggle. But in January 1644 some members at once saw the importance of the powers and personnel of the Committee. Robert Reynolds, the lawyer who represented Hindon, had suggested that most of the members of the Committee held positions in the Army and would be able to continue the war as long as they liked, and fatten their purses.[8] Though Vane opposed him[9] he did not forget the accusation.

The Commons evidently were not going to pass Vane and

---

[1] *CJ*. iii, 370.   [2] Harl. 165, f. 254. 22 December 1643.
[3] Whittaker, f. 106. 8 January 1644.
[4] Professor Notestein did not discuss this point.
[5] Clarendon, *Rebellion*, vii, 370.   [6] Ibid.
[7] D. A. Bigby, *Anglo-French Relations, 1641 to 1649* (London, 1933), 46; Harl. 165, f. 149v.
[8] Notestein, op. cit., 489. (This is from Whittaker, f. 113v.)
[9] Ibid.

St John's ordinance. Another ordinance, which prohibited the Committee from conducting peace negotiations, was therefore introduced, this time in the Lords, but exactly the same twenty-one names were put forward.[1] Vane was evidently the man behind this second ordinance, for he bore the brunt of the debate in its defence. It was not parliamentary practice for the names of a committee to be included in the draft ordinance,[2] but in this ordinance they were. Vane's group, who ordinarily had a narrow majority in the House, were ensuring their own control of the Committee by not allowing the Commons to make nominations themselves. He and Hesilrige were the tellers in favour of this unusual ordinance when it reached the Commons, Holles and Sir William Lewes were the tellers for the opposition, and were defeated, by 51 to 65 votes.[3] The Commons were now allowed to vote for or against each of the whole twenty-one, but of course they could not add names to the list. The Lords too, it may be noted, were tied down to the names in the ordinance, and the Venetian ambassador saw that the Commons were in fact nominating the Lords' representatives.[4] The peers did try to add some other names, but eventually gave way.[5] In the struggle with the Lords, Vane played the most important part. When the Lords, trying to preserve freedom of action for the earl of Essex, wanted the Committee of Both Kingdoms to 'advise and consult', not 'order and direct' the conduct of the war, Vane was one of the committee to prepare an answer in defence of the Commons' position,[6] and his line of argument was well-calculated to appeal to Parliament. He 'would not have too great a power in the soldiery, but would have them subject to the parliament, and to your committee'.[7] After two conferences with the Upper House the Commons ordered the committee which had prepared the previous answer to have a statement ready for the following morning.[8] The committee should have met that same day therefore, but apparently did not, for early next morning Vane moved that it should withdraw to do the work the House had set it.[9] He

---

[1] Ibid., 491. [2] Harl. 163, f. 285v; BM. Add. 18,779, f. 107.
[3] *CJ*. iii, 391. 7 February 1644. [4] *CSPV. 1643–47*, 74–5.
[5] Notestein, op. cit., 492. [6] *CJ*. iii, 396, 397, 398.
[7] BM. Add. 18,779, f. 64v. 9 February.
[8] *CJ*. iii, 398. [9] Harl. 166, f. 2.

returned so quickly that D'Ewes sourly concluded that Vane had 'doubtless prepared most of the reasons' for the Commons' attitude the night before.[1] Vane sat in front of D'Ewes in the House,[2] and D'Ewes probably had opportunities of observing him. To the Lords' attempts to defend the power of the earl of Essex as against the Committee Vane replied that the Committee would not command or direct anything unwise, and that Essex could always send the Committee the reason for his refusal to obey![3] This was very like insolence but the earl, with his record of defeat in the field, was in no position to reply.

The whole episode reflects Vane's character and methods. His determination and his political dexterity were clearly shown, for though his first ordinance was in effect defeated in the House, within a few days he had returned to the charge with a new ordinance so framed as to be more acceptable to the Commons. The Committee would not now have the responsibility for peace negotiations, unless Parliament so directed.[4] He was also using the Commons' awareness of the weakness of the older Committee of Safety to enable him to destroy it; with his own capacity for sustained and thorough work he probably despised the Committee's ineffectiveness, and was replacing it by a more efficient instrument for winning the war, (which the Committee of Both Kingdoms certainly was).

In the later struggle to secure for the Committee of Both Kingdoms the control of peace negotiations with the king, Vane again played a very prominent part. On 14 March 1644 the Dutch ambassadors informed the Lords that they were willing to mediate;[5] Tate 'set on', according to D'Ewes, by Vane and St John, moved next morning that the Dutch offer should be referred to the Committee of Both Kingdoms. The Commons resolved without a division that the Committee and not, be it noted, the Commons, should prepare grounds for a safe and well-grounded peace, such as both England and Scotland might consent to.[6] Vane was one of the twelve who were

---

[1] Ibid., f. 12.   [2] Ibid., f. 3v.   [3] Ibid., f. 12.

[4] The ordinance is explicit—'nothing in this ordinance shall authorize the Committee hereby appointed to advise, treat, or consult concerning any cessation of arms, or making peace, without express directions from both Houses of Parliament'. (*CJ.* iii, 392.)

[5] Gardiner, *CW.*, i, 329.   [6] Harl. 166, f. 33.

instructed to withdraw and prepare for a conference with the Lords on the subject.[1] The declaration of this committee, that the preparations for peace should be entrusted to the Committee of Both Kingdoms, on the ground that by that method the advice of the Scots would be obtained,[2] has a hollow ring, especially in view of the way the Scots on the Committee were in fact often ignored. The Commons' majority probably did not represent the country's opinion, for there was an almost overwhelming desire in the country for an end to hostilities and the Commons showed themselves aware of the suspicion at home and abroad, that Parliament did not want peace.[3] The Lords objected to allowing the Committee of Both Kingdoms to control peace negotiations; they had appointed an *ad hoc* committee of nine to manage the negotiations for peace, and another conference between the two Houses was held. Again Vane, this time with three others, managed the conference, and he reported it.[4] The committee of twelve's second answer to the Lords, which the Commons endorsed, is clever, but quite unconvincing;[5] it is clear that the Lords knew that the Committee of Both Kingdoms was hostile to peace, and so did the leading members of the Commons. The struggle continued for over a fortnight; at the end of March the Lords were still demanding a separate committee to conduct peace negotiations, but Vane retorted that, if the Lords would not approve, the Commons alone should empower the Committee of Both Kingdoms to conduct the peace negotiations.[6] On 30 March, when the vote was taken upon the Lords' request for an *ad hoc* committee to consider the Dutch offer to mediate, Vane was one of the tellers for the opposition, and only the Speaker's casting vote secured him a majority.[7]

Even before the struggle over the establishment of the Committee of Both Kingdoms, another bitter conflict had taken place between Holles's group, who were supporting the earls of Essex and Warwick, and Vane's. Early in January 1644

[1] *CJ*. iii, 428.   [2] Ibid., 429.
[3] Ibid. 'Whereas there have been many endeavours from Oxford . . . to raise a belief in the people, and in foreign parts, that they were inclined to peace, and the Parliament averse to it.'
[4] Ibid., 433.   [5] Ibid., 435–6. 23 March.
[6] Harl. 166, f. 40. 28 March.   [7] *CJ*. iii, 443.

Vane, St John and Hesilrige revealed to the Commons Sir Basil Brooke's plot to have the king's proclamation, summoning a Parliament to Oxford, published in London; this was to be accompanied by peace overtures to the Lord Mayor. How the intercepted letter that betrayed the plot was obtained is nowhere stated.[1] A Common Hall, that is, a meeting of the Liverymen of the City Companies, was called to make known the plot to the Londoners, and Vane, one of the speakers, made the occasion an opportunity to attack the king's recent proclamations.[2] He ended with a vigorous passage in which he pointed out that if the Parliament and law-courts were moved to Oxford, London would be 'desolate from all traffic [trade]', and the law-courts, 'the life and preservation of all your affairs and businesses', would be no longer there. He warned the City also that those who went to Oxford would have their estates confiscated.

Later in the same month however Vane was himself accused of being a party to a royalist plot. Lord Lovelace, who like the earl of Holland and several other peers, had left the Parliament in London and joined the king at Oxford in August 1643, suggested by letter that Vane should send an envoy to whom Lovelace might 'impart some propositions from authority, which might lead to public peace'. Vane asked the earl of Warwick's chaplain, Moses Wall, to undertake the mission; with him in the room when he did so were his usual collaborators, St John and Hesilrige, and some others, including Peter Sterry, the minister, later closely associated with Vane. Moses Wall, having been first assured that the mission was lawful, as the Speaker was acquainted with it, went to Windsor, and met Lovelace, who would put nothing in writing. But he declared that the king 'did esteem Sir Henry Vane and his party to be the honestest men of them that stuck to the parliament', and that 'the king will yield to the disannulling of laws which are made against tender consciences'. Wall on his return wrote down what Lovelace had asserted; when he did so the Speaker, Hesilrige and Samuel Browne were in the room with Vane.[3]

<hr>

[1] Ibid., 358. 6 January 1644. Whittaker, f. 105v. Baillie (ii, 133) says it 'came to the nose' of Vane.   [2] E 29(13). 16 January.

[3] HMC. *House of Lords' MSS*, 6th Rep. App. part i, p. 3. The accounts in *Anti-*

At this point Vane himself was in danger; the earls of Essex and Warwick had heard something of the Lovelace negotiations, and they proceeded to bring pressure to bear on Vane. Their plan was clever; they planned to accuse Vane under an ordinance which he and St John had themselves drawn up a year before, by which it was treason to hold intelligence with Oxford unless both Houses, or the earl of Essex, were acquainted with the negotiations.[1] Essex and Warwick thought they had Vane 'circumscribed', but they had not; Vane had somehow learnt of their plan, and before they could raise the matter in the Lords he brought it before the Commons. He defended himself not only by revealing that the negotiations were known to the Commons committee on the Brooke Plot, but also by ingeniously pleading that the ordinance of 1643 was not binding; it had not been entered on the Lords' Journal by the Clerk, owing to the cunning of some peers.[2] Vane did not dwell on the facts that he had at no time consulted the House of Lords, and that the Speaker was not the House of Commons. He won over the House, however, and the Commons voted him thanks.[3]

Further friction with the earl of Essex soon followed. Isaac Dorislaus, the advocate-general of the earl's army, had taken depositions from Lovelace's servant, who had been caught, from Moses Wall, and from another chaplain. Essex had been ordered by the Commons to establish a standing commission for trying treason suspects by martial law—it would have been ironical if Vane, one of the Commons' own leaders, had been the first victim. St John must have heard of Dorislaus's action, for he came to see him, and while Dorislaus was showing St John the draft of the martial law commission

Aulicus (E 31(17). 6 February 1644) and Whittaker (f. 216v. 17 January 1644) tally very well indeed with the depositions (by Wall, by Lovelace's servant, and by Sterry) now in the Lords' MSS. Wall, described in Vane's letter to Lovelace as 'my friend', was also a friend of John Milton.

[1] Baillie, ii, 135–6.

[2] I cannot trace this ordinance. But a similar one imposing the death penalty for holding intelligence with the royalists, was passed on 16 August 1644 (to last for four months only), and Baillie may well be right. (*A.O.I.* i, 486–8). It may be part of the Draconian legislation mentioned by Holles, *Memoirs*, 195. For the debates on it see Harl. 166, ff. 98, 106, 106v.

[3] *CJ.* iii, 358. 6 January.

Vane arrived. 'They two', said Dorislaus, 'walked aside together, and after a little time Mr. Solicitor and Sir Henry Vane came to me again.' Dorislaus seems now to have admitted to St John and Vane that the interrogations had taken place, and Vane evidently considered this an infringement of M.P.s' privileges, in that the depositions were a preparation for trying those involved, and by martial law. A day or two later the matter was raised in the Commons, and a committee was appointed, not including Vane.[1] But there the matter was allowed to drop, both by the Commons, and by Essex.

According to Baillie, Warwick and Essex were using their knowledge of the Lovelace negotiations as a form of blackmail. They knew that Vane and St John were taking steps to revive the impeachment of the earl of Holland, Warwick's half-brother, for deserting to the king at Oxford, and the earls were prepared to drop their charges if Vane and St John would spare Holland from continued attack.[2] Vane and his friend refused however. It is interesting to see from the *Journals* who were the M.P.s involved in this struggle. Vane and Hesilrige were the tellers for the impeachment; Holles and Stapleton, the friends of Essex,[3] defended Holland, as they had done in November, when his impeachment was first proposed.[4] Once more Holles was opposing Vane, and this time Holles won; Holland was reprieved.[5]

It is difficult to see why the king should have attempted to negotiate with Vane. According to Whittaker[6] the king was relying upon Vane's 'true inclination to the public good . . . knowing him to have a strong party in the House, and he the chief of it'. But none of Vane's speeches in 1643 or 1644 indicate

---

[1] Ibid., 375. 24 January 1644. The depositions are clearly those in the Lords' MSS.

[2] Baillie, loc. cit. Vane had vehemently opposed Holland's readmission to the Upper House. (BM. Add. 18,779, f. 49.)

[3] Rushworth *Historical Collections*, part iv, vol. i, 1645–7, 2.

[4] Holland's impeachment had been proposed on 7 and 11 November 1643. (*C.J.* iii, 304, 308.) A committee was set up to consider the matter; five weeks later an ordinance was twice read in the House which provided for the punishment of Holland and other deserters (an early-morning move), and both Vane and Holles were added to the previous committee. (Ibid., 349.)

[5] By 75–60 votes. (*C.J.* iii, 370. 17 January 1644.)

[6] Whittaker, f. 216v.

that he was likely to support peace proposals, and surely the king would not be so misguided as to think so. *Anti-Aulicus*,[1] one of the diurnals, thought the negotiation was intended to discredit Vane, which seems too malicious for Charles. It is possible that the king was exploiting the differences between the supporters and opponents of religious toleration, but even this explanation has its difficulties, for Vane was still co-operating with the Scottish Presbyterians in the Westminster Assembly in the spring of 1644, and had not yet appeared openly as an advocate of toleration. Probably however Vane was already working with Roger Williams to obtain religious toleration for Rhode Island, in the parliamentary committee for the colonies,[2] and this, as much else that happened in London, was known at Oxford. Whatever the king's motives they still leave Vane's to be accounted for. According to the evidence of Moses Wall, Vane hoped by continuing the negotiations to find out more about the Brooke Plot, and this seems a reasonable explanation, for Vane might conceivably find out which City men were secret royalists, or at least secret supporters of peace negotiations. Vane told Wall that he hoped to discover who was sending information to the king at Oxford; he suspected the earl of Bedford was responsible. That Vane was honestly negotiating with the king implies that he thought there were prospects of an acceptable compromise between his views and the king's, and Vane's intelligence makes this unlikely.

His part in establishing the Committee of Both Kingdoms shows that he sought power, and sometimes achieved it by dubious means. But he used that power to serve (with tireless energy) what he conceived to be the public interest. It is possible to construct almost a day-by-day diary for Vane at this time from the Committee of Both Kingdoms' Day-Book and the *Commons Journals*, and his record is impressive. Allowing for the fact that he was absent on the Committee's business, and in the summer for health reasons, for 45 days, Vane was present in 1644 on 154 out of the remaining 199 days on which the Committee met, for which the list of members present is given. In addition on nine more such days, when the clerk

[1] E 31(17), loc. cit.   [2] See below, p. 195.

gives no indication which man he is referring to, either he or his father was present. Assuming that on four of these occasions the younger Vane is meant, his total attendance rises to 158. On at least twenty days when he was not at the Committee he was in the Commons[1]—sometimes obviously because he considered the Commons were transacting particularly important business, such as naval matters,[2] peace negotiations,[3] and religious questions.[4] On four days when Vane was absent from the Committee of Both Kingdoms, committees of the Commons to which he had been nominated met, or at least had been ordered to meet. This leaves only seventeen days on which Vane was not certainly either at the House of Commons or at the Committee. But there were many occasions on which Vane had been appointed to draft documents, to interrogate suspects, or carry out other missions on behalf of the Committee of Both Kingdoms, and these may well have been responsible for some of his absences. In addition he was still Treasurer of the Navy, and though there is reason to think that his deputy did much of the work, some of the duties of the office undoubtedly devolved on Vane himself. He must have had a prodigious capacity for work.

Unfortunately the Day-Book of the Committee of Both Kingdoms does not record discussions and it gives little indication of the part played by individual members in the work of the Committee. Vane was frequently the Committee's spokesman in the Commons; sometimes he went straight from the Committee to the Commons,[5] sometimes it was a day or two more before he put the Committee's business before the House.[6] On one occasion a packet of intercepted letters had been given

---

[1] I have assumed Vane's presence in the Commons if he was named as a committee member, manager of a conference, or teller on that day. Examination of the subjects discussed in the Commons when Vane was absent from the Committee leads one to deduce that these account for his absence on those days. Baillie (ii, 230. 16 September 1644) testifies to Vane's part in discussions on religion in the House, of which one would know little from the *Journals* and diaries.

[2] *CJ*. iii, 701. 21 November 1644.

[3] Ibid., 434-5. 22 March 1644; 445-6. 3 April 1644; 713-14. 4 December 1644.

[4] Ibid., 628. 16 September 1644.

[5] E.g. *CSPD. 1644*, 44, and Whittaker, f. 122v; *CSPD. 1644*, 137, and *CJ*. iii, 483.

[6] E.g. *CSPD. 1644*, 95, and *CJ*. iii, 461; *CSPD. 1644*, 98-9, and *CJ*. iii, 453.

to him,[1] on another he delivered to the Commons one such letter which revealed that a Dutchman had been given a royal commission to destroy Parliament's ships.[2] Perhaps the 'secret service' side of the Committee's activities was particularly his responsibility. Scottish affairs were certainly his province and almost always when these had to be reported to the Commons Vane was the spokesman.[3] The House of Commons was unenthusiastic about help for the Scots, especially at the end of 1644, when a Parliament victory in the war seemed likely, and peace propositions were under way. The House was therefore reluctant to supply the financial and other needs of the Scots, and Vane or St John had to raise the matter in December 1644 several times.[4]

The attitude of the Committee of Both Kingdoms to Parliament, as revealed by Vane's activities, was a strange one. On 6 March 1644 the Committee set up a sub-committee, with a quorum of two, to draft a declaration on the king's recent peace proposals to the earl of Essex. Vane was a member.[5] It will be remembered that when the Committee of Both Kingdoms had been established, it was instructed to conduct peace negotiations only when Parliament so ordered, and Parliament had not so ordered on this occasion. The Committee evidently belatedly remembered this restriction for on 9 March, three days, that is, after the sub-committee had been set up, the Commons instructed the Committee to prepare the declaration, which, unbeknown to the House, was already in hand.[6] A similar incident took place on 2 April, when Vane was sent to the Goldsmiths' Hall committee to ask them to let the Committee at Derby House know how much money could be provided for the Scots army.[7] At the same time, evidently in the morning, Stapleton was sent off to read to the Commons the letter from the Scots commissioners about the needs of their army in the North,[8] whereupon the Commons duly ordered the Goldsmiths' Hall committee to meet that afternoon to 'make

---

[1] S.P. 21/16, p. 6.   [2] Harl. 166, f. 39.
[3] Ibid., ff. 33, 35, 47, 52v, 55, *et al.*
[4] *CSPD. 1644-45*, 172, 175; *CJ.* iii, 717, 723, 731. At this time the House was busy discussing peace proposals, the Committee of Both Kingdoms was ignoring them.
[5] *CSPD. 1644*, 36.   [6] *CJ.* iii, 423.   [7] *CSPD. 1644*, 91-2.   [8] Ibid.

provision of necessities to be sent unto our brethren in Scotland'.[1] The House was in fact 'rubber-stamping' the decisions
of the Committee of Both Kingdoms. It should be noted that
the Goldsmiths' Hall committee was asked by the House of
Commons to give particulars of what sum it could provide,
not to the Commons itself, but to the Committee of Both
Kingdoms. On 9 May the Commons instructed Vane to prepare a letter to the County Committee of Kent urging them to
maintain their cavalry, and assuring them that it would not
be employed except for the service of the county.[2] In fact the
letter had already been prepared, read, and despatched (at
the direction of the Committee) the previous day.[3] Even more
interesting is an incident in July. The Committee ordered
Vane and a 'Mr. Browne' (probably Samuel Browne) to draft
a letter to the committee of the Eastern Association to hasten
the collection of money for the earl of Manchester's army.[4]
The letter, with its clever reminder that supporting the earl's
army in the North was a means of keeping the war out of East
Anglia, was drawn up on the same day, and despatched on the
following day, the 9th.[5] Not until the day after that did the
Commons resolve that such a letter should be sent.[6] By July
the Venetian ambassador was noting the discontent of the
M.P.s who 'realise they have made a mistake in setting up the
Council of the Two Nations [sic], a body which does every-
thing without so much as participating the state of affairs in
full parliament, where some have made complaint'.[7]

On 13 May 1644 St John notified the Commons that the
Committee's term of appointment had ended; he evidently
expected the House to renew it, but the House did not.[8] Three
days later Alderman Fowke appeared with an opportune
petition from the City requesting that the Committee of Both
Kingdoms might sit again,[9] and the Commons did now send

---

[1] *CJ*. iii, 444.   [2] Ibid., 487.   [3] *CSPD. 1644*, 152–4.
[4] Ibid., 325. 8 July.   [5] Ibid., 328.   [6] *CJ*. iii, 556.
[7] *CSPV. 1643–47*, 115. Holles noted that the Committee 'did manage all the great business . . . as framing propositions for peace . . . all negotiations with foreign states'. (*Memoirs*, 221.)
[8] Harl. 166, f. 61.
[9] Ibid., f. 62. *CJ*. iii, 495. Vane, St John and others were deputed to prepare an answer.

up to the Lords an ordinance to renew the Committee's powers. But the Lords were determined to make changes in the membership of the Committee, and for a fortnight a vigorous struggle with the Commons continued on this issue. The Lords wished to add five names to those of the original seven peers on the Committee, or to be allowed to nominate whom they would. But the Commons' majority—not a large one, on 7 May only eleven votes—refused all the Lords' amendments, even the Lords' final plea, on 21 May, that two peers' names only should be added to the Committee.[1] After the last unsuccessful conference of the two Houses on 22 May the Commons' majority resorted to the trick of bringing in the first ordinance, 'the Omnipotent Ordinance', as it was called in the House, which empowered the Committee to 'order and direct' the war, and control peace negotiations, and which had been dropped at the beginning of February, after being introduced into, and passing, the Lords.[2] For this, of course, the Lords' consent was not necessary, for it had already been given. Strode reintroduced the ordinance which left the Lords helpless, and there is no evidence that Vane spoke in the 'hot debate' which D'Ewes tells us followed,[3] though one may agree with S. R. Gardiner that the political method used was 'characteristic of the leadership of Vane and St John'. The stratagem must have served to discredit Parliament in the eyes of the informed public. It may be noted that Holles was in favour of accepting the Lords' compromise offer on 21 May.[4]

In October 1644 Vane and St John, according to D'Ewes, took advantage of another City petition, to introduce a plan which would have weakened the forces of Holles's friend, the earl of Essex, and strengthened those of Hesilrige and Waller, the rivals of Essex. Some aldermen and citizens of London presented a petition containing two ordinances, one concerning trade, but the other dealing with the City Brigade.[5] St John and Vane wanted Skippon withdrawn from the earl's forces in the West to command the City's militia once again, and had, according to D'Ewes, 'cunningly wrought this to proceed from

---

[1] *CJ*. iii, 503.
[2] The dispute may be followed in Whittaker, ff. 136, 136v, 137, 137v, 139, 139v.
[3] Harl. 166, f. 64v. 22 May.   [4] *CJ*. iii, 503.   [5] Ibid., 651. 4 October.

the City petition which was contrary to their [the City's]
meaning, and soe to draw all power to Waller, Hesilrige etc.
But Glynne the Recorder discovered the knavish packing and
soe it was exploded by the House.'[1] It is interesting that the
man who delivered the petition to the House was Alderman
Fowke.[2]

It seems that for a few months Vane planned to supplant the
earl of Essex by Sir William Waller. Waller in his memoirs
asserted that Parliament was about to give him command of
its army when the news of his defeat at Cropredy in June 1644
disappointed his hopes.[3] It looks as if this plan was Vane's,
though only a few months before he had opposed allotting to
Waller's army money designated for the Scots' forces.[4] In July
1644, even after Waller's defeat, Vane pleaded earnestly with
the House to allow Waller to recruit his army, and rescind a
former order that Waller should pursue the king.[5] In August
Hesilrige and Waller's 'other friends', as D'Ewes called them,
unsuccessfully tried to persuade the House not to order Waller
to join Essex,[6] and in October St John and Vane, in the incident
just noted, were trying to strengthen Waller, at the expense of
the earl of Essex, thought D'Ewes, by withdrawing Skippon's
contingent.

Vane continued to oppose negotiations for peace. He was one
of the committee of three who drafted the very cool reply to
the Dutch offer of mediation in March 1644, and was named
first.[7] When the Committee of Both Kingdoms obtained control
of these peace negotiations, the Lords proposed that the Committee should present peace terms within four days; Vane and
Hesilrige were tellers for the opposition.[8] Holles, as so often,
was Vane's opponent. The Committee however decided that
action was called for; three days later it set up a sub-committee
to bring in a report, and either Vane or his father was a

[1] Harl. 166, f. 128v. 7 October.   [2] CJ. iii, 651, and Harl. 166, f. 128.
[3] Sir William Waller, *Recollections*, App. to *Poetry of Anna Matilda* (London,
1788), 131.
[4] Harl. 165, f. 213v. It is characteristic of the shifting loyalties of many M.P.s
that Waller, a noted supporter of Holles's 'Presbyterian' group in 1647–8, should
in 1644 be associated with Vane's.
[5] Harl. 166, f. 98v. 17 July.   [6] Ibid., f. 106. 10 August.
[7] CJ. iii, 454–6.   [8] Ibid., 458. 13 April.

member.[1] There is some doubt about the length of time the Committee was given to draft its proposed peace terms;[2] Pierrepont when he reported them to the House on 29 April thought it necessary to protest that the Committee had used all diligence,[3] and the House had to reassure the City that the Commons were in fact at work on peace terms.[4] Three days later St John was one of the tellers against a motion to discuss the peace proposals next day, and probably the only reason that Vane was not also one of the tellers was that he happened to be out of the House at the time, taking a message to the Lords.[5] D'Ewes reported that Vane, 'seeing that he could not at first divert the business of the peace negotiations, found another means to interrupt it',[6] by presenting a letter from the earl of Maitland recounting Scots' military successes. With the Commons vote of 3 May peace proposals lapsed for some weeks. The Venetian ambassador commented at this time that the Committee of Both Kingdoms had been lukewarm, and had not got its peace proposals ready.[7]

In July Waller, after his defeat at Cropredy, refused the king an answer to a peace overture, and Vane and Glyn were deputed to thank him on behalf of the House.[8] Peace proposals were discussed in the Commons at length on 1 August;[9] on the next day Vane obtained permission to leave for Kent, thus tacitly demonstrating his lack of enthusiasm for negotiations with the king.[10] All through September and early October, peace terms were discussed in the House. On 15 October the main work on the proposals was at last done, and the preamble and conclusion were referred to the Committee of Both

---

[1] *CSPD. 1644*, 122. 16 April. The elder Vane was present in the morning, both Vanes in the afternoon, and the minutes do not show which of them was appointed to the sub-committee. (S.P. 21/16, pp. 48–9.)

[2] The Committee of Both Kingdoms said (*CSPD. 1644*, 122) that the House had allowed it until 26 April to bring in the peace proposals. But the Commons did not give them this date until 22 April, following a request from the Committee itself for an extension of time (ibid., 127—'an amendment of the ordinance'— *CJ*. iii, 467). The Committee had again decided what the Commons should do.

[3] *CJ*. iii, 472.　　[4] Ibid., 478. 3 May.　　[5] Ibid.　　[6] Harl. 166, f. 55.

[7] *CSPV. 1643–47*, 94, 97. 6 May. In October Agostini was writing that Parliament had completed peace proposals, but 'their sole object is to deceive the people, and to obliterate the opinion, which has become universal, that Parliament abhors any treaty'. (Ibid., 146.)

[8] *CJ*. iii, 555. 8 July.　　[9] Ibid., 575.　　[10] See below, p. 55, n. 1.

Kingdoms;[1] the Committee did nothing and had to be sharply reminded to make its report.[2] The Committee again delayed this, but when the report was finally made to the House on 24 October Vane was its spokesman in the Commons.[3] These were the proposals that Holles and other M.P.s took to the king at Oxford, in November 1644. The Dutch ambassador again offered to mediate, and Vane was added to the committee to draw up a reply, but if one was ever made there seems to be no record of it.[4] It is obvious that Vane was utterly hostile to a negotiated peace.

His most important mission for the Committee of Both Kingdoms took place in June 1644. The Committee decided on 3 June that he and William White[5] should be sent to the Scottish and English armies outside York, to 'advise with' the parliamentary delegates to the Scottish army, and with the earl of Manchester and Lord Fairfax as to 'what course shall be taken for securing Lancashire and ruining Prince Rupert's army'.[6] The Committee had decided that part at least of the armies besieging York should be diverted to the relief of Lancashire, and in particular to Liverpool, which was in great danger and in fact fell to Prince Rupert a few days later.[7] Vane, with his usual despatch, left next day or early on the following one.[8] He paid his own expenses for the journey, so he evidently wished to go.[9] His instructions were to return to London by 22 June, or earlier if possible, but he did not return until the 30th.[10] He had asked for permission to stay longer than the time originally fixed, for reasons that do not carry conviction, saying

[1] *CJ.* iii, 665.   [2] Ibid., 668. 17 October.

[3] Ibid., 675. According to D'Ewes the Committee had altered propositions which Parliament and the Scots had already agreed to. (Harl. 166, f. 151.)

[4] Ibid., 701. 21 November.

[5] Colonel William White, later M.P. for Pontefract.   [6] *CSPD. 1644*, 197.

[7] For Liverpool's danger see *CSPD. 1644*, 193, 204. The Committee's attitude is shown in Vane's letter, ibid., 223-4.

[8] Ibid., 204. The letter from Vane and the earl of Lindsay has been wrongly dated by the Committee's clerk who copied it into the Letter-Book—Vane reported from the Committee to the Commons on 3 June (*CSPD. 1644*, 197, *CJ.* iii, 516) and could not possibly have reached York by 5 June. Vane says himself (*CSPD. 1644*, 223) that he reached York on the Sunday night, i.e. the 9th. The Committee's regular meeting time was 3 p.m., so that Vane could have left on the morning of the 5th.

[9] Harl. 166, f. 79.   [10] *CSPD. 1644*, 292.

that Parliament's representatives with the Army were not a quorum without him (but they cannot have been before his arrival either), and he wished to see the fall of York.[1] The Committee returned the firm reply that he was to return by the date fixed in his instructions.[2]

The whole incident is very odd indeed. Why should the Committee send Vane, who had no military experience at all, on a mission designed to persuade the generals of the superior wisdom of the Committee of Both Kingdoms?[3] They could have sent Stapleton. Why did Vane stay for eighteen days? Both the Venetian envoy Agostini, and Sabran, the French ambassador in England, heard that Vane's mission had another purpose than the one publicly avowed, and this was the establishment of a republican government in Britain. The Venetian envoy does not state the source of his information, but he was writing in June, only two or three days after Vane's departure.[4] Sabran's letter is dated much later, on 8 September; his informant was the earl of Holland, a frequent visitor to the French envoy. According to Sabran, Vane, finding the generals inclined to make peace with the king, told them boldly that Parliament and people could not feel themselves secure with Charles or his family, and that the form of government would have to be changed.[5] Holland could have received his information from his half-brother, the earl of Warwick, a close friend and relation of the earl of Manchester, who was at York in command of one of the armies. It would seem that the two foreign envoys'

[1] Ibid., 241.

[2] Ibid., 229. The Letter-Book is usually very complete, and all the other letters mentioned in the minutes for that day are in the Letter-Book; the letter to Vane, however, containing this instruction to return is not. It is strange too that the letter in which Vane first asked for an extension of time for his mission is also not in the Letter-Book—in his letter of 16 June he refers to a previous request for a postponement of his return; as this is not in his letter of 11 June, he must have written a letter on or about 13 June, which was not copied in the Letter-Book.

[3] Gardiner, CW., i, 368, notes this.

[4] CSPV. 1643–47, 110. Agostini's statement that Vane had gone on to Scotland in the utmost secrecy would explain Vane's overlong stay in the North. But Vane cannot have crossed the border—there are letters from Vane at York on 11, 16, 20 and 23 June; he must have started back on the 27th, and this would not have allowed time for a visit to Scotland as well.

[5] Gardiner, loc. cit., prints the relevant passage. The reference to 'the people' does add verisimilitude to the story—Vane frequently spoke and wrote in such terms.

sources of information were different, and, at the very least, this was the story that was believed about Vane in certain quarters in London.

Vane returned to London on 30 June, two days before the battle of Marston Moor. At the end of July and during August it was rumoured that there was a scheme afoot to change the government of England by making Charles Lewis, Elector Palatine, king. This was no new idea.[1] In 1641 the Venetian ambassador had heard that Charles Lewis was suggested in the Commons as a possible king.[2] No more was heard of the idea until 1644, when in August Sabran reported 'Le prompt départ du Prince palatin de la Hague n'est pas sans mistère . . . je tiens avec le commun que c'est part le convy du Parlement qu-il vient . . . enfin puisque toutes choses les plus horribles sont maintenant faisable par les gens ici, lui offrir une couronne . . .'[3] It is not unlikely that Vane senior, an old friend of the Winter Queen,[4] should have conceived the idea of making Charles Lewis king. It is more difficult to believe the younger Vane was involved in the scheme, for Parliament was not interested in Charles Lewis in 1644.[5] Moreover, when Charles Lewis had actually come to England Vane and some others spoke very bitterly against the prince's coming, 'shewing that it was against the consent or knowledge of the Houses, of the Committee of Both Kingdoms, that it was at a most unseasonable time, raysing much talke and jealousie in many men's heads and tongues'.[6] This does not sound as though Vane had invited the prince. It is certainly odd that rumours about making Charles Lewis king should circulate soon after Vane's republican schemes were said to have been defeated. It is also a coincidence that Vane returned to London, after staying somewhat longer in Kent than Parliament had authorized him to do,

[1] In 1629 one Stephan ap Evan, of Rilth, Shropshire, was accused of declaring that the king would be hunted out of the land, and that the Palsgrave would be crowned in his stead. (Judson, *Crisis of the Constitution* (New Brunswick, 1949), 306, based on *CSPD. 1629–31*, 17.)

[2] *CSPV. 1640–42*, 200.

[3] BM. Add. 5460, f. 206.

[4] See e.g. *CSPD. 1635*, 435; ibid., *1640*, 583; ibid., *1640–41*, 549.

[5] Harl. 166, f. 40. 26 March.

[6] Ibid, f. 111v. 31 August.

on the very day the Prince Elector's arrival at Gravesend was reported.[1]

The whole incident remains very obscure—perhaps, as D'Ewes asserted, the Elector had come over only to obtain the £3000 promised him by Parliament. On the other hand Sabran, a shrewd observer, thought there had been a plan to replace the king by his nephew. In October the earl of Holland, in conversation with Sabran's secretary, asserted that there had been a scheme to replace Charles I, but the Scots had objected.[2] The earl of Argyle's brother also told Sabran, in November, that the Scottish Parliament 'ne désiroient l'entremise d'aucune prince', and as Sabran went on to refer sarcastically to Charles Lewis's attendance at the Westminster Assembly, it is clear that the Palatine was meant.[3] It looks as if some such scheme was mooted by someone, but whether Vane was in any way connected with it is an open question. If he was in fact suggesting a republic in June 1644 it would be the first indication that he held 'republican' views, but Vane's 'republicanism' was of a very pragmatic variety, and it would not be at all inconsistent with his views on government that he should be a republican in June and a monarchist in August.

One of the most successful strokes achieved in Parliament by his group was the Self-Denying Ordinance, proposed by Zouch Tate, and seconded by Vane,[4] but its origins, which are interesting, have not been properly understood. On 14 November 1644 an ordinance was introduced appointing Lisle Master of St Cross Hospital at Winchester.[5] This touched off some long-smouldering impatience in the House, and a committee

---

[1] Vane had been given permission on 2 August to be absent from Parliament for health reasons for about a fortnight, but he had stayed away for twenty-seven days. (*CSPD. 1644*, 460; *CJ.* iii, 576.) That he was going to Kent is clear from *CSPD. 1644*, 387.

[2] BM. Add. 5460, f. 320. 17 October.   [3] Ibid., f. 366. 17 November.

[4] Rushworth, op. cit., part iv, vol. ii, 1645-7, 4. 9 December 1644. A petition from London followed. (Ibid., 5.) According to D'Ewes (Harl. 166, f. 151) a petition was presented on 28 October in which 'some citizens of London' thanked the House for passing a vote taking away the offices both civil and military of the members of both Houses. A heated debate followed. Could D'Ewes, who copied out his notes here, have made a mistake in the date? There seems no other mention of this petition and debate.

[5] Whittaker, f. 174. *Mercurius Aulicus* later alleged that this post was worth £800 a year. (E 465(19). 26 September–3 October 1648.)

was named to 'consider of all the offices and places of benefit
bestowed by the Parliament, what profits they that had them
did make of them, and what might be made of them for the use
of the public, the officers having a competent allowance made
out of them, and to begin with first the places conferred upon
members of each House'.[1] It is significant that Reynolds, who
had months before foreseen that some men might acquire a
vested interest in war, was put in charge of the investigation.[2]
Stapleton and Holles were on Reynolds's committee, Vane,
St John, Hesilrige and Cromwell were not. The motion
evidently did not proceed from the latter group. On the same
day, some Kentish knights and gentlemen appeared, to present
a petition of very similar tenor. It can hardly have been a
coincidence that the petition was presented on the very day
that the House discussed the offices held by M.P.s. The Kentish
petition, recalling that the petitioners had taken on the obligation of assisting Parliament's forces, continues with the very
frank statement that:

To the intent that this obligation of assistance (particularly pecuniary) so just and necessary yet so suitable to the soldiers' present
interest of making a trade of war, may not prove an occasion of
lengthening out our miseries, we shall humbly crave that some
honourable and beneficial reward may be settled to the commanders and common soldiers, to be received by them out of the
estates of delinquents at the end of the warre, as may quicken them
to a noble desire of the speedy enjoyment thereof. And in the mean-
time such competent allowance only to be made to all commanders
. . . as may reasonably defray the charge of their employment.[3]

The Press as a whole considered discretion the better part of
valour, and only two newspapers were bold enough to mention
this section of the petition; the *True Informer* lived up to its
name,[4] and the *Scottish Dove* also included an account of the
clause.[5] Thomason could obtain only a hand-written copy of
the petition, and drily adds at the end of it: 'All which was

---

[1] Whittaker, loc. cit.   [2] *CJ*. iii, 695.
[3] E 19(11). The petition is mentioned in Whitelocke, i, 329, and *CSPV. 1643–47*,
157.
[4] E 17(9).
[5] E 18(7). For newspapers omitting the news see e.g. E 18(2).

received with much thankfulness; [this was true—the House was almost fulsomely polite to the petitioners] but Mr. Rushworth durst not license it to print.'[1] In the ensuing weeks however traces of the long-suppressed suspicion and indignation of some at least of the public can be seen in the newspapers.[2] Of course a great number of the M.P.s held lucrative offices— Pym had been Master of the Ordnance,[3] Prideaux was Postmaster-General, Vane had the Navy Treasurership. They would doubtless have replied that they were sacrificing their time and talents to 'the Cause' and they had to live. The Kentish petition was quietly ignored, presumably Reynolds's committee sat throughout November, unless Cromwell's quarrel with the earl of Manchester distracted the committee's attention, until a month later, when on 14 December the Self-Denying Ordinance was introduced.

The Ordinance was in fact a clever device to stifle Reynolds's committee, appease the Kentish Petitioners, and rid the country of the unsuccessful generals, all at one stroke. Clarendon, who is confirmed by Agostini and Whitelocke, asserted that the Independents enlisted the help of the preachers to get the measure through.[4] Vane made a long speech either on the day when the motion introducing the Ordinance was made, or on the day after the fast and the eight hours of sermons which were designed to win the support of both Houses to the measure. Vane ended his speech with the offer to surrender his own office of Treasurer of the Navy, and the wish that the profits might be applied to the cost of the war.[5] Incidentally if he really declared that he did not owe his Navy Treasurership to the favour of Parliament, this was a half-truth that some M.P.s must have heard with scepticism, seeing that from December 1641 to August 1642 he had been out of the office, and had been reappointed to it only by Parliament. It may be remarked

---

[1] E 19(11).

[2] 'Divers of ours that make show to fight for religion more than pay, betray the trust reposed in them.' (E 18(4).)

[3] Harl. 166, f. 154v.

[4] Clarendon, *Rebellion*, viii, 191–2. *CSPV. 1643–47*, 166. Whitelocke, i, 351. Agostini refers to the 'scattering of seditious pamphlets'. (Op. cit., 164.)

[5] Clarendon, *Rebellion*, viii, 194. There seems to be no record of this speech elsewhere.

that in spite of the Self-Denying Ordinance, which later passed,[1] he continued to be Treasurer of the Navy, as 'Honest John Lilburne' did not fail to point out.[2] Vane, and one or two others, including the earl of Warwick, were protected from loss of their offices by a clause exempting from resignation those who had been dismissed by the king and reappointed by Parliament.[3] Vane also secured from Parliament specific reinstatement.[4]

Vane's parliamentary activities in 1644 give a clear picture of his energy and resourcefulness. He could take advantage of parliamentary procedure in a way that though legal was not completely honest—witness the introduction of the ordinances establishing the Committee of Both Kingdoms; the first was introduced into a very thin House of Lords,[5] and was later revived in order to by-pass opposition in that House. The Lovelace negotiations too could hardly have been carried on by a very scrupulous man. He continued to be a master of shrewd argument, and could defend himself or his cause with great ability. His 'leadership' of the House was a qualified one however. Undoubtedly he was a leader, and both the Committee of Both Kingdoms and the Self-Denying Ordinance can be presumed with fair certainty to be Vane's inventions. But he was not a master of the House in the same way that Pym was, nor even of the Committee of Both Kingdoms.[6] He was sometimes defeated in the Commons, and when he wanted an extension of time for his mission to York, he had to 'state his case' to the Committee, and plead for a concession. Even then he was refused.

How far the somewhat high-handed actions of the Committee of Both Kingdoms were due to Vane one does not know. It has to be remembered that he was only one member of a large committee. But certainly he was often associated with incidents in which the Committee acted without prior authorization by Parliament. He knew, up to a point, when the House of Commons must be conciliated, as when he introduced the modified

---

[1] Rushworth, op. cit., part iv, vol. i, 14–16. 3 April 1645.
[2] Haller, *Tracts*, iii, 288.   [3] Gardiner, *Const. Docs.*, 288.   [4] See below, p. 129.
[5] Opposition was expected here. (Baillie, ii, 141.)
[6] Pierrepont and Northumberland attended even more often—of course they had no other official duties outside Parliament.

ordinance establishing the Committee of Both Kingdoms, or framed the Self-Denying Ordinance. Whether he also realized that he was retaining votes, but not necessarily the good opinion of the House and the public, is doubtful.

His views on policy in the hey-day of the Committee of Both Kingdoms are not easily established, though it is clear that he consistently opposed peace negotiations. His attitude to the Lords, collectively and individually, argues that his hostility to the Upper House had also continued and even increased. There is no substantial evidence to connect Vane with a republican position at this time—his mission to York for the Committee of Both Kingdoms is a very obscure incident indeed.

With St John he was continuing to work very closely, and it is possible to identify some of his other political associates, such as Tate, Hesilrige and Samuel Browne. This cannot always be done however; even Cromwell was a teller in December 1644 against Vane.[1] Probably Vane, St John and their collaborators were not concerting by any means all their policy before presenting it to the Commons. Whether Vane endeavoured to place Charles Lewis on the throne is still an open question. In the summer of 1644 the 'war party' could look forward to victory, and would need some constructive policy for the peace. It is not impossible that Vane should for a time have considered the accession of Charles Lewis as a possible solution of the political dilemma. He was concerned with almost every other major political problem of this vitally important period.

[1] *CJ*. iii, 729. 19 December.

CHAPTER III

The Issue of Peace or War, 1645–46

THE CONTEST for power between Holles's supporters and Vane's intensified during the years 1645 and 1646, and this leads one to consider what issues divided the two groups. It is important to realize however that by no means all the members of Parliament belonged to either group, and if they did belong to one group for some months it by no means follows that they belonged to it for years. There has been a tendency to regard Parliament in the 1640s as though it were our contemporary British Parliament, with the members ranged consistently behind one or other party, whereas it was in fact more analogous to the French Revolutionary Convention, in which two-thirds of the members constituted the 'Plain', and belonged to none of the main political groups. During 1646, when the 'Recruiters' were coming in, the average number voting at divisions in the Commons was 179.[1] If Holles was right in saying that the 'Independents' could rely on some fifty M.P.s,[2] and as we know that Holles and the Presbyterians cannot have commanded more regular support than their opponents, for he was often defeated, this leaves seventy-nine M.P.s who did not 'belong' to either group. Holles in fact said this: 'Till this time [when the 'Recruiters' began to support Holles] they [St John's party] had prevailed so far . . . upon well-meaning, but not so discerning, Members of Parliament, that they were able to suppress all good motions, tending towards peace.'[3] Marten said much the same.[4]

There has been no study of the M.P.s who 'turned their coat'

[1] This figure is admittedly only a rough one, for it includes early morning and vacation-time divisions, when attendance was low; and some divisions on private matters show an unexpectedly large number of M.P.s voting.

[2] *Memoirs*, 214. [3] Ibid., 230.

[4] Quoted Yule, *The Independents in the English Civil War*, 64.

during the Civil Wars, but there were a great many of them, and it would be instructive to know their motives. But if men were prepared to make the costly decision of abandoning the royalist or parliamentary cause for its rival, there would certainly be some who would move from support of one group to the other in the House. In politics, as in religion, men's views did not remain static.[1] One must beware of assuming that because a man was a regicide or Rumper in 1649 he was an 'Independent' in 1645.

We are thus faced with a political situation of great complexity and fluidity. Nevertheless, it is true that in the 1645-8 period even more clearly than in 1644, two rival groups are clearly discernible in the House. If statistics of the tellers are relied upon, Holles would certainly seem to have led one group, for he was a teller far more than any other M.P. But if one considers his opponents' records on this basis, the surprising result is that the rival party was led by Hesilrige, who was teller in thirty-two divisions between May 1645 and December 1646, and Sir John Evelyn of Wiltshire, whose total was twenty. Vane was a teller against Holles only three times, as often as Sir John Danvers, and less often than Nathaniel Fiennes. Stapleton was Holles's most usual lieutenant, for he was a teller with Holles in thirty-one divisions, and Sir William Lewes in seven. The statistics are revealing in another way however, for on two occasions Hesilrige was a teller *with* Holles, and Stapleton was once a teller against him. Sir Walter Earle was a teller with Holles four times, but was a teller against him twice.[2] There is no reason to think that anyone at the time considered this odd.

In considering the issues which divided Holles's group from the group which evidently contained Hesilrige and Evelyn, the religious question must be examined. If divisions in the House are an indication, as they must be, of the main issues, then these are seen to be, as in 1644, not religious but political. Of the seventy divisions in which the two groups were clearly opposed to one another in 1645 and 1646, seven can be classed mainly as religious in character, sixty-three as mainly political. The

---

[1] Ibid., 20.

[2] All the figures are from *CJ*. iv and v, *passim*. Holles was a teller 58 times.

two groups of M.P.s divided most often over such questions as their attitude to the king, the House of Lords or the Scots. They also differed on policy towards delinquents, as individuals or as a class, and on how a London petition should be received. Religious issues, such as whether the ceremony of ordination should include taking the Covenant, or whether a petition from the Westminster Assembly was a breach of privilege, were much less frequent.[1] As Clarendon asserted,[2] and Holles in his memoirs more or less admitted,[3] Holles's group supported the Scots for political reasons, not for religious ones. Probably most of Hesilrige's group were also moved chiefly by political considerations, and if one thinks of St John or Pierrepont happily settling down under the Restored monarchy's religious settlement one must allow that this is probable, though no doubt some supported the Hesilrige-Evelyn group for religious reasons.[4]

According to Clarendon the names 'Presbyterian' and 'Independent' were first employed of two rival groups in Parliament after the Uxbridge negotiations, and he would date their use to about March 1645,[5] though it is true that in another passage relating to the period December 1645–March 1646 he speaks of the Independents, 'who were a faction newly grown up'.[6] Holles did not use the word Independent until he was writing of 1646,[7] though he, like Clarendon, but with less excuse, was deplorably vague in dating events.[8] One could almost believe that Holles was deliberately avoiding the term 'Independent', but a more likely explanation is that during the first three years of the war the word was little used, and Holles unconsciously reflected this. In this and the following chapters the term 'Presbyterian' has been used for the Holles-Stapleton group, and 'Independent' for the St John-Hesilrige group, in spite of the inappropriateness of such religious terms. The names were used at the time, and are still, and it is difficult

---

[1] *CJ.* iv, *passim.*   [2] Clarendon, *Rebellion*, viii, 248.   [3] *Memoirs*, 202.
[4] On the issue of toleration, for example.   [5] Clarendon, *Rebellion*, viii, 259.
[6] Ibid., ix, 167.   [7] *Memoirs*, 232.
[8] Holles was writing nearer in time to the events he described. For his inaccuracy see, for instance, his statement that the Scots were called in after the crowd surrounded the door of the Commons in August 1643, whereas Vane, Darley and the other envoys had departed for Scotland several days before. (*Memoirs*, 197.)

to find substitutes. They are employed here however in a strictly political sense of the two groups, at least some of whose members were, by June 1645, bitterly antagonistic to the leaders of the other. There is no hard and fast line between the two groups, just as there was no hard and fast line between Independents and Presbyterians in religion. It is possible however from the parliamentary diaries and other sources to draw up a list of some 40 M.P.s who can be seen to be working more or less consistently with the Independents.[1] As Holles considered his group were the moderates,[2] it seems inappropriate to use the term 'moderate' for the uncommitted M.P.s. Clarendon stated,[3] and any reader of the contemporary diurnals and diaries will confirm, that the Independents spoke more often and more persuasively than Holles's supporters; this no doubt accounts for their comparative success.

Vane continued to be one of the leaders of the group, as he had been in 1644, though as we have seen he rarely acted as a teller. It is remarkable too that Holles reserved his venom for St John as the man chiefly responsible for the Independents' policy, and though he named Cromwell, Hesilrige, Mildmay and Marten as the Independent 'teazers' or 'gang'[4] he hardly mentioned Vane. Clarendon however named Nathaniel Fiennes, Vane, Cromwell, Hesilrige and Marten as the leaders of the Independents,[5] and the diarists, the *Commons Journals* and other evidence support his view, though St John was probably equally important behind the scenes. Robert Baillie (the Scottish commissioner attending the Westminster Assembly), the Scots leaders and the king, all regarded Vane as not the least important of the Independent grandees, and on such vital matters as the appointment of Fairfax as commander-in-chief of the New Model, or the launching of the attack on Holles and Whitelocke in July 1645, Vane played a dominant part. Perhaps he did not act as teller because he could be more usefully employed in the lobby persuading M.P.s to vote for the Independent policy.

In February 1645 he was one of Parliament's commissioners at the peace negotiations at Uxbridge.[6] He had vigorously

---

[1] See Appendix A. [2] *Memoirs*, 229. [3] Clarendon, *Rebellion*, viii, 260.
[4] *Memoirs*, 220. [5] Loc. cit. [6] *CJ.* iv, 19.

opposed negotiations with the king in 1643 and 1644; it seems odd therefore that he should have been chosen to take part in the Uxbridge 'treaty'. The Uxbridge negotiations developed out of the Oxford discussions of November 1644 when Holles, Pierrepont, Lord Wenman and Whitelocke had represented the Commons.[1] Holles and Whitelocke genuinely wanted peace, going so far as to draft at the king's request an answer to Parliament which would facilitate peace (though they stoutly denied under cross-questioning later that they had done any such thing).[2] Whether Wenman and Pierrepont also wanted peace is not known. In January 1645 Vane, St John, Crew and Prideaux were added to the previous four Oxford commissioners; the Lords sent four (of whom Northumberland was one), and the Scots ten.[3] Why was Vane sent? Perhaps he had changed his mind about making peace with the king, but there is no other evidence of this. Perhaps he wished to safeguard the interests of the Independents, and to prevent the Presbyterians from making an alliance with the king. Sabran writes at this time: 'il y a lieu de craindre des étranges extremités . . . si la chambre des Communs peut disposer des Escossais et des independants, les uns et les autres desquels sont neantmoins pour se joindre au party du roi de la Grande Bretagne, les premiers s'il chasse les éveques, les autres s'il résiste aux presbiteriat'.[4]

Another explanation is also possible. The commissioners at Uxbridge would negotiate under severe disabilities—the three topics which Parliament had voted as the subjects of discussion were surely those on which agreement was least likely: religion, the militia and Ireland.[5] Moreover, Parliament's commissioners were given no room for manœuvre. They were instructed to demand such concessions from the king as the abolition of episcopacy, the acceptance of the Directory of Public Worship, and the taking of the Solemn League and Covenant not only

---

[1] Whitelocke, i, 329.   [2] Ibid., 336.   [3] See p. 65, n. 6.
[4] BM. Add. 5461, f. 98v.
[5] See Northumberland's speech, E 272(3), pp. 3 and 4, for the subjects discussed. Sabran, the French ambassador, speaking to the Scots delegates to the Uxbridge negotiations pointed out to them the difficulties caused because: 'ceux qui avoient mis les trois articles moins possible en testes de propositions sembloient l'avoir fait pour arrester le cours du traite'. (BM. Add. 5461, f. 65v.)

by the king, but also by all his subjects.[1] The commissioners of the two sides were to exchange written memoranda;[2] though discussion would have been a quicker method of interchanging propositions, and would have been less likely to use up the 21 days allowed by Parliament for negotiations. But in spite of these and other difficulties the public demand for peace was so overwhelming that an agreement might have been reached. The *Scottish Dove*, a 'Parliament' newspaper, though the most outspoken, was writing: 'Some will object . . . that the kingdome is already almost undone, and that you are not able to subsist, the taxes are great, and you have little left to live.'[3] If the dominant party in Parliament did not intend the peace negotiations to succeed, they could have sent some of their number to Uxbridge with this purpose in mind, and this was the view put forward by Agostini and Brienne.[4] Other circumstances lend colour to their opinion. The Commons would not accede to the Lords' suggestion that the fast, proclaimed for the Wednesday, the first day of the meeting, should be put back a day.[5] Therefore, though the commissioners were expected earlier, they did not arrive at Uxbridge until seven or eight in the evening.[6] They then said that they could do nothing until the Scots commissioners arrived, which postponed the talks for another day. When the king's commissioners wanted the talks extended for a further few days, Parliament's commissioners refused.[7] There is also the very damaging fact pointed out by the royalist journalist:

their Solemn League and Covenant is now only tendered to good consciences whom they hope will refuse it, and waived as often as any sort of Rebels pretend to stumble at it . . . they have now granted that their new General, Sir Thomas Fairfax, and all the officers of their intended Army, shall not have the Covenant prest upon them, and yet their commissioners at Uxbridge will have no peace unless

---

[1] See above, p. 64, n. 1.   [2] See below, n. 5.

[3] E 270(33), 21-9. February 1644-5.

[4] *CSPV. 1643-47*, 173; BM. Add. 5461, f. 120v.

[5] *The Kingdomes Weekly Intelligencer*, E 26(7).

[6] *Mercurius Aulicus*, E 271(4).

[7] Whitelocke, i, 395. Loudon, in reporting to the City, gives the same reason as Whitelocke—no progress had been made on the three subjects so far discussed. (E 273(3), p. 7.)

His Sacred Majesty sweare to this covenant and injoyne it to all his subjects.[1]

This accusation is borne out by facts, for Cromwell not a month before had been a teller for the Noes when it was moved that the Covenant should be tendered to the New Model Army.[2]

There seems to be no record of Vane's part in the negotiations at Uxbridge. The peers' reports to Parliament are laconic in the extreme,[3] and Whitelocke tells us only that Culpepper came to pay a courtesy visit to Vane, as Clarendon, Whitelocke's old friend, did to him.[4] In the early years of the Long Parliament Culpepper and Vane had several times acted as joint managers of conferences with the Lords, or on other missions for the Commons,[5] and had probably come to know each other quite well. Clarendon asserted that Vane, St John and Prideaux acted as spies on the other Parliament commissioners, and that they certainly did not desire peace.[6] On the whole the evidence lends itself to this view. It would be consistent with Vane's drawing away from the Scots at this period, and with his attempts to bring the Scots Army into England, probably to embroil them yet more deeply in the war, and thus ensure that they did not make peace with the king. It could well be that Laud was executed at this time to make the prospects of peace less likely. There is nothing definite to connect Vane with the resumed attack on Laud beyond the fact that Samuel Browne played a very prominent part,[7] and he was, as we have seen, a member of Vane's group at the time of the Lovelace negotiations.[8] Vane may have objected to the peace negotiations partly because they impeded progress in organizing the New Model—this was a reason to Clarendon for trying to

[1] See above, p. 65, n. 6.

[2] *CJ*. iv, 48. 13 February. Parliament's refusal to recognize the titles of some of the royalist commissioners—Hyde's earldom, for instance—also looks like obstructive tactics. The king overlooked this. See above, p. 65, n. 5.

[3] *LJ*. vii, 175 *seq.*   [4] Whitelocke, i, 375.   [5] *CJ*. ii, 140, 234, 238, *et al.*
[6] Clarendon, *Rebellion*, iii, 492.   [7] *CJ*. iv, 7, 12, 16.

[8] See above, Chap. II, p. 42. Samuel Browne dined with St John and Vane, and was said by Whitelocke to be 'a grandee of that [St John's] party'. (Whitelocke, i, 527.) No doubt his experience as one of the original feoffees for impropriations would predispose him to lead the attack on Laud. (C. Hill, *Economic Problems of the Church* (Oxford, 1956), 257, 259.)

prolong the discussions.[1] But probably one cause of Vane's
attitude to peace negotiations lay in his knowledge of the king's
loyalty to his Church. 'All the king's propositions are to maintain the present religion', he had declared in the Commons
early in January 1644.[2]

The grounds for identifying Vane with a 'war policy' at
Uxbridge lie not only in his attitude to peace negotiations
before and after the treaty, and in Clarendon's account of the
meeting,[3] but in the speech Vane made to the City after his
return. In this speech[4] he said much about the further prosecution of the war, but almost nothing about the blighted hopes
of peace. Parliament, he told the City, has 'sent us to you for a
double end . . . The one to give you a clear representation of
the candour of their actions and intentions in this late treaty.
[There were evidently still suspicions in some people's minds
that Parliament did not really wish for peace.] The other, the
firmness . . . of their resolutions to live and dye with you . . . in
the prosecution of this war.' It is true that at this conference at a
Common Council it was the task of the earls Northumberland
and Loudon to deal with the record of the negotiations, and
Vane's to ask for more money to prosecute the war. If he had
really regretted the failure of the 'treaty', however, one would
expect this to have been shown at some point during the speech.
He did say: 'If it pleased God, notwithstanding all the designs
of foreigners upon us, that we can but be betimes in the
field, . . . we may be able to compose these unhappy differences . . . amongst ourselves.' He went on: 'There can be no
argument I know more prevelent with you, then the shortening
of the war; the Houses of Parliament have been willing to end
it either way, by treaty or war; but they think all treaties will
be uselesse till they [Parliament] be in a posture to shew themselves able to repell that opposition that can be made against
them.' Probably the last sentence reflects Vane's true opinions,
and he was relying on the recently formed New Model Army
to secure the kind of peace that he would consider acceptable.

---

[1] Clarendon, *Rebellion*, iii, 498.   [2] BM. Add. 18,779, f. 45v.
[3] *Rebellion*, iii, 498. For Clarendon's value as a witness at this point see C. H.
Firth, 'Clarendon's History of the Rebellion', *EHR*, xix (1904), 26–54.
[4] E 273(3).

In June 1645 a report was circulated in the City by a well-known Presbyterian minister, James Cranford, that Vane and three other members, St John, Pierrepont and Crew, had constituted themselves without authority a sub-committee of the Committee of Both Kingdoms, and for three months had been secretly negotiating with the king, even bargaining with him concerning the surrender of the forts, castles and garrisons in Parliament's hands.[1] Cranford's assertions were based on something Baillie had told him about an intercepted letter to Lord Digby, containing peace propositions for the king.[2] Two days later St John told the House that there *was* a sub-committee of the Committee of Both Kingdoms, appointed, among other duties, to find out who sent to the king at Oxford news of what was done in the House.[3] The members of the sub-committee named by St John were not the same as those mentioned by Cranford, and did not include Vane. According to Baillie it was Vane and St John who were instrumental in having Cranford's allegations brought up in the Commons; information about his accusations had come to the Committee of Both Kingdoms, Vane and St John had exaggerated the matter, and reported it to the House.[4] According to Whittaker, it was the Lord Mayor, Atkins, who actually sent the information to the House,[5] perhaps another slight indication of the links between Vane and the City. A committee was set up, and after a debate in July, the Commons voted Cranford's words false and scandalous, ordered him to be imprisoned in the Tower, and to pay £500 each to the men he had maligned.[6] His arrest was

[1] *CJ.* iv, 172, 212. St John said the sub-committee was instructed to negotiate about the surrender of royalist forts, and the writer of *Manifest Truths* (see p. 69, n. 4), accepts this. The sub-committee however is one more example of the methods of the Committee of Both Kingdoms. The sub-committee's establishment is not recorded in the Day-Book, and the Scots commissioners on the main committee were not told of its appointment until nearly a month had passed. A Scots member was then appointed—but never summoned to a meeting. (Baillie, ii, 487-9, *CSPD. 1644-45*, 400-1, 460.) Stapleton and Pierrepont declared that they knew nothing of the sub-committee (Harl. 166, f. 219), though St John had stated Pierrepont was a member.

[2] Baillie, ii, 279.

[3] Whittaker, f. 215. 13 June. D'Ewes did not include Vane among those named by Cranford (Harl. 166, f. 218), but the *Journals* and Yonge (BM. Add. 18,780, f. 76v) did.

[4] Baillie, loc. cit.   [5] Whittaker, ff. 214-15.   [6] *CJ.* iv, 212-13. 19 July.

delayed however,[1] and he was released soon after at the request of the same four members.[2]

Baillie says that he did not name any particular M.P.s in his conversations with Cranford, in which case Cranford merely guessed the identity of those concerned. Apparently Vane was not one of the members of the unauthorized sub-committee of Both Kingdoms alleged to be negotiating with the king. But the Committee was so curiously constituted that its membership was not clearly established, and Vane may well have attended meetings. The accusation levelled against Cranford in the Commons by Vane and his friend may have been designed to whip up anti-Scottish feeling, or they may have decided that the best defence was attack, if they had heard something of Baillie's suspicions. It was asserted in the House that the accusation was only an Independent plot against Cranford, a strong Presbyterian.[3] The incident is chiefly important however for illustrating the continuing theme of the fear of separate Independent peace negotiations, and for Baillie's belief that St John and Vane were directing spirits in such matters as the Cranford affair. It is not known whether Cranford paid his crippling fine, though it seems unlikely that he could have done.[4] His speedy release may have been due to the generosity of the men he had 'injured', but the House may have also taken into consideration the severe epidemic of plague that was raging in London in the summer of 1645.

The Cranford affair was connected with another political struggle which took place at the same time. In July 1645 a deliberate attempt, in which Vane took part, was made, and ruthlessly pressed, to ruin Holles and Whitelocke. The two M.P.s who had taken part in the Oxford negotiations in November were accused, as has already been mentioned, of suggesting what answer the king should make to Parliament; they were also accused of distinguishing between the 'parties' in Parliament, identifying that of the earl of Essex as the friends

[1] Baillie, ii, 311.   [2] CJ. iv, 245. 18 August.   [3] Harl. 166, f. 218v.
[4] The author of Manifest Truths (E 343(1). 4 July 1646) replying to the Scots version of relations between the two kingdoms, Truth's Manifest, E 1179(5), stated that the M.P.s whom Cranford had libelled 'I beleeve regard no pecuniary benefit'. He also asserted that Cranford's allegations might have ruined the New Model Army, by discrediting those who had been active in creating it.

of peace, and the rival party as its opponents.[1] Holles was further accused of corresponding with the royalist Lord Digby.[2] John Gurdon produced the letter of accusation from Lord Savile, and according to his evidence Vane was one of the three men who were informed of Savile's letter before it was brought up in the Commons; Lord Say, Vane and Sir Nathaniel Barnardiston, who was a relation of Gurdon's, and like him a Suffolk man, were told of the letter, or were perhaps shown it, and they advised Gurdon to proceed. Gurdon pointed out that the House would be at the time in a Grand Committee, when the letter could not be received, so Vane and Barnardiston promised to call the Speaker to the chair.[3] The charges were a severe ordeal for Holles and Whitelocke, and Whitelocke says their honour, fortune and life were at stake. The methods used in prosecuting them shed a sinister light on the parliamentary tactics of the Independents. The attack was delivered entirely without warning; Gurdon had told none but Say and the two others the identity of the men he intended to accuse,[4] and Whitelocke was not even in the House.[5] Lisle was thereupon instructed to summon Whitelocke, who was at Deptford, to the House, but Lisle sent him a 'grave generall letter . . . intimating not a word of the business', which only caused Whitelocke 'amusement',[6] and gave him no idea of the serious charges that had been made. But his friends warned him, and Whitelocke realized that the opponents of the earl of Essex were 'earnestly labouring to be rid of us both, either by cutting off our heads, or at least by expelling us both from being any more members of Parliament'.[7] For several days he forbore to tell his wife, who had been ill, for fear of the anxiety it would cause her. The attack could have succeeded—the House sat until 9 p.m. one

[1] The king, in his letter to Vane of February 1646, makes an oblique reference to this—'I may not say party', he writes. (Clarendon, *S.P.*, 226–7.)

[2] Whitelocke, i, 457, 466–7, 476; Holles, *Memoirs*, 212–13.

[3] Whitelocke, loc. cit. The MS version is clearer about this. Lilburne also made charges against Holles. See e.g. Whittaker, f. 221v.

[4] Whitelocke, i, 469.   [5] Whittaker, f. 218. 2 July.

[6] BM. Add. 37,343, f. 395. 2 July. 'Amusement' here has the seventeenth-century meaning of astonishment, or misunderstanding deliberately caused. Note that the MS version of Whitelocke's *Memorials* is considerably different from the printed one for 1645. See below, pp. 71–7, 85.

[7] Whitelocke, i, 479.

day debating the matter[1]—and Holles states that it was in
this affair that his enemies came nearest to success in their
attempts to ruin him.[2] Probably Holles was the real target, for
Whitelocke asserts that friends of his had found St John and
'other great men' of the Commons investigating committee not
'so sharp' against Whitelocke as against Holles, whom they
were resolved to ruin if they could.[3] Vane was one of the
committee,[4] and certainly one of its 'great men'. It is interesting to note that Samuel Browne was chairman of the
committee,[5] and Whitelocke thought he was far from impartial.
He 'pressed matters against us more than a chairman was to
do',[6] wrote Whitelocke, and a month or so later, when Whitelocke was taking up his legal career again (doubtless it was safer
than politics), he stated: 'I am willing to believe that Mr.
Samuell Browne was the more willing to show kindness to me,
as being conscious that he had bin over severe against me in the
buisnes of the Lord Savile.'[7]

When the Commons committee was set up, care was taken,
said Whitelocke, 'that as many of our friends as we could get in,
should be of it, and Mr. Elsing, the Clarke of the Parliament,
my kind friend and a friend of the earl of Essex his party, tooke
order, about the names of those that were friends of us to bee of
this committee that so much concerned us'.[8] It would be
interesting to know what Elsing did. Perhaps he became con-
veniently deaf when certain names were called. Even so, Whitelocke was aware that he must make strenuous efforts to repel
the attack. 'Although it [20 July] was the Lord's day, yett
mercy and self-preservation requiring it, I laboured to ingage
my friends to be in the house early the next morning.'[9] Lambert
Osbaldeston, 'who had been school-master att Westminster Col-
ledge, and was much acquainted with all grandees in his time,
went this day and every day to the Sollicitor St John, and most
of the great men adversaries to Mr. Holles and me', Whitelocke tells us, 'to take them off from their severe prosecution

[1] Ibid., 480.   [2] Holles, *Memoirs*, 212.   [3] Whitelocke, i, 470–1.
[4] *CJ*. iv, 195.   [5] Ibid., 213.   [6] Whitelocke, i, 466.   [7] BM. Add. 37,344, f. 1.
[8] BM. Add. 37,343, f. 398. There is much evidence that committees were far
from impartial, and that it was important to have friends on those with which one
was concerned.
[9] Ibid., f. 406.

of us'.[1] Vane was an alumnus of Westminster school, and would certainly be among those whom Osbaldeston visited.[2] Osbaldeston did more than this, for Whitelocke seems to have had charm, as well as an instinct for survival, and his friends were many and loyal. When M.P.s came out of the house during these debates 'Mr. Osbaldeston, and some others of our friends, were attending the doore of the house, and neer there abouts to sollicite the members our friends to returne to the house.' By this means 'even the gallants who used, whatever buisnes was in agitation, to goe forth to dinner and some other of their refreshments, yett they attended constantly all the time that this buisnes was in debate, and would not stirre from it'.[3] Whitelocke's exertions were successful, and the charge of treasonable correspondence was rejected by the House, though only after protracted debates, one of which lasted four or five hours.[4] Whitelocke states that his enemies wanted the other accusations, concerning the draft reply which he and Holles had composed for the king at Oxford, postponed until a time when the House was more likely to vote against the two accused men, but the manœuvre was foiled.[5] This charge however was brought up later and used against Holles in the 1647 crisis.[6]

Doubtless as a counter-attack, it was moved that Cranford's allegations should be finally dealt with on the same day that the House was to proceed to judgement on Savile's charges.[7] It was a neat riposte, for St John, Vane and the other M.P.s named by Cranford were accused of negotiating with the king at Oxford, and so was Holles. Probably all were guilty. Holles asserts that he had seen letters from Savile to persons at Oxford,

---

[1] Ibid., f. 401.

[2] We know that Vane visited the school, and that Osbaldeston had influence upon him, for Vane's considerable financial and other help to the scholar Henry Stubbe was given as a result of an appeal by the ex-headmaster when Vane was visiting the school. (Wood, *Athenae*, iii, 1068; Stubbe, *Legends no Histories* (London, 1670), preface.)

[3] BM. Add. 37,343, f. 406v. For Hugh Peter's similar standing at a door to solicit votes in a Common Council meeting, see Pearl, *London and the outbreak of the Puritan Revolution*, 261.

[4] Harl. 166, ff. 241, 243v.   [5] Whitelocke, i, 480.   [6] Ibid., ii, 174.

[7] *CJ.* iv, 212. There was a long debate about which set of accusations should first be discussed in the House. (Harl. 166, f. 240.)

with 'many propositions made in the name of that [the Independent] party'. He names Whitelocke, the earl of Essex and others, including Sir Christopher Wray, as persons who had also seen the letters.[1] The Press as usual was discreet, and hardly mentioned the Savile affair. *A Diary or an exact Journal* frankly declared: 'I dare not wade into these deepes.'[2] The *Scottish Dove* made its sympathies clear when it wrote in the week when the Savile charges against Holles and Whitelocke were brought: 'an evill spirit is raysed, and good men are accused'.[3]

In spite of the Savile affair, Vane continued to be on friendly terms with Whitelocke. In November 1645, when the earl of Pembroke moved at a parliamentary committee that Whitelocke should be the steward of Westminster school, Vane supported this,[4] and in 1646 Vane was advising with Whitelocke about the affairs of Lord Willoughby, a mutual friend.[5]

Meanwhile, in the spring of 1645, Vane was noted by more than one observer to have taken up a very hostile attitude to the Scots, with whom Holles and his group were now working, so that on yet one more issue Vane and Holles were opponents. In February *Aulicus* claimed to have intercepted a letter from an M.P., 'Mr. Pyne', clearly John Pyne, the member for Poole.[6] Pyne had told his correspondent:

The Scots Commissioners have withdrawn their intimateness with those of the Committee of Both Kingdoms, viz. Sir Henry Vane, sen., Sir Henry Vane, jun., Mr. Solicitor [St John], Mr. Pierpoint, Lieut. General Cromwell, Sir William Waller, Sir Arthur Haslerigg, Mr. Crewe, Mr. Wallop, and have joined themselves in a seeming conspiracy and compliance with Sir Philip Stapleton and his associates; viz. Holles, the Recorder [Glyn], Clotworthy, Reynolds, Whitelocke, Maynard and the Lords; what is the design, is not yet discerned. . . . Tis hope, that 'tis only done to advance the presbyteriall government with us . . . This is a great secret, as yet known to some few; it is reported that they have some private meetings with those malignant creatures; when this is perused, burn it.[7]

[1] Holles, *Memoirs*, 212.   [2] E 292(4).   [3] E 292(5). 27 June–4 July.
[4] BM. Add. 37,344, f. 28. 25 November 1645.   [5] Ibid., f. 110. 9 September.
[6] For Pyne see Keeler, *The Long Parliament 1640–41*, 319.
[7] E 272(13). 23 February–2 March 1645. Presumably the 'malignant creatures' were Holles and his circle.

Aulicus challenged Pyne to repudiate the letter, which was not done; one can therefore presumably accept its authenticity. Sabran reported in April an outburst by Vane in the Committee of Both Kingdoms; the Scots commissioners had protested at the opening of their letters by an agent of the Committee, and according to Sabran: 'le jeune Vayne a dit qu'ils avoient médiocrement contribuez à la guerre, et au service du parlement, mais avoient tirez beaucoup de l'argent, et euz soing de bien assurez leurs affairs'.[1] The able Scots pamphleteer, David Buchanan, writing in January 1646, had his own explanation of what had happened. Some of the English, he asserted,

seeing that by the help of the Scots . . . they began to stand upon their own legs, they feel the pulse of the Scots to try if they were pliable to their phantasies and opinions, and perceiving the Scots constant to their principles and firm unto their Covenant, begin to care less for those who had raised them from the dust; yea, they begin to oppose the Scots. [Buchanan went on:] Then, in the Council of State [i.e. the Committee of Both Kingdoms] the Scots have a long time been crossed in a high measure, by those who were against their incoming; and thereafter have still been opposed by these men, and their participants, who are adverse to the settling of the Church. The Scots, with grief of mind . . . see those whom they at first conceived certainly to be right and round in this business, to have corners and bywaies.

In the same pamphlet there is an interesting reference to Vane's part in obtaining the Rhode Island charter. Buchanan wrote: 'Then a great stickler of the Independents moves the Houses of Parliament for those of his holy Society, Fraternity, and adherents, to have liberty of conscience in the transmarin plantations, thinking by these means to make a step for the same liberty at home.' It was almost certainly Vane too whom he had in mind in another passage. 'The Scots [it was argued] must be sent back in all haste . . . and this went on so far by the artifice of the Independents that it was moved in public by a great stickler of that Faction, and a venter of their plots.'[2]

---

[1] BM. Add. 5, 461, f. 176.20 April 1645.

[2] David Buchanan, *An explanation of some truths* . . . E 314(15). 3 January 1646. For Vane's connexion with the policy of sending the Scots back see pp. 75–6. Buchanan had written *Truth's Manifest* (see above, p. 69, n. 4), E 1179(5), and

It is fair to conclude that Vane had become one of the leading critics of the Scots, but his motives are not fully clear. He may genuinely have felt that the Scots Army had not done enough, and probably religious disagreements also played a part. Moreover he evidently disliked the Scots' policy of supporting negotiation with the king. This is indicated in his own letter of 23 September to his father. 'I hear the business of peace is like to be pressed very hard by our brethren', he wrote,[1] and though the words are carefully non-committal they are not those of a man who was himself hoping for peace. If Northumberland's letter of the previous day to Vane's father is any guide to opinion in their circle, it was felt there that the Scots garrisons in the Northern towns should be removed, and the Scots Army brought down south into England.[2] (Of course this would effectually put an end to Scots negotiations for peace.) Vane had reported in May 1645, and again in September, on the measures necessary to assist the Scots in their march south.[3] When soon after this the complaints of the Scots about the non-payment of their Army and the failure to establish Presbyterianism in England were discussed in the Commons, it was Vane who put forward the propositions that were adopted, that Parliament would send £2000 and 200 barrels of gunpowder to meet the Scots at Newark, which Parliament forces were besieging, provided the Scots were there by 1 November.[4] When the Commons insisted on the return of the English towns garrisoned by the Scots Vane was named first on the committee to prepare a letter to the Scots on this subject,[5] though Robert Goodwyn actually presented the draft to the House.[6] When a division took place a few months later on fixing a date for the withdrawal of the Scots from the towns in England, Vane and Pierrepont were the tellers for the motion, while

---

Histoire des derniers troubles (E 547), both of which are interesting on this period. He had to flee the country to avoid arrest by Parliament on account of his pamphlets. (BM. Add. 10,114, f. 12v.) He is noticed in *DNB* and Baillie (ii, 179, 197).

[1] *CSPD. 1645-47*, 155. D'Ewes noted that the Commons ignored the Scots' request for peace propositions to be sent to the king himself in June 1645. (Harl. 166, f. 221v.) The Scots Presbyterians were often referred to as 'brethren'.

[2] *CSPD. 1645-47*, 105.   [3] Harl. 166, ff. 214v, 239v.

[4] *CSPD. 1645-47*, 179-81; *CJ*. iv, 298. 6 October.

[5] *CJ*. iv, 340. 12 November.   [6] Ibid.

Stapleton and Holles, who wanted no definite date fixed, were tellers for the opposition, and lost.[1]

That the Scots viewed Vane's group as their leading opponents is indicated by the letter from Cheisly, secretary to the Scots commissioners in London, which had been taken from him as he was on his way to Scotland in May 1646. The letter was read in the Commons, and John Harrington recorded in his parliamentary diary: 'Mr. Solicitor [St John], Mr. Brown, Sir. H. Vane junior, Mr. Martin, Mr. White shamefully traduced.'[2] In August 1646 the Scots made suggestions for improving relations between the two countries which included measures for restricting the Press, and for the payment of the money due to them. The Scots proposals were generally approved by the Commons, though Vane 'suspected' them, but discussion was postponed for two days. In the meanwhile the Lords discussed the proposals, and framed an ordinance based on them, which they sent to the Commons, obviously hoping that better relations between the two countries could be quickly established. Vane, whether because he objected to the Scots' plans, or to the Lords' interference, or probably, to both, opposed the Lords' ordinance; Harrington wrote: 'Some obiect it is against our privilege that the Lords should offer us an ordinance in, after our moving for it. Sir H. Vane that our members erred in receiving it.'[3] (There is much other evidence of acute friction between the two Houses in 1646, though nothing else connects Vane with it specifically.[4])

There are in 1645 again indications that Vane had connexions with the City. According to the Venetian ambassador the 'war party' in December 1644 were having a petition prepared by some of the most 'seditious spirits' of London, to present to Parliament, to put away the 'charms of peace' and consider preparations for war. They might also add, Agostini thought, a demand for the Scots to advance, 'which is desired by the same party'.[5] This was exactly Vane's policy in 1645. Sabran in

---

[1] Ibid.   [2] BM. Add. 10,114, f. 15. 8 May 1646.
[3] Ibid., f. 17. 14 August 1646.   [4] BM. Add. 10,114, *passim*.
[5] *CSPV. 1643-47*, 160. 9 December 1644. The Journal of the Common Council of London records the presentation of a petition for the fortification of Windsor Castle and other places, but does not mention the Scots. (JCC. London, 40, f. 117.)

March thought he saw evidence of collusion between some in the City and one of the parliamentary groups.

La chambre des Communes [he wrote] s'est advisée d'une ruse bien subtile . . . et a demandé audit Maire et Ville de Londres, un emprunt de cent mille Jacobus, pour être recouvert sur les douanes et assises [excise], laquelle en a accordé quatre vingt mil, à condition que tous les chefs et officiers, demandez par ledit Ferfax, et accordez par ladit chambre des Communes, soient, les seuls admis . . . dont vous jugez le forte intelligence avec ladit chambre.[1]

This loan was the one that Vane had asked for when he spoke to the Common Council after the Uxbridge negotiations. There is no indication in the *Commons Journals* or in those of the Common Council of the City[2] that the City had in fact made the stipulation that Sabran speaks of, though there certainly was a conflict with the Lords, who did not wish to accept all Fairfax's list of officers for the New Model.[3]

One of the Vanes, but unfortunately the *Commons Journals* do not say which, was on a committee to prepare reasons why the Commons were adhering to Fairfax's list,[4] and Browne, Hesilrige, Glyn and Sir Peter Wentworth managed a conference with the Lords on the subject,[5] so that it is sufficiently clear which group was supporting Fairfax. It was Vane and Cromwell who were tellers for the motion that Fairfax should be commander-in-chief of the New Model, when Holles and Stapleton were tellers against, in January 1645,[6] and altogether it seems likely that if Sabran's story is true, Vane was concerned in the manœuvre. A Commons' decision to hold the 4 March conference on the loan of £100,000, with the Common Council and not a Common Hall, was maintained in spite of strong opposition from the Lords, and Vane managed a conference with the Upper House on this subject.[7] There had been

---

[1] BM. Add. 5,461, f. 138. The £80,000 loan was agreed to. (R. R. Sharpe, *London and the Kingdom* (London, 1894-5) ii, 214.) For an interesting reference to citizens meeting M.P.s to discuss the excise, see BM. Add. 37,344, f. 19. (Not in the printed Whitelocke *Memorials*.) Whitelocke does not name the M.P.s. In June there was a rumour of a plot to murder some M.P.s and 'those who was their cheif men in the Citie'. (E 339(16).)

[2] JCC. London, 40, f. 123v.

[3] *CJ*. iv, 77, 81, 83. As usual the Lords gave way.

[4] Ibid., 77.   [5] Ibid., 81.   [6] Ibid., 26.   [7] Ibid., 68.

another ordinance in December 1644 ordering the Lord Mayor and Aldermen to secure the election of 'well-affected' persons to the Common Council,[1] and it looks as though Vane and his group could rely on the Common Council far more than they could on a Common Hall, which all the Liverymen of the City Companies were entitled to attend. This finds corroboration in the appearance of that inveterate petitioner, Alderman Fowke, in June 1645 with a request from the Common Council that Fairfax should be freed from the control exercised by the Committee of Both Kingdoms, and that Cromwell should command Fairfax's cavalry.[2] This instructive contrast to the earlier attitude of Vane's group to the authority to be exercised by that Committee over the earl of Essex when he commanded Parliament's armies, is one indication that the Independents had lost control of the Committee of Both Kingdoms. It is noticeable that after March 1645 Vane was not sent to the City when Parliament had to make contact with its leaders; for example when the City was informed of Parliament's plan to capture Oxford in May,[3] nor when the City was asked to advance a month's pay for the Scots in June.[4] In April and May it is true that Vane was away from the Committee of Both Kingdoms for ten days,[5] which was unusual for him, and may mean that he was ill, but there is no obvious reason for his omission from the June committee, except his preoccupation with other affairs of state.

Vane had other duties at this time than those already mentioned; they included, for instance, the drafting of many important documents. In 1645 the Commons had much need of letters of thanks to successful generals, and of other documents connected with Parliament's victories in the field, or with the settlement of the country. Vane was often employed in such matters. In March he, Pierrepont and Whitelocke drafted a clear and sensible declaration to some mutinous soldiers,[6] and with Holles and Glyn he drew up a letter to Parliament's commissioners in Scotland about the speedy march of the Scots Army southwards.[7] When his father and the other representatives were sent to Scotland in July Vane was

---

[1] *CJ*. iii, 729.   [2] Harl. 166, f. 216.   [3] *CJ*. iv, 147.   [4] Ibid., 173.
[5] *CSPD. 1644–45*, 375 *seq.*   [6] *CJ*. iv, 69.   [7] Ibid., 167. 7 June.

on the large committee which prepared the envoys' instructions.[1] He interrupted a debate on 23 July to tell the House the good news of the fall of Bridgwater,[2] and with Reynolds was instructed to write the letter of congratulations to Fairfax.[3] But when the committee of the Army, whose leading spirit was Robert Scawen, proposed that martial law should be enforced in all counties, apparently even on civilians, it was Vane who, with Whitelocke and others, secured rejection of the plan, 'shewing that the counties of England would be brought to an intolerable bondage'. Though he might frame messages of congratulation to the generals, he was alert to the danger of Englishmen's lives, 'depending on the will of a few men', as D'Ewes put it.[4]

It seems likely then that about the summer of 1645 Vane and St John's group lost the control over the Committee of Both Kingdoms which they had so carefully planned to obtain when the Committee had been established. According to Holles this led the Independents to boycott the Committee.

Now the tide was turned; they [the Committee] had nothing to do . . . They of the Committee, who were of that [the Independent] faction seldom or never came to it; so that the Commissioners of Scotland, and the other members of it, did come and attend three or four days one after another, sometimes oftener, to no purpose, and no Committee could sit for want of a number [i.e. a quorum]; nay, they prevailed so far, as now to vilifie and show their neglect or jealousie of the Scottish Commissioners. They would sometimes get business referred to the Members of Both Houses that were of that Committee, with their [the Scots] exclusion.[5]

Unfortunately only three of the letters copied into the Letter-Book of the Committee for 1646-7 have signatures appended; from these it looks as if Holles's group predominated in October 1646.[6] Holles's allegation receives confirmation also

---

[1] Ibid., 199.   [2] Whittaker, f. 222.   [3] *CJ*. iv, 220. 26 July.   [4] Harl. 166, f. 207v.
[5] Holles, *Memoirs*, 221. Holles is as usual vague about dates.
[6] The letter of 23 October was signed by the earls of Northumberland and Manchester, Lord Wharton, Holles, Pierrepont, Lisle, Lewes, Robert Goodwin, Sir John Temple and Stapleton. Wharton and Lisle were members of the Independent group, Pierrepont a respected neutral, Northumberland a 'trimmer', Goodwin probably an Independent, but not a strong character. Four of the others were supporters of Holles at this time. Another letter in October has the signatures

from the request of Alderman Fowke and his fellow-petitioners of June 1645, that the Committee should not control Fairfax, and from an incident in the same month in which that 'fiery spirit', Peregrine Pelham, M.P. for Hull, was the central figure. Pelham was accused of declaring 'in some speeches spoken by him, that wee could not prosper soe long as wee trusted these disobliged persons in the Committee of Both Kingdoms, and that hee had named the earle of Essex, the earle of Manchester, the earle of Warwicke and Sir Philip Stapleton'. Pelham was sent for out of the Abbey, though he was taking part in a fast kept by divines of the Assembly for the good success of Sir Thomas Fairfax's army. He ingenuously confessed in the House that 'he had named the earle of Manchester and Sir Philip Stapleton, but did not remember that hee had named the earles of Essex and Warwick'.[1]

In 1646 perhaps the most important of Vane's activities was his part in the peace negotiations with the king. Charles wrote to Vane in March pointing out the advantages of an agreement between the two sides. There appears to be no full account of what led up to this development, and it is necessary therefore to look in some detail at the peace negotiations after Naseby. As Nicholas endorsed the copies of the letters to Vane in the Clarendon Papers: 'Copies of two letters sent to the Independent Party, by his Majesty's Command',[2] it is obvious that the king regarded Vane as the leader of the Independent group, and was writing to him as such. It is impossible to elucidate this important topic at all fully, for information is very scanty, but it is necessary to make some attempt.

In August 1645 the Commons decided that the House should sit on certain days each week as a Grand Committee to consider peace negotiations, and the Scots commissioners were to be informed of this.[3] Was this a victory for the peace party, or

of Manchester and Lauderdale noted; a third, in December, those of Lauderdale and Warwick (S.P. 21/23, pp. 107, 108.) If Holles is right, the absence of the Committee's records for the latter part of 1645 and for 1646 would be explained. The Fair Day-Books stop in June 1645, the Draft Day-Books (much less full than the Fair Day-Books) extend to 11 December 1645. After this there is considerably less information from the Committee's records. The Letters Sent, for instance, give no information about attendances.

[1] Harl. 166, f. 218. 11 June.   [2] Clarendon, *S.P.*, 726-7.
[3] Whitelocke, i, 496. 18 August.

for their opponents? Probably the former: Vane and St John
were absent, and there was a very thin house, partly because
many M.P.s often went out of town to visit their homes at this
time of year, and partly because of a plague epidemic in
London. The motion may perhaps have been passed as a retort
to *Aulicus*, who had in a vigorous issue accused Parliament of
being hostile to peace. He had told his readers on 13 August that
Parliament had stopped Harcourt on his way to Oxford only
because the French envoy had worked for peace, and that the
Dutch ambassadors found so much 'foule play' at London that
they had told the M.P.s: 'they had no hopes left to make them
heare of peace'.[1] On the other hand, the motion could have
been a victory for the 'war party'—it would ensure that peace
propositions would be discussed only on two days each week,
and those days were not yet fixed. Sabran thought the Commons were 'esperans avoir contenté les Escossois, en monstrans
de concourir au désir de la paix, et de dilayer toutesfois les dites
propositions'.[2] Since the motion expressly mentioned the Scots,
he may well have been right about Scots pressure; his interpretation is supported by the fact that the Commons did not
fix the days on which the peace propositions were to be debated
weekly until 13 October,[3] when Tuesdays and Thursdays were
set aside, and we know from Vane's own letter to his father that
this was in answer to a Scots request.[4]

Meanwhile Jean de Montereuil, the French envoy in Scotland, had told Mazarin in September 1645 that 'Lord
Balmerino came . . . to inform me that Prince Rupert had
brought from Bristol to Oxford, articles of peace, drawn up
between the king of Great Britain and the Independents.'[5]
(Balmerino was the commissioner appointed by the Scots to
negotiate with Montereuil.) The story of this private negotiation
between the king and the Independents rests on the unsup-
ported testimony of Balmerino alone, who does not give the
name of his informant. Vane was singularly inactive in the

---

[1] E 298(23).
[2] BM. Add. 5461, f. 335. 31 August 1645. On 30 June the judges had been
ordered to let the people know that Parliament had twice tried, and was now
trying, to obtain peace. (*CJ.* iv, 594.)
[3] Whitelocke, i, 523.   [4] *CSPD. 1645-47*, 191-2. 14 October 1645.
[5] *Montereuil, Correspondence*, i, 16. 18-28 September.

Commons that September and apart from one or two references to Northern affairs and those connected with the Scottish Army, his name hardly appears in the *Journals*.[1] It was the month when he was busy obtaining arms for Raby Castle. (It was also the month when the Commons were working out details of the Presbyterian scheme of church government for England, and perhaps Vane preferred to be absent.) Was he also preoccupied with negotiations with the king? According to Montereuil the negotiations were still going on in November.[2] On the king's side they were apparently only a manœuvre to gain time until he could obtain foreign help.[3] In Parliament itself the peace negotiations hung fire: there were only seven discussions in November, three of which took place after another Scots request for speedy consideration of peace terms had been received.[4]

In December the king approached Parliament itself. Perhaps he was already losing faith in the possibility of an arrangement with the Independents, if he ever had one. He sent a letter to the Commons, which met the uncompromising reply that the House was already discussing peace propositions to be sent to the king as parliamentary bills;[5] Parliament, that is, was allowing no discussion with the king's representatives, but was laying down its own terms. Vane appeared once in these negotiations when on 17 December he was sent to the Lords to urge that Parliament's reply should be sent quickly.[6] The Lords had hesitated about Parliament's answer to the king's letter, and the Scots commissioners disapproved of it, for they wanted an agreed peace and not a dictated one. Vane must have endorsed the majority view in the Commons, or he would not have been sent to the Lords on this mission. In October the earl of Loudon, one of the Scots members of the Committee of Both Kingdoms, had added his voice to those who believed the Parliament majority (an Independent one since the summer by-elections, according to Holles) did not want peace. He told Montereuil that he despaired of a general peace, 'seeing those

---

[1] From 5 August to 1 October. Vane's name appears twice (except on committees) in the *Commons Journals*, iv (including that on p. 267, which must refer to the younger Vane, as his father was in Scotland).

[2] Gardiner, *CW.*, ii, 12.   [3] Ibid., 17.   [4] Whitelocke, i, 533 *seq.*

[5] Ibid., 544. 10 December.   [6] *CJ.* iv, 379.

who had the most authority in the English Parliament have no inclination for it'.[1] On 27 December the king sent another letter. After debate the Commons decided not to 'treat' with the king at all, and to keep the militia wholly in Parliament's hands.[2] Again Vane was the envoy who carried this bill to the Lords, which shows that he supported this policy.[3]

In January 1646 the lagging, but to the people vital, negotiations for peace continued. Charles told Henry Killigrew, according to Montereuil,[4] that he began to see that he had very little to expect from the Independents, but whether he was referring to any secret negotiations with the Independents, or to the open transactions with Parliament, is not clear. Marten was allowed to return to the Commons in January 1646, and Whitelocke cautiously stated: 'This gave occasion to some to believe that the house began to be more averse from the king.'[5] It was Vane who found the constitutional method of restoring Marten to his place as an M.P.—he probably wanted Marten's support in attacks on the king.[6] Whitelocke's view of Marten's return is consistent with a statement by Montereuil a fortnight later that: 'What is no less secret than strange, four or five leaders of the Independent party met on Friday last and resolved that it was necessary to depose the king of Great Britain, towards which the letters they had received from him and his declaration in favour of the Irish Catholics, which had been read in parliament that same day, would give them sufficient reason.'[7] Montereuil's source of information could have been the countess of Carlisle. He mentions the 'help' she had given the French-Presbyterian plan for peace, 'in spite', he wrote, 'of what she owes to ties of blood and the interest of her brother'.[8]

---

[1] *Montereuil, Correspondence*, i, 45. 30 October–9 November 1645.

[2] Whitelocke, i, 552. 30 December. Baron Thorpe refers to the public surprise at the refusal of the king's letters. (T. Wildridge, *The Hull Letters, 1625–46* (Hull, 1886), 121.)

[3] *CJ.* iv, 393. 1 January 1646.

[4] *Montereuil, Correspondence*, i, 91. 11–21 January 1646.

[5] Whitelocke, i, 555. 6 January 1646.

[6] *Somers Tracts*, vi, 589–90. He suggested that the order of the House expelling Marten should be expunged from the *Commons Journal*, and this was done.

[7] *Montereuil, Correspondence*, i, 117. 22 January–1 February 1646. The Glamorgan treaty had been read on 16 January. (*CJ.* iv, 408.)

[8] *Montereuil, Correspondence*, loc. cit.

Her brother, the earl of Northumberland, may have been her informant. Montereuil soon wrote however that the Independents had changed their plans and they had proposed in Parliament to send the king the three Uxbridge propositions, to which they had spoken of adding four others, in order to show that they wished peace no less than the Scots.[1] It reads as though Montereuil had judged of this change of plan by what he heard had happened in Parliament, and not from any private information of the Independents' intentions.

At last the Commons got down to the task of drawing up the bill which was in effect to be an ultimatum to the king, and Vane was one of the twelve members who were to prepare it.[2] In his letter of 31 January the king had suggested that the church should be as in the days of Queen Elizabeth, 'having regard still to tender consciences'.[3] Vane's policy is clearer at this point, if one may give credit to a report by Montereuil, which is almost certainly to be relied on, for he would no doubt hear of what was said in public debates in the House.

Whatever the king may have done by this letter in trying to satisfy the Independents concerning religion, they have shown so little gratitude for it that young Vane, who has great credit among them, said openly that it was an artifice of this prince to try and detach them [the Independents] from the interests of Parliament, to which they would always remain attached, and that when matters were settled, they would much rather prefer to receive from it [Parliament] than from their king, that tranquillity for their consciences which this king offered them at present.[4]

'Openly' almost certainly means that Vane was speaking in the Commons, as it was here that the king's letter was debated. Again the House received the king's letter coldly; they voted it unsatisfactory and set up a large committee, which included Vane, to draft a reply, and frame a declaration to the kingdom.[5] He reported a conference with the Lords on the peace propositions on 20 February,[6] and when a committee was set up to

---

[1] Ibid., 124. 29 January–8 February 1646.
[2] *CJ*. iv, 423. 30 January 1646.   [3] Whitelocke, i, 567.
[4] *Montereuil, Correspondence*, i, 130–1. 5–15 February 1646.
[5] *CJ*. iv, 428. 3 February 1646.   [6] Ibid., 448. 26 February 1646.

justify to the Lords the vindictive fifth proposition, demanding the punishment of delinquents, whom Parliament would name in the future, he was one of its nine members.[1]

This was the situation when Charles wrote to Vane on 2 March 1646. His letters have been printed, and it only remains to comment briefly upon them. When Charles wrote: 'You cannot suppose the work is done, though God should suffer you to destroy the king', he was perhaps referring to what he had heard from French sources of the secret Independent meeting in January. It is interesting that Charles (in writing to Vane) laid such stress on considerations of foreign policy. There are indications that this was a sphere in which Vane was already particularly interested,[2] though there does not seem to be enough evidence to regard him as at this date Parliament's 'Foreign Secretary'. The identity of Vane's friend the 'Gentleman that was quartered with you', who is to help to persuade Parliament to allow the king to come to London, as Charles had asked in his letter of 31 December, is not known. It has often been assumed that the king was referring to Whitelocke,[3] but it was more likely Hesilrige.[4]

From February 1646 onwards it is impossible to follow Vane's policy towards peace. He was ill on 20 April, and away from

[1] Ibid., 454.   [2] See below, p. 145.

[3] The assumption that the king was referring to Whitelocke is based on an incorrectly transcribed passage in Whitelocke's *Memorials*. The editor printed the sentence: 'I lived with Sir Henry Vane, Mr. Solicitor, Mr. Browne, and other grandees of that party', in the entries for 15 and 20 October 1646, but Whitelocke wrote that he *dined* with Vane and the others, and he wrote that once only. It is quite possible that Whitelocke's editor was subconsciously remembering that Vane had let the Navy Treasury house at Deptford to Whitelocke, but there is absolutely nothing to indicate that the Vanes and Whitelocke lived there together, and Whitelocke writes as though he and his wife when in London were established in his lawyer's quarters at the Temple. He wrote the passage about dining with Vane and the other grandees at 20 October. It continues as in the printed version ('and was kindly treated by them, as I used to be by the other'), but goes on with a significant reflection which Whitelocke's editor did not print: 'in publique affairs (my children) you will find it of advantage to keep favour with all, and not to side with any faction'. In other words, Whitelocke had decided it was too dangerous to be identified with any one party. Holles had lost an influential supporter by an attack which Vane had helped to launch. (Whitelocke, i, 525, 527; BM. Add. 37,344, ff. 19-20v, 15v, *et. al.*)

[4] He is said in a 1660 pamphlet to have lived with Vane, *A dialogue between Sir Henry Vaine and Sir Arthur Heslerigg*, E 1849(2). Hesilrige could have stayed with Vane on his visits to London.

Parliament for a short time at least.[1] He was not certainly back in the House—the clerk omits for some weeks to distinguish between the two Vanes, father and son—until 11 May. On that day an amendment, insolent and humiliating to the king, was added to a resolution that the king should surrender all his garrisons; by the amendment the king, upon the demand of both Houses, should be 'delivered to be disposed as both Houses shall appoint'. Vane was one of the tellers for the amendment, Holles and Stapleton, as so often, were tellers against him, and they won, by seven votes.[2] The amendment significantly highlights Vane's attitude, but for a moment only. He was a member of various committees connected with the peace propositions in May, June and July, but none shed light on his individual position.[3]

Meanwhile the public demand for peace grew no less pressing. The *Weekly Intelligencer* adjured its readers not to be too impatient for peace.[4] The *Scottish Dove*, always the *enfant terrible* of the Press, frankly admitted: 'The people in City and Country generally have long desired Propositions might be sent to the king.'[5] The *Weekly Intelligencer* was moved by its loyalty to the king to make an unwontedly courageous stand, for in October it ventured to say: 'The king being (indeed) better beloved, then many doe apprehend he is', and to print the Covenant, so that there should be 'no diminution of his majesty's just power and greatness'.[6] This was the month in which St John moved that the peace propositions should be presented to the king, in the form of a bill;[7] Vane's name does not appear in connexion with this motion, but he and St John were probably again working together.

Information about Vane's policy in the years 1645 and 1646 is somewhat scanty, and it is understandable that his

---

[1] *CJ.* iv, 515. Vane had leave of absence for fourteen days to 'take some course for the recovery of his health'.

[2] Ibid., 542.   [3] Ibid., 558, 564, 576, 584, 587, *et al.*

[4] E 350(3). 4–11 August 1646.   [5] E 350(5). 5–12 August 1646.

[6] E 358(8). 13–20 October 1646. Article iii of the Covenant, 'We shall endeavour . . . with our estates and lives, . . . to preserve and defend the king's Majesty's person and authority', was the relevant one. A republican pamphlet of March 1646 had accused the Londoners of 'wanting the king in again upon any conditions'. (*The Last Warning to all the inhabitants of London.* E 328(24).)

[7] *Montereuil, Correspondence,* i, 280. 4 October 1646.

biographers should have resorted to general descriptions of public affairs when they came to this period of Vane's life.[1] There are several reasons for the lack of material; the records of the Committee of Both Kingdoms become thinner, and its Fair Day-Books for the second half of 1645 and for 1646 are not extant.[2] D'Ewes's notes of Commons' debates are non-existent for some days, and very brief and summarized when he does make any, for he had been discouraged by the Commons' attitude to himself,[3] and in any case probably thought it unsafe to commit too much to paper, when accusations of treason were being made with deadly purpose against men so respected and influential as Holles and Whitelocke. Whittaker had lost his first enthusiasm for keeping a diary of Commons' debates, and his record is usually very flat and uninformative. Harrington's diary[4] is fuller and much more interesting, but though it gives some information about the period from May 1646 to August 1647, there are many days of which the diarist provides no record. The newspapers were frankly timid, giving long accounts of military affairs, and hurriedly passing over parliamentary business in a few words.[5] This obviously does not apply to *Mercurius Aulicus*, but he was too occupied with the king's tragic military situation to pay much attention to the London Parliament, and not in a good position to know much about it anyway.[6] Whitelocke's views on day-to-day events in

---

[1] One of the best of Vane's biographers, J. K. Hosmer, gave six out of 517 pages to the years 1645 and 1646, and devoted three of the six pages to reprinting Vane's speech of 3 March 1645 and the king's 1646 letters to Vane. But Hosmer gave a long account, with a map, of Naseby, with which Vane was not concerned at all.

[2] See above, p. 79, n. 6.

[3] Harl. 163, f. 292v. D'Ewes had thought in the summer of 1642 that freedom of speech was disappearing, and decided not to go often to the House after this.

[4] BM. Add. 10,114.

[5] The *Scottish Dove* wrote: 'Whatsoever is devulged displeasing to unjust men, is usually questioned . . . The Prudent keep silence.' (E 322(38). 11–18 February 1646.) As an example of the attitude of the Press, one may take *Perfect Occurrences of BOTH HOUSES OF PARLIAMENT and MARTIALL affairs* (the capitals are its editor's) for a typical week, 8–15 May 1646, when out of roughly 320 lines, only some 20 refer to parliamentary business. (E 337(22).)

[6] Though the king himself was generally believed to receive accounts of Parliament's activities—see Say's statement that Holles kept up a weekly correspondence with Oxford. (Baillie, ii, 489.) See also the *Scottish Dove* (E 317(4), 14–21 January 1646): 'I shall intreat the reader to consider that his Majesty . . . have better intelligence of the Parliament's proceedings, then the Parliament have of theirs;

the Commons would have been very interesting to have, but scarcely a word of personal comment or interpretation escapes him, and he too gives a colourless summary of parliamentary affairs, though here and there he does offer a brief light on the situation. There are by chance some of Vane's own letters, interesting, but short and few, in the State Papers Domestic;[1] they were written to his father when the old man was on his parliamentary mission to Scotland in August 1645. The *Commons Journals* are as full as they usually are for the 1640s, but of course they give no speeches by individual M.P.s. There are scattered references to Vane in a number of sources, but there are many gaps in the account of Vane's activities during these years.

Nevertheless, some conclusions are possible. It is clear that in the Commons Vane pursued a tough line in his attitude to peace negotiations with the king. To judge from his speech to the City Common Council in March 1645 he considered that it was useless to treat with the king until Parliament was in a position to dictate terms. He advocated the condign punishment of the leading royalists, and a humiliating form of words for the king's surrender. His whole policy is consistent with the attitude of implacable hostility to the king implicit in Charles's first letter to Vane of March 1646. There is evidence however that Vane's attitude was not endorsed by public opinion. Of the secret negotiations between the king and the Independents nothing is known for certain. All the evidence comes from Montereuil, except for the letters from the king, which give no indication that there had been earlier peace feelers. It is quite possible that Vane had been in communication with the king from November 1645 to January 1646 and that he had the same purpose as that attributed to him in the 1644 Lovelace affair, the Machiavellian one of discovering Charles's own policy, and thus weakening the royalists, but the evidence is very uncertain. He shrewdly discerned however that the royal offer of toleration to the Independents was made merely to strengthen the king's own position.

for it is too apparent that they know at Oxford, each dayes proceedings in both houses.'

[1] *CSPD. 1645–47*, 104, 123, 138, 155, 166, 183, 191.

Contemporaries assumed that St John and Vane were working together in Parliament, and the group of M.P.s who usually viewed politics in the same light included Prideaux, Samuel Browne, Hesilrige and Cromwell. There are again indications that Hesilrige and Vane worked closely together. For instance, when John Blakiston, one of the members for Newcastle, wanted the power to appoint officers in the Army withdrawn from the Northern committee, Stapleton objected. Blakiston thereupon produced letters found after the capture of Pontefract which implicated Holles and three members of the Northern committee, William Pierrepont, Sir Christopher Wray and Sir Edward Ayscough, in correspondence with the king. When the vote was taken, Vane and Hesilrige were tellers for Blakiston's motion, Stapleton and Wray were tellers against. On this occasion the Presbyterians won,[1] perhaps because Pierrepont, a very respected figure in the House, was involved.

It is clear also that Vane had become hostile to the Scots, that he wanted them out of Carlisle and the other Northern towns and urged them to send their army south into England, but we do not know his motives. He may have wanted to end the war quickly, to save the North from continued oppression by the Scots, to put an end to Scottish negotiations with the king, or all three.

On most occasions until December 1646 the Independents carried the House with them. Vane continued to show his usual skill in 'managing' the Commons, in which timely petitions and appeals to the Commons' jealousy of the Upper House played a part. But the frequency with which he and his political friends spoke, their industry as committee members, and the cogency of their arguments, must all have been important factors in their success—there were some able members of the Commons who were not in Holles's circle, but were not among Vane and St John's regular supporters either, such men as Giles Greene, the important chairman of the Navy committee, or Sir Thomas Widdrington, the influential Northern M.P., to name only two, and these would have to be won over. It should be noted that sometimes the House was not convinced by Vane or

[1] Harl. 166, f. 267. *CJ.* iv, 295. 1 October 1645. Note that this Presbyterian victory was also won before the 'Recruiters' had come in.

his collaborators.[1] Holles and his friends felt strong enough to challenge Vane's group in the division lobby in May 1645—during the earlier part of the year there were no divisions—and lost,[2] but in August Sir William Lewes was a teller against Sir William Brereton and Edmund Prideaux, and won.[3] This was the Presbyterians' first victory, apart from the hard-fought struggle over Holles's and Whitelocke's part in the Oxford negotiations.[4] In this Vane showed the same ruthlessness in attacking his opponents that he had shown earlier in his career.

The evidence that the Independents were using their power in Parliament to reward their own supporters is conclusive, if one judges from those instances with which Vane was connected. Vane's activity on behalf of Raby Castle[5] can hardly have been justified by public interest,[6] and the restoration of his royalist relations to authority is also open to criticism.[7] He absolutely ignored the ordinance ordering him to return half his profits as Treasurer of the Navy,[8] and Lilburne's slighting reference to Vane and St John as covetous earthworms is understandable.[9] It is interesting to note in this connexion that when a motion was introduced making a ballot compulsory whenever the

---

[1] Harl. 166, f. 193. 'Mr. Sollicitor, young Fane, Perpoint and others moved to sett out some new declaration to be sett out for all men to come in upon as good termes as was proposed in the Articles of the late Treatie etc. but no vote past.' (18 March 1645.) See also f. 201v.

[2] *CJ.* iv, 136.   [3] Ibid., 238.

[4] In July. (Ibid., 213.) These division figures are much higher than usual, thus substantiating Whitelocke's assertion that his friends had canvassed support for him.

[5] *CSPD. 1645-47*, 123, 165; S.P. 10/510/159.

[6] Archaeological Soc. of Durham, *Transactions*, 1880-9, 174.

[7] His brother, Sir George, alleged by Lilburne to have been a royalist (E 387(4)), became sheriff of Durham, and receiver of the royal revenue (*CJ.* iii, 593; *Records of the Committee for Compounding with delinquent royalists in Durham and Northumberland*, ed. R. Welford, Surtees Soc. (1905), 129; E 324(7)—a leaflet published illegally). Sir George's father-in-law, a royalist until 1644, was made one of the County Committee (*CJ.* iii, 709; iv, 275; *CSPD. 1645-47*, 166). Vane's sister Anne made a surprising marriage in May 1646 to the heir of a prominent royalist, old Sir Thomas Liddell, who made his composition in the same month on very favourable terms. The marriage settlement was productive of much future litigation. (*CJ.* iv, 530; C8/92/135; C8/119/151; C33/196, ff. 17v, 70v, 98v, 151. *CSPD. 1650*, 613 is a Chancery Court order.)

[8] See below, pp. 128-9.

[9] The most recent writer to find Lilburne's accusations unintelligible is H. N. Brailsford, *The Levellers and the English Revolution* (London, 1961), 235.

House voted on appointments to be made, Cromwell was one of the tellers against it.[1] Taken in conjunction with the very considerable profits Vane was making as Navy Treasurer one would guess that in this division he voted in Cromwell's lobby.

[1] *CJ*. iv, 690.

CHAPTER IV

Relations with the Army, 1647–48

I N THIS ACCOUNT of Vane's part in the complex events of 1647–8, so far as it can be reconstructed, considerable reliance has been placed on royalist diurnals of the time, particularly on *Mercurius Pragmaticus*. *Pragmaticus* seems to have been interested in Vane, and the substantial truth of his reports has been accepted here. Sir John Cleveland, the cavalier poet and journalist, was writing *Pragmaticus* at the time, and his accounts of Vane's speeches are not always what one would expect if they were fabrications. Once or twice they are even what would in Cleveland's view be creditable to Vane. It may be added that in the 'republic of silence' which Parliament had in effect set up news of any sort was hard to come by, and what there was acquires a disproportionate importance.

The month of December 1646 was an important one for the fortunes of the Independents, and it is very strange that Vane appears to have taken little part in affairs in Parliament at that time. There is no definite evidence that he was in the Commons that month at all until 12 December, when he presented a report from the commissioners who had been sent to Scotland about the payment for the Scots Army.[1] He was one of a committee appointed two days later to draft a reply to the Scots, who had wanted some more reliable security for the payment of their £300,000 than the public faith.[2] He was as usual being employed when there was a delicate piece of formulation to be done. There is no evidence that he was present in the House again until 28 December.[3] In the interval, round about Christmas Day 1646, the Presbyterians had gained a majority in the

---

[1] *CJ.* v, 11.   [2] Ibid., 12.
[3] Ibid., 31. (One of a committee ordered to withdraw and draft a clause in the agreement with the Scots.)

House, and from then until the Army intervention in June 1647 they maintained it.[1] Vane's absence from the House in December is extraordinary. At the beginning of December one or two of the divisions were comparatively close,[2] and Vane's vote and influence one would have thought important to the Independents. Vane's record for the next five months is even more baffling. He was appointed to only seven committees, on six separate days, during the whole period. He can be said with certainty to have been in the House once only, on 11 May.[3] There is no indication of his presence in the House between 5 January and 6 February 1647 at all, and his name is missing from many committees to which one would think the House would have wished to appoint him, for example the committee of 9 January set up to examine Andrew Burrell's book about the Navy.[4] He was present at only three of the six Admiralty committee meetings in January 1647, at none after 12 January, and at only two of the twelve meetings in February. He had not been a frequent attender at this committee however, at any rate since October 1646, when the record of the committee for this period begins.[5]

The weak position of the Independents in the House during the first six months of 1647 has not received enough attention. Hesilrige and Sir John Evelyn of Wiltshire were fighting a losing battle against Holles and Stapleton, as the divisions show, and observers comment on it.[6] On 8 March Hesilrige and Evelyn were tellers against forcing the officers in Fairfax's army to conform to the government of the church established by both Houses (i.e. to the Presbyterian system).[7] On 5 March Fairfax himself was narrowly saved from being superseded as commander-in-chief by a Presbyterian, Colonel Graves.[8]

[1] See Appendix B.

[2] Ibid. On 7 December Holles had a majority of 4 only, and on 12 and 14 December was actually defeated.   [3] *CJ*. v, 167.

[4] Ibid., 47. Burrell's book, on the reformation of the Navy (E 335 (8)), resulted in the setting up of a committee to consider the building of four new frigates.

[5] Adm. 7/673, *passim*.

[6] Berkeley, *Memoirs*, 471; Wildman's *Putney Projects*, E 421(9); Bodl. Clarendon, 2417, 2495 (news-letters).

[7] *CJ*. v, 108.

[8] Ibid., 106. The name of Fairfax's rival is given in E 381(2). Gardiner describes Graves as a Presbyterian. (*CW*., iii, 259.) See also Bodl. Clarendon, 2565.

Lilburne in March rated Cromwell for 'betraying us into the tyrannical clutches of Holles and Stapleton',[1] and another pamphleteer saw a proposed order that all M.P.s should take the Covenant as a stroke by Holles and Stapleton to enable them to control the House.[2]

What then was Vane doing during these months? The Admiralty committee minutes are most instructive on this point. He was admittedly an infrequent attender during the early months of 1647, but in June and July his record is very poor indeed, for he made only one attendance during the whole of the two months. There were of course no meetings during early August, when the Army had come to London to over-throw the Presbyterians, and Parliament and City were in the throes of the crisis. He attended the committee however on 11 August when the issue between Independents and Presby-terians was still in the balance. He was not at the meetings on 13 and 14 August, when he was probably consulting with the Army. But after 16 August, when Holles and five others of the impeached Presbyterians fled and the Army ascendancy over Parliament was established, a sudden change came over Vane and he began to attend the Admiralty committee regularly. On 9 September, when the Independents with Army support had established firm control over the Commons (at least temporarily), five M.P.s, four of whom were tried and trusty Independents, Thomas Rainsborough, Sir Henry Mildmay, Nathaniel Fiennes and Marten, together with Vane senior, were added to the Admiralty committee.[3] Four peers, one of whom was Manchester, now said by *Pragmaticus* to be a close confidant of Cromwell,[4] also joined it.[5] It is obvious that the Independents were determinedly seizing control of this com-mittee. Without this it would probably have been impossible to send for Captain William Batten, the Navy's commander, whose sympathies were with Holles's group, and to dismiss him,[6] as was done a few days later. From this time until 10

---

[1] *Jonah's Cry.* E 400(5). 25 March 1647.
[2] *A warning for all the Counties of England*, E 381(13).
[3] Adm. 7/673, f. 376.   [4] E 410(19).
[5] Manchester, Mulgrave, Grey and Howard. (*LJ.* ix, 430.)
[6] Adm. 7/673, f. 381. 17 September 1647. *Pragmaticus* (E 407(18)) asserts that Batten was a man of no religion, but belonged to the Presbyterian faction, and

December 1647, when Vane had leave of absence for health
reasons, his record of attendance at the committee was much
better.

Now according to news-letters of February to April 1647
Vane and Cromwell were deliberately forbearing to attend the
Commons.[1] Holles wrote that Cromwell and his friends pur-
posely absented themselves from the Committee of Both Kingdoms at this time,[2] and there is some evidence for May 1647
to confirm this.[3] In fact because Cromwell and Vane could not
control the House and its important committees they refused to
attend as an ineffective minority. This certainly does not indicate an acceptance of the will of the majority. On the other
hand, Holles and Stapleton were not using their power over
the Commons in a wise and tolerant manner, as their determination precipitately to disband the Army, which was largely
Independent, showed. Vane in particular must have been
furiously indignant when the House ordered in February 1647
that the new defence works at Raby, which he had been at
such pains to obtain only the year before, were to be destroyed,
and the garrison sent away,[4] thus leaving the castle vulnerable
to yet another assault. It may be noted incidentally that Vane's
policy of abstention was not followed by Hesilrige, who
assiduously attended the Commons during the early months of
1647 and led the doubtless disheartened Independents. At the
Admiralty committee also[5] he was a more frequent attender
than Vane. One sees here a difference in character between the
two men.

There are numerous references during 1647 and 1648 to the
close co-operation between Vane and Cromwell, and all the
signs are that it was at this time that they became intimate.
Lilburne, writing in February 1647, accused Vane and St John,
'those worldly-wise prudentiall men', of preventing his own

this accords with Batten's own justification for joining the royalists in 1648. (*A
Declaration of Sir William Batten.* E 460(13).)

[1] *Clarke Papers*, i, preface, xviii; Bodl. Clarendon, 2504.

[2] Holles, *Memoirs*, 237–8.

[3] Letters in May from the Committee, sent to the Army, are signed by Holles,
Stapleton, and others, but not by Vane. (*Clarke Papers*, i, 107, 114, 115.) The Day-
Books of the Committee for 1646 and 1647 are not extant, and the copies of Letters
Sent (S.P. 21/23) have no signatures for this period.

[4] *CJ.* v, 98.   [5] Adm. 7/673, *passim.*

release, and accused them too of leading Cromwell by the nose, a metaphor his readers would enjoy, for Cromwell's nose was a constant subject of derision.[1] The author of *Westminster Projects*, whom Lilburne asserted was John Wildman, the Leveller, declared that: 'long before the breaking out of the army' [the impeachment of the eleven Presbyterian M.P.s in June 1647] 'Lord Say, Lord Wharton, Lieut. General Cromwell, young Sir Henry Vane, St. John, Fines and the rest, who now oppresse the people, had their private councels',[2] and that the design 'was, is, and is like to be, that these few men shall hold the raynes of Government in their own hands, not for a yeare, but for ever'. He accused the Independents of not removing Holles and his friends from the House in June, as the Army had demanded, in order to retain the help of the Presbyterians against the Levellers. He also alleged that the Independent leaders had attempted to secure the support of a leading Presbyterian, Sir Gilbert Gerrard, by making him Chancellor of the Duchy (a post which Gerrard had certainly just been given).[3]

In September 1647, Lilburne, copied within the week by *Pragmaticus*, asserted that Cromwell was 'glued in interest' to 'those foure sons of Machiavel . . . the Lord Say, the Lord Wharton, young Sir Henry Vaine, and Solicitor St. John, who, . . . never in their lives stood further for the just liberty of the Commons of England, then might helpe them to pull downe those great men that stood in the way of their own preferment'. He also declared that the Agitators had not been removed from the Army so that Cromwell might use their attitude as a threat, to make the Presbyterians of the 'Junto' (Holles's group) do and say what he pleased, and that in this design 'precious young Sir Henry Vane' was pleased to join.[4] In October *Pragmaticus*

---

[1] *Jonah's Cry*, E 400(5).   [2] E 433(15). 23 March 1648.
[3] Gerrard was voted this office on 13 February 1648. (*CJ*. v, 493.)
[4] E 407(41). *Two Letters . . . To Col. Henry Martin*. *Pragmaticus* is E 410(4), 28 September–6 October 1647. Lilburne, in another pamphlet at this time, again attacks the 'most base and wicked juglings of Lord General Cromwell, and his son Ireton; whose power and interest in the Army (by those foure grand juglers' means, viz. Lord Say, Lord Wharton, young Sir Henry Vaine, and Soliciter St. John) is now vigorously improved to support and uphold the Lords' usurpations.' (BM. 1104.a.16 (1).) It will be remembered that Cromwell called Vane a 'juggler' when the Rump was expelled in 1653.

again referred to Vane as Cromwell's spokesman in the Commons,[1] and Lilburne wrote of the two men as working closely together. 'I clearly see Cromwell's and Vaine's design, which is to keep the poore people everlastingly (if they can) in bondage and slaverie.'[2] In November *Pragmaticus* described Wharton as Cromwell's mouthpiece in the Lords, and Vane as his tool in the Commons.[3]

Vane's own political aims and activities during the struggle between Parliament and the Army in 1647 are very difficult to trace. S. R. Gardiner thought that Cromwell's decision to have the king arrested at Holmby House was due to information that Vane had given him, and which Vane had derived from his father, about a projected Scottish invasion on the king's behalf. The evidence however is not at all conclusive.[4] In June Vane was one of the commissioners appointed to go to the Army.[5] Holles was sure this was a plot, and that it had the same effect that the appointment of a committee of officer M.P.s had had earlier: it enabled the Army officers and their supporters in the Commons to come together the better to 'contrive and lay their business'.[6] He presumably meant that Vane (whom he named first among the commissioners), Robert Scawen and the other Parliament envoys played a double game, persuading the Army to follow a policy agreed among themselves but not discussed in Parliament. It is most tantalizing that there is no record of what Vane was doing while he was with the Army during the following six vital weeks. With his usual promptitude he left at once when appointed, on 2 July, and worked hard.[7] That Vane was the dominating figure among the commissioners cannot be doubted for Scawen, the leading member of the Commons Committee of the Army, and even Major General Skippon were not

---

[1] E 410(19). 5-12 October 1647.
[2] E 407(41). *Two Letters* . . . 22 September 1647.   [3] E 417(20).
[4] *Clarke Papers*, i, preface, xxv; 135; Gardiner, *CW.*, iii, 265; Dyve, *The Tower of London Letter-Book*, 56. It is interesting that in the contemporary diurnals Cornet Joyce's name was often coupled with Cromwell's.
[5] *CJ.* v, 201. 7 June.   [6] Holles, *Memoirs*, 242.
[7] In July Cromwell told Berkeley that he could not see him until ten o'clock at night, because he would be in session with Parliament's commissioners until then. (Berkeley, op. cit., 472; *CJ.* v, 264.)

politicians of his standing.[1] The London mob held Vane
responsible for the actions of the Independent party in Parliament, as shown by their threat to cut him to pieces the day after
the Independents in the Commons had opposed bringing the
king to London,[2] but in fact Vane was with the Army at St
Albans that day,[3] and it was St John, Fiennes and Hesilrige who
had opposed the Presbyterian leaders. A little later Lilburne
was saying that he would rather cut Vane's throat than
Holles's,[4] though whether on account of Vane's covetousness, or
his opposition to the Levellers, or because he was preventing
Lilburne's release, he did not say.

How far Vane was acting in co-operation with the Army
leaders, and with which leaders, we do not know. But he must
have been very close to Ireton at least,[5] for it was Vane who
presented Ireton's 'Heads of the Proposals' to the House on
6 August.[6] It is remarkable that Ireton did not do this himself;
perhaps he was not a good speaker, or perhaps it was thought
more politic for a civilian to introduce them. Wildman and
others believed, probably rightly, that the Newcastle Propositions which were submitted to the king again in September
1647 were not sent with any genuine desire for their success;
the plan was that the House, desperately anxious for peace,
would allow the 'Heads of the Proposals' to be sent to Charles,
when the members saw that the Presbyterian Newcastle
Propositions were not acceptable to the king. Wildman thought
this was another 'Machivilian' scheme on the part of the
Independent grandees. When the king once more rejected the
Newcastle Propositions, however, a proposal that no more
addresses should be made to the king was put forward in the
Commons, doubtless by the Levellers. This would have doomed
the 'Heads of the Proposals', the Army leaders' plan for a settlement, and when the issue was in doubt, there was, according
to Wildman,

---

[1] Thomas Povey, the fourth commissioner, had been a member of Parliament
only since March.

[2] *Clarke Papers*, i, 136.   [3] *CJ.* v, 210.   [4] *Clarke Papers*, i, 158.

[5] Dyve's informant (probably Lilburne) stated that Vane and Ireton were
members of the 'Junto' in September. (Dyve, op. cit., 89.)

[6] *CJ.* v, 268. Ireton was apparently not popular in Parliament. (Abbott,
Cromwell, ii, 75.)

a Cabinet Council of the Grandees . . . Sir John Eveling, Mr. William Pierpoint, and Mr. Fynes, Sir Henry Vane, Cromwell and Ireton, *cum paucis aliis*: and O how was the quintessence of their braines extracted, in plausible arguments for a new addresse to the King! . . . and I conclude from that event, that in such a cabinet councell the question was first concluded in the affirmative, and then the debate on the question was managed in the House, with much seeming solemnity.

The 'Heads of the Proposals', with its provisions for religious toleration and a powerful Council of State, had many attractions for the Independent grandees, but the House seemed disposed to vote for no addresses, whereupon, according to Wildman, 'one of the same confederacy' told the House that the Army wished for another approach to be made to the king, and so debate ended.[1] Wildman's version of Vane's attitude to the vote of no addresses finds corroboration in Berkeley, who wrote that after Marten had moved this vote in September 'both Cromwell and Ireton, with Vane and all their friends, seconded with great resolution this desire of his majesty' for a treaty.[2] Apparently Vane was adopting a generally conciliatory attitude to the king at this time, for Clarendon's correspondent Sir Edward Ford wrote of Cromwell and Ireton: 'Of late they have spoken much in the King's behalf, seconded by young Harry Vane, Mr. Solicitor, and Mr. Fiennes.'[3]

It would be interesting to know how Vane kept up the contact with Cromwell and Ireton which the passages quoted imply. He would not have to go, as *Pragmaticus* alleged Wharton did, to Putney every week to 'do homage' to the grandees of the Army,[4] for Vane still had his official position as one of Parliament's commissioners to the Army, which he could make

[1] Wildman, *Putney Projects*, E 421(19), 43. Bodl. Clarendon, 2583, 2602 (newsletters) give a similar version of events.
[2] *Berkeley*, op. cit., 43.
[3] *Clarke Papers*, i, 231, note. St John and Vane seem still to have been in agreement on policy at this time. At least St John seems also to have absented himself from Parliament a great deal in the early part of the year, and Holles believed that it was St John who arranged that the Independent M.P.s should take refuge with the Army, in July. (Holles, *Memoirs*, 275.) It is technically incorrect to say of Vane 'Fled to the Army' (Yule, *The Independents in the English Civil War*, 122), for Vane was already with the Army when the London riots of 26 July took place.
[4] E 411(23). 19–26 October.

use of when he would. On Wednesday 15 September he reported from the commissioners resident with the Army that since the previous Friday they had negotiated with the Army's commissioners, and had shown them where anything in the Army's proposals was contrary to votes of the Houses, which must mean that he was trying to work out a policy mutually acceptable to the Army officers and the Independent grandees.[1] Curiously enough, Montereuil had been told at this very time by some of the Scots that they were 'sought after' by the Independents, and that the younger Vane had offered, on the part of the Independents, to the earl of Lauderdale, all that Scotland could demand, provided that the Scots would consent to the ruin of the king.[2] Montereuil sensibly did not believe this story, for he knew that Vane would never accept Presbyterianism in the form the Scots would want, but it does reflect the position of power which many believed Vane to hold.

There is practically no evidence about Vane's part in politics during October and November 1647. In September and October he was very busy with the Admiralty committee work, for Giles Greene was ill, and had gone to the country,[3] and this probably put more responsibility on Vane. He rarely attended the committee's meetings in November however.[4] He presumably put in an appearance at the House itself on 9 October or his name would have been given as one of those absent from the roll-call ordered for that day.[5] Otherwise he seems to have attended the House only when Navy business came up; for example on 12 October when he withdrew to conduct in person, with two others, negotiations concerning a loan of £30,000 for the Navy.[6] On 10 December he had leave to go to the country for six weeks,[7] an unusually long leave, and probably an indication of the strenuous part he had been playing in events, but he had not gone next day, when Navy business came up again, and a committee of six, which included Vane, was ordered to withdraw, and manage two conferences with the Lords.[8] He was appointed to another committee on 15 December, which indicates that he was thought to be in the

---

[1] *CJ.* v, 302.   [2] *Montereuil, Correspondence*, ii, 274. 8 October.
[3] *CJ.* v, 297. 9 September.   [4] Adm. 7/673, *passim.*   [5] *CJ.* v, 330.
[6] Ibid., 331.   [7] Ibid., 378.   [8] Ibid., 379.

House.[1] Greene was back in the House by 28 December,[2] so presumably Vane could temporarily abandon naval affairs with an easy mind. The only other indications of his presence in the House in the autumn of 1647 are on 22 November, when he was instructed with three others to prepare an answer to a petition from the City and rebuke the City for its unsatisfactory collection of the assessment,[3] and on 1 December. On this latter date, Vane is said by a letter-writer to have threatened the City with a fresh military intervention, and so secured the rejection of a City petition asking for the removal of the Army to a safe distance.[4] In view of later allegations that the Independents, and Vane in particular, made similar threats against the House, there is nothing inherently improbable in this. *Pragmaticus* gibed at Vane's zeal for Cromwell and the Army at this time, declaring that Vane

upon all occasions prepares the way (like a true John-a-Baptist) . . . [for Cromwell] and then he never opens his mouth in vaine. And therefore it was, that with so much confidence hee made more reports than ever my Lord Cook did, to the House of the Proceedings of the Army, at the late rendezvous [the famous November Ware meeting], and of the resolution of the Army to serve them. He meanes as they have done heretofore, and at length turne them out of service, if they cannot serve their ends upon them.[5]

He seems to have availed himself of his six weeks' leave of absence, for there is no record of any public activity on his part during the latter half of December 1647 or the whole of January 1648. On 3 January the Derby House committee was set up to replace the Committee of Both Kingdoms, and Vane, presumably in his absence, was appointed to it.[6] There were allegations, of doubtful truth, that the House was surprised into setting up this committee at 10 p.m.,[7] but if there was any sharp practice, he may on this occasion be exonerated. *Pragmaticus* noted that Vane was a member of the committee, and

---

[1] Ibid., 385. [2] Ibid., 407. [3] Ibid., 366.
[4] Bodl. Clarendon, 2672. A number of Presbyterian M.P.s thereupon withdrew.
[5] E 417(20). [6] *CJ*. v, 415.
[7] *Mercurius Pragmaticus*, E 465(19), allegedly quoting an M.P. Rushworth too says that the House sat late that night, but the division numbers (*CJ*. v, 415) that evening do not indicate a thin House. One journalist (E 465(11)) alleged that *Pragmaticus* had an informant in the Commons.

proceeded to indulge in vituperation such as he did not often apply to Vane.[1] *Pragmaticus* obviously suspected him of being powerful behind the schemes, and calls him one who 'hath plundered Gyges his Ring, to make himselfe invisible upon all occasions'. By 1 February 1648 Vane was back in the House, according to a correspondent of the earl of Lanark;[2] this writer indicates that there were now differences between Vane and Cromwell. A letter of intelligence has similar news: 'The prevailing party are in great feares and divisions among themselves, in soe much as Sir H. Vane Junior hath left them.'[3] But Vane's estrangement from Cromwell, if it ever happened, must have been a very temporary one, for by the beginning of March *Aulicus* was again writing of him as a leader of the Commons and as one who 'thinks he is able to carry a Kingdom on his camell's back',[4] while Lilburne was describing Vane, yet again, as a confederate of Cromwell.[5] The royalists joyfully reported that the Presbyterians in the House were gathering strength,[6] and one royalist pamphleteer asserted that Lord Say, hearing that the Scots proposed to impeach the leading Independents, could only secure indemnity for his party's action in deserting Parliament in July 1647, by calling on Cromwell to speak. This writer, who gives a full list of Cromwell's and Ireton's confederates in the House at this time, had no doubt that Vane was one.[7]

In April 1648 he showed his loyalty to Cromwell by voting against the proposition that the tapestries from the royal Wardrobes should be sold, to realize the £1500 needed to pay the soldiers at the Tower—many of the royal possessions had already been disposed of. An alternative proposal had been

---

[1] Part of this may be given, as an example of royalist feeling about Vane. 'The Sainted Salamander, that hath lived hitherto in flames of zeal . . . the very floure and creame of knight-errantry, that wanders through every faction with his pedlery of all religions.'

[2] Gardiner, *CW.*, iv, 57, note.   [3] Bodl. Clarendon, 2723.

[4] E 431(20). 2–9 March 1648. Royalist writers at this period make frequent jeering references to some deformity in Vane's shoulders, which they had not done before. Had he perhaps become very round-shouldered as a result of desk-work?

[5] E 431(1). *A Whip for the present House of Lords.*

[6] *Pragmaticus*, E 431(5). 29 February–7 March 1648.

[7] *Mercurius Elencticus*, E 431(15). 1–8 March. A news-letter of 28 March speaks of Manchester, Say, Wharton and Vane as 'of that faction'. (*HMC.* 5th Rep. App., 143.)

made that the tapestries should be assigned to Cromwell, no doubt to increase the dignity of his residence, and Vane found himself opposed to his fellow-Independents, Wentworth and Brereton, but he carried the day.[1]

Another incident concerned Alderman Fowke. Again it is reported by a royalist journalist, but since it reflects credit on Vane it is hardly likely to be a fabrication. According to this writer Fowke had prevailed on Sir Henry Mildmay, whom the House had instructed to report on a dispute between Fowke and one John Bland, Receiver of the Crown rents for Yorkshire, to 'blot out' one order of the House, and falsify another, to Bland's great prejudice. But 'so notoriously base was the deportment of Sir Henry Mildmay herein, that Sir Henry Vane told him he lied'.[2] Bland, according to another royalist journalist, was Giles Greene's son-in-law; thus Vane was supporting Greene, whose sympathies lay with the Presbyterians,[3] rather than a powerful member of Vane's own group, and it seems likely that his intervention was due to a disinterested sense of justice.

According to the royalists, the English Presbyterians and the Independents were drawing together at this time, in face of their common consciousness that the Scots were about to invade,[4] and when the Presbyterians voted that the House would not alter the fundamental government of the country by King, Lords and Commons, Vane, Pierrepont and other leading Independents supported them.[5] Moreover, when the City petitioned that Major General Skippon should have command of the City militia, which they wanted restored, and that the chains which the New Model's soldiers had removed from the London streets should be replaced, Vane seconded Cromwell in supporting the City's request.[6] According to

---

[1] *CJ.* v, 532. 15 April 1648.

[2] *Mercurius Veridicus*, E 437(14). *Veridicus* described Bland merely as a receiver, but the pamphlet mentioned in note 3 described him as a receiver for Yorkshire. There is evidence in the Journals that Mildmay did fail to report the matter to the House on a date assigned, and of other delays. (*CJ.* v, 464, 515, 554.) *Veridicus* says that Bland was a Presbyterian.

[3] E 458(12). *A list of the names of the Members . . .* 14 August 1648.

[4] E 437(10). *Mercurius Elencticus*, 19–26 April 1648, p. 166. *Mercurius Bellicus*, E 433(8). 14–21 March.

[5] Gardiner, *CW.*, iv, 116, quoting *Hamilton Papers*, 190.

[6] *Mercurius Pragmaticus*, E 437(31). Gardiner, loc. cit., uses this diurnal but

Pragmaticus, again, when the City went on to ask that the Common Council should themselves nominate the members of the committee for the militia, he was one of the first to approve the motion, it being necessary for 'Sir Harry Weathercock' to 'act Sir John Presbyter, and whistle a little in disguise, in the behalf of Independency, that he may gain a good opinion among the Brethren, till the Plague of Presbytery be a little over'. *Pragmaticus* added however that the whole 'godly gang' of the Independents thought likewise.[1] Perhaps Vane's apparent changes of front were referred to by Stephen Marshall, who was always outspoken, at the Commons service of thanksgiving on 17 May, when he told the M.P.s: 'Vote not one thing this day to please one party, and then another thing, another time, to please another party.'[2] But Vane was one of the committee sent to the City to inform it that the restored militia must be so disposed of 'as to provide for the safety of the kingdom and Parliament',[3] probably meaning that Parliament should not be left exposed to violence by Presbyterian London mobs, as in July of the year before. There are several references in May 1648 to Vane as one of the Independent grandees of Cromwell's 'junto'.[4]

In that month the royalist storm broke, and the risings began, ironically enough, in Vane's own county of Kent. The Commons at once decided that Fairfax's troops must stay in London, for the M.P.s probably thought, and rightly, that the newly restored City militia could not be trusted against the royalists, and it was Vane who drafted the letter to Fairfax

mentions only the removal of Parliament's troops. There is other evidence however that the restoration of the militia and occupation of the Tower was involved. See for instance *The British Bellman*, E 422(2), 12 May 1648, *The Honest Citizen*, E 438(5), *The Weekly Intelligencer*, E 422(20).

[1] E 422(16). 9–16 May 1648.

[2] E 433(3), p. 35. Marshall was troubled at the development of parties—'if there have got among you any factions or divisions, any driving of parties [i.e. Whips] or siding with this or the other . . . throw them all in the dust'. He himself was often accused of swaying from Presbyterian to Independent, and like others, may have found it difficult to decide which group to follow. A biography of Marshall, who was practically official chaplain to the Long Parliament, is much overdue, though Prof. Trevor-Roper's 'Fast Sermons of the Long Parliament' (*Essays in British History Presented to Sir Keith Feiling* (London, 1964)) is illuminating.

[3] *CJ.* v, 565. 18 May.

[4] E.g. *Windsor Projects and Westminster Practices*, E 422(10). 15 May 1648.

about this.[1] He evidently now held that concessions to the Presbyterians had gone far enough. They had wanted to change the suggested terms which the House, at their instigation, were again to offer Charles, so that Presbyterianism should be established, not just for three years, but 'until King, Lords and Commons should alter it'. Vane was one of the tellers against this proposition, and won, in a fairly thin house, by 67 to 48 votes.[2] All through May, rising as usual to an emergency, he was occupied with the multitude of affairs that the rebellion imposed on him; he was especially concerned because of the Navy's part in the Kent revolt. *Pragmaticus* gloated over the thought that Vane's official Navy Treasury house at Deptford was likely to be attacked, and did not fail to notice Vane's assiduous attendance at the Derby House committee;[3] before the Kent rising he had attended the committee only twice during all the four months of 1648, but after the rising broke out in May he attended at least eleven times in that month,[4] and reported back to the House from the committee,[5] as he had done in 1644 from the old Committee of Both Kingdoms. The Admiralty committee however had been abruptly superseded when the revolt broke out, and the earl of Warwick had resumed the powers of Lord High Admiral.

On 1 June Vane obtained leave to accompany his wife and family to Lincolnshire,[6] but did not go for another month. His family, and that of Lady Wray, his mother-in-law, received their pass to travel on 17 June,[7] but the Derby House committee proceedings show that he attended all the numerous meetings in that month, except those on 9, 10, 19, 22 and 26 June. He was also concerned with Hull. The Derby House committee had ordered Peregrine Pelham to go there lest the naval mutiny should affect that vital port,[8] but the order was

---

[1] *CJ.* v, 574. 26 May.   [2] Ibid.

[3] E 445(21). 23-30 May. 'Sir Harry Weather-Cock, or Vaine (which you please; for, all is one), hath other businesse to doe, than sit fooling at Derby-House.' Apparently Fairlawn was attacked. (*Mercurius Publicus*, E 445(19).)

[4] *CSPD. 1648-49, passim.* He did not attend at all until 23 March, when a matter affecting the Navy (the supply of gunpowder) came up for discussion. The Kent rising was first discussed on 15 May, when he was present, and in the ensuing weeks his attendances were much more frequent.

[5] *CJ.* v, 575, 584, 610.   [6] Ibid., 581.   [7] *CSPD. 1648-49*, 132.

[8] The letter to Pelham is dated 30 May, but the order is not in the minutes for

cancelled, and instead, on 6 June, both the Hull M.P.s were directed to consult with Fairfax about the city.[1] Two days later they received new instructions; with Giles Greene they were to discuss with Fairfax means of persuading the rebellious ships to return to their parliamentary allegiance.[2] Looking ahead to the needs of the Navy, as Vane usually did, he and the other two M.P.s were also to consult with Fairfax about securing the ships and stores at Rochester and Chatham when the victorious Army had gone away. The committee of Navy and Customs (the financial committee) was hurriedly told to give the three envoys any further necessary instructions about this matter;[3] he would have to peruse those before he left, presumably on 9 June. The three M.P.s were unsuccessful in their main mission; the earl of Warwick, who was probably sceptical about the M.P.s' influence over the sailors, dryly added a footnote to one of his letters, announcing that the ships which had revolted had already left for Holland.[4] Vane did not stay to confer with Warwick, as instructed, for he was back at the committee on 11 June.[5]

Meanwhile Hull, always restless under control by the soldiers, had asked Vane and Pelham to intercede for the city with the Derby House committee to secure a *joint* watch on the town by soldiers and townsmen. The two Hull members secured a letter from the committee to Fairfax and the governor about the matter, and the payment of a part of the sum of £6000 assigned to Hull for its defence.[6] On 17 June he carried to the committee of the Navy an order from the Derby House committee providing for joint action to prevent 'evil effects' of

29 May, and those for 30 May have only the cancellation of the order. It looks as though Pelham had prevailed on the clerk not to enter the order for his departure, as he intended to have it cancelled. (Ibid., 88.)

[1] Ibid., 102. [2] Ibid., 110, 112–13. [3] Ibid., 113.

[4] Ibid., 361.

[5] For the curious allegation that the new frigates which the Admiralty had had built were waiting to take Vane and his 'conventicle' to safety abroad if the Kent rising succeeded, see E 433(37), E 445(21). Similar statements were made about other M.P.s however. (E 445(1) and (3); E 438(7); E 458(12).)

[6] *CSPD. 1648–49*, 173–8. 20 June. Baron Thorpe of the Exchequer, Recorder of Hull, had shown a letter from the mayor and corporation, especially a passage about some officers in whom the city had no confidence, to Vane, 'your burgess'. (Hull MSS, L.498, 12 June.)

the Navy revolt against Parliament.[1] He probably left for Linconshire in early July.[2]

The question of restoring the king was now, in June and July 1648, being mooted again. It is difficult in writing of the 1645-6 period in Vane's career not to take sides on the issue of the possibility of a 'safe and well grounded' peace, but for 1647-8 it is impossible. The view taken here is that it was not beyond the wit of man to devise a settlement in 1647, and still more in 1648, in spite of the untrustworthiness of the king.[3] To be lasting it would have had to be a compromise, for opinion was too deeply divided for anything else to be possible, and compromise was anathema to some of the Independent grandees, but the vote on 5 December 1648 shows that it was possible, or at any rate that a majority of M.P.s thought so.[4] At Newport in September Charles had agreed to give Parliament control of the militia for twenty years, to set up Presbyterianism for three, to let the Houses deal with Ireland as they chose. These were enormous concessions, and the king could not be expected to sign away the lives of his supporters, the 'delinquents', as well. The permanence of any settlement of course depended largely on public opinion, and on this the Independents' hold one would judge to have been very shaky, as Vane was probably aware.[5] But the feasibility of a settlement is the criterion by which his policy must largely be judged, and the assumption here made is that a settlement was possible, though whether a settlement would have lasted is open to question.

Vane's own policy however was reported in the most contradictory terms. According to one Presbyterian pamphleteer, Vane wanted to bring in the king, upon the king's own terms.

[1] *CSPD. 1648-49*, 132.

[2] He was not at the Derby House committee on 26 or 27 June. He may have gone early in July, judging from his attendances in that month. Vane's fifth child had been born at Fairlawn on 19 June (Willcock, 353); doubtless Lady Vane had intended to stay at her mother's house for the confinement.

[3] That Gardiner was aware of the dilemma is shown by his admission (*CW.*, iv, 42), that the Engagement was substantially the Restoration Settlement, but he concluded that the situation in 1647 and 1648 was radically different because of the character of the two kings.

[4] The voting was 129-83. (*CJ.* vi, 93.)

[5] Though he is said by Clarendon to have dismissed the risings as few and contemptible. (Clarendon, *Rebellion*, iv, 461.)

The quarrel between the factions in the Houses, is now not whether the king shall be brought in, but who shall bring him in, and who shall be the Princes of the People [i.e. ministers] under him, when brought in. The Royall Presbyterian and Independent, for there are such of both sorts, as Northumberland, Warwick, Say, Crumwell, Ireton, Vane, Senior, Vane iunior, etc. they would bring in the king upon their Accompt, and make such agreement with him, as might . . . advance them to honour also; the reall Presbyterian, and reall Independent, they are willing to bring in the king, but they would first have the king secure unto them Religion, Law, and the Liberties of the Nation, but alack they are but a few . . . the cry of the others is, let us use the best means we can to satisfy the king, no matter what becomes of the kingdome; and to this end they have underhand promoted and procured these tumults [the Essex, Surrey and Kent petitions], so that thereby they might force the House to an adjournment, which is the chief thing they desire, and if procured, then all the power will reside in that Committee [the Derby House committee].[1]

An anonymous letter to Fairfax of 24 May had also reported that Vane had voted for the treaty with the king. 'Sir Henry Vane Junior (upon devision of the House of this day concerning the treaty with his Majesty) voted with the Malignant partie against the honest partie.'[2] According to this writer Vane's actions were due to the persuasions of Dr Stone and Scout-Master-General Watson; the latter certainly does seem to have indulged in some rather heavy-handed intrigues in France with the royalists a little later.[3] Other versions of Vane's attitude are quite different. *Pragmaticus* has:

about the personal treaty . . . when it was first moved, that his majesty might be trusted upon his royall word at one of his houses neer London, up stood young Vane and Whimzy Mildmay[4] in the House, who living like kings in the Committee for the Revenue, and fearing that if his majesty were admitted to a treaty he might soon slip into the revenue, made bold to tell Mr. Speaker . . . that the king was a perjured man, and therefore ought in no case to be trusted.[5]

[1] *Westminster Projects, or the Mystery of Iniquity of Derby House*, E 446(5). 6 June 1648.
[2] *Clarke Papers*, ii, 17.
[3] T. Carte, ed., *A Collection of Original Letters* (1739), ii, 17.
[4] *Pragmaticus*'s usual name for Sir Henry Mildmay.   [5] E 453(11). 11–18 July 1648.

Other royalist journalists gave a similar version of Vane's attitude. 'I promised the last week', wrote *Mercurius Melancholicus*, 'to give you the names of those that were the main obstructers of a personal treaty . . . Corbet, Challoner, Vaine and others in the Commons House, that hold for the Independents and their cut-throat Army.'[1] *Mercurius Bellicus* drops into rhyme:

> Then Vane the Father, Vane the Son,
> Two Devils in conjunction . . .
> Yet these two hornets still are prest
> To be the foremost 'mongst the rest,
> Their votes are neere to seek [speak?], I, I,
> To all that banes his majesty.

These conflicting reports are puzzling; though one would guess, to judge from Vane's later attitude, that *Pragmaticus* was probably right. In the diurnal quoted above *Bellicus* says that when the City petitioned for a peace 'treaty', the Commons appointed a committee to meet with the Common Council, but 'packed together . . . those whom they know to be perfect haters of peace . . . such as Earl, Vane, senior . . .', and in this instance does not mention the son.[2]

By August 1648 Vane was alleged by a royalist writer to be plotting the king's death,[3] but on 1 September he was appointed one of the commissioners for the Newport treaty.[4] (Many journalists were pessimistic about the outcome of these negotiations, but even the royalist ones were disposed to hope.) Once more, as often in his career at important periods, there is little or no information about what one would most like to know, in this case, his personal part in the negotiations. Burnet, as is well known, declared that Vane did not really want to negotiate with the king, but that the pressure from the City and the Country was too strong to be resisted.[5] Burnet had information

---

[1] E 455(12). 24–31 July.

[2] E 452(19). 11–18 July. Similarly *The Mad Dog Rebelling*, E 452(22). 13 July.

[3] *The Royal Diurnall*, E 460(15). 14–22 August. 'heere we find the sonnes of mischiefe and errours met in counsell for the murthering of our sovereigne . . . they approach . . . by couples, 2 Vanes, 2 Challoners.'

[4] *CJ.* v, 697.

[5] Burnet, *History of My Own Time*, ed. O. Airy, i, 74. This was also the view taken by Clarendon, who based his narrative on the king's own written account

about the treaty from Holles and Sir Harbottle Grimston, who were also commissioners, but whether this particular statement derives from them we do not know. More reliable is their description to Burnet of the incident in which they begged the king on their knees to make substantial concessions straight away because they knew that Vane 'would study to draw out the treaty to a great length'; this sounds like a recollection of an event that actually took place. Both Holles and Grimston must have known Vane well. They also told Burnet that Vane, who 'declared for an unbounded liberty of conscience, would try to gain on the king's party by the offer of a toleration for the common prayer and the episcopal clergy'. Titus, who was in attendance on the king at that time, told Burnet that Vane, taking advantage of the king's belief that he could play off the Presbyterians against the Independents, 'flattered the episcopal party'. From Cromwell's letter to Colonel Robert Hammond, governor of the Isle of Wight, in October it sounds almost as though Vane was being swayed by Pierrepont towards a peace based on concessions in religion to the king. 'Some of my friends', wrote Cromwell, 'have advanced too far, and neede make an honourable retreate', and this Hammond was to tell Vane, with whom he was in close contact.[1] Cromwell was evidently conscious that Independent policy had not been consistent, in the eyes of many: 'wee have walked in this thing (whatsoever surmises are to the contrary) in plainness and godly simplicity'. S. R. Gardiner believed that Vane, Pierrepont and Hammond, 'in their alarm at the thorough-going reforms demanded by the Levellers, were anxious to come to an understanding with the king',[2] but Cromwell's cryptic letter is doubtful evidence. *Volpone*, whom S. R. Gardiner relied on at this juncture, also says:

It is to be feared (though I shall name no Body) that my Lord Say and Sir Harry Vane have appeared to some in the shape of angells.

of the Newport 'treaty'. Clarendon thought Vane was the only commissioner who did not want peace.

[1] *Clarke Papers*, ii, 49–53. Warwick told the commissioners of the Navy that one Capt. Taylor had been recommended to him for a post at Portsmouth by Vane and Hammond. (*CSPD. 1648–49*, 374.)

[2] Gardiner, *CW.*, iv, 248.

These two hate the Covenant, as they do the devill; and though my Lord says he would give halfe his estate for peace, and hath some new agents to insinuate so much unto his Majesty, yet its but a small signe, when he helps heave that main stumbling block in the way. God help us.[1]

This reads as though Say and Vane, though outwardly supporting an accommodation, were in fact demanding that the Covenant should be taken by the whole nation, and so making peace impossible.[2]

In December 1648 a major crisis, in this year of crises, presented itself, this time over the question of continuing peace negotiations with the king, and a bitter tussle took place in the Commons. The Newport commissioners presented their report on 1 December.[3] It was clear that the king could not be brought to consent to the ruin of those 'delinquents' who had supported him, though he did agree to submit their cases to process of law. Vane evidently wanted all negotiations to be broken off, for the king's concessions were not enough.[4] Fiennes, of all people, rose to the king's defence. He declared the king had 'done enough to secure religion, lawes and libertyes, in granting the militia . . . and these things having been provided for, which were the only things which the Parliament had so often declared to be the ground of their quarrell, his Majesty must needs have given satisfaction'. When the debate was resumed Vane spoke first; he labelled those who wanted to continue negotiations as royalists. 'We may do well now to consider the King's last answer upon the treaty, for, by the debate, we shall soone guesse who are our friends, and who our enemies; and to speak more plainly, we shall understand by the carriage of the busines, who are the King's Party in the House, and who for the People.'

---

[1] E 467(22). 11 October.   [2] E 470(7).   [3] *CJ.* vi, 92.

[4] If one accepts *Pragmaticus*'s version of these few days 'John Lawrence's' account of them in his letter of 4 December to Nicholas becomes intelligible. 'Young Sir Henry Vane, one of the commissioners of the Isle of Wight, was very partial in reporting to the prejudice of his majesty. But Nat. Fiennes confuted him most rationally and gallantly, arguing . . . that the king had granted enough to secure religion, laws and liberties.' (Clarendon, *S.P.*, App. p. xlviii.) 'Lawrence' said the Independent party were enraged with Fiennes.

It was a clever move, designed to forestall any demand for continued negotiations, but it met with a courageous reply. One M.P.—*Mercurius Pragmaticus* did not dare to give his name —rose and said:

Mr. Speaker, since this Gentleman hath the boldness to deal thus by way of prevention in a threatening manner, and forejudged and divided the House into two parts, I hope it is lawful for me that am no Grandee, to take the same liberty . . . you will find some that are zealous of a peace and settlement, and those are such as have lost by the warre; others you will find that are against peace, and those are such that have gained by the Wars.[1]

This reply silenced Vane, for it was the most widely believed of all the accusations made against the M.P.s,[2] and the one on which his father certainly, and himself probably, was the most vulnerable. Edmund Prideaux and Sir Peter Wentworth supported Vane in his views on continued negotiations, and wanted a decision taken then and there but the debate was again adjourned.[3] Two days later on the Monday it was resumed, and old Sir Symonds D'Ewes, Sir Benjamin Rudyard and Sir Robert Harley maintained their opinion that the concessions made by the king were sufficient to justify another attempt to negotiate. All day it was argued 'to and fro', and among the long list of M.P.s who, so *Pragmaticus* alleged, opposed D'Ewes were the two Vanes. But they and the others who thought like them based their argument now not on reason but on necessity. Fairfax and the Army had arrived at Whitehall on the Saturday, and without complying with the Resolutions of the Army[4] there could be no hope of a settlement. Mildmay said the king could not be trusted any more than a lion that had been 'raged' and set at liberty again. The House

---

[1] E 476(2). 5–12 December. Gardiner did not use this diurnal.

[2] See e.g. *The Antipodes, or Reformation with the Heeles Upward*, E 399(16).

[3] They evidently thought that the Army's approach would be a convincing argument, but the M.P.s were not so easily intimidated. Prynne wanted the question laid aside, openly declaring that they were not a free Parliament, because they were endangered by the Army's approach. (E 476(2).)

[4] Rushworth, *Historical Collections* (1647–8), part iv, vol. 2, p. 1331. This is an abbreviated version. Royalist writers comment on the verbosity of the original.

rose at eight o'clock next morning,[1] when Vane and his friends had been defeated in a full House.[2]

If this account of *Pragmaticus*'s is true, and again it has the ring of authenticity, it still leaves Vane's motives for opposing the continuance of peace negotiations unexplained. It is probable that he shared Mildmay's distrust of the king; he may also have felt that an ideal commonwealth of the tolerant type that he wished for was impossible with either the king or the Presbyterians in power. Again, he may have been moved by loyalty to Cromwell and the Army. Though he spoke for accepting the Army's Remonstrance of November, which made a negotiated peace impossible, he did not apparently wish for the death of the king—at any rate he was not a member of the committee set up on 23 December to consider 'how to proceed in any way of justice against the king',[3] though St John and Marten were, and Vane surely could have been also if he had wished. Here again Vane's distinctions were too subtle to be understood by the multitude, who would know only that he was one of the very small group, thirty, so *Elencticus* says, who were 'downright for the Army',[4] and that the Army's Remonstrance clearly implied the punishment if not the death of the king.[5] On 6 December came Pride's Purge, and the political situation changed for Vane; Giles Greene was no longer in the House,[6]

---

[1] One M.P. asserted that 'the drift of these gentlemen is, to take advantage not only of the terror now brought on us by the present approach of the Army, but also to spin out the debate of this business to an unseasonable time of night, by which meanes the more ancient gentlemen of the House (whom they look upon as most averse [to Vane's and Prideaux's views]) will be tired out, and forced to depart'. See p. 112, n. 1. D'Ewes, Rudyard and Harley were old men. The speech of Vane's mentioned by Ludlow (i, 208) is evidently, to judge from the reference to the Army, one made in the Monday debate.

[2] *Pragmaticus* gives 119-84, and is not far wrong—it was actually 129-83. (*CJ*. vi, 93.)   [3] *CJ*. vi, 102-3.

[4] *Elencticus* gives a list of them, and includes Vane, but not his father.

[5] It named among offenders the king himself, and urged that he should be brought to justice. See p. 112, n. 4.

[6] E 476(1), *The Parliament under the power of the Sword*, names Greene as one of the secluded M.P.s (11 December), though he is stated in another pamphlet (E 477(30). 19–26 December) to be one of the 'prudentiall' men, who might be 'willing to be drawn off upon advantage'. *Pragmaticus* in his issue of 12–19 December speaks of Greene as 'in Limbo'. (E 476(35).) It was Greene who had presented the petition of the 11 impeached Presbyterian members in 1647; he must have had at least some sympathy with them, and some courage. (E 399(11).)

and someone else would have to do the work he had done for the Navy. Pierrepont also was gone, though he had withdrawn voluntarily. It was likely that those who had successfully forced their policy on the House would find themselves carrying considerably more responsibilities in the future, and of course this may have been one of their objectives.

Even during this critical political phase Vane's broader interests can be seen. The university authorities at Oxford, led by their vice-chancellor, Dr John Fell of Christchurch, had coolly defied the parliamentary Visitors appointed to 'purge' the university of offending elements. The university officials had refused to appear before the Visitors, or produce their books and staves of office, and had continued to lecture though forbidden to do so. The Visitors were responsible to a parliamentary committee, who summoned the offenders to attend. They appeared on 15 November 1647, and Vane, that most independent of Independents, defended them.[1] He may have had sympathy with his old university; more probably he cared for learning,[2] and therefore valued university independence.

There are many indications that, apart from one short period of six weeks, Vane was acting with his usual energy during the 1647–8 period. It is clear that he was closely co-operating with Cromwell at the time, and was indeed the spokesman for Cromwell and the Army in the autumn of 1647 and during 1648. It seems highly likely however that Vane absented himself deliberately from Parliament and its main committees for six months from December 1646, while the Independents were in eclipse, and only returned when the Army had temporarily secured power for the Independents in June 1647. He was travelling about with the Army all that summer, and when the Army firmly established the Independents in authority in August 1647, Vane was one of those who took the reins of government into their hands. Probably his main sphere of action was the Navy, but he was prominent in the House on other matters too. His politic concessions to the king in Septem-

---

[1] He was not the only Independent to do so—Selden had helped them all he could, as one might expect, and Whitelocke and Fiennes also spoke for them at the committee. (Camden Soc., *Visitors Registers of the University of Oxford* (1853), lxxi.)

[2] His interest in the Camden House manuscripts, noted earlier, is another case in point.

ber 1647 and to the City in 1648 cannot have improved his reputation for honesty. Whether he really leaned towards an agreement with the king in the summer and autumn of 1648, or whether he was, at Westminster and Newport, dissembling his real wishes is not clear; since the evidence is scanty and conflicting much must depend on one's estimate of Vane's character, and it seems likely that the royalist view of Vane as a disciple of Machiavelli is not far from the truth. A desire for power, an outstanding capacity for hard work, intelligence of a high order, which led him sometimes to stand apart from personal and party loyalties, mark Vane in this period as always, and help to explain both his unpopularity and his stormy political career.

CHAPTER V

Vane's Part in Naval Administration, 1640–48

THROUGHOUT the Long Parliament the Navy was to occupy much of Vane's time and energy, and his first recorded speech dealt with the subject. The House of Commons was discussing financing the Army in the North, on 23 December 1640, when Sir Robert Pye, the member for Woodstock and Auditor of the Exchequer, raised the question of supply for the Navy. Doubtless this was by prearrangement, for Vane promptly rose with a 'paper' to give details of the Navy's financial needs.[1] Though he was concerned almost entirely with money matters, one can see in his warning: '60,000£ presently supplied for the navy, or our walls will be much broken', something of the broader view and the vigour that were to mark many of his later speeches.[2] Six days later he again urged that money should be voted for the Navy, speedily, and gave details of what was required.[3] Still the Commons, who were preoccupied with the needs of the Army, did nothing for the Fleet, and he had to return to the charge three weeks later,[4] criticizing by implication the inaction of the House. The Fleet however remained unprovided for. In February and March 1641 he spoke again on its needs,[5] and at last, on 11 March, the House decided that the Victualler and Treasurer[6] of the Navy should be sent for, to see if they would advance ready money for its use.[7] The Commons were in fact proposing to use the method the crown had long adopted. Six

---

[1] Notestein, *D'Ewes*, 106.   [2] Ibid., 186.   [3] Northcote, *Notebook*, 115.
[4] Notestein, *D'Ewes*, 266. 20 January 1641.   [5] Ibid., 339, 429.
[6] Vane was already in the House, so that his fellow-Treasurer, Sir William Russell, was being sent for.
[7] *CJ.* ii, 102.

days later, in a trenchant speech, Vane again explained in detail the number of ships that were necessary and the amount of money required. 'The French intend this year a fleet of eighty sail', he declared, 'we shall loose the regallitie of the seas otherwise', and, 'our strength hath bin in being able to governe the seas'.[1] He made a reference to 'the care of the lord admirall' for the Fleet, but the conviction of the speech marks it as Vane's own.

On the following day the elder Vane raised the question of providing for the Fleet. His son had been to see his fellow-Treasurer, Sir William Russell (who had gout, and therefore probably could not come to the House). Russell had made what D'Ewes called only a 'slight offer' to supply the Fleet, and D'Ewes, when he rose to speak, more than hinted that the Navy's ill-preparedness was due to Russell, and made significant references to the wealth Russell had acquired.[2] He cast no similar aspersions on Vane however. A committee was set up to consider finance for the Navy, and Russell finally offered to lend £6000, he and his fellow-Treasurer jointly agreeing to pledge their personal credit for the rest of the £20,000 required.[3]

The House decided to assign tunnage and poundage (and not a subsidy) for the needs of the Navy, presumably preferring indirect taxation to direct, and the money for twenty ships was provided by April 1641.[4] The vessels were then fitted and were ready for sea, except for the crews. Northumberland, the lord admiral, wrote to the king that: 'having lately had occasion to presse forty men for your majesty's service, only one man of them appeared, who ran away the next day'.[5] The old severe penalties for resisting impressment in the Navy had been

[1] Notestein, *D'Ewes*, 498–9.

[2] Ibid., 505–6. Russell had been Navy Treasurer since 1618, with some intervals.

[3] Ibid., 518–19.

[4] For Vane's later statement that the Navy's services in protecting merchant shipping were the grounds for assigning tunnage and poundage to the Navy, see Burton, iii, 445.

[5] Bodl. Tanner, 66, f. 48. Northumberland told the king: 'The principall officers of your majesty's navy have advertised mee . . .' This could mean Vane. For pressing as carried on in the 1630s see Hollond, *Discourses*, 134, and for the 1640s, *The humble remonstrance of Andrewes Burrell*, E 335(6). J. R. Hutchinson, *The Press-Gang, Afloat and Ashore* (London, 1913), has little information about the seventeenth century, but does mention the proclamation of 1623, which merely admonished the pressed seaman to do his duty.

abolished in 1623, but mere exhortation was ineffective. Northumberland wrote to the king, that: 'if some other course bee not speedily taken, to make marriners obedient to the presse, the great expense in preparing of this fleete will be totally lost, the seas left unguarded this sommer . . . leaving the provision of a remedy to your majesty's wisdome'[1]

Perhaps Northumberland hoped for another royal proclamation, but Vane preferred to rely on Parliament. In words almost identical to those Northumberland had used in his letter to the king Vane urged in the Commons that unless the House took some course that sailors might be 'pressed' the cost already incurred in victualling and furnishing the ships would be lost. A sharp debate followed. Some members 'would by noe meanes have anie mariners prest as being against the lawes and libertie of the subject'.[2] Nothing was decided about the matter that day, and on the next day, although motion was made for taking up the matter again, it was 'laid aside'.[3] Clearly the House disliked the idea of forcing sailors to serve against their will, and for the time being Vane was defeated.

Not until 7 May was the subject raised again, on a day when the excitement about the first Army Plot and the Protestation was running high, and at the time for the mid-day meal, when many M.P.s would be absent.[4] This time John Wyld, the respected member for Worcestershire, was ordered to bring in a bill for the 'pressing' of sailors, but only 'for this occasion'. The House was evidently still uneasy about the measure. It seems however that the House had been 'managed', by choosing a time when members' minds were full of other subjects, and when their numbers were depleted.[5] The bill now went rapidly ahead. It was read twice and committed the next day,[6] and a committee was appointed, with Vane named second after Glyn, to meet with the Lords.[7] On 11 May the bill passed the

---

[1] Tanner, loc. cit.   [2] Harl. 163, f. 55–55v. 16 April 1641.
[3] Ibid., 63.   [4] *CJ.* ii, 138.
[5] *Mercurius Pragmaticus* asserted that this trick was resorted to in 1648. A motion was started 'after 12 o'clock (the usuall time when the House rises) when most members that they feared would hinder it were gone to dinner, and by this trick carried it'. (E 470(35). 21–8 November.)
[6] Peyton, f. 117. 8 May 1641 (a.m.)
[7] *CJ.* ii, 140–2. The committee met that afternoon, though the House was sitting at the time—the bill was being rushed through.

Commons,[1] and shortly received the royal assent. Vane seems also to have supported the conscription of soldiers. In December 1641 when discussion on this subject had been interrupted by a summons to the royal presence, it was he who moved the resumption of the debate on the engrossing of the bill.[2]

In November 1641, when the lord admiral desired an ordinance of Parliament as his warrant in carrying out a Commons' request to provide four ships to defend Ireland, Vane appeared as his spokesman. He presented the ordinance ready drafted, and the House passed it. The Lords were probably troubled at the way in which the royal authority was being ignored, and they apparently contemplated an amendment to the effect that the action was taken in accordance with the king's directions.[3] D'Ewes was aware of the Commons' assumption of responsibility for the Navy; he wrote in June 1642 that: 'we tooke upon us the care of it [the Navy] for about the space of two years since'.[4]

It was Vane who moved that the ships that were assigned to the Irish coast should be hastened away, and that money should be borrowed from the City at once for this purpose. The Court of Aldermen authorized payment next day.[5] A week later Samuel Vassall, the well-known London merchant, proposed that the sailors of the merchant ships lent to the Royal Navy should be paid at the rate of twenty-eight days to the month, and not thirty,[6] so that the merchant ships' sailors should not suffer financially while serving in the Royal Navy, where the pay was lower,[7] but Vane and others opposed Vassall's suggestion. It would be interesting to know on what grounds. Possibly

---

[1] Harl. 163, f. 164.

[2] Coates, *D'Ewes*, 224. Maynard, again Vane's opponent, attacked the compulsion in the bill very cogently—'presse he would nott, because that was a kind of contract, to which noe man could bee compelled'. (Peyton, f. 162. 11 December 1641.)

[3] Coates, *D'Ewes*, 165.   [4] Harl. 163, f. 146. 4 June 1642.

[5] Coates, *D'Ewes*, 183. 22 November.   [6] Ibid., 208.

[7] Harl. 163, f. 55. Some members, when the conscription of sailors was proposed, held that the service would be more attractive if 'ther wages might bee encreased and ther persons better used then formerlie'. (Ibid., ff. 55–6.) This implies that Royal Navy pay was lower, and Slyngesby (Hollond, *Discourses*, 351–2) states this was so in 1660. Sir Thomas Roe said that food in the State's Navy was better than in merchant ships, but work and discipline was harder—higher pay would not solve the problem. Perhaps this was Vane's view.

it was feared that sailors would desert from merchant ships, but on this there is no information.

Vane lost his post as Treasurer of the Navy in December 1641; a Commons committee later stated that he had been punished for his part in Strafford's trial in the previous April.[1] It is odd that the dismissal had not come much earlier. He had taken no part in the famous Grand Remonstrance debate of 22 November, nor on those of the previous days, though it is true that he had probably drafted part of the document,[2] and this may have been known to the king.

Henceforward he was less active in Navy affairs, though he was still concerned with them. On 7 March he reported to the Commons from the lord admiral that the king had proposed that one larger ship, the *Prince*, should take the place of two that the House had recently decided should be sent to the Irish sea. The matter was referred, after a division,[3] to the committee of the Navy.[4] Giles Greene, its chairman, who was the member for Corfe Castle, and a prominent merchant of Weymouth, visited Northumberland, who declared the *Prince* unfit for service. The House decided to ignore the king's proposal, and to send the two ships, but Vane now argued that in place of one of these ships, of 400–500 tons each, several smaller ones, of 50–60 tons each, would be more useful, and Sir Walter Earle seconded him.[5]

The committee of the Navy just mentioned had become very important in naval administration.[6] It was one of the many *ad hoc* committees set up in 1641 to deal with naval affairs, and had been instructed to prepare a tunnage and poundage bill, and consider how money should be provided for the Navy.[7] Most of its members were also on a committee of Customs which did yeoman service in drawing up a Book of Rates,[8] so

---

[1] Whittaker, f. 220v, says of Vane that he had the Treasurership 'taken from him upon the question of the earl of Strafford'. (15 July 1645.)

[2] See below, p. 194.

[3] No doubt because the king's wishes were being defied.

[4] Ibid., ff. 21v, 22v.   [5] Ibid., f. 31v.

[6] For the MS sources for the Navy committees, 1642–53, see Appendix C.

[7] *CJ.* ii, 107. 18 March.

[8] Giles Greene, *A Declaration in Vindication . . . of the Committee of the Navy and Customs*, E 405 (8). 1 September 1647 (Thomason's date).

useful that it continued in force until after the Restoration.[1]
It was the only Navy committee to survive the 1641 recess, when
all committees lapsed by order of the House, except those
specifically revived.[2] As the Navy was paid for out of some
customs duties, including tunnage and poundage, the decision
of the House to amalgamate the two committees in 1643 is
understandable.[3] Thus the 'committee of Navy and Customs'
was created.

With the Navy and Customs committee was associated a
network of other Navy committees. Greene, Vane and four
merchants were unpaid commissioners of the Navy; with the
paid commissioners they took over in September 1642 the
duties which the Surveyor, Comptroller and Clerk of the Acts
had performed hitherto.[4] Shortly after, in October, six of the
Navy and Customs committee and three peers were given the
jurisdictional function of the lord high admiral; the earl of
Northumberland had been dismissed by the king, and though
the House appointed the earl of Warwick commander-in-
chief, it put the Admiralty itself into commission.[5] Both Vane
and his father were on this Admiralty committee, and Greene,
the earls of Northumberland and Warwick were fellow-
members. The jurisdictional duties of the Admiralty put further
responsibility upon six of the same men who already had a
heavy financial burden as members of the Navy and Customs
committee; as Greene put it later, they 'did wade through
those intricate cases which fell out in that first year'.[6] Almost
the same men were a committee of Excise and a Foreign Affairs
committee. The committee of Excise dealt with disputes
arising out of ships and goods taken by reprisal; this also
involved many intricate law-cases, and was, according to
Greene, 'a distracted work'. The committee for Foreign Affairs

[1] C. D. Chandaman, *The English Public Revenue, 1660–88* (unpublished Ph.D.
thesis, London, 1954), 58.
[2] *CJ.* ii, 304.   [3] *CJ.* iii, 299. 2 November 1643.
[4] For a brief outline of naval administration of the Interregnum, 1641–59, see
A. C. Dewar, R.N., *Mariner's Mirror*, xii (1926), 406. I owe this, and the reference
to those of Vane's accounts for 1642–9 as Navy Treasurer which are in the Public
Record Office, to the kindness of Mr D. E. Kennedy of the University of Melbourne.
[5] *CJ.* ii, 812, 813. 19 October 1642.
[6] Greene, loc. cit.

dealt with complaints from the ambassadors of Spain, France and Holland, and was kept busy.[1]

The central figure in all these committees was Giles Greene, as is clear from the diaries and *Commons Journals*.[2] Vane, though a member of these committees, played a secondary role. The fact that he lost his office as Navy Treasurer in December 1641 was partly responsible for this, no doubt, but the major factor must have been his preoccupation with general policy. From March 1642 to the end of 1643 he appears not to have spoken on the Navy or naval matters more than twice. In June 1642 he delivered a petition presented by ships' captains who brought ammunition from Hull to London,[3] and in March 1643 he was the spokesman of the Navy committee, Greene on this occasion acting only as his seconder. This last is a curious incident. Vane informed the Commons that the commissioners the House had lately appointed to receive the customs, who were certain London aldermen, would not lend the £30,000 requested by the committee of the Navy, but £20,000 only. The committee thought that the House should press the merchants to lend the whole sum. The merchants were called in, the Speaker addressed them, and presumably rebuked them, for D'Ewes was surprised to see the London citizens who had been, as he says, so much responsible for the civil war, 'soe roughly dealt withall'. He concluded that 'they had some secret plott to make some advantage of this request of ours, which fell out accordinglie the day following, for Mr. Greene preferred an ordinance on ther behalfe to be past both houses extremelie to ther advantage'.[4] (The aldermen were to retain the receivership of the customs for a certain time and had power to dismiss and employ all officers, which might be a profitable right.)[5] It would seem that the public rebuke administered to the citizens was designed to cover up the fact that substantial concessions

---

[1] Ibid.   [2] See below, p. 125.

[3] *CJ*. ii, 627 states that the ships came from Kingston-upon-Hull, which would explain Vane's presenting the petition and is probably correct. D'Ewes states that the ships were from Berwick (Harl. 163, f. 164v); he gives Vane's name as the person presenting the petition.

[4] Harl. 164, f. 327. 14 March. D'Ewes says these 'fiery spirits' among the citizens had been the main instruments with Hampden and the other 'violent men' to 'blow up the flame of our present civil wars'.

[5] Ibid., f. 331.

were to be made to their demands. Alternatively they may
have been allowed to state their objections, though D'Ewes
does not assert this, and by so doing prepare the House for an
ordinance meeting their grievances. Certainly if Vane and
Greene's intentions were merely to overawe the commissioners,
one would hardly expect the ordinance to follow the next day,
as it did. It is not clear why Vane, and not Greene, represented
the committee's views to the Commons. Perhaps he was a more
persuasive speaker, though Greene was a very able man. By this
time however Vane was one of those most concerned with the
relations of the House to the City, and this may be the reason
that he brought the matter up in the Commons.

Meanwhile he had been restored by Parliament to his former
office as Navy Treasurer. A week after the members had heard
of Vane's dismissal by the king, Walter Yonge rose to move that:
'Sir H. Vane bee putt into the next Bill off Tunnage and
Poundage to bee continued Treasurer of the Navy'.[1] That the
House should control the appointment of royal officials was an
extraordinary suggestion[2] and the method suggested, by which
Vane's re-appointment was the condition for granting tunnage
and poundage, savoured of blackmail. Sir John Holland, the
parliamentary diarist, does not record any debate on Yonge's
suggestion, and no action was taken. On 12 March 1642 Vane,
whom Sir Thomas Peyton in his account of the day's proceedings still calls Treasurer of the Navy, moved that the House
should make financial provision for the Fleet.[3] It was another of
his lucid speeches, and evidently reminded the House that he
had lost his official position, for on 18 March D'Ewes came into
the House and found a debate in progress 'touching the naming
of Sir Henry Fane the younger in the Bill of Tonnage and
Poundage to be one of the Treasurers of the navie'. D'Ewes
thought that it was 'referred to the Committee that was to
drawe the bill for Tonnage & Poundage to present a clause to
the House whereby that place might bee settled upon him'.[4]
The clerk however had understood differently. 'It shall be

---

[1] Coates, *D'Ewes*, 312. 18 December 1641.

[2] An act disabling royal officials from sitting in Parliament had actually been
introduced, but evidently the separation of powers did not commend itself. (Harl.
163, f. 256. 3 June 1641.)

[3] Peyton, f. 102.   [4] Harl. 163, f. 37.

referred to the *consideration of the Committee*, to insert a clause in this bill for the making Sir H. Vane junior one of the Treasurers of the Navy.'[1] The clerk was evidently right, for neither of the two tunnage and poundage acts of the period concerned has anything about continuing Vane in office.[2] It would have been difficult to do—as it was, the earl of Warwick sent by Pym, four days later, a petition detailing the offices such as that of chief postmaster which had been taken from him,[3] and, luckier than Vane, was re-instated by order of the House.[4] But if Vane had been similarly favoured a host of other disgruntled ex-officials might have besieged the House. Warwick's services to the country and his rank put him in a different class. The tunnage and poundage committee may have considered that the tenth of the Nineteen Propositions sent to the king at York in June 1642, was a more regular way of obtaining redress for Vane;[5] Parliament asked that any peer or M.P. who had been dismissed from his office should be re-appointed, if the House to which he belonged petitioned the king on the member's behalf. It seems Vane tried to prevent Warwick from regaining his lost office of postmaster, for the earl wrote to his son-in-law Lord Mandevile requesting him to further Warwick's interests in the House of Commons, in respect of the Letter Office, which Vane wished 'to continue in sequestration'.[6]

In August 1642 however, by ordinance of Parliament, Vane again became Treasurer, and this time sole Treasurer, of the Navy.[7] He had received some help in the matter from White-locke, who wrote in May 1644 in an unpublished passage: 'I therefore spake to Sir Henry Vane the Younger, for whom I did some service in Parliament in drawing and passing his Ordinance touching the office of Treasurer of the Navy, that he would lend me the house at Deptford belonging to that office, and whereof he himselfe then made no use.'[8] Two days after the ordinance took effect, a clerk began to record, in a book now in the Bodleian Library,[9] the orders which the committee of Navy and Customs gave Vane. The Committee of Both

---

[1] *CJ.* ii, 485.　　[2] *Statutes of the Realm*, v, 144, 175.　　[3] Harl. 163, f. 42v.
[4] Ibid., 52v.　　[5] *LJ.* v, 97.　　[6] HMC. *8th Rep.* App. ii, 58.
[7] *CJ.* ii, 705. 5 August 1642.　　[8] BM. Add. 37,343, f. 300v.
[9] Bodl. Rawl. A 220. 10 August.

Kingdoms also instructed him to make payments for Navy purposes.[1] But when the Commons wanted a report on the general state of the Navy[2] they called on Giles Greene, the chairman of the Navy and Customs committee, whose orders Greene signed.[3] Greene also made frequent reports from the committee to the Commons.[4] There is even some evidence that Vane was not carrying out in person his duties as Navy Treasurer—when in the spring of 1645 Greene's committee wished to know what money was owing for ships hired for transport duties, it was the deputy-Treasurer, Richard Hutchinson, who was summoned before it.[5] The Admiralty committee had lapsed in December 1643; Parliament's fortunes were then at a desperately low ebb, the earl of Warwick was appointed lord admiral, and he exercised the powers the committee had formerly had.[6]

There were no further significant changes in naval administration until 1645, but in these Vane was closely concerned. After the Self-Denying Ordinance had been introduced, and the 'New-Modelling' of the Army had begun, it was natural for Parliament to consider the control of the Navy also, and in February 1645 an ordinance was brought in to the House, by which naval administration was to be reformed. A committee was set up, to send for the commission formerly granted for carrying on naval affairs (the October 1642 ordinance appointing the nine Admiralty commissioners, of whom Vane was one), and to consider what officials were necessary for the Navy. together with their salaries and privileges.[7] The committee was a large one; Greene was named first, but Vane was not a member, no doubt because he was at Uxbridge. As soon as he returned, on 27 February, he was added to the committee.[8] In April, as a result of the Self-Denying Ordinance, the earl of Warwick resigned the office of lord admiral. The powers of the office were again put into the hands of a committee, this

---

[1] E.g. *CSPD. 1644–45*, 124; *CJ*. iii, 628.   [2] E.g. *CJ*. iii, 507.

[3] S.P. 16/509/17, 37, 43.

[4] E.g. Harl. 166, ff. 31v, 33v, 41, 58v, 150v, 153v (this last was a two-hour report).

[5] *CSPD. 1644–45*, 632. 8 March.   [6] *CJ*. iii, 329.   [7] *CJ*. iv, 21 February 1645.

[8] Ibid., 64. In Vane's case, he was not added to committees when the House knew he was absent.

time of eighteen, among whom Vane was not included.[1] It is very difficult to account for his omission. The new Admiralty committee's composition was probably a triumph for Holles's faction; of the eighteen members eight or nine belonged to Holles's group, and only two to Vane's.[2] But why should Holles's group wish to humiliate Warwick, whose sympathies were with their group, by putting the Admiralty into commission? Perhaps this was the plan of Vane and St John's group, but Holles and his followers had won one of their occasional successes when the Admiralty committee was actually nominated. It seems unlikely that Vane wished to give up some of his Navy work, and was therefore not nominated, for in October he became a member. If his exclusion was indeed a political matter, why should Holles be so powerful in April 1645? It is possible that Vane was ill; there is practically no information about him that month. He did not attend the Committee of Both Kingdoms, he made no reports in the House, and apart from Sabran's statement that Vane had denounced the Scots, there is no evidence of activity on his part at all.

The new Admiralty committee was instructed to name a commander-in-chief for the Navy, and a political struggle ensued; when the Committee met two days later it resolved that both Houses should be informed that the Self-Denying Ordinance made it impossible to nominate a suitable person.[3] Holles, who was instructed to inform the Commons of the committee's decision, and Warwick, who was to inform the Lords, were in fact continuing the fight against the ordinance

---

[1] *LJ.* vii, 327; *A.O.I.* i, 669.

[2] I assume that the earls of Pembroke, North and Warwick belonged to Holles's group, and the M.P.s Stapleton, Whitelocke, Sir Christopher Wray and Sir John Evelyn of Surrey. With Holles himself this makes a total of eight, and probably Greene leaned to the Presbyterians (see above, p. 113). Only Say certainly belonged to Vane's group. For evidence as to Holles's associates see Whitelocke's *Memorials*, his MS and Holles's *Memoirs*.

[3] Bodl. Rawl. C 416, f. 2 (the committee's Minutes), 21 April. It would seem from D'Ewes (Harl. 166, f. 209v) that the Admiralty committee wanted Warwick as commander, as one would expect, but D'Ewes is not clear on this. (Cf. f. 205v.) Yonge reports Holles as saying that the committee considered that the Fleet should be under the command of one man, but could not think of anyone fit for so great a trust. Sir Robert Pye then moved that Warwick should be appointed. (BM. Add. 18,780, f. 5.)

which they hated. *Aulicus* noted the extraordinary arrangement of dividing the admiral's power among eighteen commissioners, but added: 'Yet for all this power is cut into 18
parcells, you may see it gathering into one single person, which
if you will observe who leads up the other seventeen, is no hard
discovery.'[1] Perhaps *Aulicus* thought Greene would dominate
the new committee; if so, he was right. Within a week however
of setting up the committee of eighteen, Parliament, 'seeing
their distractions increase and their forces diminish', as *Aulicus*
put it,[2] appointed Warwick as commander-in-chief, and the
circumstances in which this was done are interesting. It was
seriously proposed that a committee of three should command
the navy, of whom Warwick was to be one, Peregrine Pelham
and Alexander Bence his coadjutators.[3] According to Whittaker, Pelham and Bence were experienced seamen, but really
Aulicus was more accurate when he called them 'two most
famous, eminent, unheard-of-gentlemen',[4] though Bence
worked very hard on the Navy and Customs committee.[5]
Neither M.P. however can be said to have had the training or
experience necessary to command the Navy. But Pelham
belonged to the Independent group, Warwick to the Presbyterians, and probably Bence was to hold the balance. Actually,
after a long debate the Commons negatived Bence; this left
Warwick and Pelham, and the Lords rejected Pelham,[6] a
decision which the Commons accepted. When it came to
appointing a commander for the summer's expedition there
was another trial of strength between the two rival parties;
D'Ewes suggested that Batten, the vice-admiral, should command the Fleet,[7] and there was a proposal that the Lords should
be asked to agree to this. Vane, always hostile to the Lords,
and Sir William Waller, probably still hoping for favours from

---

[1] E 284(20). 20–7 April.   [2] E 286(17). 4–11 May.
[3] Whittaker, f. 207–207v, Harl. 166, f. 205v. Whitelocke, like Whittaker,
thought that all three were nominated successfully, 'after long debate', and
Pelham certainly took it for granted that he and the two others were appointed,
but it seems clear from the *Commons Journal* that Bence was negatived. (Whitelocke, i, 427, *CJ*. iv, 125.) Blake, Deane and Monk later formed a successful
triumvirate at sea, but they were better qualified to command than Bence and
Pelham.
[4] See above, n. 2.   [5] Bodl. Rawl. A 221, *passim*, e.g. ff. 11v and 130.
[6] *Aulicus*, loc. cit.   [7] Harl. 166, f. 209v.

the Independents, were the tellers against this, and were defeated, by the narrow margin of two votes.[1]

The minutes of the Admiralty committee set up in April[2] show that it was dominated by Holles's group, with Warwick often in the chair, but in October Vane was added to it.[3] This may be connected with the election of the new 'Recruiter' M.P.s. According to Holles, after the failure of the Savile accusations against himself and Whitelocke, the Independents were afraid they would lose control of the House, and therefore in the long summer vacation, when many members were away, they raised the question of filling the vacant places and, even so, carried their motion by only three votes.[4] Perhaps Vane's election to the Admiralty committee was one of the fruits of the Independents' increased hold on the House after the new elections.

An important incident, referred to by Vane's first biographer, George Sikes, writing in 1662, occurred in July 1645. The Commons resolved that Vane should keep his office of Navy Treasurer 'during the continuance of the war, and no longer', as the House stipulated, provided that he paid over to the Receiver-General one half of the clear profits, for the benefit of the nation.[5] Some months before, a committee had been set up to consider what salaries should be allowed the new holders of offices vacated by M.P.s under the Self-Denying Ordinance;[6] presumably it was this committee which reported on the Navy Treasurership. At the end of June the House had voted that the Ordnance Office should be regulated 'for the best advantage of the State',[7] and this new attitude to administration was bound to affect naval administration also sooner or later.

Vane's post as Navy Treasurer had been protected, as we have seen, by the last clause of the Self-Denying Ordinance, which stated that 'Those members of either House, who had offices by grant from his Majesty before this Parliament, and were by his Majesty displaced sitting this Parliament, and have

[1] *CJ*. iv, 144. 15 May.   [2] Bodl. Rawl. C 416.   [3] *CJ*. iv, 297.
[4] Holles, *Memoirs*, 214, 221. It is true that the House did not decide to order elections to be held until August, though the matter had been raised seven months before. See R. N. Kershaw, 'The Recruiting of the Long Parliament', *History*, viii, no. 23 (October 1923).
[5] *CJ*. iv, 207. 15 July.   [6] Ibid., iv, 62, 82.   [7] BM. Add. 18,780, f. 58.

since by authority of both Houses been restored, shall not by this Ordinance be discharged from their said offices or profits thereof, but shall enjoy the same.'[1] But now he obtained express confirmation of his post, and his re-appointment was dated from 12 May, when the Self-Denying Ordinance came into force. His accounts from May 1645 therefore run from that date.[2] At least once later, in April 1647, when party feeling was running high,[3] Vane's somewhat anomalous position was challenged, but he continued to hold the post.

It is remarkable that, as Oppenheim stated,[4] Vane did not return to the State one penny of his profits as Navy Treasurer for 1645–50. In fact, he ignored the ordinance of July 1645 entirely as far as this was concerned. His accounts for May 1645 to December 1646, which were not presented until December 1650, show that his poundage was £4909 17s 6d for this period, or some £3000 a year. If he had paid any of this over to the Receiver-General it would have been mentioned in his voluminous declared accounts, but there is no indication of this whatever, and one must conclude that Oppenheim's strictures on Vane were justified. Perhaps Vane found that he could not meet his necessary expenses without the whole poundage, but in that case he should have put his case before Parliament. Perhaps he never intended the July ordinance to be more than a means of placating public criticism that those in public places were enriching themselves at public expense. It is odd that Parliament did not demand that he should return the half of his profits, but of course the M.P.s may have innocently believed that their injunction was being carried out. It should be noted, for comparison with Vane's £3000, that those M.P.s who were in need were allowed by the House £200 a year.[5] No doubt Vane would claim that he was faithfully serving the country in many different ways, and with the Raby estates

<hr />

[1] Gardiner, *Const. Docs.*, 288.

[2] A.O.I. 1706/90. 13 May 1645 to 31 December 1646.

[3] BM. Add. 10,114, f. 23. 29 April. 'Sir H. Vane junior not restored though prest for.'

[4] Oppenheim, *A History of the administration of the Royal Navy*, 295–6. Oppenheim noticed Sikes's *Life* only, and overlooked the Commons ordinance.

[5] *CJ.* iv, 161. For comparative figures on wages to M.P.s see R. C. Latham, 'The payment of Parliamentary wages—the last phase', *EHR* (1951), 27–30.

and the Cockfield and Chester-le-Street mines yielding little or nothing he (and his father) had to rely on their income from official sources.

The Navy Treasurer's house at Deptford, which Vane had let to Whitelocke, Lady Vane now wanted returned. 'I came with my wife and Mr. Hall and his wife to Detford', wrote Whitelocke, 'and my Lady Willoughby told us that my Lady Vane desired to make use of Detford house herself, a recompense not very gratefull for my labour in doing service for Sir Henry Vane about his office, to which this house belongeth.'[1] Vane apparently agreed, for in October Whitelocke wrote: 'I visited Mr. Holles, who was not well, and meeting Sir Henry Vane by the way he went thither with me, and made a large apology to me concerning his house at Detford.'[2] The house was worth £20 a year in the 1630s,[3] and it too, if let, would add to the Treasurer's income.

On 27 October 1645 Vane moved that Giles Greene should have payment for his services to the Navy; he proposed that Greene should have the sum of £500 a year, and arrears for three years.[4] Greene had lost his whole estate to the royalists, and had been maintained by his children, but even so Whitelocke was envious; it was, he said, a reward for committee services that few others obtained.[5] About the same time Cornelius Holland was given an extensive grant of royal lands in Buckinghamshire to compensate him for the offices he had lost by his support of Parliament's cause,[6] and Vane's group[7] must have been one of those in Holles's mind when he wrote, 'they [the dominant Independent group] had power over all the money of the kingdom, pleasured and recompensed whom

---

[1] BM. Add. 37,344, f. 3. 12 August 1645.

[2] Ibid., f. 18v. 11 October 1645.

[3] Aylmer, *The King's Servants*, 19.

[4] *CJ.* iv, 322. (Vane senior was in the North, so Elsing must have meant the younger.) The ordinance accords Greene no official position.

[5] Whitelocke, i, 529.

[6] *CJ.* iv, 270. 11 September 1645. Royalist pamphleteers often referred to Holland's financial gains. Holland bought bishops' lands for £807 os 7d (Bodl. Rawl. B 239). Vane bought none, but acquired church lands in another way, explained below (Chap. VII).

[7] Though Greene was probably politically a neutral with Presbyterian leanings, he is regarded here as coming under Vane's protection.

they would; which were none to be sure but their creatures, or such as were willing to become so'.[1] In justice to the Independents one must point out that avarice did not mark all the group. Many of them were in such financial straits that they claimed the £200 a year which Parliament allowed M.P.s in need, and Greene had served for three years on the Navy committee before he received a penny for his services. Moreover there were some who stayed in town all through August 1645 to carry on the nation's business, although plague was raging in the capital, and Greene was one. Vane was not.[2]

At the end of 1646 Vane planned to give up the office of Treasurer of the Navy, which he had held for eight exacting years. His decision is understandable, and there are several possible motives for it. His health may have suffered from the years of strenuous activity, he may have found difficulty in working with a predominantly Presbyterian Admiralty committee, he may have wished to give more time to other activities. What is remarkable is that he intended to sell his office. There is no other explanation of the fact that he asked the House to give him power to surrender the office, 'with all his interest therein', and to nominate someone in his place.[3] One of Clarendon's correspondents wrote that Vane had sold the position,[4] which shows how contemporaries interpreted his action. It is difficult to account for the House's consent, for no other 'royal' official was similarly allowed to dispose of his post. The motion was introduced very early one morning, and was pushed through with great speed, the Lords agreeing straight away,[5] so perhaps it had been arranged that only Vane's friends should be present. The Presbyterians had gained what proved to be a stable majority in the House only a day or two before, and one would expect them to have opposed Vane's motion vigorously. Of course Vane, or his father on Vane's behalf, had bought the office in 1639, and they wanted to recoup themselves, but one would not have expected the House to acquiesce. However, he continued to hold the post until

---

[1] Holles, *Memoirs*, 193.   [2] *CJ.* iv, 251 *et al.*   [3] *CJ.* v, 30. 28 December 1646.
[4] Bodl. Clarendon, 2417, 14–24 January 1647 (Letter of intelligence from London). Whitelocke (ii, 98) notes the passing of the ordinance.
[5] *CJ.* v, 31.

December 1650, so he evidently thought better of his decision.

It has already been noted that Vane was an infrequent attender at the Admiralty committee meetings in 1647 until his party gained control of the committee in September.[1] By an interesting coincidence in time, Greene was given leave of absence from the Commons on the very day that the Independents were added to the committee[2]—did he not want to work with them, or were they taking advantage of his departure? As we have seen,[3] the Independents used their control of the committee to dispense with Captain Batten's services as vice-admiral. Batten did not like Vane,[4] and one cannot help making a connexion between Greene's departure, Vane's assiduous attendances, and Batten's virtual dismissal. Batten declared that he could not understand why he was displaced,[5] but his sympathy with Holles's group is explanation enough. He had also, in November 1646, brought a charge against a ship's captain of uttering 'scandalous words' against the king and his issue, which some members of the Admiralty committee may have thought ill-judged enthusiasm.[6]

Batten was astonished that 'another (such another!) was thrust in to be my successor as till then I never imagined would be Vice-Admiral of a navy'.[7] This was Colonel Thomas Rainsborough, the Leveller, and Vane was concerned, according to Sir Lewis Dyve,[8] in the extraordinary incidents leading to Rainsborough's appointment. Dyve had heard, doubtless from Lilburne, his fellow-prisoner, that Rainsborough was confident of obtaining Batten's position, but Cromwell and others, jealous of Rainsborough's popularity with the soldiers, and

---

[1] Appendix C and pp. 94–5. [2] *CJ.* v, 297. 9 September 1647.
[3] Above, p. 94.

[4] To judge from his sarcastic comment on Vane's absence from the Navy Office in October 1641, which Batten attributed to the dearth of money in the Office. (*CSPD. 1641–43*, 139.) Vane was very busy with public affairs at that time. Pepys gives an unfavourable picture of Batten's own avarice.

[5] E 460(13). [6] Adm. 7/673, f. 41. 12 November.

[7] Probably because Rainsborough had started as a cabin-boy? (BM. Add. 11,602, f. 39; *Mercurius Pragmaticus*, E 435(42).)

[8] Dyve, *The Tower of London Letter-Book*, 84–5, 89. Lilburne wrote in 1649 that Cromwell had tried to 'worm' Rainsborough out of the Navy. (E 552(15); E 568(20).)

afraid of his independence of character, planned to appoint the less popular, and more flexible, Richard Deane. They could then 'place or displace him at pleasure'. As Cromwell and Rainsborough were friends, however, it was arranged that Cromwell should not appear openly in opposition to Rainsborough's appointment. But Rainsborough knew of the plot, and a fortnight later came to a meeting of Cromwell, Ireton, Vane and St John, whereupon a violent quarrel ensued. Rainsborough got his way, and was appointed.

Lilburne's connexions with the Army were close, and the month's delay in appointing a successor to Batten certainly requires explanation.[1] But Deane's claim to the command was strong, for he was a fine seaman, and the objections to Rainsborough's appointment could have been on service grounds, particularly since, as time was to show, Rainsborough was certainly not popular among the sailors. Vane signed the committee order appointing Rainsborough,[2] but he signed other Admiralty orders occasionally, and one cannot deduce from this one fact that he was supporting Rainsborough's appointment. In the conflict with the Upper House over the appointment of this notorious Leveller, to whom the Lords strongly objected, Vane's name is not mentioned. It is true however that though the dispute continued from October 1647 to March 1648, when the Lords finally gave way, there was only one division on the question,[3] and therefore little indication of the attitude of individual M.P.s. *Pragmaticus* cynically suggested that Rainsborough was being sent to sea because he had had a major hand in drawing up the *Agreement of the People*, one item of which called for an account by the M.P.s of how the kingdom's money had been spent![4]

Before Giles Greene left for the country in September 1647, he published the judicious and able pamphlet, already referred to,[5] which sheds some light on Vane as Treasurer of the Navy.

---

[1] *Pragmaticus* (E 410(4)) had heard by 9 October that Rainsborough was to be appointed; not until ten days later did the committee's minute-book record the appointment. This is another instance of *Pragmaticus*'s 'inside information'.

[2] Adm. 7/673, ff. 413–14.

[3] *CJ.* v, 405, 413, 417, 503. Northumberland supported Batten, according to one news-letter writer. (Bodl. Clar. 2605.)

[4] E 421(1). 14–21 December 1647.   [5] Above, p. 120, n. 8.

Greene explained how the committee had power to order payment from the customs to the Treasurer. 'The moneys being so settled in his hands, they were all to be issued out by him, by the only order of that committee; which trust I dare confidently affirm he hath discharged with as much clearnesse and freedome from any corruption as ever Treasurer did.' This is a valuable testimony to Vane's honesty in administration, for Greene was an independent-minded M.P., who although he usually supported Vane's views in 1645–6, showed Presbyterian sympathies in the following years. The pamphlet demonstrates the sound policies of Greene's committee, that, for instance, they 'took along with them the concurrent advice and full consent of the Commissioners of the Navy, Victuallers of the Navy, Officers of the Ordnance'. Greene asserted that the ship-yards, storehouses and ships were very efficiently provided, and, which was largely true, that no complaints from sailors were heard at the doors of Parliament. This was a remarkable achievement when one remembers how often soldiers were driven to make their protests in person in this way.[1] Some at least of the credit for this must go to Vane.

It may be that he was inspired by similar motives to those of Greene: the desire to give the country better government, and to earn respect for Parliament.[2] Greene stated categorically that in filling vacant offices neither he nor any members of the committee received a penny for any appointment made. As Vane sometimes made such recommendations[3] Greene's assertion is interesting. *Pragmaticus* did accuse Greene and Corbet, another prominent member of the committee, of 'licking their fingers',[4] but his only charge against Vane was repeated from a pamphlet by *Elencticus*, in which the Navy Treasurership was said to be worth at least £6000 a

[1] See for instance *CJ*. v, 526. It is true however that John Hollond (140) asserts that several ships' companies came to the Parliament door to clamour for their pay in 1644.

[2] '. . . next that duty I owe to God and to the Parliament and to my country . . . to make me account no labour too great, nor care too much, to be any way instrumentall in so great and glorious a work as the Reformation in Church and State . . . next . . . to manage that work . . . as that on the one side the King, on the other side the people, might be in love with Parliaments . . .'

[3] E.g. Adm. 7/673, ff. 4, 394, 413.

[4] E 435(12). 4–11 April 1648.

year in time of war,[1] and one cannot treat this assertion seriously.[2]

The year 1648 saw Vane's accounts as Treasurer of the Navy brought in at last, but only for 1642–5.[3] Royalist writers and others had continued to criticize Parliament for not insisting on the production of the public accounts,[4] and the belief that M.P.s were reaping financial advantage from the country's suffering was more widespread than ever.[5] Probably as a result of the pressure of public opinion, the Navy and Army Treasurers and the Master of the Ordnance were ordered on 12 April 1648 to bring in their accounts[6] thirteen days later. 25 April came and went, but nothing was heard of the accounts. The subject was next raised on 5 August,[7] being doubtless brought to mind by that other hardy perennial, the question of the offices held by M.P.s contrary to the Self-Denying Ordinance.[8] Again nothing was done, but on 4 September the House ordered that the first business on Friday 8 September should be the accounts of Vane and the other two officials.[9] They were given yet another day's

---

[1] E 465(13). *The Second Centurie*, n.d.

[2] See Appendix D for details of Vane's actual profits.

[3] *CJ*. vi, 14. 9 September. This can be only a summary of Vane's original accounts—the later ones in the Public Record Office are rolls of enormous size, and practically exposés of the work of the Navy. All money spent on the Navy went through the Treasurer's hands.

[4] *The poore Committee Man's accompt*, BM. 669, f. 11 (n.d. but among 1647 pamphlets); *Mercurius Pragmaticus*, E 421(1). 14–21 December 1647; *The Antipodes* [a tract addressed to the Army] E 399(16). 22 July 1647; *Mystery of the Two Juntoes*, E 393(29). 24 June 1647.

[5] See Milton's disillusion, *Hist. of Britain*, Bohn's standard ed., 1853, v, 236–7. For Bellièvre's bribery of M.P.s see *Montereuil, Correspondence*, ii, 109. Other complaints about accounts not being presented include E 442(2), *British Bellman*. As late as November 1648 Col. Rich's regiment in its petition to Parliament was still asking for State accounts to be presented by those who had been entrusted with the State's money. (E 472(3).)

[6] *CJ*. v, 527. The order instructing M.P.s to bring in their accounts to the Committee of Accounts is *CJ*. v, 204–5, 10 June 1647. No M.P. was to receive any profit from an office given by Parliament.   [7] Ibid., 662.

[8] E 458(25). *Mercurius Pragmaticus* asserted that when it was moved that 4 August might be a day of humiliation, one M.P. said that the preparation for a fast should be the putting aside of pride, vainglory etc., and therefore moved that the Self-Denying Ordinance should be reinforced. The House agreed to debate this on 9 August but put it off; *Pragmaticus* is right here (*CJ*. v, 665). On 9 August it was postponed for a week, on 16 August for another week, on 23 August it was not raised, and the matter was dropped. This was a subject that the House did not like.

[9] *CJ*. vi, 6.

grace,[1] but on 9 September the accounts were finally presented to the House, with the certificates of the committee of Accounts appended. Vane's accounts for the early period of the war, now that they were at last forthcoming,[2] are surprising. Between August 1642 and May 1645 he had paid out for Navy purposes, if the account is to be believed (and surely any discrepancy would not have escaped the eagle eye of William Prynne, who signed the account), some £640,000. He had received, chiefly from the commissioners of excise, some £641,000. He had in fact taken for himself only about £617 for the thirty-three months covered by the accounts. He should have been receiving some £3300 a year as poundage and for other allowances due to him; he had actually taken only some £200 a year. (It should be noted however that he ultimately drew every penny that was due to him.)

But in June 1648 an order of the Commons instructed Vane to pay towards the cost of defending the Isle of Wight the amount of £500, for which he should reimburse himself 'out of that moiety of the profits of the place of Treasurer of the Navy, which he pays in to the Committee of the Revenue'.[3] The same order subsequently referred to the £500 as being advanced 'voluntarily' by Vane. It may be remarked that the rest of the £2500 required for the Isle of Wight was to come from John Bland, whom Vane had defended, according to *Mercurius Veridicus*, in the dispute with Fowke and Mildmay already noted.[4] The summer of 1648 was the period when the Presbyterians were said to be regaining power in the House of Commons, and Cromwell and Vane were making concessions to them. It looks as though the Presbyterians were pursuing Vane with some vindictiveness. Of course the chairman of the committee of the Revenue was Vane's own father, so he may have found means of avoiding this payment, as he did for the rest of the half of his profits as Navy Treasurer!

In February 1648 Vane raised in the Admiralty committee

---

[1] Ibid., 10.

[2] Ibid., 14. Oppenheim, *Administration*, 296, said that Vane's accounts for 1642–5 were missing. He had evidently once more overlooked the *Commons Journals* record. In the 1647–50 period accounts were going to the committee of Accounts, and not to the Audit Office of the Exchequer (see p. 135, n. 6).

[3] *CJ.* v, 582. 2 June.   [4] See above, p. 103.

the question of the deputy-Treasurer's office.[1] The committee
minute runs:

Sir Henry Vane, knight, Treasurer of the Navy, having this day
represented to this Committee that whereas he is appointed Treasurer
of the Navy . . . to execute the same by himself, his sufficient deputie
or deputies, and therefore that a constant personall attendance
may be given to the severall trusts and duties belonging to the said
office, which cannot by reason of his relation to the publique be so
well performed by himselfe, hath . . . appointed Charles Vane, Esq.,
his brother, a person well affected unto the Parliament and of
abilitye, for the dischargeing of the said service to be his deputy.

The Committee approved of the appointment, and by Vane's
desire a record was made in the minutes. It was witnessed by
two men; the first name is that of Richard Hutchinson, Anne
Hutchinson's brother-in-law, who had come back from
Massachusetts with Vane, and who had been the deputy-
treasurer.[2] He must have signed resentfully; he had probably
done a great deal of the financial work that was nominally
done by Vane.[3] It has been shown earlier that he had been
sent for on one occasion by the Navy committee when accounts
were to be produced,[4] and he was similarly sent for this very
month of 1648,[5] and the document recording this refers to the
Treasurers of the Navy,[6] which may mean that he was thought
of as joint Treasurer with Vane. Vane had no doubt become
aware of the position of importance which his erstwhile 'menial
servant' had acquired, and his jealousy was well-founded, for
Hutchinson later replaced him as Treasurer, in face of opposition

---

[1] Adm. 7/673, f. 510. 8 February.

[2] Hutchinson had been employed by the Navy and Customs committee to
discover arrears of customs due before the committee was set up. (Bodl. Rawl. A
221, f. 53v; A 222, f. 30v.) He had presumably done this work efficiently, and had
come to be familiar with Navy accounts thereby. He was described as Vane's
'menial servant' in 1644 (*Calendar of the Proceedings of the Committee for the Advance of
Money*, i, 34), but had become 'Clarke to the Treasurer of the Navy' in Vane's 1647
accounts (E 351/2286), and 'Ric. Hutchinson, Esq., Paymaster to the Accomptant',
in 1652. (E 351/2288.)

[3] In Vane's accounts for 1648–9, presented in 1650, there is recorded a payment
to a Navy messenger for 'attending the Pay-Master and Clerks whilst they were
making upp the Treasurer's Accompts'. Hutchinson is described earlier in the
document as Paymaster to Vane. (E 251/2287.)

[4] P. 125.   [5] *CSPD. 1648–49*, 355.   [6] Ibid.

from Vane himself. But it was evidently too difficult for a new-comer to take over the complex duties of deputy-Treasurer, for by February 1649 Hutchinson had regained the position.[1]

During all the period reviewed in this chapter, with the exception of eight months from December 1641 to August 1642, Vane was Treasurer of the Navy. He was also a member of the important committee of Navy and Customs, and of the Admiralty committee for most of the period of its existence. Giles Greene testified that Vane did not use his position as Treasurer to sell appointments, and Vane's accounts show that he had made an almost ludicrously small profit from the office by May 1645, though by December 1650 the position was very different. Though his second and third accounts as Treasurer, and probably the earlier one too, were drawn up by Richard Hutchinson, Vane's first speeches in the Long Parliament show that he was himself expert in Navy finance, and from the beginning spoke on it with authority. He also saw the Navy's inportance in foreign policy, as one would expect him to do, in view of his diplomatic experience. In naval matters, as in other spheres, he supported the transference of power from the king to Parliament, nor did he shrink from reducing the rights of the individual if he judged this necessary for efficiency. He was not the central figure in naval administration during this period—Giles Greene was that—and there were members of the Navy committees who worked very hard, probably indeed harder than Vane, whose political duties absorbed much of his time. If the period before 1640 saw Vane's apprenticeship to naval administration, the years 1640–8 saw him as the journeyman; he was to emerge in 1649–53 as the unequalled master of this field of national policy.

[1] Bodl. Rawl. A 224, ff. 20v, 27v.

CHAPTER VI

The Republican Statesman, 1649–53

V ANE WITHDREW from Parliament some time in December 1648, and did not reappear for about six weeks. Later he gave widely differing reasons for his withdrawal, saying on one occasion that he had objected to putting the king on trial, but on another declaring that he had opposed Pride's Purge.[1] The first is the more likely explanation. However, he was back at the Admiralty Office on 30 January,[2] the very day of the king's execution, and his attendance that day was to prove damning evidence against him at his own trial for treason in 1662. He was named to committees of Parliament on 1 and 2 February,[3] and may therefore have taken his seat there by that time, but he did not appear at the Council of State until 23 February.[4] It is true that Darnall, under-clerk of the House, stated in his evidence at Vane's trial in 1662 that the Council of State was set up on 7 February, and that Vane was a member.[5] But this is one of the many half-truths that his enemies resorted to in order to secure his conviction, for Vane was not appointed a member until 14 February,[6] and the fact that he did not take his seat there for nine days lends support to his protestation at the trial that he was appointed to the Council without his consent.[7]

In the vital political question before this Parliament, that

---

[1] Burton, *Diary*, iii, 174; *Tryal*, 31.
[2] Bodl. Rawl. A 224, f. 8v. 30 January 1649.
[3] *CJ*. vi, 127, 130. [4] *CSPD*. 1649–50, 13.
[5] *Tryal*, 27. Darnall may have had a personal reason for giving evidence against Vane; in 1647 he had obtained the grant of part of the *sub-poena* office in chancery, but had had to surrender it, as it had been previously granted to the elder Vane who had, as already noted (above, p. 10), given it to his eldest son. (*Calendar of the Proceedings of the Committee for the Advance of Money, 1642–56*, ed. M. A. E. Green (1888), i, 62.)
[6] *CJ*. vi, 141. [7] *Tryal*, 31.

of establishing a new representative body, he was early given important responsibilities. On 15 May 1649 he and one other M.P. were given the 'special care' of the work of a committee on regulating elections and putting an end to the Long Parliament.[1] This was one matter with which he did not, or could not, deal with his usual despatch, and the debates were interminable. As chairman of this committee he did report in October 1649 a letter he had received concerning Henry Nevile's election for Abingdon, and this led to an order by the House that the committee should sit every day.[2] The committee did not do so, however, and the Army's impatience with the lack of action on this subject is well known.

But there was much other work for Vane to do. Both the Council of State and Parliament turned to Vane as they had done in previous years, to draft documents to be presented to Parliament or to the public. On 5 January 1650, for instance, the Council instructed Vane, the Commissioners of the Great Seal and three others, to draw up a statement of the 'state of the nation', to be presented to Parliament when the Council's term of office expired on 3 February.[3] On 9 July of that year the 'special care' of the narrative of a battle at Scariffhollis in Ireland was entrusted to him,[4] though Scot actually reported it —probably because this was the month in which Vane was preoccupied with his surrender of the Navy Treasurership and the resulting business transactions. Ten days later, when a bill against atheist opinions was being discussed, he was one of those instructed to withdraw and draft a clause for inclusion in the bill.[5] On 10 September 1650, a committee was instructed to prepare a narrative of the battle of Dunbar, together with an act fixing a day of thanksgiving for the victory, and though Salwey had the 'special care' of this,[6] it was evidently Vane

[1] *CJ.* vi, 210.   [2] Ibid., 305.
[3] *CSPD. 1649–50*, 469. The MS S.P. 25/5 adds the supplementary information.
[4] *CJ.* vi, 438, 440.
[5] Ibid., 443. 19 July. He was teller for omitting a clause from this bill, on 9 August (ibid., 453), but the diurnals have no information on this. E 778(19), *Severall Proceedings . . .* gives an account of the act, but does not mention the clause opposed by Vane. His intervention must have been designed to mitigate the severity of the act which, among other things, imposed a penalty of six months' imprisonment merely for asserting that drunkenness and swearing were not unholy.
[6] *CJ.* vi, 464, 465.

who took charge, for a week later he reported the act and the account of the victory to the House.[1] The drafting committee was small—it consisted of only three men, so that Vane's share was probably considerable, and the 'narrative'[2] is most interesting. It frankly admitted the straits to which Parliament had been reduced before the victory—Vane was said in May 1650 to have spoken very pessimistically of Parliament's situation[3]—and it shrewdly assessed the importance of Dunbar. But no thanks at all were given to Cromwell for the victory; the praise was for God alone, and though Cromwell could hardly in public have disparaged God's efforts in comparison with his own, Vane's attitude may well have rankled. Cromwell may also have resented Parliament's vote about this time that part of the excise receipts assigned to the Army by a 1644 ordinance, should be paid to the Treasurer of the Navy; this was for the use of the fleet which was to recapture Barbados for the Commonwealth, but Cromwell in Scotland had his own pressing need for money.[4]

Irish and Scottish policy was critically important as soon as the Republic was established, for Cromwell was about to embark on the conquest of Ireland, and Scotland had to be kept quiescent. Here too Vane was a leading figure as soon as he appeared at the Council of State in February 1649.[5] On several of the relevant committees Cromwell also sat, and doubtless Vane's zeal was quickened by the knowledge of the importance of their work to his friend. It was natural that when the 'Irish and Scottish committee' was set up in March 1651 Vane should be a member.

This proved to be a very important committee whose purview included a number of subjects not obviously connected with those two countries. The poorly paid clerk, Matthew

---

[1] Ibid., 468.

[2] E 780(8), *Severall Proceedings* . . . E 612(11) has some information on this incident, but has been wrongly bound, and pp. 9 *seq.* are in E 612(3).

[3] Gardiner, *CP.*, i, 277. Vane's remarks were made at dinner with Baron Thorpe, the Recorder of Hull.

[4] *CJ.* vi, 482. 11 October 1650.

[5] *CSPD. 1649–50*, 22, 25, 58, 62, 97, 217, 302, and S.P. 25/2, 18 May 1649. This last is doubtless the letter referred to by the counterfeit *Mercurius Pragmaticus* who noted that Vane was drawing up a conciliatory letter to the Scots. (E 556(25).)

Locke, later Monck's secretary,[1] and the commissary William
Dobbins,[2] who gave evidence at Vane's trial, stated that in 1651
and 1652 they several times saw him sit in the committee for
Irish and Scottish affairs, where he was often in the chair.[3]
Some of Vane's ex-colleagues, such as St John, could have
given fuller particulars of Vane's work on the committees, but
that would have been embarrassing as they had made their
peace with the king. This Irish and Scottish committee[4] soon
absorbed the Ordnance committee[5] of which Vane was also a
member,[6] and an extraordinary variety of business was referred
to it. In 1651, for instance, the Council of State instructed it to
consider the state of Parliament's guard,[7] to consider where
money could be obtained for the Council's expenses, and for
carrying on the affairs of the Commonwealth,[8] to report how
the militia in Kent and adjoining districts should be ordered,[9]
and to deal with the published account of Britain's war with
Portugal, since there were passages in it which the House had
ordered to be kept secret.[10] The Committee examined a man
who had retained £600 of excise money,[11] it reported to the
Council on the amount of ready cash in the Excise Office,[12] and
was instructed to plan the disposal of the £20,000 left in the
hands of the Goldsmiths' Hall committee,[13] which had been
wound up in the previous year. This was in addition to dealing
with numerous petitions,[14] and of course the business one would
expect it to despatch concerning Ireland and Scotland. The
committee seems to have worked hard, sitting, sometimes at
least, at 7 a.m.,[15] and how Vane fitted in the sessions of this
committee with his work on the Council of State, whose meetings he rarely missed until July,[16] and with his unremitting
attendances at the Admiralty committee, it is difficult to see.
He had a great deal of other business to do as well, and his

---

[1] For Locke's later career see below, p. 237.

[2] William Dobbins was a commissary, supplying provisions for Scotland and
Ireland. (*CSPD. 1651-52*, 584, 594, 621.)

[3] *Tryal*, 28.   [4] *CSPD. 1651*, 66-7.   [5] Ibid., 68.   [6] *CJ.* vi, 533.
[7] *CSPD. 1651*, 358.   [8] Ibid., 99.   [9] Ibid., 125.   [10] Ibid., 184.
[11] Ibid., 522.   [12] Ibid., 342.   [13] Ibid., 449.
[14] E.g. ibid., 496, 500.   [15] Ibid., 455.

[16] He went to Lincolnshire for a well-earned holiday in August, but within a
couple of weeks the Council of State were requesting his speedy return. (*CSPD.
1651*, 341.)

complaint to Cromwell in August, that his family duties and his health had suffered, must have been well justified. It is not surprising that when Francis Rous wrote in June 1651 appealing to him to urge Parliament to secure the payment of Pym's debts, still unpaid after more than seven years, he began his letter: 'I know you want not work'.[1] It is typical of Vane that he went straight to the House next day, and secured an order for the release of the estates, assigned by Parliament years before for payment of the debts, but now held by the committee for Compounding.[2]

The energy which he brought to committee work is well illustrated by another matter which eventually found its way to the same 'maid of all work', the Irish and Scottish committee. Parliament in March 1650 referred the question of the nation's postal system to the Council of State, which did nothing about it. On 30 September 1651 Parliament requested a report 'forthwith' from the Council, which hastily set up a sub-committee. Three days passed, and again nothing was done. On 3 October however Vane, Hesilrige and Fielder were added to this sub-committee. It met next day, and fixed days for meeting, to hear claims and propositions for improvement. By 7 November the sub-committee had taken its decision that the posts should be farmed.[3]

In the early months of 1652 the affairs of Scotland called for skilled handling; it was necessary to pacify that conquered country, and re-organize its government, now that Parliament had decided on the union with England. Several men were appointed to do the work, among them Vane and St John, and Rushworth wrote as though these two were in charge, as one would expect.[4] It was Vane who with Fenwick was sent back early in March, when most of the Scottish constituencies had accepted the commissioners' plan, to report it to Parliament.[5] He found time to attend the Admiralty committee on the day

[1] H. Cary, ed., *Memorials of the great civil war* (London, 1842), ii, 277. 16 June.

[2] *CJ.* vi, 589.

[3] *CSPD. 1652–53*, 109–11. Parliament did not accept the decision.

[4] *Calendar of the Proceedings of the Committee for Compounding*, ed. M. A. E. Green (1889–92), i, 535.

[5] C. S. Terry, *The Cromwellian Union* (Edinburgh, 1902), pp. xvii–xliii.

before he made his report to the House,[1] but was too busy to attend the committee again for the next few days; the M.P.s who were also members of the Council of State had the task of drafting the Act of Union, and probably the brunt of this work fell on Vane, who had for years been Parliament's leading 'expert' on Scotland. Certainly it was he who reported the bill to Parliament about a week later.[2]

In addition to being in effect (as will be shown later) First Lord of the Admiralty under the republic, it would seem that Vane was also Foreign Secretary. He had long been interested in foreign affairs, and the king in his letters to Vane had assumed his interest in this subject.[3] But from early in 1649 onwards Vane was a dominating influence in foreign policy. In March 1649 he was one of a sub-committee of the Council to consider to what alliances the king had been committed, and which of these should be continued.[4] The Council asked five of its members, including Vane, to consider whether the Commonwealth ought to send an agent to Spain.[5] This evidently took a long time to decide, for it was two months before the Council resolved to despatch an envoy, and the decision was taken just after Vane came in one day in December;[6] probably he reported from the committee. It was some time before the Spaniards returned the compliment by offering to send an ambassador, but the activity of the Commonwealth Navy changed the attitudes of foreign powers to the new republic. An interesting letter to Cromwell in December 1650 gives a glimpse of Vane's motives and characteristic subtlety. After recounting with pride how Blake's seven ships, which had entered the Mediterranean the month before, were likely to ruin Rupert's fleet and strike terror to the French, Vane told Cromwell that the British victories had caused the Spanish government to send an ambassador.

The Portuguese likewise stands knocking at the door for audience, and we pause upon it a little, that he may be sensible of his error in so rashly engaging against us . . . but by degrees, we shall hear what he will say, and play our game the best we can between them

---

[1] Bodl. Rawl. A 226, f. 98v. 15 March.   [2] *CJ*. vii, 105.
[3] See above, p. 85.   [4] *CSPD. 1649-50*, 36.   [5] Ibid., 329. 3 October.
[6] Ibid., 434-5.

both for the interest of England. The French and Dutch will not sit out long, unless they resolve to sit out altogether, and turn downright enemies, which we hope they will think on twice before they resolve on it.[1]

The *Commons Journals* bear out Vane's words. He was a teller against allowing the Portuguese ambassador to come to London to negotiate a treaty after Blake's victories.[2] He was defeated however on this question, in which Henry Marten was his opponent. About the same time he was named first to a committee to draft an answer to the Spanish ambassador, but Marten had the 'particular care' of it[3]—perhaps the House was more anxious than Vane was to conclude treaties of friendship as speedily as possible.

In the vital negotiations with Holland Vane also played an important part. He had shown interest in the United Provinces as early as 1643,[4] but in 1649 he began to be deeply involved in England's relations with her commercial rival and religious ally. After the murder of Isaac Dorislaus, one of the Commonwealth's envoys at The Hague, who was assassinated by royalists in revenge for his part in the trial of Charles I, Vane had much work to do. He made the arrangements for the funeral, which became a military demonstration.[5] But according to his first biographer he strove to prevent the war with Holland,[6] and certainly when the House divided on the question of sending St John and Strickland as ambassadors-extraordinary to the Netherlands Vane was one of the tellers in favour of the project.[7] Whether he was also the author of the

---

[1] Nickolls, *Original Letters*, 39–40, 41.

[2] *CJ*. vi, 511.   [3] Ibid., 516. 27 December.

[4] It was Vane who moved in 1643 that the Westminster Assembly should be asked to write letters to some ministers of churches in Zeeland and Holland, who would thus learn of 'the artifices and disguises of his majesty's agents in those parts'. (Harl. 165, f. 214v. *CJ*. iii, 317. 22 November.) An entry in the *Commons Journals* for November 1642 records that the two Vanes, Pym and four others were to form a committee to 'consider propositions for a league with Holland', but nothing seems to have come of this. (*CJ*. ii, 865.)

[5] *CSPD. 1649–50*, 131, 137, 144, 147; *CJ*. vi, 209, 212; S.P. 25/2.

[6] [G. Sikes], *The Life and Death of Sir Henry Vane* (London, 1662), 96.

[7] *CJ*. vi, 528. Some thought it was wrong to 'fall at the feet of those that have spurned and abused us', remembering Amboyna and Dorislaus's murder. (Nickolls, op. cit., 55.) Vane was one of the committee to draft the envoys' instructions. (*CSPD. 1651*, 53.)

bold plan of union between the two countries which St John went to Holland to negotiate in April 1651 we do not know.[1] St John later stated that he had been unwilling to go to Holland, but had been compelled to do so,[2] which sounds as though the plan was not his. In January 1651, before St John's mission had been finally decided upon, the Council of State named Vane first to a committee set up to examine the relations between England and Holland,[3] and evidently he took charge, for when the Council wanted the *Magnus Intercursus* of 1496, on which the Dutch view of their rights was partly based, translated into English, the document was in Vane's possession.[4] Early in April, when St John and Strickland were still in Holland, he was ordered to prepare a letter to them from Parliament,[5] a task of some difficulty no doubt, for their reception had been far from encouraging to the supporters of a close alliance.

The negotiations with the Dutch continued to be largely in Vane's hands; he informed the House of the letters from Pauw, the aged Dutch envoy-extraordinary, who was anxiously striving to prevent full-scale war between the two countries,[6] and on 18 June Vane reported the meeting between Pauw and the Council's delegates.[7] On the next day however the Council of State allowed Vane no part in drafting the English reply to the Dutch envoys,[8] and five days later there was a remarkable development, for when the earl of Pembroke reported to Parliament the Council of State's reply to Pauw's representations, Vane acted as teller *against* the Council's statement, which was decisively rejected by the House.[9] A new statement was ordered to be drawn up, was brought into Parliament immediately after prayers next day, and passed, but Vane had had no hand

[1] There is an account of the negotiations in J. Geddes, *The History of the Administration of De Witt* (London, 1879), 170–1. The Dutch agreed to a closer union, but would not give up their treaties of alliance, or surrender the royalist refugees in Holland.

[2] O. St John, *The Case of Oliver St John, Esq.* (London, 1660). E 1035(5).

[3] *CSPD. 1651*, 19.

[4] Ibid., 116. He was ordered to give it to Milton; their first recorded contact had been in March 1649. (Ibid., *1649–50*, 36.)

[5] *CJ.* vi, 554. It is assumed that the younger Vane was named.

[6] *CJ.* vii, 135.   [7] Ibid., 143.   [8] See below, p. 154.

[9] *C.J.* vii, 145. The clerk does not indicate which of the Vanes was acting as teller on this occasion, but as Purefoy was Vane's fellow-teller, it seems more likely to have been the younger—Purefoy is found supporting him on other occasions.

in this. He had absented himself from the Council the day it was discussed there, on 25 June.[1] What is more, he failed to appear either in Parliament, the Council of State, or the Admiralty committee for more than two months, from 1 July onwards.[2] This very public disagreement with the Council requires explanation, and the most likely one seems to be that he, like Cromwell, wanted peace with the Dutch, and thought the Council's reply not conciliatory enough. If he knew that he could not carry the Council with him, this would explain his absence from its meeting on 25 June. It is true that the Council's revised, and surely no less intransigent reply, passed the House without a division when it was brought in next day,[3] but the Council may have rallied its supporters. Certain it is that Vane withdrew from public affairs until 9 September, when he attended a Council meeting,[4] and there is no information of value about him for these two months,[5] though there is an interesting passage in an August letter from the royalist, Sir George Radcliffe, Strafford's friend, who stated that he had heard Vane mentioned as ambassador to Holland.[6] This would tally well with pacific views on Vane's part, but Radcliffe's informant is unknown, and his statement stands quite alone. Vane's absence certainly was unusual. The Admiralty committee was sitting every day,[7] and July and August were critical months for the Commonwealth, with Blake hunting the Dutch East India vessels and Ayscough lying in wait for their ships from the New World, the famous 'Silver Fleet'. It is incomprehensible that Vane should not have been at his post at such a time. There are three possible explanations. Either he was ill, or he was interviewing De Retz in Paris, on the mysterious mission discussed below, or he was deliberately absenting himself in silent protest against a policy of which he disapproved. The last fits in best with Sikes's account of Vane's

---

[1] *CSPD. 1651-52*, xli.

[2] Ibid., xlii; *CJ*. vii, 145 *seq.*; Bodl. Rawl. A 226, ff. 161-94v, *passim*.

[3] *CJ*. vii, 145.   [4] *CSPD. 1651-52*, xliv.

[5] Except that his accounts as Navy Treasurer for 1649-50 were declared on 26 June (E 351/2288), and that Milton's sonnet to Vane belongs to July—was the sonnet a gesture of sympathy?

[6] Radcliffe to Colonel Holles, St Germain, 23 August 1652. HMC. *Bath MSS*, ii, 106.

[7] Bodl. Rawl. A 226, loc. cit.

attitude to the Dutch War, and with what is suspected to have been his policy in 1647, when he had found himself in a minority.[1] A visit to France at this time would have been dangerous[2] (with De Ruyter cruising off Calais with twenty-two warships, and Blake seizing a French squadron early in September), but perhaps not impossible. There is no reference to ill-health on Vane's part at this time, but this is inconclusive. On the whole voluntary withdrawal seems the most likely explanation of this obscure episode.

The occasion for a visit to De Retz could have been the letter of credence from the Prince de Condé for his envoy, which was read in Parliament in March 1652; both letter and emissary were referred to the Council of State.[3] This secret embassy of Vane, known only from the memoirs of the cardinal, who gives it no date,[4] is wrapped in mystery, both as to its purpose and its duration.[5] Vane was hostile at this time to Spain,[6] and may have hoped for some sort of alliance with France directed against Spain, though from De Retz's cryptic account it sounds as though the projected treaty was more an anti-Roman Catholic one. But there is so little information about the incident that one can only speculate.

During the years 1649-51 many letters passed between Cromwell and Vane, though only a few remain. Cromwell wrote to Vane when he wanted to secure Parliament's attention for matters in which he was personally interested,[7] and Vane

---

[1] See above, Chap. IV.

[2] Roger Williams, writing in July, mentions the danger in the Channel from French and Dutch attacks. (Knowles, *Memoir of Roger Williams*, 146.)

[3] *CJ.* vii, 118.

[4] J. F. P. de Gondi, Cardinal de Retz, *Mémoires* (Paris, 1956), 375.

[5] Abbott, *Cromwell*, ii, 525, relying on the Council of State attendances, rightly questions Gardiner's date (October or November 1651) for the De Retz visit, and suggests that Vane may have gone to Paris after his return from Scotland. The Admiralty committee records (Bodl. Rawl. A 225, ff. 70–158; A 226, ff. 1–52v) rule out the 1651 dates, and narrow the 1652 possibilities to April–May, or July–August. Abbott's conjecture that the elder Vane may have been the envoy must be rejected—De Retz states that the envoy was Cromwell's intimate confidant, which the elder Vane never was.

[6] According to the Spanish ambassador, Cardenas. 'In the absence of Harry Vane, who has just set out as commissioner to Scotland, and who is a man of great influence, and moreover very hostile to Spain, I have determined to request an audience from the Council of State.' Guizot, *Cromwell*, i, 468.

[7] *Calendar of the Committee for Compounding*, ii, 1432.

kept Cromwell informed of the news from London.[1] After Dunbar he wrote appreciatively of Cromwell's 'honest and despised army', but in his reference to the Parliament there is both condescension and a hint of his policy of keeping it in session. 'I never knew anything take a deeper and more kindly impression than Dunbar upon the Parliament, who in general have good aims, and are capable of improvement upon such wonderful deliverances as these vouchsafed to them.'[2] His letter of December 1650 with its account of naval victories and policy towards Portugal has already been mentioned. In the spring and summer of 1651, Cromwell wrote several times to Vane requesting supplies for his Scottish campaign;[3] he, like a number of other people, evidently thought that if he wanted Parliament or a committee to deal with some business speedily, Vane was the man to interest. On one occasion the general wrote to his wife: 'Mind Sir Henry Vane of the businesse of my estate.'[4] (The son of the marquis of Worcester was trying to secure from Parliament part of the family property seques-tered on account of his father's delinquency, and assigned to Cromwell.) The case of Christopher Love, the Presbyterian minister involved in a royalist plot, prompted letters to Crom-well from Vane at this time,[5] and early in August 1651 Vane was assuring Cromwell that the men and supplies he had asked for, and more, were being despatched.[6] This letter is an interest-ing one in many ways, for it shows his conscientious attitude to his duties, his assumption that August was 'vacation time', and his impatience with those who were not so quick as himself to see what was needed. It also reveals the friction between some Council or committee members. Another letter passed between the two in August,[7] but if there were any letters after that month they have not survived.

In an oblique style, which he could assume on occasion, he indicated in the letter written on 2 August 1651, before he went on holiday, that there was some difference of opinion between Cromwell and himself. He assured Cromwell that he 'answers your heart's desire in all things, except he be esteemed even

---

[1] Nickolls, op. cit., 17. July 1650.   [2] Ibid., 19. 10 September 1650.
[3] Abbott, op. cit., ii, 402-3, 411-12, 428.   [4] Ibid., 405.
[5] See below, p. 156.   [6] Nickolls, op. cit., 79.   [7] Abbott, op. cit., ii, 447.

by you in principles too high to fathom'. The meaning of this
is not clear; the subjects on which the two men were probably in
disagreement at this time, the army's strength and the continuance of the Rump, could hardly have been referred to in
these terms. It sounds more like a difference on religious
matters. The vital votes on the future of the Rump took place
in Parliament in November 1651[1] and, though there is no
positive evidence that Vane took part in the debate, there
is no reason to doubt the accepted view of his attitude, that he
wished the Rump to continue to sit, and opposed Cromwell's
plan of an early dissolution. He was not one of those M.P.s
and officers who met at Lenthall's house on 10 December to
discuss the future form of government, which indicates that
Cromwell thought his views on the Rump were not shared
by Vane.

His exclusion however in August 1652 from the committee
for the 'new representative' may not have been a deliberate
slight, since he had been absent from London when the Army
officers' petition demanding immediate new elections was
presented, and this may well account for his exclusion from
the committee set up to consider this question.[2] It was this same
committee which was instructed to draw up a bill on the plan
for a new Parliament, but again Vane's exclusion need not
have been so complete as some historians have assumed, for
'all that come, to have voices' was the rule for this committee,
so that Vane could have attended if he chose.[3] During October
Cromwell and the Army officers were having discussions with
M.P.s;[4] almost certainly Vane, as one of the leading men in the
House, would have been there, but there is no evidence on this.
If the late-November vote for the new Council of State, in an
unusually full Parliament, is an index to members' popularity
at the time, Vane's stood high; only Cromwell's, Whitelocke's,
St John's and Rolle's stood higher, and in the case of St John
and Rolle this is hard to understand.[5] In that month Vane was

---

[1] Ibid., 499.   [2] *CJ.* vii, 164. See above, p. 147.   [3] Ibid., 178.
[4] Abbott, op. cit., ii, 584. The diurnals show an awareness that there were
dissensions among the politicians. See E 799(17) and (22).
[5] *CJ.* vii, 220. 24 November 1652. Whitelocke had many friends, and obviously
was popular. Reynolds spoke of St John as a favourite of Parliament (Burton, iv,
297), but was referring to an incident early in the Long Parliament. From Claren-

almost continuously occupied with the Navy finance and administration, and is only twice recorded to have interested himself in other subjects.[1] Early in December the new Navy commissioners were appointed, and he was immersed in naval matters until the end of March 1653.

On 6 January 1653, when Vane was working with great energy to strengthen the Navy, and was in fact at Chatham, responsibility for the committee drawing up the bill for a new Parliament was transferred from John Carew, to whom it had earlier been assigned, to Major General Harrison. Carew was Vane's fellow-commissioner for the Navy. Like him Carew was at Chatham, and possibly this was the excuse for the change of convener. Both men would still have been entitled to attend the committee under the 'all that come, to have voices' rule, but both were working hard to supply the Navy's needs, much of the time at Chatham, and cannot have had time to spare for the Parliament bill. On 30 March however, with Blake's victory off Portland safely behind him, Vane had time to give to other matters, and was in the House when the bill 'for a new representative' was discussed[2]—the House had gone back, during the anxious days of the Dutch War, to debating this subject once a week only. When the House divided on the question of fixing a high property qualification (estate to the value of £200 a year) for the franchise, Vane and Bond were tellers for *not* putting the question.[3] Defeated on this, they were tellers in favour of this very restrictive franchise. Presumably Vane had guessed he would be defeated, in the very thin House,[4] on the

don's description of St John one would not expect him to command a large following, but he may have obtained credit as a moderate. (See his letter to Cromwell, Nickolls, op. cit., 26, and St John's own account of his attitude at the time, E 1035(5).) But why Rolle?

[1] The treaty with Portugal (*CJ*. vii, 223) and ex-lord mayor Gurney's fine. (Ibid., 214.)

[2] *CJ*. vii, 244. Abbott, who stated (op. cit., 571) that Harrison replaced Vane in charge of the bill, failed to notice the August committee. For Vane and Carew at Chatham, see below, p. 182, and Bodl. Rawl. A 227, f. 9v. Harrison was absent from the Council for the whole of the second half of February (Abbott, op. cit., ii, 619), and it seems unlikely therefore that he really took charge of the bill.

[3] *CJ*. vii, 273.

[4] For the numbers in the House at this time see Masson, *Milton*, iv, 398–9. Masson says that after December 1652 a House of over 50 was a good one. 38 voted in this division.

franchise clause, and hence his opposition to putting the question.

There are several indications that by 1650 Henry Marten was among Vane's political opponents. According to *Mercurius Pragmaticus* Marten defended and Vane attacked Lilburne at a Council of State meeting in March 1650.[1] Certainly Marten and Vane were tellers for opposite sides in divisions in Parliament in September and December 1650.[2] And when Parliament voted on the composition of the new Council of State in January 1650, though old Sir Henry Vane's name was one of the five at the top of the list in the secret ballot of the House, the nominations had to be confirmed by open voting, and in this old Sir Henry was rejected, Marten being one of the tellers against him.[3] This may well have been the occasion recounted by John Aubrey[4] on which Marten criticized the elder Vane in Parliament; on no other name was there a division, so that some special attack must have been made on the old man. It will be remembered that the younger Vane himself did not escape a barbed comment from Marten: 'If young Sir Harry lives to be old, he will be old Sir Harry.' This was a bold speech to make when the younger Vane was at the height of his power. But Aubrey gives no date. The quarrel between the committee of the Navy (the financial committee) and what became known as the 'Merchants committee' may have added fuel to the flames. The latter committee had been set up after the king's execution to purge the Navy and the customs service of royalists, and to abolish useless offices in the two branches of government administration. In fact, so John Hollond, the Surveyor of the Navy alleged, the committee members used their authority to give positions in the customs, which were profitable, to their friends and relations.[5] Such charges were freely bandied about

---

[1] E 596(12). 19–26 March. ' "No faith with Lilburne", cries young Vane.'

[2] *CJ*. vi, 468. 17 September; 511. 18 December.

[3] Ibid., 369. Sir William Armyn, Vane's friend, was one of the tellers for Vane senior.

[4] *Brief Lives*, ed. O. L. Dick (1962), 266.

[5] Hollond, *Discourses*, 117, 120, 122. (Oppenheim wrongly identified the committee of the Navy (financial) with the committee of Merchants, 'The Navy of the Commonwealth, 1649–60', *EHR*, xi, 571. The nomenclature of the various Navy committees is complicated and often defeated even contemporaries. For the quarrel between the two committees, see *CJ*. vi, 400, 401. Ap. 1650.) Marten owned a ship

in this period, but Parliament was evidently persuaded to take a critical view of the committee of Merchants, for it abolished it on 23 April 1650. Marten was a member of the Merchants' committee.

After his return from Scotland in 1652 Vane clashed several times with Marten. On the first occasion the subject under discussion was the complicated one of the Holland Fen dispute. The earl of Lindsey had begun the drainage of the fen in the 1630s, and in 1641 the Fen-men had taken forcible possession of the lands already drained. Lindsey had sold part of his interest to Sir William Killigrew, who appeared as spokesman for those who had promoted the scheme and who wrote numerous pamphlets in the 1640s and 1650s on their behalf. Killigrew wanted the restoration of the land seized by the Commoners, and the completion of the whole project. The Fen-men repudiated the promoters' title to the land, and wanted no more than a 'settlement' between themselves and Lindsey's group. A committee of Parliament of which John Goodwin was chairman had sensibly recommended in 1649 that the parties to the dispute should come to a settlement, but the Commoners had responded by offering to negotiate on the basis of their own admission to the scheme as partners. Killigrew indignantly refused, claiming that he and Lindsey had spent thousands of pounds already, and the Commoners would be receiving a share of the land which Lindsey and himself had paid to drain. Petitions, deputations and full debates at a large parliamentary committee during 1651 followed, but the bill drawn up on the lines desired by Killigrew was not brought in until April 1652, and it looks as though he had waited for Vane's return from Scotland. It is clear what Vane's policy was; he supported Killigrew and the promoters, who wanted to regain the drained lands and to continue with the project, as opposed to the Commoners, who wanted their title to the recovered land established, but no more drainage undertaken. Vane's position was weak, for the Fen-men made great play with the fact that Killigrew, Lindsey and their partners had been active royalists, whereas the Fen-men had nearly all

(the *Marten*, Bodl. Rawl. A 221, f. 7v), had belonged to earlier Admiralty committees (BM. Add. 9305, *passim*), and knew something of naval affairs.

fought for Parliament. Vane was therefore roundly defeated, and Marten (who with Lilburne had been championing the Fen-men) was with John Goodwin authorized to bring in a bill merely 'settling' the fens already drained.[1] Whether Vane, when he acquired so much of the earl of Lindsey's other property,[2] acquired also his title to the drained fenlands, is not known, but it seems probable, though Killigrew never mentions Vane's name. Killigrew made out a strong case for completing the project, but the Fen-men's arguments were also convincingly presented in the contemporary pamphlets, and Vane may have been moved either by private or public interest, or both. It is to be noted however that he was once more championing the less democratic side.[3]

He was Marten's opponent on a number of other subjects. On 21 May 1652, for instance, Hesilrige and Marten wanted to continue a debate on the Irish settlement, while Vane was a teller against this.[4] Probably he was anxious to get on with the urgent Navy business for that day, and did not want this delayed by a long and wearisome debate on religious toleration for Ireland. He prevailed, and the debate was postponed for ten days. On the day of the resumed debate Vane found himself in the same lobby as Marten, for both wanted religious toleration for Ireland, and the House accepted this bold policy.[5] But on other matters they continued to differ, for instance over the transfer of the powers of the old committee of Indemnity to the Goldsmiths' Hall committee.[6] On 19 June there was the clash mentioned above, in the Council of State, on the negotiations with Holland; the Council decided that a three-man committee, and not the committee for Foreign Affairs, which had been in charge of the negotiations, was to draw up the second answer to Pauw, the Dutch envoy.[7] Vane had been the leading figure on the Foreign Affairs committee in this matter,[8]

---

[1] *CJ.* vii, 118. 9 April 1652.   [2] See below, pp 171–2.

[3] The 1649–52 phase of the Lindsey Level dispute can be followed chronologically in: BM. 725 c. 37; 669, f. 19 (63); 515, f. 21 (10x and 10); 669, f. 19 (59) and (62).

[4] *CJ.* vii, 134. Vane had returned to Parliament on 14 May (ibid., 132). There was a good attendance (66) in the House on 21 May, so Vane's attitude cannot have been due to a desire to have a fuller House.

[5] Ibid., 137.   [6] Ibid., 144.   [7] *CSPD. 1652–53*, 298.   [8] Ibid., 297.

but Marten, Bradshaw and Scot formed the new committee, and Vane was pointedly excluded. At the critical debate in the House, five days later, Marten was one of the tellers against Vane.[1]

Vane was always on the alert to prevent political enemies of the Commonwealth from undermining its security. According to *Pragmaticus*, it was Vane and his father who moved for an act prohibiting royalists from staying within twenty miles of London.[2] The Council of State instructed Vane in September 1650 to report to Parliament the Council's view that the residence in England of the wives of prominent royalists then abroad was dangerous.[3] The attack on Barbados, for which he asked Parliament for money in the same month, was said to be due to the desire to prevent royalists from seeking asylum there.[4]

The same ruthlessness to political opponents which Vane had shown to those involved in Waller's plot in 1643, and to Holles and his friends in 1646, was evinced again in 1651. The popular young Presbyterian preacher, Christopher Love, was one of several ministers implicated in plotting a London rising, part of a nation-wide royalist conspiracy. Love was deeply involved, but he was only 30, his wife was expecting a child, and his trial was far from just.[5] In spite of these mitigating factors, Vane relentlessly opposed every attempt, in Parliament and out, to save Love's life. When it was proposed that Love's case should be postponed, Vane was a teller against this.[6] Two days later, after Love had been condemned, petitions on Love's behalf poured into the House, and it was moved that the execution should be postponed for a month, but Vane opposed this also. Love's sympathizers now suggested banishment, as an alternative to execution. Vane, still inflexible, prevented this

---

[1] *CJ.* vii, 145.   [2] E 595(8). 12–19 March 1650.
[3] *CSPD. 1650*, 352. 23 September.
[4] C. Wilson, *Profit and Power* (London, 1957), 45.
[5] E 790(1) *Mr. Love's Case*. See also E 790(2) *A Short Plea for the Commonwealth*, and E 790(5) *A Vindication of Mr. Love*. Love said that his envoy to Cromwell was arrested, and his letters to Cromwell seized. He prophesied that 'those who have gotten power into their hands by policy, and use it by cruelty, they will lose it with ignominy', and, in what must have been a warning to Vane, declared: 'I see men hunger after my flesh, and thirst after my blood, which will hasten my happiness and their ruine.' (E 790(1).)
[6] *CJ.* vi, 599. 9 July.

too.[1] He had had a safe majority on each division, and wanted to have Love's fate settled beyond all doubt: he was therefore a teller *for* putting the motion that Love should be pardoned, for he knew it would be lost. Love's friends abandoned the struggle for the time being; they did not even call for a division, and the motion was negatived,[2] though four days later, in the teeth of opposition from Vane, they secured the reprieve of one month, after petitions from Love and his wife had been read.[3] Vane had twice written to Cromwell, warning him against any clemency to Love,[4] and in August the minister was executed. Neither the Commonwealth Government, nor Vane, can have enhanced their reputation by their attitude to this famous case.

It is clear that in the period 1649 to 1653 Marten and Vane were at odds with one another, and probably Marten's support for the Leveller doctrines which he had championed for several years accounts for this. Certainly it would explain Vane's attitude to the Lindsey Fen dispute, and would be consonant with his support for a property franchise. There are hints also in the contemporary Press that Vane was hostile to Lilburne. Vane did not however, in spite of Lilburne's attacks, pursue him vindictively—Vane might have said, like Richelieu, that his enemies were those of the State. Though his father had been vehemently criticized in Lilburne's 1649 pamphlets,[5] Vane was not present when Lilburne's case first came before the Council of State in September 1649, and on succeeding days preferred to attend the Admiralty committee and to see to other business rather than to hear Lilburne's case debated.[6] By 1651 he was at odds with his old friend Hesilrige, which is unexpected, but the Rhode Island dispute may account for this.[7]

Vane was determined to defend the Commonwealth against

---

[1] Ibid., 603.   [2] Ibid.   [3] Ibid.   [4] Nickolls, op. cit., 84.

[5] *Legall Fundamentall Liberties* E 560(14); *An impeachment of High Treason* E 568(20).

[6] He was absent from the morning session of 19 September, though it is true that he attended in the afternoon. (S.P. 25/3.) When Lilburne's case came up again on 20 and 22 October, Vane was not at the Council. He attended an Admiralty committee meeting on the 20th (S.P. 18/3), and on the night of the 22nd he read to the Council of State the account of the nation's finances which he delivered to Parliament on the 23rd, and which must have taken him considerable time to prepare. This probably explains his non-attendance at the Council of State on the 22nd. (*CSPD. 1649-50*, 357. The MS (S.P. 25/3) gives 'night'.)

[7] See below, Chap. IX.

its enemies, both within and without. He was probably aware that the régime was insecurely based in the loyalties of the nation, and this would explain the ruthlessness with which he pursued Christopher Love. Probably he did not realize the odium he was thereby incurring, or perhaps his own popularity was not a matter of moment to him. In December 1651 when a parliamentary committee advised that only beer or ale brewed by common brewers or sold by inn-keepers should be excisable,[1] Vane was one of the tellers against the proposal. It would have needed an army of officials to check on all the home-brewed beer in the country, and Vane was roundly defeated. If he cared about his own popularity, he would hardly have taken the attitude he did on this trivial matter.

During the 1649–53 period no other member of the Long Parliament took a leading part in so many aspects of government. Perhaps Marten comes nearest to Vane in this respect, but Marten was not interested in Scottish affairs or in the colonies. Vane directed, or helped to direct, so many of the Council's and Parliament's activities that he must have been the most important single member of the Parliament. Planning with Roger Williams how to counter Hesilrige's schemes for Rhode Island, drafting the union with Scotland, directing relations with Portugal and Holland, probably with Spain also, giving unremitting attention to Navy administration, it is again difficult to see how Vane could possibly accomplish all the work he did. With it went a multitude of minor tasks, uncompleted or too unimportant to consider here, such as meetings in connexion with riots in York[2] or Kent,[3] and the early stages of the plan for co-ordinating all the revenue into one receipt,[4] one of the Commonwealth's most urgent problems. Vane's prodigious industry always compels one's admiration.

---

[1] *CJ*. vi, 50. 12 December. There must have been some ambiguity about the 1650 ordinance mentioned by Dr Ashley. (*Financial and Commercial Policy of the Protectorate* (London, 1962), 68.)

[2] *CSPD. 1649–50*, 233.   [3] Ibid., 172. S.P. 25/2.   [4] S.P. 25/3; *CJ*. vi, 310.

CHAPTER VII

The Admiralty Committee of the Council of State, February 1649 to December 1652

As WE HAVE SEEN, the first indication that Vane had returned to his previous duties after his absence from public affairs in December 1648 and January 1649 is his signature on a Navy committee letter on the very day of the king's execution.[1] He signed other Navy orders on 10 and 14 February 1649,[2] and it may be an indication of his concern for the Navy that he appeared at the Council the day after Parliament had assigned to that body responsibility for the admiralty function of the Navy,[3] for Vane arrived at the afternoon session, at which the vital matter of the command at sea was discussed, and much other naval business also.[4] Professor Abbott however attributed Vane's attendance to the fact that Parliament had that day revised the oath required by the Engagement,[5] and members had no longer to express approval of the king's execution. He was at once given important work to do for the Navy. William Jessop and Robert Coytmore, the secretaries of the Admiralty committee which had lapsed in May 1648, brought the old committee's records with them, and Vane, Colonel Valentine Walton, Cromwell's brother-in-law, and Thomas Scot had the task of reading them, evidently to decide what powers should be given to the three newly appointed colonels, Robert Blake, Richard Deane and Edward Popham.[6]

Henceforward Vane's arrival at the Council of State was

---

[1] See above, p. 139. [2] Rawl. A 224, ff. 8v, 15v, 18.
[3] CJ. vi, 149. Warwick resigned as Lord High Admiral the same day.
[4] CSPD. 1649–50, 13. [5] Abbott, Cromwell, ii, 19.
[6] See above, n. 4, and S.P. 25/1.

generally, though not invariably, the signal for naval business to be discussed, and it seems as though the Council was spurred into action for improving the Navy as soon as he began to attend. Certainly *Mercurius Pragmaticus*, which in February 1649 was referring to the Navy as 'Miles Corbet's fleet',[1] and in early April was asserting that Parliament had no ships ready to go to sea,[2] was writing in mid-May as though it was Vane who was striving to produce a fleet to defend the Commonwealth.[3] A spate of letters on naval matters began to be despatched from the Council after he made his appearance there,[4] and much naval business fell to him.

On 5 March 1649, for instance, Vane, Walton and two others were instructed to meet the Navy commissioners on the following day about preparing eight ships for sea. They did so, and a letter from the Council the very next day instructed the commissioners to put carpenters to work.[5] (*Mercurius Pragmaticus* had early notice of this activity and reported that sailors were being 'pressed' into the Navy's service all the next week.[6]) But meanwhile the Council of State had evidently decided that it was a waste of time for the whole Council to debate Navy affairs, and on 12 March took the important step of appointing Vane, Walton and the London alderman Rowland Wilson as a committee of three to sit daily on Admiralty affairs.[7] It looks as though it was Vane who recommended Coytmore as secretary to the three-man Admiralty committee, for Coytmore's appointment followed immediately after Vane's arrival at the afternoon session next day.[8] A committee of three would hardly

---

[1] E 545(15). 20–7 February. Corbet was one of the key members of the Navy and Customs committee, and his name is often coupled with Greene's in the *Diurnalls*. The Admiralty committee had lapsed when Warwick was appointed admiral in May 1648, Greene disappeared from public affairs at Pride's Purge, and Corbet and the Navy and Customs committee took responsibility for naval matters generally for a few weeks. Corbet continued to report from the financial committee for some months after the February committee of Council was established, but was then sent to Ireland. (*CJ*. vi, 161 (10 March), 234 (16 June *et al.*))

[2] E 549(13). 27 March–3 April.   [3] E 555(10). 7–14 May.
[4] *CSPD. 1649–50*, 14 *seq*.   [5] Ibid. 28. S.P. 25/2.
[6] E 548(3). 13–20 March.
[7] *CSPD. 1649–50*, 34. Coytmore evidently considered that this three-man committee was a continuation of the old Admiralty committee set up in 1645. (Ibid., 346.)
[8] Ibid., 36.

need two secretaries, and Jessop's appointment was terminated.[1] On 21 March Vane on instructions from the Council gave a major report to Parliament on the Fleet's state of readiness. The new Admiralty committee was well aware of the importance of incentives to the Navy, and in this speech Vane dealt with an increase in the pay of officers at sea.[2]

He made another report on the Navy two days later,[3] and on the following day, when the House debated the important question of the new tax assessments (on which the Navy was largely to depend for financial support), Vane was in the chair at a Grand Committee,[4] for the first time in his career. The Council of State did not sit as usual that day; evidently the members' attendance at the Commons was considered vital. At the end of March the Council took the decision to have five new ships built.[5] This meant finding ready money, and someone solved the problem by suggesting that the fines of the royalists who had taken part in the 1648 rising in South Wales, and which had been allocated to the Army, should instead be handed over for the temporary use of the Navy.[6] Vane had come early that day, and it was he who was instructed to report to Parliament on the plan, and probably therefore he suggested it. Parliament agreed, and that very same day Vane was reporting back to the Admiralty committee of the Council on the matter[7] —one more instance of his speed in administration. The Council had been concerned at intervals for some weeks with the act brought in by Corbet's Navy committee, for the 'encouragement' of seamen, and the minutes for 14 April record a resolution: 'that the Gentlemen of this Counsel doe endeavour on Monday next to procure the reading of the act which is to be brought in by Sir Henry Vane concerning the amendment of the act for the encouragement of seamen'.[8] The Council

---

[1] He found employment with the Goldsmiths' Hall committee. See below for a suggested reason why the Council preferred Coytmore.

[2] CSPD. 1649-50, 48.   [3] CJ. vi, 171.   [4] Ibid., 172.

[5] Ibid., 59. Printed in the calendar as 'fire-ships' but the MS has 'five', and subsequent references confirm this reading.

[6] CSPD. 1649-50, 59; CJ. vi, 176. Cromwell intervened, and secured the return of the money to the Army. (Abbott, op. cit., ii, 67.) The later hostility between the two men may have had one of its roots in service rivalry.

[7] CSPD. 1649-50, 51.

[8] S.P. 25/2. Deane, writing to the Speaker a few days later to urge the passing

members were evidently successful—Vane reported to the
House on the subject on the 16th, and the amendments were
passed next day. Vane's act differed from Corbet's in the
important particular that it provided financial rewards, and
medals, for those who distinguished themselves in an action
at sea, and one-tenth of the proceeds from captured enemy ships
was to be set aside for this purpose.[1]

In one of his important speeches in March he had persuaded
the House to maintain the summer Fleet in service for eight
months instead of the customary six,[2] but on 23 April he
reported some difficulties with the commissioners of customs
over the money for the extra two months, and the Council had
to authorize letters of credit.[3] Vane, evidently feeling that not a
day should be lost, instructed Coytmore, immediately the
Council's order had been passed, to write to the Navy commissioners for an estimate of what money would be needed to fit
out three of the four 'great ships' on which the carpenters had
earlier been set to work.[4] Coytmore, in this letter to the commissioners, wrote, not for the last time, as though Vane constituted the whole Admiralty committee, and made no mention
of Walton or Wilson.

On 22 June a letter reflecting the Council's pride in putting
such a great fleet to sea, as by its strenuous efforts it had
succeeded in achieving, went out to the three admirals.[5] Vane
was at the Council when it was decided that the letter should
be sent, and it would be interesting to know who drafted it, for
the masterly final letter is much superior to the Council's brief
outline.[6] The emphasis on finance—the Council doubted,

of this act, thought the act was in Vane's hands. (J. B. Deane, *Life of Richard
Deane* (London, 1870), 400–2.)

[1] *CJ.* vi, 187, 188. Vane's act is a very long one, and must have taken some time
to draft; he may have been working on it on 14 April, when he did not attend
the Council meeting. Vane's act is in *A.O.I.* ii, 66–75, Corbet's, ibid., 9–13.

[2] *CJ.* vi, 171, 23 March.   [3] S.P. 25/2.

[4] *CSPD. 1649–50*, 107. The Navy commissioners at this period were also devoted
and efficient (Oppenheim, *A History of the Administration of the Royal Navy*, 347), and
Vane reported their estimate back to Parliament only three days later; the Council
had already considered their figures, and on the 26th instructed Vane to inform
Parliament of the importance of sending out the ships—he did so the same day.
(S.P. 25/2. 26 April.)

[5] *CSPD. 1649–50*, 202–3.

[6] The Council's instructions were: 'That a letter be written to the generals at

understandably, whether the country would be able to shoulder a similar expense in future years—could well have come from Vane, and the description of 'our own forces at sea' as 'so many good ships . . . as have not formerly been set out in any one year',[1] is certainly a tribute to his efforts.

On 14 July Vane wrote to Colonel Richard Deane, one of the three admirals appointed to command the Fleet some five months before, discussing Navy finance with his usual authority.[2] Deane passed Vane's letter to Colonel Popham, Deane's colleague, who thereupon wrote somewhat sharply of Vane's under-estimate of the Fleet's financial needs.[3] But this did not prevent Vane from realizing that Popham's judgement was to be relied upon in the matter of victualling the Fleet off the Irish coast, and he wrote next day to the Navy commissioners to have the previous estimate revised.[4] The Navy commissioners, having been rapped over the knuckles, for the original mistake in the estimate was theirs, complained to Popham for reporting their error to the Council of State, and not first of all to themselves. Popham's reply is instructive. 'I only wrote a private letter to Sir Henry Vane, desiring his opinion, as a person best able to rectify a mistake in point of money . . . had I known you could have given me better satisfaction than Sir Henry Vane, I should not have applied to him.'[5]

That Vane was having to 'manage' the Council of State itself in the interests of the Fleet is clear from one of his letters to Popham. Characteristically he replied on the day he received Popham's. 'If you and Col. Deane do not write to the Council

sea to let them know how much it concerns the State that the utmost improvement there may be of ther present fleet . . . least if ther fleet be not broken this summer they [the royalists] may prove very prejudiciall to trade. To desire them to doe what they can for that purpose but to leave the manner to them upon the place.' (S.P. 25/2. 21 June.)

[1] See above, p. 161 n. 5.   [2] HMC. *Leyborne-Popham MSS*, 1899, 21.   [3] Ibid.
[4] That the letter, ostensibly from the Admiralty committee (*CSPD. 1649–50*, 240), was actually from Vane, is shown by Coytmore's letter to Popham of 19 July (HMC. *Leyborne-Popham MSS*, 22) and is another instance of Vane's acting as though he were the whole Admiralty committee. For Vane's belief in giving the men on the spot a free hand, see *CSPD. 1649–50*, 311, 319, 420, and below. He was also prompt in carrying out what they thought necessary. See Popham's letter to Vane requiring £3000 to be sent to him in *specie*, which the Council of State at once did. (Ibid., 227, and HMC. *Leyborne-Popham MSS*, 20.)
[5] *CSPD. 1649–50*, 248. 25 July.

of State', he wrote, 'that care be taken to provide monies timely to pay off the mariners' wages against their coming in we shall be exceedingly to seek . . . the Council of State may be slow if they be not quickened by you.' His shrewdness is shown in the advice he gave to Popham, to 'let our winter guard be out and this summer's service first be over before you mention the next summer's fleet, lest we be overwhelmed by the thought of charge before we be able to overcome it'.[1]

In August Coytmore was again writing as though Vane were not merely the Admiralty committee but could speak for the whole Council of State.[2] Ten days later the Navy commissioners, who were reluctant to cut down the trees in the royal park at Theobalds, in Hertfordshire, wrote to the Admiralty committee about this. Coytmore replied: 'The Admiralty committee had risen before yours came, but Sir Henry Vane wonders you should boggle in cutting elm timber in Theobalds Park, as you are empowered thereto by Parliament, and wishes you to go in hand with speed.'[3] Vane did not wait to consult his two fellow-members about this, though the Admiralty committee met next day, and he was present.[4] Admittedly he was sure of his facts.[5]

Vane believed in taking an August holiday and, as often before, he did not carry out his official duties for a few days in August and September 1649. He did not attend the Council of State from 25 August to 4 September; he ought perhaps to have been preparing his accounts as Treasurer of the Navy, for Parliament had called for them on 3 August,[6] but as he did not present them for another fifteen months, evidently he did not allow this task to interrupt his holiday.

A letter from Coytmore shows that Vane could differ in opinion from the Council on occasion. Captain Penrose, of the ship *Mary Rose*, had been ordered by the Council of State to convoy merchant ships to Spain; he had made an excuse for not doing this, which the Council had accepted.[7] Vane however did not 'take well' from Penrose the assertion that his ship was foul and in want of stores.[8] It is of interest in this

[1] HMC. *Leyborne-Popham MSS*, 22.   [2] *CSPD. 1649-50*, 276.
[3] Ibid., 288. 23 August.   [4] Rawl. A 224, f. 101v.   [5] *CSPD. 1649-50*, 288.
[6] *CJ*. vi, 274.   [7] *CSPD. 1649-50*, 321.
[8] HMC. *Leyborne-Popham MSS*, 41.

connexion that convoys had been difficult to obtain, and expensive, but in 1649 were supplied free of charge for the first time.[1] Was this also Vane's work?

In November 1649 the Council of State took an important decision, behind which Vane's hand is almost certainly to be seen. The generals-at-sea had written that there was a great need for a winter guard for the coasts.[2] On 14 November the Council of State, at a meeting which Vane attended, entrusted the task of organizing the guard to its Admiralty committee.[3] The Admiralty committee met next day,[4] and on 16 November the Council took the important decision to build six more new frigates.[5] The Council left it to the Admiralty committee to decide where and how the vessels should be built, and the committee acted with its usual despatch, meeting that very same day, and promptly ordering Peter and Christopher Pett, the well-known master shipwrights, to attend three days later.[6] This meeting with the Petts was on Friday, and on Saturday Vane attended both the Council and the Admiralty committee.[7] He was, understandably, feeling the pressure of work, and on the Monday he made another attempt to get his brother Charles installed as deputy-Treasurer of the Navy.[8] But again Charles Vane cannot have mastered the work, for in January 1650 he was sent off to Portugal as British Agent, and Hutchinson continued to be an important figure in the Navy office.[9]

Vane was at Council of State meetings, and probably Admiralty committees too, during the following days, and on his arrival at the Council on 27 November a number of Navy matters were discussed.[10] The problem of paying for the six new ships was formidable, and probably it was the Admiralty committee which suggested selling old ships to pay for the new ones. It was Vane who was instructed to ask Parliament for the necessary authority.[11] Generally only when Vane attended the

[1] Hollond, *Discourses*, 355.   [2] *CSPD. 1649–50*, 364.

[3] *CJ.* vi, 32; *CSPD. 1649–50*, 391; S.P. 25/3.   [4] *CSPD. 1649–50*, 395.

[5] Ibid., 396; S.P. 25/3. 16 November.   [6] *CSPD. 1649–50*, 396.

[7] Ibid., 397; S.P. 25/3. 17 November.   [8] S.P. 25/3. 19 November.

[9] See above, pp. 137–8.

[10] He came in after item 6; items 7, 8, 9 and 10 were Navy matters. (S.P. 25/3. 27 November.)

[11] S.P. 25/2. 27 November.

Council of State was Navy business brought up; in his absence Navy matters were not dealt with.[1]

On one matter about this time Vane did not act with his usual speed. Coytmore wrote to Colonel Popham in September asking Popham to use his influence with Vane, Walton, and Popham's other friends, to secure Coytmore an adequate allowance,[2] but it was two months later before the Admiralty committee decided to recommend an increase in its secretary's salary[3] and even then it was only a third or less of what Coytmore had hoped for. Coytmore was not particularly efficient, and was somewhat self-important.[4] The Admiralty committee's 'drive' did not spring from him.

In the latter part of December 1649 Vane continued to attend the Admiralty committee, though not always the Council of State; on 17 and 18 December for instance he was present at the committee, though not at the Council meetings on those days.[5] On 20 December he came in to the Council with a letter about the unauthorized felling of timber in the Forest of Dean by the woodmen of Herefordshire, a matter which was of importance to the Navy.[6] During the rest of the month there was comparatively little Navy business transacted in the Council, except that the accounts for the next summer's guard were presented to the House; this was done by Walton, who had

[1] On 3 December, when Vane was there, a number of Navy items were discussed, but on 5 December, when he was absent, no Navy business was considered. (*CSPD. 1649-50*, 421, 425-6). On 8 December he came at item 5, when Admiralty matters began (S.P. 25/3; *CSPD. 1649-50*, 429-30), though when Vane was away on 1 December one or two Navy items were discussed. (Ibid.. 417.) No important decisions were taken however.

[2] HMC. *Leyborne-Popham MSS*, 37.

[3] *CSPD. 1649-50*, 395. 15 November. The increase was confirmed by the Council of State about a month later. (Ibid., 433, 434.) Coytmore did not get the increase he had hoped for, £150 or £200, but only £50 p.a.

[4] Popham to Vane: 'It is not unusual for Mr. Coytmore to mistake "winter" for "summer" guard.' (HMC. *Leyborne-Popham MSS*, 21.) Deane complained that Coytmore was opening letters he had no authority to read. (Ibid., 24.) Probably Coytmore had been retained as secretary rather than Jessop because Jessop was in the '30s very much Warwick's man, and had been the earl's secretary. After the Restoration Coytmore gave evidence against the regicides.

[5] S.P. 18/3, f. 101. (Letter signed by Vane.) *CSPD. 1649-50*, lxvii-lxix.

[6] Vane came in at item 8, and items 9 and 10 are concerned with the timber. (S.P. 25/2. 20 December.) Information about the incident had been sent to Vane (*CSPD. 1649-50*, 464); and one can assume therefore that he raised it.

become the key figure on the Navy and Customs committee.[1] Walton in fact made an important contribution to the work of the Commonwealth Navy, and Vane did not carry the burden alone, either at this time or later. In the period March 1649 to February 1650 122 letters from the Admiralty committee were signed by Vane, 91 by Walton, and 60 by Colonel John Jones[2] (an active member of the Council of State, a future son-in-law of Cromwell, and a regicide). Probably the figures roughly reflect the respective shares of responsibility shouldered by the three men.

In 1650, for an unknown reason, the clerk keeping the minute book of the Admiralty committee began to record, on 26 February, the names of those attending the meetings,[3] and he continued to do so until the series of volumes ends in August 1653. From these entries, as the accompanying table demonstrates,[4] it is quite clear that Vane was the mainspring of this committee. He is shown to have attended 114 meetings for which attendances were recorded during the period 26 February–31 December 1650, and to have signed Admiralty committee letters on 12 other days. His total attendances for the period, for he must have been at least briefly present on the days on which he signed letters, were 126. Dennis Bond, the member for Dorchester, who was playing a very prominent part in parliamentary affairs at this time, attended at least 67 meetings of the committee, and, in addition, signed 10 letters; from August 1650 onwards his record of attendances is impressive. The third highest attendance was Walton's, with 57 recorded attendances and letters signed on 8 other days. Thomas Challoner was nearly as reliable—the clerk records his presence at 42 meetings, and he signed letters on 16 other days. But the attendances of none of the three compare with Vane's, and it is clear beyond doubt that he must have been the person on whom most of the committee work devolved.

---

[1] Ibid., 451. *CJ.* vi, 339. 28 December.   [2] *CSPD. 1649–50*, xxii.
[3] The minute-book for 25 February 1649–19 October 1650 is S.P. 25/123. This MS is numbered by pages. If there was any idea that a written record of attendances would encourage committee members to appear more regularly at the meetings, the Council were disappointed—the numbers attending did not increase. After 26 February 1649 the clerk does not so often indicate who signed the committee's letters.   [4] Appendix E.

The Council of State may indeed have thought either that the Admiralty committee was too hard-worked, or that Vane had too much influence on it, for the Council decided that the committee quorum was to be three (after March 1650),[1] and not two, as in 1649; they also enlarged the new committee to eight members.[2] Incidentally, the standing order about the quorum was not taken too seriously, and on two occasions when only Vane and Walton were present, they still proceeded to transact the business.[3] The committee was somewhat informal in another way also; in 1649 and 1650 Dennis Bond signed 5 letters, and attended at least one other committee meeting, before he was officially appointed to the committee![4]

Obviously the work done by the committee must have been largely Vane's, and individual items from the committee's letter-books only underline this. Thus on 7 January 1650 Walton and he came to the afternoon session of the Council of State together, and almost immediately the Council discussed a proposition from the Navy commissioners for building the six new ships.[5] During this and the following months, as so often before, the Council of State transacted no naval business if he was away, but if he was present naval affairs were taken up immediately or soon after his arrival.[6] Sometimes, as in 1649, he came in to the Council of State with one of his fellow-members of the Admiralty committee, as though they had come together from the committee.[7] On 8 April the committee went to Woolwich to confer with the 'generals of the Fleet'.[8] On 27 April Vane wrote to Popham to hasten the Fleet's departure for Portugal, and incidentally to ask Popham to take care for

[1] S.P. 25/123, p. 12. 2 March.   [2] Ibid.
[3] Ibid., pp. 273 (20 March), 292 (6 April).
[4] He was added to the committee on 9 April. (Ibid., p. 12.) He had signed letters on 16 January, 17 January, 16 February (3 letters), 22 February, 13 March, 3 April. (Ibid., pp. 222, 223, 241, 248, 263, 289.)
[5] CSPD. 1649–50, 470–2. S.P. 18/3.
[6] Any careful reading of S.P. 18/3, CSPD. 1649–50, and S.P. 25/123 will confirm this. One may take as examples 26 February, when the act for the impressment of seamen was discussed just after Vane had come in, alone, or 1 March, when Admiralty business followed immediately after Vane's arrival. An actual instruction to Vane to report from the committee to the Council, on a very important matter, is given in Bodl. Rawl. A 225, f. 24v. 3 December 1650.
[7] See above, n. 5, but many other examples could be given.
[8] S.P. 25/123, 292.

the safety of Vane's brother Charles, the Commonwealth's envoy to that country.[1] Meanwhile, the Council of State was much exercised about providing the necessary money for the Portuguese expedition, and Vane was ordered on 13 April to report to Parliament the need for money.[2] For once it was five days before he carried out his mission, but then it was in specific terms—that the Army and Navy should each have £50,000 out of the next £200,000 coming into the excise.[3] But this was not enough, and on 15 May he reported to Parliament that it would be necessary to borrow £200,000 on the security of the customs, to which Parliament agreed.[4] It looks as though he was the government's expert on defence expenditure.

In August 1650, though he had not himself attended the Council of State that day,[5] he was ordered to report to Parliament an encounter between one Captain Wyard and some royalist ships. Wyard had distinguished himself in the action and Vane must have done justice to Wyard's crew, for these were the first ordinary sailors in British history to receive medals for their services.[6] On 13 August the Admiralty committee order book for once gives some indication of an actual debate at one of the meetings; the entry begins 'Debated at the Committee', and proceeds to list the subjects discussed: the number of ships to patrol Portuguese waters, how many ships were to be ready to support the Army and how many to be convoys, and how many were to protect the East Anglian and Scottish coasts.[7] (Vane was present, as was usual.) Coytmore wrote once more, in September, as though Vane were the whole Admiralty committee,[8] and a week later Vane reported to Parliament an estimate of the cost of the Fleet, from what is called in the *Commons Journals* the committee of the Navy,[9] and may have been so, for the Navy and Customs committee

---

[1] HMC. *Leyborne-Popham MSS*, 72. Vane wrote that the Council of State would send instructions about this, and they did so two days later.

[2] *CSPD. 1650*, 101.   [3] *CJ.* vi, 400.   [4] Ibid., 412.

[5] *CSPD. 1650*, intro., xv–xli.

[6] Ibid., 277, 8 August. Wyard had beaten off a royalist attack when convoying ten Hull ships to London and Rotterdam. (E 778(19).) For the medals see Oppenheim, 'The Navy of the Commonwealth, 1649-60', *EHR*, xi, 44.

[7] S.P. 25/123, 429–30.   [8] *CSPD. 1650*, 328. 5 September.

[9] *CJ.* vi, 467. He had made another report on Council instructions the day before, on naval matters.

continued to function[1] though, unfortunately, its minutes for this year (1650) have not survived. He made another report to Parliament a few days later on the need for a supplementary estimate for the Fleet off Portugal[2] and, on the last day of September, Coytmore wrote to the Navy commissioners to inform them that if they considered the ship *Liberty* should go to Lisbon: 'Sir Henry Vane conceives it best to pay the men on board [i.e. not on shore] that you may preserve them together.'[3] (Vane had no doubt foreseen that once the men had their pay in their hands on shore they would disappear to their homes or the ale-houses.)

Deane had written to him that there was a great want of three or four 'nimble ketches' for the Scottish coast,[4] thus showing that the generals-at-sea thought Vane was most likely to further their requests, and Deane came up for a conference with the Admiralty committee in October.[5] Again one sees the system of personal consultation and consideration, in which the committee, or more probably Vane, believed. He signed a number of the usual Admiralty committee letters in November 1650,[6] but was busy with a multitude of other, including personal, affairs, though he reported to Parliament on the situation in Portugal on 26 and 30 November,[7] and on 10 December the Council instructed him to urge Parliament to press on with the Trinity House bill which Vane, among his innumerable official duties, had found time to help draft.[8]

At the end of 1650, his long tenure of office as Treasurer of the Navy came to an end. The circumstances are significant. On 27 June a petition from Vane, first brought in a week before,

---

[1] It is mentioned quite often in Bodl. Rawl. A 225. See also *CSPD. 1650*, 326, where Col. Thomson, now its chairman, is mentioned, and p. 170 below. The indications are that this committee met less often than the Admiralty committee, had a more changeable membership, and dealt only with the authorization of payments. S.P. 46/102 contains many of these; they are signed by Thomson and several others, but not by Vane. As Treasurer of the Navy he acknowledged receipt of many of these payments (ibid., *passim*), and he could hardly have authorized payments to himself. He could however presumably have attended the committee's meetings.

[2] *CJ*. vi, 473. 26 September.   [3] *CSPD. 1650*, 365.   [4] Ibid.
[5] Bodl. Rawl. A 225, f. 7v. 30 October.   [6] Ibid., ff. 9v *seq*.
[7] *CJ*. vii, 473. *CSPD. 1650*, 448.   [8] *CJ*. vi, 465 and 183 (30 May).

was read in Parliament.[1] According to the diurnals he stated that he was anxious that the profits of the Treasurer's office should redound to the State, and the office be well managed, though with the least charge to the public.[2] But he must also have asked that he should be awarded compensation for surrendering his office, for the committee of the Navy (the financial committee) which was instructed to consider how the office of Treasurer was to be managed in the future, was also to consider what compensation should be given to the petitioner. Colonel George Thomson, its chairman, reported from the Navy committee nearly three weeks later—hardly with the 'all speed' which had been ordered. The committee recommended that 'fit compensation' should be given Vane for the surrender of his right to the office and, 'in consideration of the profit to the State', £1200 p.a. out of the Deans' and Chapters' lands should be paid him. The committee also recommended that 'there shall be one fit and able person appointed Treasurer of the Navy . . . who . . . shall personally attend upon that employment; and be allowed, for the entertainment and salary of himself, his deputies and clerks, £1,000 p.a., which shall be in lieu of all salaries, fees, and other profits, formerly belonging to the place of treasurer of the navy'.[3]

The emphasis placed upon the personal carrying out of duties indicates that, as we have seen, Vane's work as Treasurer had been largely performed by his deputy. In view of Vane's innumerable other duties, it is hard to see what else could have been done. The act embodying the committee's proposals was passed on 19 July.[4] Incidentally, it is interesting to find that Vane was absent from the Council of State from 1 July onwards,[5] though he attended the Admiralty committee as usual,[6] and was in Parliament at least occasionally[7]—was he canvassing support for his Navy Treasurership bill? On 10

---

[1] Ibid., 427, 432. The petition is not in the House of Lords' MSS, and does not appear to be extant.

[2] E 777(27), *Severall Proceedings in Parliament. A Perfect Diurnall.* E 777(30) has almost the same wording. *The Weekly Intelligencer* is briefer, but states that Vane was 'sollicitous' that the profits should redound to the State (E 608(9)). The order about Vane's office was accompanied by a special committee to consider what offices were burdensome to the people—the two subjects were obviously connected.

[3] *CJ.* vi, 440.   [4] Ibid., 444.   [5] *CSPD. 1650*, intro. xv–xli.

[6] S.P. 25/123, 369 *seq.*   [7] *CJ.* vi, 438–40.

October, three months after his resignation was first mooted, Parliament discussed the appointment of a new Treasurer, and Hutchinson was proposed; there was a division. Vane was one of the tellers for the Noes, and was defeated.[1] On 18 October an act was brought in for 'removing obstructions in the sale of Dean and Chapters' lands',[2] and eight days later the commissioners for the sale of these lands granted to Vane the manors of Cheddar and Chicknalls in Somerset, and much property in Topsham, Devon. The former owners had been the Deans and Chapters of Exeter and Wells cathedrals. From the Close Roll[3] it appears that the lands were worth not the £1200 that Parliament had granted Vane, but £1864 8s 5¾d a year, though, in fairness to Vane and the commissioners, it may be supposed that in the circumstances of the time he might not have been able to sell the lands for their ordinary market value.[4] He would have known the amount of money available from the Deans' and Chapters' lands. As far back as March 1650 he and two other members of Parliament had been appointed by the Council of State to examine the receipts from this source,[5] and he was one of those appointed in November 1650 to view the accounts of the surveyors of these lands.[6]

The Close Roll records the transfer of various Lincolnshire rectories by the earl of Lindsey to Vane and Thomas Lister, the

---

[1] Ibid., 482. Perhaps Vane was hoping that his brother Charles might still obtain the office. Charles Vane had been generously paid for his services as Parliament's envoy to Portugal. He received £1200 for his embassage before he left England, and £200 on his return. (CSPD. 1650, 230, 580, 597; ibid., 1649–50, 508.) In November 1651 a sub-committee of the Admiralty committee recommended the payment of £500 to Charles Vane for his services in Portugal. (Bodl. Rawl. A 226, ff. 48, 49v.) Vane was not a member of the sub-committee. Charles Vane shortly afterwards bought from the trustees for the sale of Crown Lands an estate at Chopwell, Northumberland, which his family had formerly leased from the Crown. (Records of C.C. Durham, 358.) He was already (1646) part-owner of a colliery in Durham. (R. K. Galloway, Annals of Coal Mining and the Coal Trade (London, 1898), 133.)

[2] CJ. vi, 485. This was the very day that the act concerning the Navy Treasurership became law, and the two were connected. Vane was named first on the 'obstructions' committee.

[3] C54/3550.

[4] Dr Thirsk quotes Clement Walker's allegation that Cromwell acquired lands worth 50 per cent more than the grant Parliament allowed him. (I. J. Thirsk, Sale of Delinquents' Estates, Ph.D. thesis (London, 1950), 125.)

[5] CSPD. 1650, 37.   [6] Ibid., 434.

member for Lincoln, in November.[1] A few days before, Vane had requested the Council of State to allow Lindsey to come to town, to enable him to effect a sale of his lands 'in which a very well-affected person is much concerned'.[2] The well-affected person was Vane himself: a chancery bill and answer records the sale of the manors of Belleau, Aby and Swaby, with other property in Lincolnshire, to Vane, for the sum of £8500.[3] Four times after the first request the Council gave Lindsey permission to stay on in London, the last licence being granted in February 1651.[4] Vane shortly added local offices in Lincolnshire to his many other commitments: he became a militia commissioner and a J.P.,[5] and by the end of January 1651 was a vice-admiral for the county.[6]

The state gained a considerable sum in replacing poundage by a fixed annual payment to the Navy Treasurer. Vane's accounts for 12 May 1649 to 31 December 1650[7] show that he had drawn £8253 14s 6d as poundage, or some £4949 4s od per annum. In addition he had drawn over £1000 porterage money, and allowances for his clerks and other officials. One may note that it required a man of strong mental fibre, which Hutchinson was not, to be Navy Treasurer at this period of the Navy's history. He was probably an efficient civil servant, but no more. The corruption and inefficiency in the Navy nearly

[1] C54/3589. The Goldsmiths' Hall committee had stipulated that Lindsey should settle the rectories on Vane and others. Armyn, a trustee for the earl's sisters, was a party to the transaction. (*Calendar of Committee for Compounding*, ii, 503.) For Lister see *DNB*. He was Armyn's son-in-law.

[2] *CSPD. 1650*, 565.

[3] C10/9/93 (Chancery Bills and Answers). Lindsey was deeply in debt, and Vane wanted to make sure the property was not burdened with any mortgages etc. The fact that Vane's suit was not the beginning of a conventional lawsuit is shown by the speed with which Lindsey replied to Vane's bill of complaint. Normally the answer was presented weeks or even months later, but Lindsey's was returned the following day. For chancery procedure, see W. Phillimore, *Calendar of Chancery Proceedings: bills and answers filed in the reign of King Charles I* (London, 1889), i, preface. Lindsey later alleged that his property was much undervalued in the sale. (S.P. 29/56/62.) Vane's profits from his office as Treasurer of the Navy from May 1649 to December 1650 were within £250 of the sum he paid Lindsey.

[4] *CSPD. 1650*, 566. 23 November; 567 (2 December); ibid., *1651*, 32 (3 February); 58 (24 February.)

[5] Ibid., 479.

[6] Bodl. Rawl. A 225, f. 56v. One hopes that Vane had efficient deputies—Lincolnshire was a long way from London.

[7] E 351/2288.

drove him mad, and in spite of a large increase in the salary of £1000 a year that Parliament had allowed him in 1650, in April 1653 he was piteously begging the Admiralty committee to find a successor.[1]

Vane still continued to attend the Council of State Admiralty sub-committee regularly, except when he was away from London. The committee went on with its usual work, new ships were built, petitions were received, guns ordered, rewards assigned and victualling orders given.[2] The committee was further enlarged in March 1651 to eleven[3] and in July two more names were added.[4] This may have prompted Vane's attempt in June of that year to wrest control of the Navy from the Council of State. A bill was introduced in that month providing that the office and affairs of the Admiralty should be vested in commissioners, and he was one of the tellers for the bill. To secure autonomy for the new commissioners, under the bill they and the Navy commissioners were also to control all stores, magazines and provisions relating to the Navy, so that the officials of the Board of Ordnance would also lose authority. Vane and Dennis Bond wanted the bill brought in with despatch, and were therefore against sending it to a committee. But they lost, and the whole plan was abandoned, an act being quickly brought in to continue the Admiralty powers in the Council of State.[5] It is quite likely that Vane found the process of reporting back from the Admiralty sub-committee to the Council of State, who then reported to Parliament, intolerably slow. He may also have found it irksome to work with a large committee, many members of which knew little or nothing of naval affairs; in this way the Council of State committee was in marked contrast with the 1643-4 committee of Navy and Customs, some of whose members were merchants and shipowners.[6] Vane's predominance on the later committee may be partly due to this change. Parliament's decision in May that orders by a committee should be signed by at least the

---

[1] *CSPD. 1652-53*, 265. He had actually been arrested in 1651. (*CJ.* vi, 547.)

[2] Bodl. Rawl. A 225, 226, *passim.*   [3] Ibid., f. 70.   [4] Ibid.   [5] *CJ.* vi, 592.

[6] Of the March 1651 committee only Bond, Walton, Vane himself and Col. Thomson (if this is George Thomson, Navy commissioner, which seems doubtful), had any considerable knowledge of naval matters. The 1643 committee included the two Bences, Greene, Moyer and Vassall. (Bodl. Rawl. A 221, *passim.*)

quorum[1] made little difference to the Admiralty committee, for its letters were almost always signed by at least three members, or sent on behalf of the committee by its secretary, Coytmore.[2] On rare occasions, in 1651 and 1652, as in 1650, men attended who were not members of the committee, and even signed letters.[3] Committees had proliferated so much that perhaps it was difficult to remember just which committees one belonged to.

Though he reported sometimes in 1651 from the committee to the Council of State, he was not the only member to do so, and during that year Dennis Bond reported far more often than Vane.[4] In August Bond alone, in spite of Parliament's order of 1 May,[5] ordered one warrant to be issued. In the same month the Council, evidently considering that the planned reduction in the Army should be paralleled by a similar reduction in the Fleet, ordered the Admiralty committee to consider how the 'great charge' of the Navy could be lessened,[6] and the committee, in a letter signed first by Vane, did order Colonel Deane, off the Scottish coast, to reduce his squadron, but no further effort at economy was made, and in view of the worsening relations with Holland, could hardly have been. In March 1651, an entry in the committee's order-book again shows who was regarded as the leading member of the committee: 'Dr. Walker [Walter Walker, the Admiralty lawyer] returned his report according to the Committee's order yesterday. The Committee not sitting, it was sent into the Council to Sir

---

[1] *CJ.* vi, 569. 1 May. An attempt was made at the same time to prevent the authority of the Council of State from being exercised by a few members, but the House negatived the proposal that acts of the Council should be signed by at least five members. Later, however, when Vane was reporting to Parliament in November about recording all payments of money in a book, opportunity was taken to insert a clause that all such payments, and warrants for imprisonment, must be signed by five Council members. (Ibid., 43.) Vane alone signed one Admiralty committee letter in May 1651. (Bodl. Rawl. A 225, f. 127v.)

[2] Bodl. Rawl. A 225, *passim.*

[3] Sir Henry Mildmay, not a member of the committee, signed a committee letter on 21 May, ibid., f. 114. Alderman Pennington attended as a committee member on 6 September 1652, but was not added to the committee until the next day. (Bodl. Rawl. A 226, ff. 191, 192.)

[4] Vane reported six times to Bond's twenty. (Bodl. Rawl. A 225, *passim.*)

[5] Bodl. Rawl. A 226, f. 2v. 9 August.

[6] Bodl. Rawl. A 225, f. 82.

Henry Vane.'[1] Similarly, Colonel Popham, off Dunkirk, wrote to Vane about his position and Vane passed on the information to the Council.[2]

Vane's absence in Scotland, from Christmas Day 1651 to the beginning of 1652, accounts for his failure to attend the Admiralty committee during this period, though he appeared at the committee the day before he reported the Scottish settlement to Parliament.[3] Just over a week later, while still working on the act of Union, he reappeared at the committee,[4] and attended regularly until 16 April, when he was not present.[5] After that date he did not attend the committee until 12 May, but from then onwards attended regularly for some weeks.[6] From 30 June however until 10 September 1652 Vane withdrew from the committee,[7] as from Parliament; this unusually long absence has been discussed above.[8]

The months of March–May 1652 were important ones for the Navy; on 25 March an 'extraordinary' meeting of the Admiralty committee was held, attended by several Council members who were not normally members of that committee. The main subject was the provision of guns for the whole Fleet.[9] In May the clerk sometimes forgot to record the names of those attending the Admiralty committee, but whenever he did inscribe the names, Vane's is one.[10] This was the time of Blake's first encounter with Tromp in the Downs, and in the committee some important decisions were taken—to hire forty merchant ships, for example, and to offer suitable financial inducements to captains of Commonwealth ships who remained on board their vessels when they reached port instead of decamping as soon as they could.[11] It was Vane who reported to Parliament the decision to hire the merchant ships and requested the necessary money. He gave an account of the battle in the Downs, and presented information about this from Cromwell and Bond, who were now at Dover.[12] He reported, and probably drafted, the account of the battle which

[1] Bodl. Rawl. A 226, f. 2v. 9 August.   [2] *CSPD. 1651*, 254.
[3] Bodl. Rawl. A 226, f. 98v. 15 March.   [4] Ibid., f. 104. 23 March.
[5] Ibid., ff. 104–21v.   [6] Ibid., ff. 121v–32, 132–60.   [7] Ibid., ff. 160–94v.
[8] Pp. 147 *seq.*   [9] Bodl. Rawl. A 226, f. 105v.
[10] Ibid., ff. 132 *seq.* 12 May onwards.   [11] Ibid., f. 138v. 24 May.
[12] *CJ.* vii, 135.

was released for the Press.[1] For several weeks he was occupied with the crucial problem of the Commonwealth's relations with Holland, and then came his long absence from public affairs, already discussed.

By 9 September Vane was back in London, and attending a meeting of the Council.[2] Next day he resumed his regular attendance at the Admiralty committee.[3] There is no evidence that he was back in Parliament however until 28 September, when he reported on naval matters from the Council. An important speech was made that day by some member of the House; Parliament's approval was asked for the building of the quite unprecedented number of thirty new frigates.[4] Evidently the government had decided that the Fleet should not be so dependent on the hired merchant ships, which probably were not of the new three-decker design, which had first appeared in the '30s. It is significant that the decision to build this great number of ships was taken in the fortnight or so after Vane's re-appearance at the Council table. The *Commons Journals* are even more uninformative at this period than they are for the years 1647–9—the clerk was deliberately filling his pages with unimportant material[5]—and it is nowhere stated who put the plan before Parliament; it may well have been Vane. He now also returned to the attack on the administration of the Navy. At the end of July, after Vane had gone, Salwey had reported on two matters with which Vane had been connected, one of which was consideration of the 'executive part' of the Navy.[6] On 30 September Salwey was deputed by the Council of State to urge Parliament to resume discussion on the re-organization of the Admiralty,[7] and went down to the House next day to do so. There was a division on whether the committee of the Navy should be allowed to nominate M.P.s among the special Admiralty commissioners now to be appointed if the new plan was adopted, and Vane was a teller against.[8] He was perhaps hoping that, as in the case of the Self-Denying

---

[1] Ibid., 139.   [2] *CSPD. 1651–52*, 328.   [3] Bodl. Rawl. A 226, f. 194v.
[4] *CJ.* vii, 186.   [5] See e.g. ibid., 179–82.   [6] Ibid., 159.
[7] *CSPD. 1651–52*, 424.
[8] *CJ.* vii, 188. These proposed Admiralty commissioners are not to be confused with their agents, the Navy commissioners, Willoughby, Bourne and others.

Ordinance, he himself would be excepted. Or perhaps he thought that the loss of himself as a commissioner would be a small price to pay for purging the administration of the Navy from the amateurs who strolled in to the meetings of the Council of State Admiralty sub-committee.[1] He was defeated on this however. The Navy committee was instructed to report the bill in a week's time, but it did not do so.[2]

Early in October Vane, Dixwell, and Lisle went down to Blake at Dover to confer with him about the Council's dispositions for the fleet.[3] (This was just before the Kentish Knock battle.) Their instructions were prepared by the Council's Foreign Affairs committee, a large committee, of which Vane was also a member.[4] On 4 November the Council ordered Vane to report to the House a letter from Blake[5] (who was expecting another encounter with the Dutch), and the Council's dispositions for the ships, which Vane did straight away the same day.[6] The House adjourned that day from Friday 5 November to the Tuesday, obviously to give those concerned time to consider the financial problem, for Colonel Thomson had reported from the Navy and Customs committee on the Navy's debts and financial needs.

On Tuesday 9 November Vane presented to Parliament a lucid account of the receipts from the sale of delinquents' and Bishops' lands and from the excise. The document occupies nearly one and a half pages in the *Journals*[7] and Vane had expounded it to the Council of State the day before,[8] so pre-

---

[1] Such as Lord Grey (Bodl. Rawl. A 225, f. 100v. *et al.*) Hesilrige (ibid., f. 114v).

[2] Presumably this is the financial committee of Navy and Customs, though again this is by no means certain. Its warrant was signed by Thomson, Walton, a Popham, Aldwort and Boone in January 1651. (S.P. 46/102, f. 219.) In September 1652 its warrant was signed by Sir J. Danvers, Gilbert Millington, James Nelthorpe, Nathaniel Hollowe and Algernon Sydney. (Ibid., f. 241.) The first committee might be expected to make a wise choice of special commissioners for the Navy, the second not.

[3] *CSPD. 1651–52*, 430.   [4] Ibid., 67.   [5] Ibid., 473.

[6] *CJ*. vii, 210. According to the Council of State's Order-Book (see above, n. 5), he should have reported on the Navy's financial needs also, but Thomson did this. He was the most active member of the Navy and Customs committee in 1650 and 1651 (S.P. 46/102, ff. 219, 223, 226, 230, 235), and he and Vane may have decided it was more appropriate for Thomson to deal with this subject. Thomson figures in Pepys's diary as a self-styled Navy expert.

[7] *CJ*. vii, 210–12. 9 November.   [8] *CSPD. 1651–52*, 482.

sumably he and others had been working hard over the week-
end. It is interesting that this duty fell to Vane's lot, for one
would have imagined that one of the more frequent attenders
at the committee for Navy and Customs would do it, but it was
evidently thought that as the account concerned so many
different departments of State, Vane would be the best person
for the task. He secured the approval of the House for using the
money in hand from delinquents' estates for the immediate use
of the Navy, and next day the House also agreed that the
purchasers of Bishops' lands, who were in default to the tune of
over £15,000, should be compelled to pay what they owed.[1]
He was energetically procuring money for the Fleet, but the
Commons' long weekend—it rose on Fridays until Tuesdays
at this period—was an obstacle to a quick settlement, and
though he was twice a teller in favour of the House's sitting
temporarily on Saturdays and Mondays, Parliament would
not agree to do this.[2] On the same day he reported back to the
Council from its Admiralty sub-committee on the size of the
squadron to defend the Straits,[3] the vital area if Tromp decided
on a winter campaign. On 23 November he sustained another
defeat; the House again voted that the Admiralty powers
should be settled in the Council of State, though it did take
authority over convoys from the committee of Navy and
Customs and transfer it to the Council.[4] Obviously convoys in
wartime would have to be correlated to general naval strategy.
Still the special naval commissioners whom Vane had wanted
were not authorized, and on 2 December 1652 Vane was named
first to the Admiralty sub-committee (this time of twelve
members) of the Council of State.[5] Only two days later this
committee was superseded. Blake's defeat off Dungeness by
Admiral Tromp, when Parliament had assimilated the dismal
news, accomplished what Vane and Salwey had long failed to
achieve; the House decided to establish a small committee,
responsible to Parliament alone, to organize the provision of
ships for the Navy, and the necessary supplies.[6] The bill was
rushed through the House in one day, on 10 December.[7] It was

---

[1] *CJ.* vii, 212.   [2] Ibid., 214. 11 November.
[3] Bodl. Rawl. A 226, f. 241. 11 November.   [4] Ibid., 219.
[5] *CSPD. 1652-53*, 2.   [6] *CJ.* vii, 225.   [7] Ibid., 228.

laid down that there should be four M.P.s on the committee
(two were not to be members of the Council of State, which is
an interesting provision), the three generals of the fleet (Blake,
Deane and Monck), and two other men who were not M.P.s. At
last Vane had a small, expert committee, with freedom of
action, an instrument fit for the work it had to do.

CHAPTER VIII

The Admiralty Commission of Parliament, December 1652 to April 1653

No writer on the naval history of this period has noted the December change in naval administration, but it was highly important. It was this committee which was referred to in the 1662 biography of Vane. 'In this war, after some dubious fights, (while the immediate care of the fleet was in other hands) he with five others[1] were appointed by the parliament to attend that affaire.' 'Hereupon', the author asserted, Vane became 'the happy and speedy contriver of that successful fleet that did our work in a very critical season, when the Hollanders . . . took prizes at pleasure, hovered about our ports, and were ready to spoil all.'[2] Vane, who had long wanted such a committee, was naturally nominated as one of the members. Probably many in touch with naval matters would have echoed the sentiments of Robert Coytmore, who wrote to Robert Blackborne, the new commissioners' secretary: 'I believe the honourable commissioners and yourself have your hands full to bring the affairs of the navy into order.' He ended on a warning note, 'All is expected from you.'[3]

From the first the new commissioners' Letter-Book gives a different impression from that of the Council's Admiralty sub-committee.[4] Five of the commissioners[5] wrote to Blake on 17

---

[1] Sikes was omitting the three generals-at-sea, who were on active service most of the time.

[2] [G. Sikes], *The Life and Death of Sir Henry Vane* (London, 1662), 96.

[3] S.P. 46/114, f. 66.

[4] Roger Williams noticed the religious enthusiasm of the committee. 'The mighty war with the Dutch . . . hath made the Parliament set Sir Henry Vane and two or three more as commissioners to manage the war, which they have done, with much engaging the name of God with them.' (Knowles, *Memoir of Roger Williams*, 258.)

[5] Vane and Salwey were the Council members, George Thomson and John

December, three days after the act came into force, clearly setting out their plans.

> We . . . are preparing . . . inducements and encouragements to seamen cheerfully to engage in their service. We are also taking care how victuals may be provided for the next year's service . . . seeing the fleet well officered that is now in preparation . . . we think it requisite to have a meeting and conference with yourself, and to that end doe (God willing) resolve to make our repaire down to you either on ship board or some convenient place ashore.[1]

The last sentence sets the keynote of their policy, and is underlined by letters a few days later, in which the new commissioners told Blake they were glad he approved the way of 'consulting personally with you',[2] and that they desired 'in this as in all particulars that concern the service to have frequent and mutual correspondence with you in all freedom for the good of the service'.[3] Already they had been busy on a new act for the 'encouragement to seamen',[4] raising their wages and prize-money and taking particular care for the sick and wounded. Next they turned to the Ordinances for War, and on this Vane once more clashed with Marten.[5]

At the end of the month the commissioners assured Blake they were doing their utmost that 'provisions and necessaries may be speeded to you'.[6] (The very friendly and pious tone which marks many of their letters is quite unlike those from the old Admiralty sub-committee of the Council of State.) They had been anxious to go down to Blake at Portsmouth ever since they had been appointed,[7] but had been detained by the necessity of seeing through Parliament the 'encouragement to seamen' act, the Ordinances for War, and the measures for supplying

Carew the M.P.s, Langley the only other acting member, apart from the generals-at-sea when they were available.

[1] Bodl. Rawl. A 227, f. 1.   [2] Ibid., f. 2v. 23 December.   [3] Ibid., ff. 2v-3.
[4] The Council appointed Vane to put this matter before Parliament, but actually Whitelocke did so. (*CSPD. 1652-53*, 39; *CJ.* vii, 231.)
[5] *CJ.* vii, 235. Art. xxiv, over which Vane and Marten differed, is given in S. R. Gardiner, and S. T. Atkinson, ed., *Letters and Papers relating to the First Dutch War*, Navy Records Soc. (London, 1906), iii, 298, but there is no indication of the cause of the disagreement. These articles were the first codification of naval law. (W. M. Clowes, *Royal Navy* (London, 1898), ii, 98-101.)
[6] Bodl. Rawl. A 227, f. 3v. 27 December.   [7] Ibid., f. 1.

the Fleet with money. On 29 December, however, they wrote that they hoped to leave on 3 January and ended their letter by piously congratulating themselves on the good relations prevailing between the generals of the Fleet and themselves.[1] On the principle of trusting God and keeping your powder dry, a letter of the same day accedes to Commissioner Pett's request that the shipwrights should be allowed to work on Sundays.[2]

By 4 January 1653 Vane and the other new commissioners were at Chatham, instructing Hutchinson, the Navy Treasurer, to send down £12,000 in their coaches, which they had sent back to London for the purpose.[3] They reported to the Council of State that they found the seamen 'in some distempers, calling for their pay, being many months due to them'.[4] But they did not pay the sailors all their due, for the men would promptly have gone home, but kept back two months' pay and disbursed the rest on shipboard, and then only after the ships had been put into condition.[5] The commissioners decided that political agitation was behind the sailors' discontent—the men were mutinous 'upon pretence of their pay, but in truth desirous upon the receiving of their money to get out of the service at present, set on, as may be suspected, by malignant spirits disaffected to parliament'.

On 8 January they were back at Whitehall; it was a Saturday, but they were at work, sending Blake intelligence.[6] A week later they were telling him that in view of the news from Holland he would understand 'what great concernment it is to the State' to have a Fleet speedily at sea to intercept the return of Admiral Tromp,[7] who was escorting the Dutch merchant fleet from the Caribbean back to Holland. The usual work of victualling and providing other supplies went on, and on the 26th they were back at Chatham again, conferring with Blake (arriving inopportunely on a day of prayer),[8] appointing new clerks of the Cheque[9] and writing urgent letters to the Treasury commissioners representing the need for money.[10] The lighthouse keepers, who had been instructed to confuse the Dutch

---

[1] Ibid., f. 4v.   [2] Ibid., f. 5.   [3] Ibid., f. 6.   [4] Ibid., f. 7v.   [5] Ibid., ff. 10v-11.
[6] Ibid., f. 12.   [7] Ibid., f. 14.   [8] Ibid., f. 20.   [9] Ibid.
[10] Ibid., f. 23. The Navy Treasurer's agents, they wrote: 'dare hardly show their faces, or keep in the office'.

by changing their lights, were ordered to restore them to their
old positions now that the English fleet was putting to sea.[1]
The commissioners informed the Council of State that they were
sending one or more of their number to consult with the
Council about the command of the Fleet. The commissioners
would arrive at 8 or 9 p.m. and if that was too late for the
Council, could an early morning meeting be arranged?[2]
Salwey was sent to London, and did a magnificent job, finding
men for the Fleet, and what was nearly as important, clothes
and beds for them.[3] The other commissioners went on board
the flagship, to 'hasten their putting to sea', at Queenborough,[4]
and then back at Chatham wrote at midnight to Blake, telling
him the good news that one thousand soldiers from Cromwell's
and Ingoldsby's regiments were coming to the fleet, the Irish
and Scottish committee having this in hand.[5] The generals-
at-sea were anxious about the proportion of sailors to landsmen,
and the commissioners replied: 'As soon as we received your
letter the last night we ordered your desires put in execution
concerning the proportion of land soldiers unto each ship in the
list you sent up.'[6] They wrote to Blake to tell him that Tromp
intended to convey the merchant ships home before the English
Fleet could get out of port, and therefore urged him to put to
sea.[7]

On the Saturday morning following their midnight letter
to the generals they left for London,[8] having first written to
Blake.[9] They reported to the Council that afternoon.[10] Later
that evening they wrote again to the Generals, commenting
with asperity that they had met on their way to London one
Captain Harris, 'distempered in drink', and had moved the
Council of State to dismiss him.[11] They had written to Parliament the same day from Chatham.[12] Vane signed every single

---

[1] Ibid., f. 24.

[2] Ibid., f. 22. All three generals were eager to take part in the expedition against
Tromp.

[3] Ibid., ff. 26v–7.   [4] Ibid., ff. 26–26v. 3 February.   [5] Ibid., f. 27v.

[6] Ibid., ff. 28–28v. 4 February.   [7] Ibid., f. 27v. 2 February.   [8] Ibid., f. 29.

[9] Ibid., f. 28.

[10] Ibid., f. 29v. The clerk failed to enter all the letters on the proper day at this
time—doubtless the pressure of business was too great.

[11] Ibid., f. 29.   [12] Ibid., f. 29v.

letter, but so did Langley and Carew, and Salwey when he was not 'on mission'.[1]

When Parliament met after the weekend, on Tuesday, Vane reported on the state of the Fleet, and on what the commissioners had been doing. The House evidently appreciated, as well it might, how great had been his efforts, those of his fellow-members of the December committee, the Navy commissioners, and the shipwrights, and warm thanks were given to them all.[2] The five parliamentary commissioners wrote the same day to the generals, despatching the votes of thanks, and asking how the commissioners could be kept in touch with the Fleet at sea.[3] They also wrote on the same day to the Navy commissioners, instructing them to obtain £400 on imprest from Hutchinson for the sick and wounded; Vane had been deputed by the Council of State to ask Parliament to provide money for this need—he had evidently spoken of it at the Saturday afternoon meeting.[4]

The correspondence continued in full spate all through February, giving a vivid picture of the industry and efficiency of the new commissioners. One sees them finding officers, 'men fearing God, faithful to the State', for a Dutch prize, arranging means of keeping in touch with the generals-at-sea, sending them news of Tromp's whereabouts, enquiring why ships assigned to the Fleet have not yet arrived, ordering ammunition to be brought from Hull[5]—a ceaseless stream of letters was pouring out of the Navy Office. Obviously the same five men, Vane, Carew, Salwey, Thomson and Langley, were working night and day.[6] Between 18 and 20 February the two-day battle off Portland was fought, and a moving letter from General Deane was sent, not to the Admiralty commissioners in general, but to Vane, appealing to him to take steps to assist the families of the dead and wounded.[7] The Admiralty

---

[1] Ibid., *passim.*   [2] *CJ.* vii, 256. 8 February.   [3] Bodl. Rawl. A 227, f. 29v.
[4] Ibid., f. 30; *CSPD. 1652–53*, 154.   [5] Bodl. Rawl. A 227, ff. 35v, 36v, 33v, 37v.
[6] One letter of 14 February has 'Sat. night' by the date.
[7] S.P. 46/114, f. 123. 'I know your affection to the poor widows of the seamen now slaine . . . is such that you need neither provocation nor anie remembrance, yet fearing lest multitude of business may prevent the speedy settling thereof, I have therefore presumed to offer to your thoughts whether a present order of parliament to the effect following may not be necessary.' n.d. but the letters below are obviously answers to it.

commissioners wrote straight away to the generals-at-sea to
reassure them on this head,[1] and at the same time to Navy
commissioner Willoughby at Portsmouth,[2] with full instructions on this matter. The next day was a Monday, and Parliament was not sitting, but when it met on Tuesday, Vane
delivered an account of the battle.[3] While he was in the Commons the other three signed letters,[4] but he returned later in
the day.[5] Next day they wrote that refitting the Fleet would be
an 'extraordinary difficulty',[6] nevertheless they set to work to do
so, instructing mayors of port towns to obtain seamen,[7] and
trying to obtain ordnance,[8] but not relaxing their care for the
sick and wounded.[9] The large numbers of Dutch prisoners had
also to be dealt with.[10]

On 1 March the commissioners hurried down to Portsmouth,[11]
to see the situation there for themselves, reporting back to
London the almost overwhelming needs of the Fleet, and doing
much other work besides.[12] They left four days later, writing
en route to London, at Guildford, to the Council of State about
sending another physician to Blake.[13] On Tuesday 8 March
Vane was present at the Council of State, when the Council
sanctioned resolutions jointly agreed upon at Portsmouth
between the generals and the four Admiralty commissioners.[14]
During the following days, the old tasks of obtaining ordnance,
men and provisions were carried on, and careful scrutiny was
made of the list of officers drawn up by Deane and Monck.[15]
The need for crews was desperate, and a new act for pressing
seamen was rushed through Parliament in one day,[16] giving
the press-masters and others wider powers. The commissioners
now had to see that the act was put into force,[17] but fish for the
Fleet, appointments of ships' officers, and the investigation of
the burning of the *Fairfax* figured almost as largely in their
correspondence.[18] At last they found time to express their

---

[1] Bodl. Rawl. A 227, ff. 40–1. 20 February.   [2] Ibid., f. 41.
[3] CJ. vii, 261. The Council of State had ordered him to do so earlier that day.
(CSPD. 1652–53, 177.)
[4] Bodl. Rawl. A 227, ff. 42–42v.   [5] Ibid., and f. 43.   [6] Ibid., f. 44.
[7] Ibid., f. 46.   [8] Ibid.   [9] Ibid., f. 46v. Ibid., ff. 47–47v.   [10] Ibid., f. 47.
[11] Ibid., ff. 48, 50.   [12] Ibid., ff. 48v–49v.   [13] Ibid., f. 50.
[14] Ibid., f. 52v.   [15] Ibid., ff. 50–6.   [16] CJ. vii, 269. 18 March.
[17] Bodl. Rawl. A 227, f. 56v.   [18] Ibid., ff. 57, 57v, 58.

appreciation of the beer with which a kindly Army colonel had supplied them when they were at Portsmouth more than a fortnight before, and a hogshead of French wine (together with the two empty beer hogsheads and a hamper of bottles) was despatched to him.[1] On 24 March Vane was not with his fellow-commissioners,[2] doubtless because peace overtures from Holland and Zeeland were being discussed in the House,[3] but he was back next day.[4] The work of supplying the Fleet and transmitting intelligence went on; some days were more difficult than others; for instance, when the captains of the hired merchant ships would not accept the terms offered them.[5]

Towards the end of March 1653 the Dutch planned an attack on England's vulnerable point—the Newcastle coal-trade. Vice-Admiral William Penn's Fleet, which normally escorted the colliers, was ordered to join Vice-Admiral John Lawson's as convoy for the coal-ships, and on 7 April the commissioners went down to Gravesend to hasten the preparations of the hired merchant ships which were to be part of the Fleet which Penn was to command.[6] After what was doubtless an exhausting day, Vane and his fellow-commissioners were roused between 3 and 4 a.m. by John Fielder and Thomas Scot, who had been sent down by the Council of State with intelligence from Scarborough and the Low Countries, and with instructions to consult with the four commissioners. There was 'debate' on all this, and by 7 a.m. a messenger was on his way to Penn.[7] The instructions now sent to Penn could not have been phrased in more general terms. He was to use the best means he could 'being upon the place' to secure or rescue the colliers; Penn, if he ever received the letter, must have been mystified as to why it had been sent, for of course he knew what his objective was. The four commissioners now dictated a letter to the Council of State whose tone is strongly reminiscent of Vane's sarcastic remarks on other occasions.

My Lords, [said the commissioners] Colonel Fielder and Mr. Scot were with us this morning between three and four of the clocke and have communicated unto us your lordships' instructions . . . whereupon we immediately in obedience to your commands sent the letter

[1] Ibid., f. 59.   [2] Ibid., ff. 59v, 60.   [3] *C.J.* vii, 271.
[4] Bodl. Rawl. A 227, ff. 60v-1.   [5] Ibid.   [6] Ibid., f. 64.   [7] Ibid., ff. 65, 65v.

enclosed to Vice-admiral Penn, that he may be losing no time till he shall receive your lordships' orders in so weighty and important a juncture as this is, more particularly to guide him than we find ourselves able to give him, who have heard nothing of the posture of his fleet since our coming to this place. We have desired Sir Henry Vane, one of our number, to attend the Council in company of Mr. Scot and Col. Fielder, as well to represent to them the state of affairs here in reference to the ships that are to go out of the river, as to offer to the Council such things as are necessary for the fitting them with men, which is their great want.[1]

Vane carried with him to Whitehall a memorandum, four of whose points are connected solely with the manning and officering of the Fleet. The fifth, however, reflects the irritation which had shown itself in the letter, for he was to 'represent to the Council that we find that the giving of orders to the fleet when at sea is a great hindrance to us in the speedy setting forth of the ships in the service, which is the executive part of the navy, wherewith we are entrusted'.[2] It is clear that the commissioners wanted to leave naval tactics to the man-on-the-spot, having provided him with the means of carrying them out, while the Council of State, on the other hand, thought it should have a hand in these important decisions. Significantly it was Vane who was sent to argue with the Council. Later that day the commissioners still at Gravesend wrote to Vane at Whitehall to tell him that Penn had left Margate before the messenger arrived that morning, so: 'although we doubt not but the Council have sent their orders before this comes to your hands, yet lest any neglect might lie upon us, we presently despatched away the messenger in a ketch, which we hope if the wind hold will be at Sole before tomorrow night'.[3] The Council of State record[4] is completely colourless, and tells us nothing of the lively interview that must have taken place between Vane and the Council.

He did not stay in London, for he was back at Gravesend next day.[5] He must have returned to the capital, however, on that day, a Saturday, or on the Sunday, for on Monday he and

---

[1] Ibid., f. 65v.   [2] Ibid., f. 66.   [3] Ibid., f. 66v.   [4] CSPD. 1652–53, 268.
[5] Bodl. Rawl. A 227, f. 66v. 9 April.

three other commissioners were at the Navy Office, whence a very sharp letter to Cromwell himself was despatched.[1] Cromwell had been asked on 1 April to order that the men of Ingoldsby's regiment who were to join the Fleet should be despatched to Portsmouth,[2] and later the men from his own regiment had also been sent. He was now tartly informed that his soldiers had been accompanied by no officers and that no clothes or bedding had been provided for them. He was requested to give orders that those soldiers who had already gone and those who might be sent later, should be properly supplied.

Next day the commissioners wrote to the generals of the Fleet explaining the reason for their personal visits to the ports, 'we finding by experience', they regretfully admitted, 'that the captains are slow enough in their preparations, unless they be under a continual inspection'.[3] Navy pay, fish and other victuals, intelligence, congratulations to Navy commissioner Nehemiah Bourne, are the subjects of letters in the following week.[4] The last letter signed by Vane is dated 18 April.

The 19th was a Sunday, and that afternoon there was a meeting between members of Parliament and army officers; there had been ten or twelve such conferences since October. This one continued for hours; Cromwell argued in favour of his plan of dissolving the Parliament and governing the country through a group of officers and M.P.s who were 'well-affected to religion and the nation'—it would clearly be a body very like the powerful Committee of Both Kingdoms of 1644 and 1645—but no agreement was reached. The House had been debating the future of Parliament weekly, on Mondays, but three or four of the leading M.P.s at the meeting on the 19th promised to try to secure a postponement of the next day's debate until another discussion with the officers should take place. Whether Vane was one of the twenty or so M.P.s at the Sunday conference is not known. But he was in the House next morning—when Parliament's bill for a 'new Representative' was rushed through in a House where some 100 members,

[1] Ibid., f. 67. 11 April.
[2] Ibid., f. 62. It may be significant that he had to be asked to do this.
[3] Ibid., f. 67v. 12 April.   [4] Ibid., ff. 68–9v.

instead of the usual 50, had taken their seats! One would give much to know the details of this bill, but when Cromwell dissolved the Rump, he put the bill under his cloak, and it has never come to light. It would have prolonged the life of the Rump, however, and made Cromwell's suggested 'Council' impossible.

The sequel is well known—Cromwell's march to the House at the head of a force of soldiers, his sudden interruption of the proceedings, just as the Speaker was about to put the question for the passing of the bill, his tirade against the Parliament, and his exchange with Vane, who protested, when he saw the musketeers enter the House, that this action was against common honesty, only to hear Cromwell's 'railing' at him— 'O Sir Henry Vane, Sir Henry Vane, the Lord deliver me from Sir Henry Vane!'

There has been much speculation about Vane's part in the events of the previous critical twenty-four hours. Cromwell declared at the time that Vane might have prevented the 'extraordinary course' of Monday's events, and that it was Vane who had not so much as common honesty. Someone must have alerted the members to the threat to Parliament, and made arrangements to rush the bill through. It could well have been Vane, but on this there is no evidence. Much remains obscure about the whole episode.[1]

Of course Vane could not be expected to carry on as Admiralty commissioner under the authority of the Army, and he left for the country. On 22 April Salwey and Langley wrote to Blake, Deane and Monck. Deane had written wondering whether anyone at this time worried about the Fleet, and the two commissioners replied:

Sir Henry Vane being gone to the country. and Col. Thomson being not at present with us, who yet we expect suddenly with us, and Mr. Langley being ill, we are necessitated to despatch this to you from ourselves,[2] to let you know that through God's assistance

---

[1] Whitelocke mentions Ingoldsby alone among the officers who were with Cromwell that week-end, and mentions him twice. Was Ingoldsby, many of whose regiment had been sent to the Fleet, especially hostile to the Parliament?

[2] They were not a quorum, which required three members, of whom one must be an M.P. (*CJ.* vii, 228.)

care will be continued for your encouragement and furtherance in the present service.[1]

Later that day Thomson re-appeared,[2] Langley returned after a brief absence,[3] and the work went on as before, though perhaps not with quite the same energy.[4]

The re-organization of the Navy which took place in the critical five months December 1652–April 1653 was clearly the work of the special commissioners for the Admiralty and Navy appointed in December 1652. It depended on a careful survey and mobilization of resources of man-power and materials, a keen appreciation of the paramount importance of finance, and, as its foundation, personal consultation with the commanders, and personal supervision of the work in the ports and dockyards. The replacement of the clumsy Admiralty committee of the Council of State by a more workable group of five or six knowledgeable commissioners made the task easier, and was at least partly due to Vane. The successive phases of Civil War and Commonwealth administration of the State Navy become clearer when the extant records of its committees are examined. It is hardly possible to doubt that the devotion and energies of the commissioners of the Admiralty and Navy, who were given a fairly free hand in December 1652, were largely responsible for the later English victories in the first Dutch War, and that among these men Vane held the premier place.

---

[1] A briefer version is in *CSPD. 1652–53*, 289. Bodl. Rawl. A 227, f. 70 gives the letter in full.

[2] Ibid., ff. 70–1.   [3] Ibid., f. 71v. 25 April.

[4] Ibid., ff. 72 *seq*. The four months before Vane's dismissal occupy 70 folios in Bodl. Rawl. A 227, the four months after his dismissal only 56.

CHAPTER IX

Religious Policy, 1640–53

THOUGH HE WAS APPOINTED to one or two committees on church matters in the first two months of the Long Parliament,[1] Vane did not play a leading role in religious affairs as early as in naval policy. For instance he was not a member of the important committee of Twenty-Four set up on 10 November 1640 to frame a 'Declaration of the State of the Kingdom'[2] (the genesis of the Grand Remonstrance), though the declaration was clearly to cover ecclesiastical as well as political grievances. By early February 1641, however, the House had a higher opinion of him; when the London petition on episcopacy was discussed, and referred to the committee of Twenty-Four, six members were added to the committee, and Vane was one.[3] This was no doubt an attempt by the anti-episcopal members to strengthen their hand.[4] Sir Edward Dering, the well-known member for Kent, was one of the tellers for the opposition to the six, which makes his later acceptance of the Root and Branch Bill abolishing episcopacy, from the hands of Vane, Hesilrige and Cromwell, all the more strange.

On 27 May 1641 the Root and Branch Bill was put forward by Dering. The fact that the bill was thrust into Dering's hands by Hesilrige, Vane and Cromwell rests on Dering's evidence alone,[5] but it is difficult to believe that he would have fabricated such a story. The incident reveals something of Vane's position at the time; neither he, Hesilrige nor Cromwell carried enough weight in the House to present a bill, but Dering did. It also shows that the three men were acting thus early in collaboration. Dering's purpose was to use the bill as a lever to force the

[1] *CJ.* ii, 24, 52, 54.   [2] Ibid., 25.   [3] Ibid., 81.
[4] Shaw, *History of the English Church*, i, 42.   [5] E 197.

Lords to give way and allow the exclusion of the bishops from secular jurisdiction.[1] He does not indicate that Vane, Cromwell and Hesilrige had any such similar moderate intention. It must be remembered that Dering's version of the incident appeared in a collection of his speeches, which was hotly attacked in the House, and he was censured for it.[2] Presumably Hesilrige, Vane and Cromwell did not accept Dering's version of events. Incidentally Sir Christopher Wray, Vane's father-in-law, was one of the tellers for those who wished to censure Dering, and it was Cromwell who moved that the book should be burnt, which was done.[3]

A speech on 11 June 1641, during the debates on the Root and Branch Bill, was published as Vane's,[4] and has been accepted by all his modern biographers,[5] but there is no other record of the speech,[6] and it seems highly doubtful whether Vane ever delivered it. As printed, this lucid, carefully arranged speech, with its very telling arguments, is certainly a very able attack on episcopacy. It is understandable that Vane, or one of his friends, should want it printed. It is to be noted that it marks an earlier phase of his religious thought, when he accepted that lay authorities must be responsible for organizing church government, in contrast with his later view that the State should not interfere in religious matters at all.

[1] A. Everitt, *Kent and its Gentry, 1640–60*, Ph.D. thesis (London, 1957), 111–12; Shaw, op. cit., i, 79.

[2] Harl. 162, f. 366. 2 February 1642.

[3] Ibid., f. 366v. Dr Everitt quotes Dering as asserting that the Kent petition for Root and Branch abolition of episcopacy was founded on a copy sent down from London (op. cit., 108–9). Was this also organized by the promoters of the Root and Branch bill? The opportunity for Dering's presentation of the bill was provided by a petition from Lincolnshire presented by Sir Edward Ayscough (*CJ*. ii, 159), who was Sir Christopher Wray's brother-in-law. Dering says that the petition was a 'fair invitement' to him to 'issue forth the bill then in my hand'. (Shaw, loc. cit.)

[4] E 198(2). If spoken at all the speech must have been delivered on 12 June, for it reminded its hearers that the day before the House had voted episcopacy to be an impediment to the perfect reformation and growth of religion. This resolution was passed on 11 June (*CJ*. ii, 173). Shaw assigns Vane's speech to 12 June, presumably for this reason. (Shaw, op. cit., i, 86.)

[5] E.g. Hosmer, 142; Willcock, 104–5.

[6] It is not in D'Ewes (Harl. 163, f. 306), nor in Peyton's diary. All Vane's longer speeches seem, like this one, to have an extremely logical arrangement which is covertly or overtly mathematical. He marshals his arguments under numbered headings, and it is easy to see that he had financial ability.

On 21 June he brought in his important amendment to the Root and Branch Bill by which 'some of the clergie and some of the laitie' were 'to exercise Ecclesiasticall jurisdiction in everie shire for a time'.[1] The proposal was a revolutionary one, and D'Ewes's first note, later erased, called it 'a new government of the church', but the house adopted it on 12 July in an even more radical form under which all the commissioners would be laymen.[2]

His resentment against the bishops showed itself without disguise in August of that year when he moved that the House might 'fall upon the impeachment of the Bishopps to give their offence a name or stile'.[3] The charges against the bishops had so far spoken only of 'oppression of the clergy of this realm, and other his majesty's subjects, and in contempt of the king, and laws of this kingdom'.[4] Peregrine Pelham, his fellow-member for Hull, followed immediately after Vane, in a way which gives a strong impression of prearrangement, to declare that: 'They that did anything that is against the prerogative of the king . . . the rights of parliament . . . is treason, which he conceived that this is.' To impeach the bishops on a charge of treason would have been to endanger their lives; the presumption is that Vane would have been willing to go thus far. Serjeant Wyld argued strongly for making the charge one of *Praemunire*, but the House was evidently unwilling to categorize its charges against the bishops more precisely than it had done, and when the matter was brought up again in October the House declined to name the bishops' offence, or to fix a day for discussing the subject.[5] There was also a proviso that if the matter were brought up again it must be after 10 a.m., so perhaps Pelham and those who thought like him had tried to take advantage of a half-empty House.

A few weeks later Vane spoke in favour of sequestering the votes in the Lords of the bishops who had been impeached, and was seconded by Cromwell.[6] On 20 November, when the Commons had decided that certain named papists should be arrested[7] (an aftermath of the Irish rebellion), Vane moved

[1] Harl. 163, f. 337.   [2] Ibid., f. 393v.
[3] Harl. 164, f. 8. 8 August. Shaw does not deal with this incident.
[4] *CJ*. ii, 235.   [5] Ibid., 295.   [6] Coates, *D'Ewes*, 40.   [1] Ibid., 177.

that their names should be sent to the Lords, so that the Lords'
concurrence in the arrests should be obtained, and he was sent
as the messenger to the Upper House.[1]

In February 1641, as we have seen, he was added to the
original committee which ultimately drafted the Grand
Remonstrance,[2] but this enlarged committee also did nothing,
and on 23 July it was ordered to draft a remonstrance and
present it to the House four days later.[3] On that day the House
was occupied with many important matters, including the
Army estimates, and the Root and Branch Bill, and no remonstrance appeared.[4] By 3 August the plan had changed; a committee of eight, including Pym, Hampden and Vane, were to
bring in, by Friday 6 August 'peremptorily', the remonstrances
'of the State of the Kingdom and of the Church'.[5] Two separate
documents were thus projected. But still the documents were
not presented to the House; on 12 August, four of the original
eight members were ordered to bring in two days later the
remonstrance concerning the State, and two others, Fiennes
and Vane, that concerning the Church.[6] After the recess it was
decided to revert to the original plan for one remonstrance;
on 25 October it was ordered that the 'Declaration concerning
the State of the Kingdom' be presented to the House on 29
October.[7] This was done, and throughout November the
debates went on with a single document under discussion.
Godfrey Davies noted that clauses 181–204, nearly all of which
deal with church matters, are, according to internal evidence,
by a different hand;[8] presumably these formed Fiennes and
Vane's remonstrance, incorporated with Pym's. Strangely
enough, Vane is not reported to have taken any part in the
debates on the Grand Remonstrance,[9] as one would certainly
expect him to have done.

In 1642 and for most of the following year he did not speak
again on religious subjects, except for two requests for lecturers
to be appointed at St Martin-in-the-Fields, and at the church
at Isleworth; and these may have had a political purpose.
There were a number of such requests to Parliament at the

[1] Ibid.   [2] See above, p. 191.   [3] *CJ.* ii, 221.   [4] Ibid., 225–6.
[5] Ibid., 234.   [6] Ibid., 253.   [7] Ibid., 294.   [8] *Early Stuarts* (Oxford, 1938), 117.
[9] Coates, *D'Ewes*, 185.

time, and the sermons were probably needed to enlist support for Parliament's cause. The Irish rebellion, the attempted arrest of the Five Members, and many other political problems, were diverting members' minds from purely religious questions, and it is not surprising that Vane ceased to devote so much time in Parliament to these subjects. It is to be noted that he had not always carried the House with him; the Root and Branch Bill was dropped, and the treason charge against the bishops rejected.

In September 1644 he appeared for the first time as the open champion of toleration. He had taken part earlier in a discussion between himself and other members of the Westminster Assembly who were endeavouring to find a *modus vivendi* in religious matters between Presbyterians and Independents, but though he had not shown open sympathy with the latter, Baillie had begun to suspect where Vane's true loyalties lay. 'Sir Harie Vane, whatever be his judgement, yet less nor more, does not own them [the Independents], and gives them no encouragement', wrote Baillie.[1] After his return from Kent however at the end of August in that year Vane twice argued at the Westminster Assembly for a full liberty of conscience.[2] On 13 September the 'Accommodation Order', which held out the possibility of toleration for the sects, was introduced; he and St John, according to Baillie, were responsible for this challenge to Presbyterianism.[3] Baillie wrote that Vane and St John had disagreed about the Order, and that Vane had not wanted the differences about church government mentioned, but only the theological differences about free grace. He would apparently have left freedom of church government to be inferred by omitting all mention of this topic.[4] This is important, for when he had secured the charter for Rhode Island six months earlier he used the very same indirect, but nevertheless effective method of achieving religious liberty. The charter

---

[1] Baillie, i, 145–6. 2 April 1644. All Vane's biographers assume that Roger Williams was referring to a speech by Vane in favour of toleration, when in the *Bloody Tenent*, published on 15 July 1644 (Thomason's date), he quoted a 'heavenly speech' he had heard in the House of Commons. (E 661(6).) The speech may well have been made by Vane, but there is no proof of this.

[2] Baillie, ii, 235–6. 25 October.

[3] Ibid., 230. 16 September. *CJ.* iii, 626.   [4] Baillie, loc. cit.

made no mention of the civil government's connexion with religious matters,[1] an omission which in the circumstances of Rhode Island's quarrel with Massachusetts, must have infuriated his old colony. Vane's biographers have failed to notice that his policy in relation to the charter is consistent with his writings, in which he advocated that the State should refrain from concerning itself at all with church matters.[2] The Rhode Island charter was his first victory.

In the same month in which the 'Accommodation Order' was discussed, the Commons, following a petition from London Presbyterian clergy, considered the form of ordination to be used in the new national church. The debates went on through September and early October, and on 1 October Vane and St John were tellers against a clause which would have enjoined the congregations to 'obey and submit' to their ministers, who were 'over their flocks in the Lord'.[3] According to Baillie, Vane also opposed the compulsory subscription of the Covenant by newly ordained ministers.[4] Meanwhile the 'Accommodation Order' had been put into force, and resulted in the appointment of a sub-committee of the Westminster Assembly, which had the task of considering the difference between Presbyterians and Independents. This sub-committee discussed a plan whereby church government should be administered by county boards, composed of local ministers and lay governors, who would be named by Parliament.[5] This is exactly Vane's old plan of June 1641, and he must surely have been responsible for reviving it.[6] When the Assembly's sub-committee reported to the committee of Parliament set up under the 'Accommodation Order', Vane and Lord Say secured a narrow victory by one vote for the Independents' view.[7]

---

[1] Haller, *Liberty and Reformation in the Puritan Revolution* (New York, 1955), 159; Gammell, *Life of Roger Williams*, 119; Knowles, *Memoir of Roger Williams*, 146, 414-16; *Rhode Island Records*, i, 143. The charter is dated 14 March 1644.

[2] *A Healing Question*, 6-7, *Retired Man's Meditations*, 387-8.

[3] *CJ*. iii, 647. Baillie, ii, 235-6.   [4] Ibid.

[5] Jordan, *Development of Religious Toleration in England, 1640-1660* (London, 1932-1940), ii, 57. Shaw, op. cit., 37-43.

[6] Perhaps through the independent minister, Philip Nye, who had been Vane's colleague in Scotland when the Solemn League and Covenant had been negotiated, and who was a member of this sub-committee.

[7] Shaw, loc. cit.

Baillie was bitterly disillusioned with Vane; his attack on the intolerant Presbyterianism of the Scots came as a bombshell to the Scottish delegates.[1] That he was now openly professing what he had all along believed is the generally accepted view, and can hardly be denied. His change in religious policy may have been due to Parliament's increasing independence of Scots military aid; and if he had indeed found the Scots hostile to his plans for setting up a different king, or a republic, this too may have played its part. Certainly when D'Ewes wanted the officer who carried the letters from Cromwell and his fellow-generals describing the Marston Moor victory brought into the House, so that recognition could be given to the Scots' contribution to the battle, Vane, 'alledging that the three generalls had written as much as they thought fit', advised against calling in the officer.[2]

There is curiously little evidence of his religious views in the next few months of 1644 and 1645. He was not one of the Independents who co-operated in the establishment of Presbyterianism; at least his name is not on any existing list of elders. In Yonge's and D'Ewes's diaries there is, however, one glimpse of his religious attitude at this time. In September 1645 Selden had argued vigorously against allowing ministers to withhold the sacrament from offenders. Vane supported him, declaring that it would be better to convince the offender of the grievousness of his sin, and thus bring about his reformation. He showed, according to D'Ewes, that: 'We ought not to place an arbitrary power in any but the parliament.'[3] His speech must have been influential, for D'Ewes added: 'And soe all power was taken from them [the ministers] and soe they were not to judge but to represent it to the parliament.' The debate went on until five o'clock, D'Ewes tells us.

Some months later Vane befriended John Biddle, the Unitarian scholar, who had appealed to him for help, by moving that Biddle should either have his case heard in the House, or be set at liberty. Biddle was released, but in September 1647 was again imprisoned for a bold pamphlet he had written, and this time Vane could not, or did not, save him,

[1] Baillie, ii, 231, 235-6.　　　[2] Harl. 166, f. 81v. 10 July.
[3] Ibid. f., 266; BM. Add. 18,870, f. 114v.

though Biddle prefixed the pamphlet by a letter to him.[1] During the years of negotiations with the defeated king such indications as there are of Vane's religious views are inextricably bound up with the political developments already considered.

In May 1650 Vane struck another vigorous blow for religious freedom, this time in a country where many M.P.s might well have thought it a most dangerous innovation. The House were debating the settlement of Ireland, and discussing a clause which declared that Parliament's commissioners did not intend to force anyone to worship contrary to their conscience. Vane and Marten went into the lobby as tellers in favour of toleration. Sir Henry Mildmay and Masham, normally among Vane's supporters, understandably were against. By a narrow majority, in a thin House, Vane won.[2]

In January 1651 the House discussed a book by John Fry, one of the members. It was a lively, anti-clerical, somewhat rationalist treatise, which at one point actually demonstrated how small the differences were between Catholics and Protestants. Vane was a teller against allowing extracts from the book to be read, and was defeated, and when the House divided on the question of whether the book was scandalous, Vane was a teller against condemning the book, and won.[3] On both divisions, his friend Sir William Armyn was a teller for the opposite side. Hesilrige also was a teller against Vane on the first division. This was not the last time in 1651 that the two men were opponents, for when Hesilrige wanted Newcastle's market day changed from Monday to Tuesday, Vane twice acted as teller against him.[4] Public opposition to his old colleague upon such a petty issue probably indicates some underlying impatience with Hesilrige on Vane's part; and this is borne out by a passage in one of Roger Williams's letters.[5] Williams had come to England to secure a new charter for Rhode Island. One of the prominent citizens of the colony, William Coddington, had obtained a charter in 1651, by

[1] *DNB*, art. *sub* Biddle.   [2] *CJ*. vii, 137.
[3] *CJ*. vi, 529. 31 January 1651. J. Fry, *The Clergy in their Colours*, E 1378(5). Fry ater became a Quaker.
[4] *CJ*. vi, 589. 18 June.   [5] See below, p. 199.

which the island settlement of Aquidneck became independent of the mainland colony, and he himself became the island's governor for life. This had naturally caused friction among the settlers,[1] and Williams wanted Coddington's grant withdrawn. He probably did not know that Vane had been sent to Scotland, for although Williams arrived in England at the end of 1651 or the beginning of 1652,[2] he waited until April before presenting his petition to the Council of State.[3] The Council referred the matter to its committee for Foreign Affairs, of which Vane was a member,[4] and through his help Coddington's charter was revoked, and the old one temporarily confirmed.[5] Williams and Vane jointly drew up the Council's answer to the Rhode Island petition,[6] one more indication of the way in which business was done by the Council committees.

Williams could not obtain all he wanted. The confirmation of the 1644 charter was to be in force only until the differences between Coddington and the colonists were settled, and this, Williams told the colonists,[7] was hindered by two things, one being the Dutch war. The other obstruction was

the opposition of our enemies, Sir Arthur Hesilrige and Col. Fenwicke, who hath married his daughter, Mr. Winslow,[8] and Mr. Hopkins, both in great place; and all the friends they can make in Parliament and Council, and all the priests, both Presbyterian and Independent; so that we stand as two armies, ready to engage, observing the postures and motions of each of the other, and yet shy each of other.

The letter gives an interesting glimpse of the factions within the Council. Perhaps their divided opinions on the Massachusetts-Rhode Island controversy explain the hostility between Hesilrige and Vane at this time.

Williams could not remain in England without taking part in the religious controversies of the day, but he waited for

---

[1] Gammell, op. cit., 134, 147.

[2] He left New England in November 1651, ibid., 146.

[3] Knowles, op. cit., 252.

[4] Ibid. Vane's part in the committee's activities is seen in its proceedings, *CSPD. 1651–52*, 242.

[5] Knowles, op. cit., 146, 258–9.   [6] Ibid.   [7] Ibid.

[8] Massachusetts' agent in England.

Vane's return from Scotland before bursting into print. At the end of March 1652 he contributed an 'explanation' to a small pamphlet in defence of religious toleration, a statement submitted to the parliamentary committee for the Propagation of the Gospel by six men, one of whom was Charles Vane.[1] Williams published at least three more tracts during the year.[2] When Vane went down to Portsmouth on Navy matters Williams accompanied Lady Vane to Belleau, and dedicated one of his pamphlets to her.[3] Vane faithfully promised Williams that he would 'observe the motion of the New England business' while Williams stayed some ten weeks with Lady Vane in Lincolnshire. This was one more duty for Vane, and at a time when Navy affairs must have been taxing all his energies. But Williams seems to have rendered Vane a reciprocal service, for in the winter of 1652 the minister gave personal help towards alleviating the sufferings and discontent of the miners in Northumberland and Durham.[4] It must surely have been Vane who called Williams's attention to the needs of the people in this area, where most of the Vane and Liddell families' collieries were.

Vane's guiding principles in religious policy seem to have been two: a rooted distrust of clerical power, whether of bishops or presbyters, and a belief that the State should abstain from interference in church matters altogether. The latter belief, which he shared with his friend Roger Williams, is well illustrated in the Rhode Island charter. His friendship with Williams seems to have been responsible for the rift with Hesilrige, which began to appear in 1651. The Solemn League and Covenant was probably, as generally recognized, a temporary reversal of his usual attitude, made necessary by the political emergency. His support for the imposition of

---

[1] *The Fourth Paper presented by Major Butler* . . . 30 March (Thomason's date) 1652. E 1378(5). The pamphlet declared the licensing and payment of ministers to be wrong, and claims the right of Jews to live freely among the nation. If Vane was known to be associated with the demand for freedom for Jews, it would explain the occasional references to Jews in ballads aimed at him.

[2] Gammell, op. cit., 153.

[3] Knowles, loc. cit. Masson, *Milton*, iv, 530. Vane went down to Portsmouth on 2 March. (Bodl. Rawl. A 227, f. 48.)

[4] Gammell, op. cit., 153.

severe penalties on those who refused the Covenant, which has hitherto passed unnoticed, is a more significant deviation, and equally revealing of Vane's character. The fuller development of his religious ideas however belongs to the later 1650s.

CHAPTER X

The Last Years, 1653–62

AFTER THE DISMISSAL of the Rump, Vane left for Lincolnshire.[1] Oddly enough, in view of Cromwell's outburst against Vane on 20 April in the House, he was offered a seat in the Little Parliament,[2] if a royalist report is to be trusted, and he was apparently still regarded as an influential figure.[3] Of the next five years of his life however very little is known except from his own writings at the time. He could not be expected to be inactive, and he now turned to authorship. In April 1655 he finished his first book, *The Retired Man's Meditations*.[4] This was a largely theological work of 428 octavo pages packed with biblical quotations, which sheds little light on his attitude to contemporary events. But in his references to the earthly triumphs of the sons of Belial over God's saints,[5] and the ecstatic prophecies of Christ's thousand-year kingdom,[6] one can detect in his thought a new note, a certain hysteria, indicative of some mental unbalance. His fall from power in 1653 must have been a cruel blow to his pride, and no doubt the millenarian views then becoming widely current had a new attraction for him. He did not urge disobedience to Cromwell's government however. Governments should be obeyed, he declared, unless they were found in 'fixed enmity' to Christ and his Saints.[7] A wise and statesman-

---

[1] His fifth son, Christopher, was born there on 21 May.

[2] *Thurloe S.P.*, i, 265.

[3] Roger Williams wrote in July 1654 that Vane was 'daily missed and courted for his assistance'. (Knowles, *Memoir of Roger Williams*, 263.)

[4] Preface, *Retired Man's Meditations*.

[5] When magistracy is transformed, the sons of Belial, 'as so many thornes that have laine goading in the sides of God's suffering saints, for a long time', will be 'thrust away'. (Ibid., p. 387.) There are many indications that Vane in the 1655–9 period had suddenly become a highly excitable person.

[6] Ibid., 383–4.   [7] Ibid., 388–9.

like letter of February 1654 to Rhode Island shows that Vane
was still interested in the welfare of that colony, and his advice
was taken.[1] He was not elected to the first Protectorate Parliament; according to his brother in Holland, people there were
surprised at this.[2] Old Sir Henry Vane however was a member,
and there are other indications that he and his eldest son were
not on the best of terms.

In January 1649, just before the king's death, the elder Vane
had written a paper setting out the benefits he had bestowed
on his eldest son; he showed a certain doubt whether young
Sir Henry would cheerfully assume the debts and care for the
family with which the older man's death would burden his
heir.[3] The elder Vane died in May 1655, and according to a
letter which Roger Williams received from England,[4] which is
confirmed by a statement in Clarendon,[5] the old man at his
death was estranged from his son, whom he would have
deprived of at least part of the inheritance, had he lived longer.
Whether the two had quarrelled over politics, or over some
other subject, such as religion, is not known. Vane did refuse
the executorship of his father's estate,[6] but he did not refuse the
burden of the £10,000 debts.[7] Soon after the death of his father
he went to Raby to deal with the estate,[8] where he found the
garrison, which he had been at pains to secure for the castle
during the First Civil War, still in occupation. He now sought
to have it removed, for there was no danger now of a royalist
attack on the castle, and the presence of the soldiers was
unwelcome. But no doubt there were those in the government

[1] Knowles, op. cit., 260-1. He warned the colonists that their quarrels would
make them a prey to their enemies, and suggested the appointment of commissioners from both sides to settle the disputes.

[2] *Thurloe S.P.*, iv, 546. 28 August 1654.

[3] Dalton, *Wrays of Glentworth*, ii, 112. 'If therefore at my death I charge the
estate with £10,000 debts and legacys, I do hope and promise myself that he will
cheerfully undertake the payment thereof according to my last will and testamente
and be a Father to his brothers and sisters which God put into his hearte.'

[4] Knowles, op. cit., 287-8. 'But though his father cast him off yet he hath not
lost in temporals, by being cast off for God.'

[5] Clarendon, *Rebellion*, vi, 411.

[6] Will of Sir Henry Vane the elder. P.C.C. Aylett 159.

[7] *Proceeds of the Protector*. BM. E 937(2*).

[8] He took back Gaunt's Colliery, on Cockfield Moor near Raby, from the
tenants at this time. (Raby deeds. 18 August 1655.)

who remembered how he had obtained arms for Raby at a time when they were hard to come by in 1645, and when Vane went back to Belleau, Raby Castle was searched for arms and they were removed.[1] Vane wrote to Thurloe to request that the soldiers and not the arms alone should be removed;[2] he was probably successful.[3]

Cromwell's attitude to Vane was hardening; Vane's reputed refusal of the seat in Barebone's Parliament might account for this, though Ludlow asserts that the government was trying to bring pressure to bear on Vane to support the régime.[4] For whatever reason, in the autumn of 1655 Vane's right to Teesdale Forest in Durham was legally questioned.[5] Though Vane's title to the forest would seem to have been somewhat weak, he returned a haughty answer to the challenge.[6] When Thurloe sent to Vane a letter from Cromwell himself, Vane did not condescend to write a direct reply, but sent only a stiffly courteous letter through the secretary.[7]

In May 1656 appeared Vane's *Healing Question*.[8] This, in welcome contrast to the *Retired Man's Meditations*, is as clear in its meaning as Vane's fondness for inordinately long sentences allows. It is also much shorter.[9] The general political argument of the pamphlet was simple: the divisions among the supporters of the 'Good Old Cause' would disappear if the Army were once more subjected to the 'Supreme Judicature', and sovereignty were established in the whole body of the people that had adhered to the 'Cause'. There were interesting suggestions that a standing National Council, appointed for life, should issue orders in the intervals between Parliaments, and that if Parliament chose to place power in the hands of one person, or 'some few', righteous government might be established.[10] There were some honeyed words about the Army, 'considered as it is in the hands of an honest and wise general, and sober faithful officers, embodied with the rest of the party of honest men'.[11]

---

[1] *CSPD. 1655*, 315; *Thurloe S.P.*, iii, 745.   [2] Ibid.   [3] See below, p. 226, n. 2.
[4] Ludlow, ii, 30; Clarendon *S.P.*, ii, 213.
[5] C. H. Firth, 'Cromwell and Sir Henry Vane', *EHR*, xxvi, 751-3.
[6] Vane declared that the forest had been granted to his father 'by a special royal grant'. This would hardly prove Vane's own claim to the lease. (Ibid.)
[7] *Thurloe S.P.*, iv, 329.   [8] BM. E 879(5). 12 May (Thomason's date).
[9] 24 pages and a postscript.   [10] *Healing Question*, 15, 16, 18, 20.   [11] Ibid., 18.

No doubt Vane hoped these words would save him from the penalty which his trenchant attacks on the military dictatorship, in other parts of the pamphlet, would incur. If even the 'good party' could not be trusted with a share in government, he asked, why had this not been thought of before so much blood and treasure was spent in war?[1] There was a pretty broad hint that private gain was behind the action of the Army in April 1653.[2] The longer the whole body of the 'good party' had no part in government, the stronger would be the suspicion that a section intended to monopolize power.[3] If a particular member of the 'good party', or a number of them, imposed themselves as the competent judge of the safety and good of the whole, 'this is that anarchy that is the first rise and step to tyranny'.[4] All in all, it is surprising that Vane remained at liberty as long as he did. Not until the writs for the second Protectorate Parliament were issued did Cromwell take action, however. Then, either because of plots against the government,[5] or because the Protector had heard that Vane was standing for Parliament,[6] he was summoned before the Council on account of his 'seditious book'.[7] Bradshaw, Ludlow and Colonel Nathaniel Rich were summoned at the same time.[8]

The other three duly appeared before Cromwell and the Council of State on the day stated, but not Vane.[9] On receiving the summons at Belleau, he sent the messenger back with a cutting message saying that when England was a monarchy, Parliament had declared it illegal for the king to command a man to attend him at the royal pleasure, and Vane hoped he could claim the same liberty. He would however travel to London, to his house in the Strand, in a few days' time, 'which is as soon as I can well expect to have a coach to meet me

---

[1] Ibid., 13.   [2] Ibid., 14.   [3] Ibid.   [4] Ibid., 16.

[5] The fact that Rich was arrested at the same time does lend support to this view. He had been negotiating with the Fifth Monarchy men in the summer. (P. G. Rogers, *The Fifth Monarchy Men* (London, 1966), 73.)

[6] *Thurloe S.P.*, v, 296, 299; *CSPV. 1655-56*, 264. One news-letter writer thought he was already elected, on 5 August (*Clarke Papers*, iii, 68-69.) Why Vane should have changed his mind about sitting in one of Cromwell's parliaments, if he did, is not known.

[7] *Proceeds of the Protector.* The summons was issued on 29 July, and Vane was to appear before the Council on 12 August.

[8] Ludlow, ii, 10.   [9] Ibid.

half-way, this very hot season for travel, my own being in no condition to perform so long a journey upon so short a warning given'.[1] Eight days after the date assigned, Vane wrote to William Jessop, the Clerk of the Council, that he had been at his house in the Strand since Thursday night, and was ready to appear when sent for.[2] He was at once summoned before the Council, and ordered to give bail of £5000 for his good conduct. This he courageously refused to produce, for he would not acknowledge the authority of the Council, whose votes and orders he boldly declared had not the binding force of law. He announced his intention of spending a few days with his relations in Kent, which the Council were humane enough to allow him to do, but on 4 September he was arrested and imprisoned in Carisbrooke, Isle of Wight. He made a vigorous and outspoken protest to Cromwell, and roundly declared that nothing of truth and righteousness remained in the land but the name. The Army and Cromwell, he asserted, were given their authority by the nation by whom they were paid, and the Protector was no more than an appointed official. But Cromwell was aiming at the throne 'in spirituals as well as in temporals'; and this became clearer every day. He ended with another almost hysterical prophecy of the coming triumph of the 'suffering Saints, to whom not only this Nation's wisdom in their Supreme Assembly, but the ruling Powers of the whole world shall yield subjection'.[3] He was becoming subject to delusions of grandeur. Vane's fellow-prisoner in Carisbrooke was a well-known Fifth Monarchist preacher, John Rogers, and another, Christopher Feake, was also imprisoned on the island.[4] Certainly by 1659 Vane was connected in many people's minds with the Fifth Monarchists. The Lord Mayor in the summer of that year sent Fleetwood a broadside in which Vane was said to be about to lead a Fifth Monarchist rising,[5] and clearly Whitelocke by the end of 1659 also believed that Vane was a Fifth Monarchist, for his curious statement that Vane

---

[1] *Proceeds of the Protector.*   [2] Ibid.   [3] Ibid.

[4] L. F. Brown, *The Political Activities of the Baptists and Fifth Monarchy Men in England during the Interregnum*, 89. Feake was at Sandown, Rogers at Carisbrooke itself.

[5] Ibid., 186, 189. A correspondent of Hyde referred to Vane as the Counsellor of the Fifth Monarchists. (Bodl. Clar. 61, f. 103.)

proposed to change the laws, magistracy, ministry and government of the nation, is only explicable in this way.[1] The Fifth Monarchists were thought to be aiming at replacing the laws of England by the Mosaic code. Vane obviously shared a number of Fifth Monarchist ideas—we have seen that he was expressing millenarian views before he met Rogers and Feake, and he shared the Fifth Monarchist enthusiasm for religious toleration. The desire which Feake had expressed in 1653 to spread the rule of Christ to the Continent, by way of a victory of the British Navy over the Dutch,[2] would harmonize with Vane's own earlier support for a union between England and Holland. Government by the elect was also a Fifth Monarchy tenet,[3] and Vane may well have been influenced by them in the direction of doubting the morality of oath-taking.[4] The enlistment of sectaries in Vane's regiment in 1659[5] would be explicable by his friendship with such ministers as Feake and Rogers. The view of the royalist Lord Mordaunt that Vane's religion was 'to make a party, and solely interest leads him', is not necessarily to be accepted.[6]

After nearly four months in Carisbrooke Vane was released, and probably went to Raby, but there is very little information about him in 1657 and the first eight months of 1658, though we do know that he bought a lead-mine in Teesdale in 1658,[7] and in the same year met George Fox at Raby.[8] Fox and he had an altercation, and Fox told Vane he was not the man he once had been.

In September 1658 Cromwell died, and for Vane the political landscape at once changed. Bristol Corporation, evidently realizing that he might once more be a power in the land, hastily sent him £20[9]—part of the arrears of the honorarium

---

[1] Whitelocke, iv, 367-8.   [2] L. F. Brown, op. cit., 24.   [3] Ibid., 25.
[4] Ibid., 189. See below, p. 220.   [5] CSPD. 1659–60, 156.
[6] Bodl. Clar. 61, ff. 114-15. 6 June 1659.
[7] Raby Deeds, 15 July. The mine cost only £390, payable over five years.
[8] George Fox, Journal, ed. J. L. Nickalls (Cambridge, 1952), 334–6. 'Friends that were with me stranged to see his darkness and impatience . . . And I did see he was vain, and high, and proud, and conceited, and that the Lord would blast him . . . [to Vane] thou hast known something formerly but now there is a mountain of earth and imaginations up in thee . . . thou art not the man as thou wast formerly.'
[9] Latimer, The Annals of Bristol in the Seventeenth Century (Bristol, 1900), 283.

that was his due as High Steward of the borough, but which
they had prudently forborne to pay in the days of his disgrace.
Ludlow states that Vane sought election to Richard Cromwell's
Parliament both at Hull and at Bristol, but was defeated at
both places by the use of 'government' influence.[1] The Bristol
archives provide no information,[2] but he was certainly a
candidate at Hull,[3] and in a later letter to the Corporation
referred to the 'unjust practices' which had deprived him of
the seat.[4] By this time[5] he can have had little hope of a seat,
but at the last moment Robert Wallop secured his return for
the 'rotten borough' of Whitchurch[6] in Hampshire. He perhaps
had to face opposition here from one of Richard Cromwell's
relations, a brother of John Dunch, whom the Protector had
urged to stand.[7] Vane later declared in the Parliament that his
election was a 'special testimony of God's providence', which
sounds as though he had not been sure of securing the seat.[8]

Even before the election results were known, meetings of
those who wanted to overthrow the Protectorate were taking
place at Vane's house at Charing Cross. They would accept
seats in the Parliament, they decided, and, with a nostalgia
for the Rump that few of the population can have shared, they
upheld the rights of the Long Parliament, which 'though under
a force, yet was never legally dissolved'.[9] No doubt Vane heartily
concurred.

Oddly enough, though he was elected on 21 January,[10] and the
Parliament met on the 27th, Vane did not take his seat until
8 February.[11] This long delay requires explanation, and there are
two likely ones; either he was reluctant to take the oath of
loyalty to Richard Cromwell—he never did take it[12]—and

[1] Ludlow, ii, 50.

[2] *Ex. inf.* kindly supplied by Miss S. Lang, Assistant Archivist, Bristol Record
Office.

[3] Hull City MSS, Bench Book, vi, f. 277.   [4] Ibid., L. 635.

[5] The Hull election took place on 10 January. See above, n. 3.

[6] Ludlow, loc. cit. Ludlow was Wallop's 'cousin', and therefore probably well-
informed about his relation's affairs. In 1640 a grand total of eight voters voted at
the Whitchurch election. (Keeler, *The Long Parliament, 1640–41*, 50.)

[7] Davies, *Elections*, 493.   [8] Burton, iii, 181.   [9] Ludlow, ii, 50.

[10] *Return of M.P.s*, i, 509. Only 3 counties and 4 boroughs sent in a later return.

[11] BM. Lansdowne, 823, f. 212. Gilbert Mabbott to Henry Cromwell.

[12] Ibid. f. 221.

waited until the commissioners appointed to supervise this no longer attended, or he was organizing support for the petition which some 'well-affected' citizens of Westminster intended to present on the day that Vane first appeared in the House. This petition was the very same one that Oliver Cromwell, on a morning in Febuary 1658, had dissolved Parliament to avoid. It was printed in the following month, when George Thomason, the bookseller, obtained a copy. The title-page named the author as 'E.H.'[1] but it could well have been written by Vane himself. The author shows a fervent respect for Parliament, and a nostalgia for the Long Parliament and its achievements that one would expect only from certain members of the Rump. The audacious appeal to Cromwell, to 'call on God for wisdom, that you may be taught and enabled to establish such a sure foundation of Right, Freedom, and Justice', is worthy of Vane himself, whose own imprisonment might well have led him to demand also that 'none may be . . . proceeded against by imprisonment, or otherwise, but such who shall be really found transgressors of the law'. Certainly Vane was not alone in regarding 'the people' as 'the original of all just power',[2] but that, and the belief that 'private and selfish and arbitrary interest' accounted for opposition to righteous views, is in line with his thought in the '50s. The appeal for 'tender consciences' would obviously be consonant with Vane's authorship, and so would the disillusion,[3] and the surprise that 'old friends, who for years together engaged their lives and estates for the nation's freedome . . . should express trouble and dislike' for the petition. If an Army chaplain wrote it, as Firth surmised, it is odd that so little space was given to the Army's grievances. The petition was to have been presented by 'under a score, though signed

---

[1] E 396(5). C. H. Firth ('Letters concerning the dissolution of Cromwell's last parliament', *EHR*, vii, 107) says that the author was probably Edward Harrison, sometime chaplain to Major-General Harrison's regiment. When John Canne became official news-writer to the restored Rump, in May 1659, which implies at least the blessing of Vane, Edward Harrison, Canne and another Baptist pastor, jointly wrote an article in Canne's first issue of the *Publick Intelligencer*. (L. F. Brown, op. cit., 182.)

[2] Vane harped on the phrase in 1659. (Burton, iii, 174, 176; iv, 71.)

[3] 'The good people expect and hope for better things in God's good time, to whom alone they desire to look, having learned in some good measure to cease from man.'

by many thousands', to Oliver's last Parliament.[1] It was brought
to the House in 1659 on 8 February,[2] the day Vane first took his
seat in Richard Cromwell's Parliament, and on the next day
also, but the House declared it was too busy to receive it.
(Samuel Moyer, the well-known London mercer and member
of the Levant Company, with about twenty more citizens,
presented it on the 9th.) It was brought in again on the 15th,
when, in spite of the support of Vane and Hesilrige, it had a
frigid reception.[3]

It is very interesting that it was Livewell Chapman, the
stationer, who distributed the pamphlet when it was printed
in 1658.[4] Chapman was associated with Thomas Brewster,[5]
who is known to have printed at least two of Vane's works.[6]
Mrs Chapman (probably carrying on the business during her
husband's imprisonment) was stated in 1663 to have printed
one of Vane's pamphlets.[7]

---

[1] E 936(5). Note that in 1658 support for the petition in Parliament was organized. (Firth, op. cit., 108.)

[2] *CJ.* vii, 601; BM. Lansdowne, 823, f. 212. It seems that William Kiffin, the Baptist minister, came with the petition on 8 February, but Samuel Moyer, who doubtless carried more weight with the House, came next day, and on the 15th.

[3] Ibid., f. 219. It was 'ill-resented by the House in general', and the M.P.s voted that the mention of thanks and good affections should be left out of the House's reply. (Francis Aungier, M.P., to Henry Cromwell.) Aungier says that the petition was from 'Barebone's gang', and one contemporary at least suspected Vane's hand in it, for one of the 'Rump Songs' runs:

> Mongst whom there is one,
> That to Devil Barebone,
> For his ugly petition gave thanks . . .
> Whose petition was drawn
> By Alcoran Vane,
> Or else by Corbet the Jew. . . .
> $\qquad$ *Rump Songs*, ii, 161.

[4] E 936(5).

[5] *CSPD. 1661-62*, 23. Thomas Creake stated that he printed the *Phoenix of the Solemn League and Covenant* by order of Chapman, Giles Calvert (who published many Quaker pamphlets), and Thomas Brewster, 'they saying they were sharers in the pamphlets'. (Ibid., *1663-64*, 180.)

[6] *Retired Man's Meditation*, 1655; *Healing Question*, 1656, 1660.

[7] S.P. 29/67/161 n.d. but about February 1663. Professor Woolrych (*Cambridge Historical Journal*, xiii, 2 (1957), 138) thinks that the pamphlet *XXV Queries* may have emanated from Vane's group. It seems unlikely however that the major part was Vane's own work for the following reasons among others: the author refers to the Engagement of January 1649, which 'we' took, but Vane had refused it, and refers to the 'inconsiderable sums' which the purchasers gave for the Deans' and

According to Thurloe the 'Commonwealth's men' had decided at their November meetings to question Richard Cromwell's authority, in the hope of re-establishing a republic under Parliament alone.[1] Vane's speeches in the House, as soon as he took his seat, are certainly consonant with this.[2] He sometimes spoke at inordinate length, indeed to judge from the space which Burton gives them in his diary his speeches were hardly shorter than Hesilrige's, one of which we know went on for two hours.[3] This was 'filibustering', and it had a double purpose. At least one-half and probably two-thirds of the M.P.s were new to Parliament,[4] and these inexperienced M.P.s might, through these long speeches, be brought to see the political situation from the 'republican' standpoint, and to abolish the Protectorate. The lengthy speeches also served to postpone the grant of subsidies, and thus, by leaving the Army unpaid, render its support for Richard Cromwell more uncertain. These considerations account for Vane's long reminiscences about the Long Parliament, irrelevancies which did not go unchallenged.[5] His objection to the Protectorate seems to have been based on his belief that if it was allowed to continue with the power that Oliver Cromwell had enjoyed, it would soon lead to the restoration of the monarchy;[6] he wanted Parliament unequivocally to assert its own sovereignty.[7] But he was soundly defeated on the recognition of the Protectorate,[8] and he then tried to reduce the Protector's power by denying him the veto.[9] Though defeated on this too, he doggedly returned to the charge several times.[10]

Chapters' lands. Vane would hardly write in this way, in view of his own transactions in these lands. It should be noted that *XXV Queries* was printed by Livewell Chapman. (Professor Woolrych used the Harleian Miscellany reprint which does not name the printer.)

[1] Davies, *Restoration*.

[2] Burton, iii, 178, 180, 192 *et al.*

[3] BM. Lansdowne, 823, f. 212; Burton, iii, 171.

[4] Davies, *Elections*, 497.

[5] Burton, iv, 123. 'Be a person never so great, he ought not to wander so far in the debate.' (Maynard speaking); 231 (Bodurda).

[6] Burton, iii, 178; iv, 71.

[7] Ibid., 'You [the Commons] are now in clear rightful possession of this government, which cannot be disposed of but by your consent.'

[8] Davies, *Elections*, 499.   [9] Burton, iii, 319, 343.

[10] Ibid., 366, 368; iv, 292.

As many contemporaries noted,[1] Hesilrige and Vane were working together in this Parliament,[2] and the old animosity of 1652 was apparently forgotten. Together they sought to reduce the 'Court's' majority by having the lawyers, who were notoriously supporters of Richard Cromwell,[3] withdrawn from Parliament. Hesilrige therefore argued that the assizes, which had been postponed, should take place, and Vane seconded him,[4] though it is difficult to believe that he was thinking more of the nation's needs than of his own political advantage, especially as attendance at the assizes would have removed the formidable Sir John Maynard. Both men also denounced the admission to Parliament of the Irish and Scottish M.P.s, who were 'Court' nominees.[5] Vane shrewdly pointed out the inconsistency of summoning the English M.P.s to Richard Cromwell's Parliament under the old pre-Protectorate constitution, and the Scottish M.P.s at the same time under the Humble Petition and Advice arrangements.[6] But the 'Commonwealth's men' were in a minority in the House, and they lost the day on both issues.

It should be noted that Vane once more faced in Sir John Maynard a most able opponent. After a lengthy speech by Vane, the day after he appeared in the House, Maynard returned a cutting reply—stories about the Long Parliament, he declared, were not relevant, and he reminded the House (in contradiction of Vane's eulogy) that the Long Parliament had countenanced great oppressions, and the protection of delinquents.[7] Those who had told stories about the Long Parlia-

---

[1] Clarendon *S.P.*, iii, 267, 403; M. Sylvester (ed.), *Reliquiae Baxterianae* (1696), 75; Burton, iv, 221–2. Richard Cromwell, asked who the 'Commonwealth's men' were in the House, replied: 'Sir Arthur Hasselrigge and Sir Henry Vane.' (Bodl. Clar. 60, f. 358.)

[2] For a few examples among many see Burton, iii, 346, 366, 369, 442. Hesilrige, like Vane, saw the Rump through rose-coloured spectacles (ibid., 97), and he expressed unbounded admiration for Vane's part in it (ibid., 442).

[3] Slingsby told Hyde that the Commonwealth party hoped to rid themselves of the lawyers, who were all of the Court party, by this means. (Bodl. Clar. 60, f. 135.)

[4] Burton, iii, 327. 'A delay of justice is of great consequence', Vane declared.

[5] Arthur Annesley, himself an M.P., thought that the attack on the Irish and Scottish M.P.s was a direct result of their vote in favour of recognizing the House of Lords. (BM. Lansdowne, 823, f. 239.)

[6] Burton, iv, 180.   [7] A covert reference to Vane's own family?

ment were themselves a large part of the late troubles. This last was in Latin, but many of the members would have enjoyed it.[1] On another occasion Vane was arguing that the Humble Petition and Advice was not legal because it was drawn up by a Parliament which was subject to the use of force; Maynard cut the ground from under Vane's feet by pointing out that the actions of the Long Parliament after Pride's Purge were similarly illegal.[2] This would be gall and wormwood to Vane, for the years 1649-53 had been the great days of his power.

He was still interested, as one would expect, in the nation's finances,[3] and deeply interested in foreign policy. The situation in the Baltic was critical, as Thurloe explained to the House on 21 February: if the Swedish king were allowed to capture Copenhagen the Sound might be closed to British vessels, but if the Dutch saved it they would be 'insupportably insolent'. Thurloe hoped for a subsidy from Parliament, but there was silence for a while after he sat down, for the subject was very complex, and most of the M.P.s inexperienced. Vane spoke first, freely admitting his own perplexity, but he had seen that Thurloe had carefully omitted to mention which of the two Scandinavian rulers was the aggressor. No doubt Vane knew that it was Charles X of Sweden who had disturbed the peace; Richard Cromwell's advisers however were intending, by and large, to support the Swedish king against the Danes and their allies the Dutch. Vane was suspicious that Richard Cromwell was trying to obtain money from Parliament by a subterfuge, and unconvinced that Britain ought to support Sweden: 'If it be our interest that Sweden ought to be emperor of the Baltic seas, I should be very glad to understand how.' He was not satisfied that Britain should aim at taking possession of some part of the Baltic—'like birds of prey' as he witheringly put it—

[1] Burton, iii, 181.

[2] Ibid., 182. When Gewen declared that Richard Cromwell was king to all intents and purposes, Vane at once reminded him that it was still treason to proclaim anyone to be king. Maynard dryly retorted that Gewen had said only that Richard exercised the kingly power, 'and if he do not, you must hang up all your judges in Westminster Hall'. (Ibid., 534.) When Vane was arguing vehemently against allowing Richard to nominate the Upper House, Maynard was his chief opponent. (Ibid., 565; iv, 70-1, 74.)

[3] Ibid., iii, 305.

or that Holland was already our enemy.[1] It was one of his most brilliant speeches, in spite of the absence of a definite constructive policy. He took a prominent part in a later debate on the Baltic, now supporting the creation of a large Navy, but unwilling to give to the Protector authority over it or the troops it would carry.[2] He had obviously followed Oliver Cromwell's foreign policy with acute attention and disapproval. 'I see this affair all along managed to support the interest of a single person, and not for the public good, the people's interest.' He argued that co-operation with Holland would have been the best policy for the late Protector to follow, but that if it was decided that Holland must be prevented from dominating the Baltic, then the attack on Jamaica, 'where you have left your dead men to your reproach', should not have been undertaken. He disliked Cromwell's pro-French policy.[3] The House, led by Vane, agreed later to provide the ships required for intervention in the Baltic, but the problem was not settled when this Parliament was dissolved.[4]

As the weeks wore on, though the House adopted his views on the Navy and foreign policy,[5] Vane could not fail to see that on all other matters he and Hesilrige were in a minority in the House. The gulf between the Army and Parliament was widening; a majority in Parliament was opposed to religious toleration, and was thought to be considering the reduction of the Army's strength and the restoration of the king. Vane's policy towards the Army is not easy to understand. Late in the session, he advocated paying the soldiers their arrears,[6] a move which would be popular with the Army, but five days later he was seconding the impeachment of the unpopular Major-General Boteler,[7] whose actions many of the Army would feel were no more illegal than their own. More than once at this time Vane admitted he was confused, and perhaps he was not following a consistent line. From his writings one would guess

---

[1] Ibid., 401. For the position in the Baltic at this time see Davies, *Restoration*, Chap. xi.

[2] Burton, iii, 441.　　　　　　　　　　[3] Ibid., 489–90.

[4] In the end it was the French who forced a settlement on the Northern Powers. (Davies, *Restoration*, loc. cit.) See also below, p. 221.

[5] *CJ*. vii, 606.　　　　　　　　　　[6] Burton, iv, 365. 7 April.

[7] Ibid., 412.

that he would be in favour of paying an Army which would support, but be subordinate to, a 'godly' government, but Boteler had exceeded the limits which would be set by such a government for a military authority.

Meanwhile the hostility of the House to Vane himself was hardening.[1] When he commented one evening during a late session, 'We are not able to hold out sitting thus in the night', an M.P. remarked scathingly, 'He might well be spared.'[2] During the whole session he had never moderated his language,[3] and his speeches show no awareness on Vane's part of the many enemies he had in the House, though Richard Cromwell's 'Court', the Presbyterians, the 'moderates' and the royalists were all his opponents. The M.P.s recognized his delaying tactics; when he and Hesilrige wanted a free debate on putting the militia under Richard Cromwell's control, one M.P. impatiently declared that this would mean a ten-day discussion, 'till the nation, and the House, be about your ears'.[4] His eloquent plea for religious toleration went unheeded by the House.[5] As usual, it is difficult to say how many M.P.s took Vane's line; Brodrick counted 47 'true patriots',[6] as he sarcastically described Vane's group, out of the 300–400 M.P.s, and this minority group grew no larger as the session wore on. In

---

[1] One M.P. accused Hesilrige of trying to make himself and Vane 'the great Hogens-Mogens'. (Ibid., 221–2.) There are many disparaging remarks about Vane from M.P.s other than Maynard during the latter part of the session. The term Vanists was, according to John Rogers (*A Christian Concertation*, see below), invented by Baxter about this time, in the summer of 1659. It is certainly not used in the 1640s and earlier 1650s.

[2] Ibid., 139.

[3] See his reference to 'sneaking counsellors' of the Protector. (BM. Lansdowne, 823, f. 245.)

[4] Burton, iv, 472.

[5] Ibid., 329. 2 April. This was the occasion on which, seeing that the House intended to denounce magistrates who neglected to punish those guilty of holding heretical opinions, Vane exclaimed, 'All is lost! It is co-ercing the conscience.'

[6] Brodrick estimated that 23 of the 47 'patriots' were 'highly exasperated' with Richard Cromwell's government. (Davies, *Elections*, 500.) One of Nicholas's correspondents had been told that 9 leading men obstructed the 'Court' party. (*Nicholas Papers*, ed. G. F. Warner, Camden Series (London, 1920), iv, 81.) The absence of party discipline meant that M.P.s voted in what seems to us an inconsistent way, and even Maynard, on minor issues, sometimes voted with Vane. (Burton, iii, 346, 348.) There were over 400 M.P.s present in February 1659. (BM. Lansdowne, 823, f. 231v.)

March Vane was actually summoned to the bar for some disrespectful words he had used of the House.[1]

In this situation one would suspect that Vane might have invited the intervention of the Army, but here the evidence is conflicting. Ludlow states that it was the Army leaders who made the first approach to Vane and Hesilrige, through Ludlow himself, and that the two friends replied that they would assist the officers when they saw it was 'seasonable'.[2] This should be more reliable evidence than that of the royalist correspondent who informed Nicholas that Vane and his party had 'contrived the disorder' of the dissolution.[3]

But Major Nehemiah Bourne, the Navy commissioner, who claimed to be in the counsels of the Army, and who sympathized with the Anti-Cromwellians and supported religious toleration, also wrote that the 'honest party' in the House, not being able to carry even one vote, were 'stirred by the Lord' to 'apply to the officers of the Army'.[4] Bourne's view would make sense of Vane's policy—when the attempt to refuse recognition of the Protectorate failed, he then tried to reduce the 'Court' majority by excluding the lawyers and the Irish and Scottish members, but when that too was defeated, in desperation he turned to the Army, hoping to put the clock back, and secure the return of his much-admired Long Parliament, and with it, of course, his own supremacy.

It is certainly a remarkable fact that, of the Press appeals to the Army to recall the Rump,[5] noted by modern historians,[6] all but one emanated from the same publisher, Livewell

---

[1] Ibid., f. 274. 29 March. Vane had denied that the Parliament was a true Parliament.

[2] Ludlow, ii, 45. (Ludlow as usual gives no dates.) Vane, Hesilrige and Scot opposed Parliament's votes of 18 April, which were obnoxious to the Army.

[3] *Nicholas Papers*, iv, 12. Slingsby told Clarendon that the 'Commonwealth's men' used the Declaration for the fast, which presaged religious intolerance, to insinuate the fear of such a policy into the Army. (Bodl. Clar. 60, f. 354.)

[4] *Clarke Papers*, iii, 210.

[5] These are: E 979(5), (8); 980(5), (11), (15), (16), (17); 669, f. 21 (24), (26), (27), (28). E 980(1), discussed below, was a very violent effusion, and understandably has no means of identifying either printer or publisher.

[6] Davies, *Restoration*; Woolrych, op. cit., 151. Professor Woolrych noticed that three of the pamphlets listed above were published by Chapman, and surmised that Chapman's responsibility for the change of government might well have been considerable.

Chapman, who had issued the 1658 petition, and had indirect connexions with Vane. Even the one pamphlet which has no indication of its printer or publisher may well also have owed its publication to Chapman. No other publisher rushed into print to plead for the Rump's return, nor, indeed, in view of the widespread detestation of the Rump by 1653, is this surprising. In these circumstances one naturally looks at the pamphlets to see if Vane himself was the author of any of them. There are strong reasons for thinking that Vane wrote at least two, and that he probably had a hand in several more. It is difficult to believe that any politician other than Vane would have spoken of foreign affairs at this crisis, as did the author of *Some reasons humbly offered to the Officers of the Army, for the speedy re-admission of the Long Parliament,*[1] and other passages in this pamphlet, such as the intemperate terms in which the majority groups in Richard Cromwell's Parliament are referred to, the necessity for experienced administrators, the harmful effects on trade of the political uncertainty,[2] also read like Vane's work. A week later another pamphlet appeared,[3] which in style (with the numbered points that Vane sometimes favoured in his published speeches), its contemptuous references to Richard Cromwell, and its reminder of the experiences of those who had suffered under his father, indicate Vane as its likely author. Two other pamphlets read very like Vane's work;[4] three others were by ministers.[5] One of these was Christopher Feake, the

[1] E 979(8).

[2] He had said in April that 'merchants break every day, ten at a time'. (Burton, iv, 365.)

[3] E 980(17). *Reasons against a Single Person.* (To Fleetwood and the Army.) 5 May.

[4] E 669, f. 21 (27). *A Declaration of the well-affected to the Good Old Cause in the cities of London, Westminster and the Borough of Southwark . . .*; E 979(5). *The humble representation of divers well-affected Persons of the City of Westminster and parts adjacent.*

[5] I am assuming this, on internal evidence, in the case of E 979(4) and E 980(15). Christopher Feake's is E 980(5); in his preface Feake says that he wrote it on 20 March: he recounts the achievements of the Long Parliament, and if he was connected with Vane, the date is significant, for it looks as though Vane's circle was preparing the public for the return of the Rump by 20 March.
One pamphlet at this time (E 980(12)), *The Armies Dutie,* has no publisher named, but since it was printed and to be sold in Popeshead Alley, where Livewell Chapman's premises were, it is a fair assumption that he printed it. This did not demand the return of the Rump, though the authors did not oppose this. It was by H.M. (Henry Marton?), H.N. (Henry Nevile?) and several others, and was a plea for a

Fifth Monarchist, whom Richard Baxter assumes associated with Vane in 1659.[1] The pamphlet, which contains no name of printer or publisher, was a vituperative effusion in which the authors promised to bring 2000 men to support the Army.[2] This last was from Southwark, a part of London in which Vane was interested.[3]

The political vacuum following the dissolution of the Parliament on 22 April lasted a week; then the Army leaders met Vane, Hesilrige, Salwey and Ludlow at Vane's house at Charing Cross.[4] One can hazard a guess as to which articles of agreement between the Army and the politicians received Vane's strong support—religious and civil rights for 'the people', liberty of conscience, the establishment of a commonwealth, perhaps the 'maintenance of schools of learning'. The next meeting was at Fleetwood's house, and then or a day later Vane and seven others were appointed to draft a constitution for the country, to be submitted to the Army leaders.[5]

There is no source for the restored Rump of 1659 comparable to Burton's vivid and detailed diary of Richard Cromwell's Parliament, and Vane's part has to be reconstructed from a number of sources. The House immediately set up, on 9 May for eight days only, a Committee of Safety, with Vane as one

new constitution. Vane himself was deeply interested in ideal constitutions, and probably would not have objected to republican theories on this subject being ventilated.

The extraordinary letter, which must be a forgery, in the *State Papers Domestic* in which Desborough and one R. Hughes tell Livewell Chapman: 'Sir H. Vane seems born for such a time as this', and 'We hope you received the arms and ammunition sent', is intelligible if the writer believed that Chapman was Vane's publisher, and that both were Fifth Monarchists. It also hints that Brewster was involved in a plot to murder the king. Some person, one feels, knew enough about Chapman's activities to think this letter was a plausible way of incriminating him. It does not appear to have convinced the authorities; Williamson wrote on his copy, 'query if not from Sir Samuel Morland'. Morland was a royalist spy in 1659, and an important one, but his connexions with Vane were close. (*CSPD. 1659-60*, 409-11.) Another slightly different copy is in Stowe MSS, 185, f. 168 onwards.

[1] Quoted M. Weinstock, *The position of London in national affairs 1658-60*, unpublished M.A. thesis (London, 1934), 80.

[2] E 980(1). *To the Officers . . . the humble petition and Advice of divers well-affected to the Good Old Cause, Inhabitants in and about the Borough of Southwark.*

[3] *CSPD. 1645-47*, 123. See below, p. 221.

[4] Ludlow, ii, 74.   [5] *Clarke Papers*, iv, 6-7.

of its ten members.[1] No judge was allowed to take his seat, so Maynard was adroitly disposed of.[2] A committee was set up to consider those imprisoned for religious reasons, and though Vane, the chairman, stood out for his right to 'hat honour', it did release a number of Quakers.[3] The House set up a new Admiralty committee[4]—the old one was said to be hostile to the Rump—and the new membership is strikingly reminiscent of the 1649–53 Admiralty committee,[5] though there is no evidence that Vane played much part in it, no doubt because he was so preoccupied with the Baltic question, itself so vital to English sea-power. However, when the Council of State was anxious for more ships to be fitted out for sea, since the main Fleet had been sent to the Sound, and more money was needed for the Navy, Vane was asked to report on this to the House.[6] When the Council decided that sailors would have to be conscripted again, Morley reported to the House, but this was, no doubt, because it was on one of the few days on which Vane did not attend either session of the Council.[7]

Within a fortnight of its return the restored Rump had replaced the Committee of Safety by a Council of State, of which Vane was a member. It worked hard, sometimes meeting at 7 a.m., and sometimes in the evening; there were even some Sunday sessions![8] Twelve members appeared on the first day,

[1] Ludlow, ii, 79–80.

[2] Ibid., 80. Under the transparent pretext that the judges might hinder the reform of the law! Maynard was appointed as assize judge by the Council of State. (Bodl. Rawl. C 179, p. 68.)

[3] W. C. Braithwaite, *Beginnings of Quakerism* (London, 1923), 457–8. Quakers refused to take off their hats to their social superiors.

[4] Ludlow, ii, 81; *CJ*. vii, 666. 26 May.

[5] In addition to Vane, George Thompson, John Carew, Valentine Walton, William Say, John Langley and Richard Salwey were members. Salwey's close association with Vane belongs to 1659.

[6] Bodl. Rawl. C 179, p. 18. The bewildering changes in government were understandably too much for some Navy officials; the officers of the ordnance at Portsmouth, under the mistaken impression that no Admiralty commissioners were sitting, wrote to Vane at the end of May, for permission to provide arms for the ship *President* which had just put into port. They evidently assumed that Vane was once more in authority over the Navy. (*CSPD. 1658–59*, 568.)

[7] Ibid., 76. Vane reported on authorizing Admiralty judges to sit again, though the Council had told Morley to do this. (*CJ*. viii, 657.)

[8] Bodl. Rawl. C 179, *passim*. This MS, like other Admiralty records, has its folios numbered like pages. Note that the record of Council of State attendances in

and Hesilrige, Sydenham, Sir James Harrington and all the rest except Vane and Dixwell took the oath appointed by Parliament against government by the single person.[1] Perhaps this accounts for the fact that Vane did not appear for the next three days—though Dixwell did.[2] Since Vane was vehemently opposed to government by a single person, one must conclude that he had adopted the Fifth Monarchist objection to oaths as such. He re-appeared on the fourth day, however, and seems to have made it his practice to attend one or other of the daily sessions of the Council, but usually not both.[3] He, with Scot, Fleetwood and Sydenham were the committee for 'discovering designs against the commonwealth', and the 'secret service' committee,[4] but in practice Scot and Vane took charge of this.[5] He was also on the committee for Examinations, i.e. for examining suspected persons,[6] and it was in this capacity that he and Hesilrige several times examined Sir George Booth, after Booth's unsuccessful rising in August.[7] The Council of State took impressively thorough precautions against royalist revolts; boats were even anchored above and below London Bridge to prevent access to the City, and without such efficient steps the summer risings would have been far more serious than they were. There are indications that some of the Council's efficiency in these matters was due to Vane.[8] He should

CSPD. 1659-60, xxiii, is quite inaccurate. For instance in July 1659 Vane did not attend four times, but twenty-five, as recorded in Rawl. C 179. Vane had his share, with other Council members, of deer from the royal parks. (Rawl. C 179, pp. 90, 142.) At one point the Council gave its attention to a report that cock-fights were intended at Staindrop, the village at the gates of Raby Castle, and one feels this information must have come from Vane. (Ibid., p. 88.) The new Council turned out all the supporters of Cromwell from their lodgings in Whitehall, and Vane was given the rooms he had had in 1649-53, with some additional stabling. (Ibid., pp. 155, 212.)

[1] Ibid., p. 1. The list, drawn up after the Restoration, of those who did take the oath of abjuration (to renounce the line of King James I for ever) does not include Vane. (BM. Stowe, 185, f. 156.) St John, by the way, did take the oath.

[2] Bodl. Rawl. C 179, p. 1.   [3] Ibid., passim.   [4] Ibid., p. 12.

[5] Mordaunt, 25; Bodl. Clar. 65, f. 122.

[6] Bodl. Rawl. C 179, p. 193. 20 July.

[7] Bodl. Clar. 64, f. 114. Booth gave nothing away, however.

[8] When the members of the Council of State who had been entrusted with the task of deciding who should command the militia in London, Westminster, Southwark and other boroughs, were to expedite their report, the clerk sent the message to Vane, who had been absent. (Rawl. C 179, p. 5.) On 9 August he

not, by the way, rightly have belonged to the Council's Committee of Safety, set up on 29 July, since the Committee was to consist of those members of the Council who were Army officers which Vane then was not. He seems to have added himself to the Committee however, for he reported from it on 9 August.[1] Perhaps he felt that when he became the 'honorary' colonel of a Southwark regiment of volunteers on 1 August he was justified in joining the Committee![2]

As Vane was almost the only man among the twenty-one members of the Council of State who had any considerable knowledge of foreign affairs,[3] it was natural that he should be virtually the 'Foreign Secretary' of the restored Rump.[4] The Council as soon as it was appointed began to consider the Baltic problem. It very soon endorsed the statesmanlike policy already advocated by Vane in Richard Cromwell's Parliament, of co-operating with Holland to obtain peace and free trade in the Baltic, and to this was added a 'lasting peace and nearest union with Holland'—perhaps an echo of the 1652 plan? The Dutch were advancing somewhat similar propositions of co-operation, and Vane steered the negotiations so successfully that he was able to announce to Parliament on 30 July that a treaty with the United Provinces had been signed.[5] Among the matters discussed with the Dutch was joint action against pirates,[6] an interesting early example of international co-operation at sea. Vane had been an inevitable member of every committee of the Council to interview the Dutch, Danish or Swedish ambassadors, and whenever the Council wished a report made to Parliament on foreign policy, it was he who was appointed to give it.[7] The Council's clerk for foreign affairs, who was

announced the disposition of forces in London, a lengthy report, to the Council of State. (Ibid., p. 404.)

[1] Ibid., pp. 230, 404.   [2] See below, p. 225.

[3] The names of the members are in *CSPD. 1658–59*, 349. Bradshaw was ill, and St John not a foreign affairs expert. Whitelocke however was presumably well-versed in Baltic problems, and sometimes, with Vane, received the foreign envoys, though not as often as one would expect. Honeywood, the Queen of Bohemia's steward, knew Holland well.

[4] Vane's leading part in the negotiations can be traced in several sources, among them: Rawl. C 179, *passim*; *Thurloe S.P.*, vii, 676–83.

[5] F. P. G. Guizot, *History of Richard Cromwell and the Restoration of Charles II*, trans. A. R. Scoble (London, 1856), i, 483.

[6] Rawl. C 179, p. 414.   [7] Ibid., *passim*.

described in its records as its 'foreign secretary', was Samuel Morland,[1] the mathematician; this no doubt accounts for the fact that he knew enough about Vane to be asked to be a Crown witness at Vane's trial.[2]

In the late summer Parliament sent two plenipotentiaries, Vane's brother-in-law, Sir Robert Honeywood, and the Navy commissioner, Thomas Boone, to the kings of Sweden and Denmark.[3] Vane's eldest son, a cornet in the Life Guard, was one of their retinue.[4] Meanwhile the French envoy, Bordeaux, was addressing Vane as though he were the man who really mattered in diplomatic affairs,[5] there were important negotiations with Portugal to be dealt with, reports to be made to the House on foreign policy in general, and also on the attitude of Lockhart, the governor of Dunkirk.[6] Vane had power in his hands again, and brought to his tasks, as before, his extraordinary energy and clear intelligence.[7]

The restored Rump had no coherent party pattern; 'Parties are like so many floating islands, sometimes ioyning and appearing like a continent, when the next flod or ebb separates [so] that they can hardly be known, where they will be next', wrote a correspondent to Hyde.[8] Prynne's courageous attempt to take his seat had been frustrated, by a combination of artifice and force in which Vane played a large part. On the Monday after the Rump had assembled, Prynne got into the House, and saw Hesilrige, who told him, but one feels without much conviction, that he had no right to be there. Now however Vane arrived; he went up to Prynne, and said 'in a menacing manner': 'Mr.

---

[1] Ibid., pp. 225, 266, 310.   [2] See below, p. 237.   [3] *CSPD. 1659-60*, 1, 17, 270.

[4] Ibid., Will of Sir Henry Vane's eldest son, P.C.C. Laud 120. Young Vane made his will at Copenhagen in June 1660 (perhaps because he had been given jewels by the kings of Sweden and Denmark?), but died at Hampstead three months after his father's execution.

[5] Guizot, *Cromwell*, i, 437, 443.   [6] *CJ*. vii, 652, 657.

[7] He was also reporting to the House on Henry Cromwell in Ireland (*CJ*. vii, 663), and on letters from Monck (ibid., 736), supporting the plan to sell Hampton Court (Ludlow, ii, 101), and bringing in a petition from Hull (*CJ*. vii, 689, 690). This last may have been from the Independent congregation in the town. They obtained permission from the Council of State to use the chancel of the church there, as formerly (the Presbyterians were using the rest of the building). (Bodl. Rawl. C 179, f. 315.)

[8] Quoted G. H. Brown, *The Place of Sir Arthur Hesilrige in English Politics, 1659-60*, B.Litt. thesis (Oxford, 1949), 104.

Prynne, what make you here? You ought not to come into this House, being formerly voted out. I wish you as a friend quietly to depart hence, else some course will presently be taken with you for your presumption.' Prynne stoutly defended his right to sit, and took his usual place, 'resolved not to stir'. Meanwhile Hesilrige and Vane, joined now by some other members, withdrew to the Committee Chamber to consult on this embarrassing situation. After half an hour they all came down. Seeing Prynne still ensconced in his seat, Hesilrige and Vane, 'after some whisperings with the Speaker and others next them', settled on their plan. As a result the House decided not to sit until one o'clock, and when Prynne reappeared there were soldiers to keep him out.[1]

However it was not long before the first signs of a rift between Hesilrige and Vane appeared. On 13 May, six days after the Rump had re-assembled, Hesilrige advocated that the Commons should grant all officers' commissions, whereas Ludlow, Vane and Salwey saw the consequences of a step so likely to antagonize the Army leaders.[2] Vane sat on the committee though, and fell into an 'unusual passion'—another outburst— when he failed to obtain the appointment of Captain George Bishop as a militia commissioner for Bristol.[3] Bishop was a Quaker,[4] but the House accepted the appointment of other Quakers in Bristol as militia commissioners. Bishop however had been prominent in the prosecution of Christopher Love, and by vetoing him the House was covertly censuring Vane, as Vane no doubt realized. Vane was in close touch with Edward Burrough and other Quaker leaders during this summer and

---

[1] E 761(1). Prynne's *A True and Perfect Narrative*.

[2] Ludlow, ii, 89.

[3] *CJ*. vii, 717. 14 July. Bodl. Clarendon MS, 62, f. 187. Brodrick asserted that Vane 'declynes in reputation to that degree' that he was defeated on this minor issue, though he was 'seconded by Salwey and all whom his power of persuasion could in any way prevayle upon'. Massey wrote (*Nicholas Papers*, iv, 165) that the M.P.s were defeating Vane, 'sometimes for noe other reason but that he shall take notice that he *is* outvoted'. Bishop was a supporter of the restored Rump (W. A. Cole, *The Quakers and Politics, 1652–1660*, unpublished Cambridge Ph.D thesis (1955), 94), and may have had close connexions with Vane. (Ibid., 157.) He wrote a letter to the Army Council on 27 April urging the recall of the Rump. (George Bishop, *The Warning of the Lord to the Men of this Generation* (1660).)

[4] For Bishop see Cole, op. cit., 326–32.

autumn.[1] This was natural, for Vane was the champion of religious toleration, which the Quakers put in the forefront of their programme, and he introduced a motion providing for the elimination of tithes,[2] a form of taxation which the Friends resolutely opposed.

Hesilrige leaned to the Presbyterian position, but differences on the future of the country's government widened the rift between the two old friends. The restored Rump had voted to dissolve itself after a year[3] (though bets were laid at first that it would not last a fortnight), and there was much discussion about the form a new government should take. Massey wrote to Nicholas: 'Some of the grandees are for a general comprehensive state of all men of all religions, but Sir Henry Vane is stiffe for the guifted men allone, and those onely such as his owne holiness shall deeme soe.'[4] He told Nicholas later: 'Sir Henry Vayne lookes upon the nation as unacquainted with its own good, and unfitt to be trusted with power . . . he would have some few refyned spiritts (and those of his owne nomination) sitt at helme of State togeather with the Councill, till the people be made familiar with a Republique and in love with it, that is, until he ceases to be.'[5] If royalist reports are to be believed, and they are confirmed by Parliament's attitude to Vane in 1660, most of the M.P.s disliked and despised him.[6] No doubt in his case, as in Ludlow's, his opposition to the grant of Army commissions by Parliament had something to do with this.[7] One royalist wrote in July that Vane and Salwey had been deserted by many of their party, and had not more than sixteen or seventeen M.P.s—there were forty to fifty in the restored Rump—that they could rely upon. It was rumoured, so this correspondent asserted, that Vane's group wanted the whole House adjourned, 'that the whole manage of affairs might pass by the council, where they believe themselves more

---

[1] Ibid., 160, 193. For a letter sent to Vane about the persecution of Quakers in Massachusetts, see Bishop, op. cit. Burrough in his letter to Vane, probably in September, warns him not to 'rule by your craft and policy'. (Ellwood MSS, Friends House Library, London, ii, ff. 27-9.)

[2] Ibid., 138.   [3] Davies, *Restoration*, 106.   [4] *Nicholas Papers*, iv, 157.

[5] Ibid., 161. (Massey may have been deducing Vane's attitude not from his speeches in Parliament but from the pamphlet, *A Needful Corrective*—the words he uses are an echo of that.) See below, p. 227.

[6] Ibid., 165. 1 July.   [7] Ludlow, ii, 89.

prevalent'. Hesilrige opposed this 'very smartly'; he wanted a summons to all M.P.s who were absent, followed by a settlement of the nation.[1] Hesilrige failed to perceive the self-evident truth, only too clear to Vane, that a freely elected Parliament would contain a royalist majority, and be hostile to the Army. One would like to have evidence on the two men's views other than short passages in royalist letters, but Vane's opinions on government by an élite, as expressed in his pamphlets in the 1650s, are corroborative testimony.

In this same month Ludlow, who had secured with Vane's help parliament's permission to return from his new command in Ireland as soon as he had settled affairs there, was about to propose that Vane should be appointed as colonel of Ludlow's old regiment, but Vane's opponents were too quick, and the House appointed Colonel Morley, who belonged to Hesilrige's group, instead.[2] Ludlow could see the storm coming; he had discussed his fears of an Army *coup d'état* with Vane and had begged Vane, Hesilrige and the Army leaders to keep on good terms with one another. Vane recognized the wisdom of Ludlow's advice, and within a fortnight had effected a reconciliation between Hesilrige and Lambert, whose bitter exchange of words on the Act of Indemnity, which the Army thought gave the soldiers little security, is well known.[3]

In August Sir George Booth's rising presented the government with a minor crisis, and a number of men, including Skippon and Colonel George Thomson, were authorized by the Council of State to raise regiments in defence of the republic. Vane was one of the new colonels,[4] and the only one later to pay with his life for this action. He raised his regiment in Southwark,[5] though of the 360 men he was authorized to recruit, at least 60 failed to appear.[6] He was very busy at the time with foreign affairs,[7] but he took on himself new duties in connexion with the rising, reporting to Parliament in commendation of the officer who was dealing with potential rebels in Lincolnshire,[8] and examining prisoners, including Booth, him-

---

[1] *Thurloe S.P.*, vii, 704.
[2] Ludlow, ii, 94-5. The *Commons Journals* give some evidence of Morley's hostility to Vane.
[3] Ibid., 55, 100, 112.   [4] *CSPD. 1659-60*, 94, 563.   [5] *Tryal*. See below, pp. 237-8.
[6] *CSPD. 1659-60*, 239.   [7] Ibid., 213.   [8] Ibid., 77.

self.[1] At the height of the crisis the Council of State ordered that Raby Castle (that strategic fortress) was to be provided for,[2] and one can guess whose initiative secured this edict. He must also have been hard at work on the accounts for the Army and Navy, which he presented to the Rump on 28 July.[3]

On 3 September there was another violent quarrel with Hesilrige,[4] when Hesilrige wanted a new oath to be put to militia officers, and Vane did not. On 27 September his group tried to prevent the City from holding free elections, and were soundly beaten.[5] (The Common Council elections justified their fears in December.) Meanwhile the Army's discontent was growing ominous; the Derby petition had been brought to the attention of the House by an irate Hesilrige, and had been bitterly denounced. But no satisfactory steps to pay the Army had been taken, and another Army petition, with very forthright demands, was presented to Parliament on 5 October.[6] Parliament's gestures of defiance, nullifying all that the House had done since the Army intervention of April 1653, led to Lambert's expulsion of the Rump. There had been rumours during the previous week that Vane, who had for some months been associating with Lambert,[7] was advocating a military dictatorship with Lambert at its head.[8] It is hard to believe this, when one remembers the fervour with which Vane had expounded the right of Parliament to govern, but perhaps he did contemplate this expedient, as the only way in which he could maintain his own power. He was said to have declared that Lambert's action in expelling the Rump was the only way to save the Good Old Cause, and to have seen in Lambert's triumph signs of the Messiah's Second Coming.[9] He was

---

[1] Ibid., 142, 214.   [2] Ibid., 94.   [3] *CJ.* vii, 737-8.

[4] Nicholas told Ormond that the two men had been 'like to fall to blows'. (*CSPD. 1659-60*, 207.) The oath was against the government by 'a single person', which makes it seem likely that Vane was objecting to oath-taking either on religious principles or on grounds of expediency.

[5] Salwey and Rich were tellers against Marten and another M.P. (What little information there is indicates that Marten and Vane were again not seeing eye to eye.) (*CJ.* vii, 788.)

[6] Davies, *Restoration*, 154.

[7] Mordaunt, 23. 16 June; Ludlow, ii, 111. Many lampoons in 1660 and 1661 refer to their association.

[8] Ibid., 64-6.   [9] Davies, *Restoration*, 157.

certainly supporting Lambert in some way—perhaps he expected Lambert immediately to summon a sanhedrim of the kind that he wanted. But he had few adherents. Salwey was still loyal; Hesilrige, Nevile, and Milton however were all resolutely opposed to the new development.[1] Baxter had been attacking Vane in print since May, provoking Vane's anger to such an extent that Vane had even denounced him in the House.[2]

Baxter's *Key for Catholics* and *Holy Commonwealth* were two shots in the pamphlet war of 1659 in which Vane was closely involved. Vane seems himself to have written, in addition to the April and May pamphlets already mentioned, a reply to Harrington's *Oceana*;[3] at least Baxter, Anthony à Wood, and modern authorities accept it as Vane's own work, and nothing in the pamphlet contradicts this. In this the main tenor of his argument was that voting for the legislature should be restricted 'for a season'. He sadly recognized that the great difficulty facing the constitution-makers was to ensure that 'the depraved, corrupted and self-interested will of man, in the great body which we call the people, being once left to its own free motion, shall be prevailed with to espouse their true public interest'. So, he argued, none should be admitted to 'the exercise of the right and privilege of a free citizen, for a season, but either such as are free-born, in respect of their holy and righteous principles . . . or else who, by their tried affection and faithfulness to common right and public freedom, have deserved to be trusted with the keeping or bearing their own arms in the public defence'. (He omitted to mention who was to judge which citizens conformed to either of these standards.)

John Rogers valiantly took up the cudgels on Vane's behalf against not only Harrington, but also Prynne and the redoubtable Baxter.[4] Rogers has some shrewd arguments, a wealth of

---

[1] Ibid., 154–5. St John, described by one of Clarendon's correspondents as 'a wiser man than to believe he can ever settle a republic' (Bodl. Clar. 69, f. 129v), and Pierrepont were negotiating for a return of the king on the basis of the Isle of Wight terms, according to Mordaunt. (Mordaunt, 95.)

[2] Baxter, *Reliquiae*, 75–6.

[3] *A Needful Corrective or Ballance in Popular Government*, n.d., and no printer or publisher given. (Bodl.)

[4] *A Christian Concertation with Mr. Prin, Mr. Baxter, Mr. Harrington* . . . BM. E 995 (25). n.d., but about August 1659. It also was printed by Livewell Chapman, who

learning, and an almost sycophantic admiration for Vane, whom he describes as 'a man of such eminency for piety and prudence, honour, abilities, self-denials and sufferings in the service of Christ and of his DEAR country, as is not so meet to mention while he lives'. In Rogers's eyes, Vane's whole group, Fleetwood, Ludlow, Hesilrige and the rest, were incomparable for their 'sparkling virtues, and twinkling lustre, like stars up above the upper region'. Defending Vane with conviction against Baxter's absurd charge of Roman Catholicism (largely based on Vane's advocacy of wide religious toleration), he declared that Vane and his family could be called 'a Church, a Court, and a University of the highest, best and most liberal sciences that appertain to men or Christians'. It is certainly interesting that Vane's circle included the learned Henry Stubbe, who was also writing pamphlets in defence of Vane at this time,[1] George Sikes, a scientist as well as a theologian, and young Sir Thomas Liddell, who was interested in new mining techniques, though there is no evidence in Vane's own writings of scientific leanings.

Vane seems to have realized very soon after Lambert's expulsion of the Rump that the Army could not govern without some kind of public authority to support it, and he tried to persuade the Army leaders to recall the Rump. There was little difference now between his policy and Hesilrige's, except that Vane would not condemn Lambert, and was the only civilian appointed by the Army to commission officers.[2] Vane's proposal would have had the merit of bringing Hesilrige and the Rump supporters back from their voluntary exile, and allowing some sort of compromise to be worked out, but the Army leaders refused. Instead, yet again, they set up a Council of State; Vane was elected, though not unanimously—even the Army grandees

seems to have been in financial difficulties—Rogers says these held up the pamphlet for six weeks, 'till the help of a silver clyster-pipe set it [the press] a-work again'. Prynne replied, of course, to Rogers.

[1] *An Essay in defence of the Good Old Cause . . . and a vindication of the hon. Sir H.V. from the false aspersion of Mr. Baxter.* E 1841(1); *A Light shining out of Darkness . . .* E 987(2). Stubbe, an interesting character, was not ashamed ten years later to have written in defence of Vane—'I am ashamed rather to have done so little, than that I have done so much for him that so frankly obliged a stranger, and a childe.' (*Legends no Histories*, 1670.)

[2] Bodl. Clar. 65, f. 257.

could not be relied upon to support him.[1] Some of Vane's old
colleagues, Walter Strickland and Cornelius Holland among
them, were members, and attended the Council from time to
time, but Vane did not,[2] and it looks as though Lambert had
acted without Vane's approval on 13 October, when his troops
surrounded the Parliament. In fact, Vane's days of power were
over, and he never again directed affairs of State. He was
careful however to obtain from the Army authority for himself
and Salwey to continue to act as Navy commissioners,[3] for even
in this time of anarchy, the needs of the Navy must not be
forgotten. He was even accused at his trial of issuing a warrant
in December as Treasurer of the Navy,[4] but this was a mistake.
He persuaded Lambert and the other Army leaders to confer
with Ludlow, Salwey and himself at the end of October; but
the Army leaders could not satisfy Vane and his friends that
the Army was furthering the 'common cause' though what this
meant Ludlow does not explain.[5] So Vane still absented himself
from the Army Council of State,[6] though he was eager to see
the anarchy brought to an end, and consented to serve on a
committee of fourteen set up by the Army to draft a new
constitution.[7]

The times called for action however, not for political and
religious theory, and while Vane was arguing about ideal
constitutions[8] Hesilrige was acting. Portsmouth declared for the
Rump on 3 December; the apprentices of the City, which was
intensely hostile to Army rule, rioted two days later, and a

[1] Davies, *Restoration*, 157.
[2] *Clarke Papers*, iv, 92–3. Confirmed by the record of warrants issued by the
Committee of Safety between 1 November and 20 December. (Bodl. Rawl. A 259,
pp. 138 *seq.*)
[3] Ludlow, ii, 157. I assume that Vane took the initiative in obtaining the order.
[4] *Tryal.* See below, p. 238. Hutchinson's accounts for 1 January 1657 to 7 July
1660 (E 351/2296), when he handed over his office to Sir George Carteret, make
it clear that Hutchinson held his office for the whole 3½ years, without an interval.
Vane's authorization of expenditure had no doubt been given in his capacity as
Navy commissioner (see above, n. 3), and the prosecution had become confused.
Hutchinson's accounts as Navy Treasurer, by the way, are inferior to Vane's in
volume and lucidity.
[5] Ludlow, ii, 144.
[6] Nicholas was curious to know whether Vane and Salwey had 'given over
meddling with business'. (*CSPD. 1659–60*, 280.)
[7] Ludlow, ii, 149. 1 November.   [8] Whitelocke, iv, 376.

coroner's jury declared the officers who had put down the riot guilty of murder.[1] The unkindest cut of all for Vane was no doubt the line taken by the Fleet in the Downs, which declared that the Rump should be recalled. Now at last Vane took action, for the Fleet protected England against the return of the Stuarts;[2] he, Salwey and two others set off to interview Vice-Admiral Lawson.[3] (Lawson was a Fifth Monarchist, and, so Clarendon averred, a dependant of Vane.) But Lawson was determined to make contact with the City, and Vane could not persuade him to weigh anchor until he reached Gravesend. Ironically, it was now Vane's task to argue that the Rump should not be restored—it was the Army, he held, which was safeguarding the Good Old Cause. Scot and Okey represented Hesilrige's views to Lawson however, and they prevailed.[4]

The Army and the constitutional committee still continued to debate the fundamentals of liberty,[5] but the tide of events left them far behind. On 21 December the soldiers sent to besiege Hesilrige and his supporters, who were demanding the recall of the Rump and had taken Portsmouth, went over to the side of the besieged. While this bombshell was being discussed at Wallingford House Vane and Salwey entered with the devastating news that the elections for the Common Council in the City had returned a Council full of malignants.[6] Vane's last important political act was to persuade Fleetwood not to treat with the exiled king.[7]

The Rump, which met once more on 26 December, was in no mood to look kindly on those who had associated with Lambert and the Army. The Council of State acted quickly against Vane's recently recruited regiment, which was disbanded;[8] they perhaps feared that the men might try actively to defend their colonel. Four days after the first steps were taken against

---

[1] Weinstock, op. cit., 130.

[2] Mordaunt, 156. It would be the Fleet in the Downs which would have to intercept a royalist invasion.

[3] L. F. Brown, op. cit., 108, 117; Clarendon, *Rebellion*, xvi, 106.

[4] Davies, *Restoration*, 184.   [5] Ibid., 185.

[6] Ibid., 187. From first to last Vane's City connexions, though far from clear, are significant.

[7] Whitelocke, iv, 382. 23 December.

[8] *CSPD. 1659–60*, 300, 342, 350. The meaning of the first two entries is rather obscure.

his regiment Vane was summoned before Parliament, and charged with issuing orders to the Navy without Parliament's authorization.[1] He defended himself ably,[2] but he was expelled from the House, and ordered to retire to Raby Castle. He did not obey, but stayed on in London, at his house at Charing Cross. According to Morland, Hesilrige was so much opposed to Vane's expulsion that he wept when he saw he could not prevent it;[3] he realized belatedly that his course of action had paved the way for the Stuarts, and that none of his beloved oaths of loyalty would stem the tide.

He now strove to have Vane re-introduced to the Rump. A petition in Vane's favour was presented by Lawson, but its only result was to lose the Vice-Admiral his command—the Rump was irreconcilable.[4] Late in January 1660 one of Clarendon's correspondents reported that Hesilrige, Vane and Lambert had met and agreed to 'join interests', and to 'raise all the sectaries they can'.[5] Royalists saw Vane as the implacable enemy of monarchy,[6] and some, even in February 1660, as a man who might yet return to power;[7] this explains Monck's request to Parliament[8] that Vane should obey its order and leave London. Ten days later Monck repeated his complaint—he had excellent spies, and declared that Hesilrige and Colonel Rich were seen to go into Vane's house on 10 February. Hesilrige plaintively denied the charge,[9] but the Rump was

---

[1] *CJ.* vii, 806. There is nothing to indicate that he had sat in Parliament since it re-assembled on 26 December.

[2] Whitelocke (iv, 388) says that Vane made an 'ingenious' answer. Salwey fared worse than Vane for a time, for he was sent to the Tower.

[3] Bodl. Clar. 68, f. 104. Hesilrige's magnanimous attitude to Lambert (*CJ.* vii, 802) tends to confirm these allegations.

[4] Bodl. Clar. 68, f. 159.   [5] Bodl. Clar. 69, f. 116.

[6] E.g. Bodl. Clar. 68, f. 159. (Hesilrige and Nevile endeavouring to introduce Vane again into the House.) 'The strength of their argument receiving force from his being irreconcilable to your Majesty's interest and family.'

[7] Bodl. Clar. 69, f. 131. 'This kind of unusuall proceedings of the parliament, in no more executing the former order, after so manifest a contempt in him . . . is evidence enough, that he hath a body of friends there, and if the sense of it doth not work upon Monke, I shall wonder if after all this downfall Lambert and Vane and all that party, doth not once more take the opportunity out of Monke's hands.'

[8] Davies, *Restoration*, 281.

[9] G. H. Brown, op. cit., 163. Hesilrige and Rich were working together in Parliament. (*CJ.* vii, 802.)

forced to act; the Serjeant-at-arms was instructed to conduct Vane to Belleau, as a first stage on the journey to Raby.[1]

Vane must have realized in what direction events were moving but he did nothing during the spring of 1660 to protect himself. He did not flee from the country, and though submissive and contrite petitions poured in to the restored king,[2] there was none from Vane. In the summer the Convention Parliament discussed whether the Act of Indemnity should cover Vane or not. He was listed among the twenty men who, though not regicides, were deserving of punishment for their 'mischievous activity'. The Commons were divided as to whether Vane should lose his life; Holles, his old rival, pleaded that he should not. The Lords however wanted Vane put to death, and in the end, after negotiations between the two Houses, the Commons were persuaded to rely on an appeal by petition to the king's mercy, if Vane and Lambert should be declared guilty of treason, and this was drafted.[3]

Some time between February and July 1660[4] Vane leased or bought the secluded house in Hampstead, part of which was still known, until its recent demolition, by his name, though he had spent far more time at Charing Cross House, Fairlawn in Kent, and even Raby, than ever he was to spend at Hampstead. The move to Hampstead is very understandable; his presence so near to the spot where Charles I had been executed[5] would be a constant reminder to the new king and his supporters of the part Vane had played in the events leading up to, and succeeding, the king's death. He may also have felt too that if he decided to fly the country, as many other supporters of the 'Good Old Cause' did in 1660, he could do so more easily from

---

[1] *CJ.* vii, 841.   [2] *CSPD. 1660–61*, 8.   [3] Willcock, 315.

[4] Mordaunt's informant (see above, p. 231), who saw Hesilrige going into Vane's house in February, could hardly have done so if Vane were already at Hampstead. The Hampstead house was well back from the road, and in extensive grounds. Sir James Harrington was his near neighbour, at Ken Wood.

[5] His house at Charing Cross was quite a small one, next door to Northumberland House, between the modern Northumberland Street and Craven Street. (*Survey of London*, ed. G. Gater and W. H. Godfrey (London, 1937), xviii, 19.) The Vane family retained it until 1679, when Vane's son Christopher sold it to a goldsmith, who retained part as his residence, but part became a tavern, 'The Standard'. (Ibid.) (There is still a winehouse on the site.) The extravagance of Vane's great-great-grandson led to the sale of Fairlawn in the eighteenth century. The building was destroyed in the same century, and a new house built on the site.

Hampstead than from Charing Cross, where he was under constant surveillance. There was an underground passage—one wonders whether perhaps Vane had it made?—from the brewhouse at the Hampstead house to an obscure door on the road.[1] Charing Cross House was leased by Secretary Nicholas,[2] and Lady Vane approached him for favours,[3] so perhaps the terms of the lease were advantageous to both parties. It was to the Hampstead house that Vane returned after his brief sojourn at Raby in the summer of 1660. He would probably have been wiser to stay in the North, where the king and his other enemies might have forgotten him. As it was, the Court decided to arrest Vane, on a trumped-up charge, and hold him for trial until a more vindictive Parliament than the Convention should agree to his execution, and on 1 July he was arrested at Hampstead.[4] There were different stories handed down by tradition about his arrest. One was that he had been hidden disguised as a 'carman' (wagoner) at Ken Wood House, while the pursuivants were searching for him, and was found there; the other that he was walking under the fine avenue of elms which led up to his own house (admiring the sunset) and while his agitated servants gathered round him, seeing the troops approach, he calmly turned to the soldiers and asked their business.[5]

Vane was confined in the Tower until October 1661. He had friends who visited him there; Thomas Taylor, a minister, said to have been appointed to a living by Vane, went to see him in the Tower in December, and was promptly arraigned before the justices for saying in October 1659 that he would maintain a government of which Vane was high constable![6] Of

---

[1] *Hampstead Record*, 6 September 1890. The plaque on the recently demolished house, which was part of the one Vane lived in, was erected by the Royal Society of Arts in 1898, following correspondence in a local newspaper.

[2] *Survey of London*, loc. cit. BM. Eg. 2538, f. 278v, makes it clear that it was Vane's house which Nicholas had leased.

[3] *CSPD. 1661–62*, 145.   [4] Ludlow, ii, 340.

[5] The first story is in an inaccurate eighteenth-century copy of some papers then belonging to the Vane family. (Highgate Public Library, Heal Collection, iii, 143.) The other is in T. J. Barratt, *Annals of Hampstead* (London, 1912), i, 132.

[6] *CSPD. 1660–61*, 482. The Venetian ambassador (*CSPV. 1659–61*, 173) had heard in July 1660 that no-one was allowed to communicate with the prisoners in the Tower, but he was evidently mistaken.

course the vultures gathered, and petition after petition requested the king to make grants of Vane's estates in Kent or Durham.[1] His anxious young brother-in-law, Sir William Wray, petitioned the king to secure him in possession of the estates, of which Vane was trustee.[2]

The Cavalier Parliament, when it met, obediently voted that Vane and Lambert should be tried for treason, and in October 1661 he was moved to the Scilly Isles, out of reach of republican plotters and of *habeas corpus*. It was not until April 1662 that Vane was brought before a Middlesex Grand Jury on the charge of treason, and it is not at all clear why the government acted just when they did. Contemporaries assumed that the Fifth Monarchy rising in January 1661 led to the government's determination to proceed against Vane,[3] but the fourteen months that elapsed after the rising before Vane was brought before the Grand Jury seems too long, even allowing for the law's delays. The charge of 'traitorously imagining and intending etc. the death of the king' was supported by the facts that 'the prisoner sate with others in several councils or rather confederacies, incroached the government, levied forces, appointed officers, and at last levied open and actual war, in the head of a regiment'.[4]

The verdict against him was not obtained without difficulty; according to Vane, the Solicitor, his old enemy Sir John Maynard, had a 'long whisper' with the foreman, and told him Vane must be a 'sacrifice for the nation'.[5] Most of the half-hour that the jury took to consider their verdict must have been taken up in listening to the prosecuting counsel, who had the effrontery to go in to the jury to browbeat them. Vane alleged also that the jurors protested that they were being asked to pronounce not only whether certain acts had been committed, but to accept that the acts constituted treason. If this is true the jury showed some spirit.

The Middlesex Grand Jury however found a true bill against Vane for treason, on the grounds that he had levied war against the king. Vane now carefully prepared a defence of his actions as far back as May 1642. He must have been taken

---

[1] *CSPD. 1660–61*, 240, 261, 345, 365.   [2] Ibid., 328.
[3] Willcock, 318–19.   [4] *Tryal*, 26–7.   [5] Ibid., 73.

utterly by surprise[1] when he heard the actual terms of the indictment, which were unknown to him until he appeared in court in June to face his trial; he was accused of committing treason not against Charles I, but against Charles II, and all the charges related to the period 1649–59.[2] Vane's accusers, who included his fellow ex-members of Parliament Sir Geoffrey Palmer and Sir John Maynard, had been exceedingly astute. Not only had they presented Vane with completely unexpected charges, but they had made it impossible for him to call as witnesses such Long Parliament members as Holles or St John —or Maynard himself. Vane, obviously needing time to think, asked for the charge to be read a second time, which was done, and then that it should be read in Latin, which the judges refused.[3] Already he had thought out objections to the indictment itself. He argued that the 'forces' levied in 1659 during Booth's rising, of whom one regiment was in name under Vane's colonelcy, did not amount to 'waging war' as the prosecution alleged, no particulars of the place where the troops had assembled, or of other people concerned, had been given, the indictment itself declaring only that he and others had assembled 'in a warlike manner'.[4] The judges disregarded his objections, and urged him to plead or confess. He pleaded 'Not Guilty', and was given only four days to prepare his defence.

As Vane contemptuously said, it would have been better to have executed him by 'special command' than to pretend to give him the benefit of the law.[5] As the charge was one of treason he was not allowed counsel. Even his attorneys, and those employed in his legal affairs, were not allowed access to him.[6] When he asked to be allowed to *sub-poena* witnesses, the

---

[1] This is made clear by 'The true copy of the prisoner's own papers', printed in the *Tryal*, 36 *seq.*, which begins with an account of Vane's actions from November 1640 onwards.

[2] The official explanation (*Kingdomes Intelligencer*, 2–9 June 1662, p. 367) was that 'There being so much to be said against him, twas thought fit not to trouble the Court with any of his crimes before that fatal year of 1648.'

[3] *Tryal*, 52.   [4] Ibid., 20.   [5] Ibid., 25.

[6] He must have had some law books with him in the Tower. At least there seems to be no evidence in his earlier career of such wide knowledge of the law as he showed in this trial. One would think too that he must have had some papers relating to the history of the Long Parliament with him, unless he had a prodigious memory. Perhaps the person who smuggled his trial notes out, smuggled some books and papers in.

judges had the effrontery to reply that the jury were to be
without food or drink until their verdict was given, and time
for summoning witnesses could not therefore be granted him.
Vane, whose biting wit had not deserted him, commented that
he was reminded of the more than forty Jews, who resolved not
to eat and drink until they had murdered St Paul, as recorded
in the 23rd chapter of Acts.[1] He had argued that as the judges
were members of the House of Lords, and as it was the peers
who had struck out the proviso by which the Commons would
have spared his life, in the bill of Indemnity, the judges had
prejudged his case. Certainly there is little doubt that the
judges had made up their minds what the verdict was to be
before the trial began. As he angrily pointed out, men had
begged his estates from the king before he was condemned.[2] In
these circumstances, one can only admire the more the masterly
defence he presented, and—which people had not expected
of him[3]—his courage. For ten hours he defended himself
against his prosecutors, and his judges, with consummate skill.

The accounts which he had so carefully compiled of his
actions between 1640 and 1649 now had little relevance, but
many of the principles he advanced in them were applicable
also to the period 1649–60. His sarcastic remark: 'I would
gladly know that person in England of estate and fortune, and
of age, that hath not counselled, aided or abetted . . . and
submitted to the Laws and Government of the Powers that
then were', summed up his defence that in carrying out the
orders of a *de facto* government he had done no more than
millions of others had done.[4] It is remarkable that he did not
name some of the other men who had acted with him, but who
now, having adroitly changed their coats, were sitting in the
seats of power, as for example St John, raised to the peerage,
and building his £40,000 house in the Fens, or Samuel Browne,
appointed a judge of the Court of Common Pleas.[5]

In substantiation of the charge that Vane planned to destroy
the king (Charles II) and government, the counsel for the
prosecution produced a warrant to Navy officials which Vane
had issued on the day of Charles I's death, and charged Vane

[1] He gave chapter and verse. (*Tryal*, 67.)   [2] See above, p. 234. *Tryal*, 24.
[3] Baxter, op. cit., 76.   [4] *Tryal*, 44.   [5] *CSPD. 1663–64*, 489, 494.

with being a member of the 1649 Council of State. His accusers
knew where to look for evidence of his activities; they alleged
that he reported from that Council of State in March 1649 on
the allocation of money for the Navy.[1] There were also accusations that he attended the Council and its committee for Irish
and Scottish affairs, and that he reported the form of the oath
of secrecy to be used by the Council. Warrants were produced
signed by him as president of the Council in June 1652, and as a
Navy commissioner. Vane managed to produce witnesses,[2] who
must have been men of courage, to testify that his signature had
often been forged. If witnesses to his signature had had to be
sought, it would have given him precious time, but Judge
Wyndham told the jury it was incredible that anyone should
forge Vane's signature to a warrant setting out ships for sea,
and no delay on this score was allowed. Vane reiterated that
no witness had seen him sign the warrants alleged to be his,
and further, that no witness had actually seen him in the
Council of State. As for his reports from the Council of State,
the messenger, he said, did not always agree with the message
he had to deliver. In any case, he had signed the warrants by
instructions from the Council of State, and, 'where such great
changes take place, as happened in troubled times, a man could
not proceed according to all the formalities of law'. King, Lords
and Commons had fallen out, and when this happened, he had
decided it was the best policy to 'preserve the government in
its root, to wit, the Commons'. One can see why Vane thought
that to bring a charge of treason against him alone was patently
unjust. As he truly said, if he had committed treason, others
had committed it with him.[3]

The command of the regiment, 'an imployment, which I
can in truth affirm, mine own inclinations, nature and breeding

---

[1] *Tryal*, 28.

[2] Vane alleged (ibid., 71) that Monck had brought much pressure to bear on
one officer who had been involved in the Southwark 'assembly', to testify against
Vane. It is interesting that Matthew Locke, the clerk who gave evidence against
Vane, and who had become Monck's secretary (HMC, *Leyborne-Popham MSS*,
122, 137), was granted jointly with Monck in 1664 lands which had escheated to
the Crown. (*CSPD. 1663–64*, 495, 571.) Samuel Morland resisted pressure from
Finch to testify against Vane, and burnt some of Vane's papers which might have
incriminated Sir Henry. (Willcock, 379.)

[3] *Tryal*, 32.

little fitted me for', as he said, Vane contended was a command in name only. The Council of State nominated him to it, and the only proof of the 'warlike manner' in which Vane and the men were alleged to have assembled was that Vane had given the troops five pounds to spend in drink.[1] He had, he said, when he saw the proceedings of the Army, interesting themselves in the civil government of the nation, 'which I utterly disliked', persuaded the officers to lay down their charge, and he was able to produce some Army officers as witnesses to this. From first to last he had defended himself with astonishing legal acumen, considering that he was not a lawyer by profession.[2] He even pointed out that he was being tried in Middlesex for an offence that had been committed in Surrey, i.e. Southwark.[3] He ingeniously argued that the Southwark raising of troops could have been done for the king's restoration—no hostility or injury had been offered to anyone. And how could adherence to the Long Parliament be interpreted as adherence to the king's enemies, unless the Act of Indemnity were overthrown?

The king's counsel were driven to accepting his contention that many of his actions had been authorized by what he called a Parliament, but when Vane, as they no doubt expected, then challenged them to prove that he had ever acted in the 1659 Council of State after Lambert had expelled the Rump, the prosecution were ready for him, and produced a warrant he was alleged to have signed as Treasurer of the Navy in November 1659. The Solicitor General, Finch, argued cogently that the 'Parliament' which had authorized Vane's actions in this and other matters consisted of not one-eighth of the House of Commons, and that for Vane to claim that he was justified in obeying such a body was not an excuse but an aggravation of his offence. Finch pointed out that any rebels who happened to be successful for a time, could claim that they were only

[1] Ibid., 49.

[2] Though the official newspaper's report states (*Kingdomes Intelligencer*, 368) that his pauses were 'so many and frequent' that they 'much exercised the patience of the Court', and that he appeared 'amazed and speechless, complaining often of his broken memory and long imprisonment'. The pauses cannot have been so long, however, for the whole trial lasted ten hours, and there were, according to the same authority, 'a cloud of witnesses' against him. He was not allowed to take any food or drink, though it was brought for him.

[3] *Tryal*, 33.

obeying a *de facto* government, and so justify themselves.[1]
Justice Wyndham concurred with Finch; if a House was under
the constraint of force, and some members were kept out, some
let in, its actions were null in law. The other judges agreed.[2]
The jury gave the verdict that the Crown wanted, and five
days afterwards Vane was condemned to be hanged, drawn and
quartered at Tyburn.[3]

Vane pleaded ably for a stay of execution, and asked for
counsel, so that it could be argued legally whether a Parliament
was accountable to any inferior court, and whether the king,
being out of possession, and the Power Regent in others—but
at this point the judges interrupted him, to say that they did
not admit that the king was ever out of possession. In a characteristic retort Vane reminded them that the words of the indictment against him ran, 'that he endeavoured to keep out his
majesty'. How could he keep the king out of the realm if he were
not out?[4] But the judges would not listen, nor would they, as he
asserted they legally should have done, put their seal to his
'bill of exceptions' against the charges. As he was taken out
of the court he declared, 'I gave no general offence; whom man
judges, God will not condemn.'[5] The last phrase was the very
one used by Venner at his trial the year before, and can have
done nothing to soften the hearts of Vane's enemies.

He had argued at this trial 'as if he had not been standing
at the Bar, but sitting in the Rump or Committee of Safety'.[6]
He had told a friend, 'I bless God that enabled me to make a
stand for this Cause; for I saw the Court resolved to run it
down, and (through the assistance of God) I resolved they
should run over my life and blood first!'[7] His courage cost
him his life; though Parliament had as we have seen petitioned
Charles II that Vane and Lambert, excepted from the Act of
Indemnity, should yet not lose their lives, and the king had
agreed, there was no reprieve for Vane. Lambert on the other
hand was spared; brought to trial three days after Vane, 'his
carriage was much different from him that was tried on Friday

[1] Ibid., 33–4.   [2] Ibid., 34–5.   [3] Ibid., 52.   [4] Ibid., 54.
[5] *Mercurius Publicus*, 5–12 June, p. 368.
[6] *Kingdomes Intelligencer*, 2–9 June, p. 368.
[7] *Tryal*, 77.

last, not troubling the Court with seditious queries'.[1] Of course one does not know whether Vane would have preferred the twenty-one years of imprisonment that were Lambert's lot, to his own swift despatch.

Sir Henry, back in the Tower, was urged to make some submission to the king, to obtain a reprieve, but he refused. 'As for that glorious Cause . . . in which so many righteous souls have lost their lives, and so many have engaged by my countenance and encouragement, shall I now give it up, and so declare them all rebels and murderers? No, I will never do it.'[2] Nor would he offer the 'some thousands of pounds', which friends suggested might buy his pardon. He would not give a thousand farthings, he declared.[3] He wrote, in a document that the court refused to receive, 'Had nothing been in it, but the care to preserve my own life, I needed not have stayed in England, but might have taken my opportunity to have withdrawn myself into foreign parts, to provide for my own safety.' His steadfast religious faith and his patriotism are impressive. As George Sikes put it: 'He had for any time these two years made death familiar to him, and being shut up from the world, he said, he had been shut up with God, and that he did know what was the mind of God to him in this great matter.'[4] 'I have also taken notice', he declared, 'in the little reading that I have had of history, how glorious the very heathens have rendered their names to posterity, in the contempt they have shewed of death (when the laying down of their life has appeared to be their duty) from the love which they have owed their country.'[5] Even after three centuries have passed, the account of Vane's trial and his last days in the Tower still has power to move the reader.

The Lord Chief Justice had told Vane when sentence was pronounced that 'had not the prisoner's high crimes been heightened by his very ill deportment, he might have had some

---

[1] *Mercurius Publicus*, 5–12 June, p. 366.

[2] *Tryal*, 80. This statement is rather at odds with another he made in the papers he prepared for his trial, in which he said that in the changes and revolutions that had passed: 'I was never a first mover, but always a follower, choosing rather to adhere to things than persons.' (Ibid., 44.)

[3] Ibid., 81.   [4] Ibid., 77.

[5] Ibid., 63.

hopes of mercy'.[1] Judge Forster, in similar vein, declared that 'God . . . yet intended his mercy only to the penitent'.[2] The king was moved not only by Vane's defiance[3] at the trial, but, as is well known, by his belief that Vane was 'too dangerous a man to let live if we can honestly put him out of the way'. No doubt his views influenced the judges in deciding on their sentence.

The hideously cruel hanging, drawing and quartering were not carried out. 'At the request of some of Sir Henry Vane's relations (whose loyalty and sufferings for his majesty and his blessed father were as eminent, if possible, as Sir Henry's crimes), his majesty consented Sir Henry should be beheaded on Tower Hill (just there where the renowned earl of Strafford was put to death).'[4] Vane perhaps remembered the hapless Tomkins and Challenor, hanged with even more expedition after their court martial for taking part in Waller's plot in 1643. But their execution had taken place in wartime, and without what Vane called the 'two years cool blood'[5] which his own long imprisonment had allowed. The date of Vane's execution had been carefully chosen, for it was the anniversary of the battle of Naseby. 'Who can forget', enquired the news-writer, 'how Sir Henry himself seventeen years since (for 'twas then printed) moved for a thanksgiving for this very day, the day of that fatal battle of Naseby?'[6] On the scaffold Sir Henry, in a black suit and cloak, with scarlet waistcoat, denounced the mockery of a trial to which he had been subjected, and declared, 'I am come to seal that with my blood, that I have done', and gave what was no doubt in his own eyes his final justification. 'In all respects, wherein I have been concerned as to the publick, my design hath been to accomplish good things for these nations.'[7] When the Lieutenant of the Tower tried to seize the papers from which Vane was reading, he tore them into pieces, 'with more choler', says the news-writer, 'than could be

---

[1] *Mercurius Publicus*, 5-12 June, p. 368.   [2] *Tryal*, 55.

[3] The letter is printed in Burnet's *History of my Own Times*, ed. O. Airy (Oxford, 1897), i, 286, n. 2.

[4] *Mercurius Publicus*, 12-19 June, pp. 370-1. His brother Sir Walter Vane is generally assumed to have been the intermediary.

[5] *Tryal*, 25.   [6] *Mercurius Publicus*, loc. cit.

[7] *Tryal*, 88.

expected in a dying man'.[1] He was steadfast to the end in his refusal to admit that he had committed any offence; almost his last words were, 'I bless the Lord I have not deserted the righteous cause for which I suffer.'[2] Significantly, his very last words were of England—'Father, glorify Thy servant in the sight of men, that he may glorify Thee in the discharge of his duty to Thee and to his country.'[3]

Perhaps Vane's family were able to assure him before he died about their financial future—they were allowed to keep Raby Castle, Charing Cross House, and Fairlawn; Belleau alone had to be given back.[4] One feels that his heart was at Fairlawn, with its beautiful formal gardens; certainly it was here that his headless ghost was reputed to walk, in a grove of yews, at least until a century ago.[5]

Vane's wife, and nine of his thirteen children, six girls and three boys, survived him. The youngest, a girl, was only four. One has the impression that they were a lively and affectionate family. According to Henry Stubbe's elegant Latin tribute,[6] the eldest son was gentle, intelligent, and industrious; the young man's will, made less than a month before his father's arrest, evinces his strong family affection. 'I bequeath unto my most deare mother the Lady Vane the case of dyamonds which enclosed the King of Swede's picture; desiring if she please to put therein my father's picture', and he left jewels or a casket to each of his sisters except the baby Katherine.[7] Vane's words to his children, as he kissed them farewell in the Tower, were those of a man who felt the parting deeply—'The Lord bless you, He will be a better father to you. I must now forget that ever I knew you'[8]—and he prayed that the spirits of those that loved him should be drawn towards his family, left desolate.[9]

---

[1] *Mercurius Publicus*, 12–19 June, p. 371.

[2] *Tryal*, 95.   [3] Ibid.   [4] *CSPD. 1661–62*, 409.

[5] Article by Lady Vane, *The Sketch*, 25 January 1899. Lady Vane stated that when staying at Fairlawn in 1869, she heard footsteps one night on the flagged walk where Vane's dining-room had been, but was not alarmed, and heard only later of the ghost.

[6] Printed at Oxford in 1656. *Illustrissimo, summaque spei . . .*

[7] P.C.C. Laud 120.   [8] *Tryal*, 79.   [9] Ibid., 84.

Charles II's government however still regarded the family with suspicion, though Vane was dead; a letter from his daughter Albinia was opened in November 1663, and she was questioned.[1] About the same time two of his brothers-in-law who had been too closely connected with his actions, or too sympathetic to his views, thought it wiser to leave the country; Sir Robert Honeywood went to Holland, presumably for good;[2] Sir Thomas Liddell obtained passes for an eighteen months' stay abroad.[3] The book Vane finished writing just before his execution was published, anonymously, in 1664.[4] He had asked the Fifth Monarchy men to pray for him before his execution, so it was said,[5] and certainly this book is very reminiscent of their teaching. The Vane family remained patrons of nonconformity in religion,[6] and when James II was trying to conciliate the dissenters in 1688, he made Christopher Vane, heir to Sir Henry, a Privy Councillor.[7] In 1698 Christopher Vane became Baron Barnard of Barnard Castle,[8] and the earl of Lindsey was even afraid that Vane's attainder would be reversed.[9] This however never happened.

The last nine years of his life must have been tragically difficult for Vane, deprived of power over the nation's affairs for all but a few months in 1659. Only during the period of the restored Rump, in May–October 1659, was he at the helm of state, and one has the feeling that Vane was then triumphing over the dead Cromwell—the Council of State was working industriously, as it did in 1649–53, the Navy committee's personnel was much as it had been in the earlier period. But his victory was a hollow one, for the Rump lacked any solid basis of support in the nation's esteem, and he could not carry even the Rump with him. Vane's writings and actions show that he realized where the loyalties of most of the nation were, and he wrestled with the dilemma of producing a government

---

[1] *CSPD. 1663–64*, 338.   [2] Ibid., 292.

[3] Ibid., 129, 227. Liddell had raised a regiment of 1000 in Durham to defend the republic at the time of Booth's rising. (Bodl. Rawl. C 179, ff. 286, 303.)

[4] *A Pilgrimage into the Land of Promise*, 1664.   [5] *CSPD. 1661–62*, 397.

[6] G. Lyon Turner, *Original Records of Early Nonconformity*, London, 1911, ii, 1002.

[7] Willcock, 345.

[8] G.E.C. *Complete Peerage*, ed. V. Gibbs (London, 1910), i, 425.

[9] *CSPD. 1699–1700*, 283.

in which 'the people' had a share, but which would follow the policies of which he approved. It was a dilemma he could not solve, however, in spite of his use of the Press. All the indications are that not only the publications he acknowledged as his own, but a number of others, particularly in the period April–May 1659, were Vane's, either directly or by inspiration.

Richard Baxter shows that many people regarded Vane as the man most responsible for what the country had suffered in the 1640s and 1650s, and Baillie's vindictive pleasure at Vane's death reveals what bitter hatred he had inspired in some. Nevertheless, had he chosen to show what the triumphant royalists considered appropriate remorse, he need not have lost his life, for he was certainly not a regicide. But he would not stoop to the hypocrisy of denying his real convictions, as so many did, and Vane's severest critic could not deny that in the last nine troubled years of his life his loyalty to his beliefs and his personal courage gave a lustre to his fame which his long years of power and success had never quite earned.

Conclusion

V ANE'S brief term of office as governor of Massachusetts had revealed some of his qualities as a politician. He had evinced a generous open-mindedness in religious matters, courage in maintaining his principles, and a rare gift for expressing them lucidly and vigorously. He had made some firm friends. But he had also shown his lack of patience; when defeated at an election and deprived of office he had gone back to England, leaving others to carry on the struggle. He had aroused bitter antagonism in the colony. There had not been time for him to demonstrate the extraordinary ability and energy he possessed in administration.

His comparative youth, and perhaps the unhappy Massachusetts episode, probably account for the fact that for the first three years of the Long Parliament, he did not initiate measures, but contented himself with supporting Pym, Hampden, St John, Strode and other leaders. There are indications that he and Marten occasionally assisted one another during this early period, but this does not mean that Vane was a republican, merely that the two men took a similar attitude to peace negotiations and the House of Lords, and co-operated on these matters only.

But in the autumn of 1643, when he returned from Scotland, having successfully negotiated the Solemn League and Covenant, he was listened to as one of the leaders of the House. Pym was already ill, and the consequent collapse of his main executive committee, the Committee of Safety, allowed Vane and St John to create the instrument by means of which their group would control Parliament—the Committee of Both Kingdoms. By this time some of the M.P.s who had originally supported the war, such as Holles and Stapleton, together with a large section of the public, were now eager for peace negotiations. Vane and those who were working with him opposed such negotiations; they therefore tried to wrest from the Commons the authority to conduct peace discussions, and vest it in the Committee of Both Kingdoms, which they planned their group should control. In all the manœuvres associated with this Vane was a key figure. At this period he collaborated closely with St John, and received support from Hesilrige, Samuel Browne and Cromwell; probably John Lisle and Zouch Tate were on occasion instruments of his policy.

The relations between the Committee of Both Kingdoms and Parliament are important, for the Committee in fact used Parliament merely to ratify decisions that the Committee, the real policy-making body, had already made. Vane was frequently involved when the Committee of Both Kingdoms treated Parliament in this disrespectful fashion; he would doubtless have pleaded the war emergency as his excuse. But very probably also he found the slow working of parliamentary government trying. He favoured government by a small group, and in his pamphlet of 1656, *A Healing Question*, he suggested that government should be carried on by a standing Council of State, to be chosen for life; its orders should be binding in the intervals of 'Supreme National Assemblies', or Parliaments.[1]

For a brief time in 1644 and 1645 Vane was trying to increase the authority of Sir William Waller, in the hope of replacing the earl of Essex by Waller as commander of Parliament's forces. Waller was later a member of Holles's group, and this is one more instance of the important but little remarked fact that political allegiances often changed during this period.

By January 1644 the struggle for political and military power was beginning to take on a bitter character; Vane was consistently hostile to Essex's group, and they retaliated by accusing Vane and St John of treason, in that they had negotiated with the king's emissary, Lord Lovelace. The tension between the two groups was acute, and in 1645 Vane was one of those who launched a surprise attack in the Commons on Holles and Whitelocke. The two M.P.s were given no inkling of the charges beforehand, and the episode was a critical one for their fortunes. Whitelocke's manuscript memoirs give a vivid picture[2] of the

---

[1] *A Healing Question*, 18.   [2] BM. Add. 37,343, ff. 395 *seq.*

danger he and his friend faced; they exerted themselves however to organize their defence, and Vane and his collaborators,
St John, Lisle and Samuel Browne, were defeated.

There are indications, such as the pointed omission of Vane
from the new Admiralty committee set up in April 1645, that
the Independents' control of the House was precarious by this
time. But in the autumn the 'recruiters' began to come in, and
possibly this accounts for Vane's return to the Admiralty
committee. The Committee of Both Kingdoms had also been
won over to Holles's view, and some of the leading Independents, including Vane, boycotted committees they could not
control. This may explain the absence of the Draft Day-Books
of the Committee of Both Kingdoms after December 1645,
for the Committee's quorum was seven, and this was probably
unobtainable without its Independent members. By the end
of 1646 the Independents had lost control of Parliament itself
to Holles's group, and the indications are that Vane, like
Cromwell, now boycotted Parliament as he had earlier boycotted the Committee. When the Army restored the Independents to power in 1647 Vane began once again to attend the
Admiralty committee, which he had been neglecting.

There is little information about his political attitude during
the vital summer of 1647, but what there is indicates that he,
with St John, Say and Wharton negotiated with some of the
Army leaders, and we know that Vane presented Ireton's
'Heads of the Proposals' to Parliament. But the vote of 'no
addresses' of September 1647 was a Leveller move; Vane, with
Cromwell and the other leading Independents, thereupon
adopted a more conciliatory attitude to the king. Vane showed
himself no friend to the Levellers both now and in the following
years. His policy in the early months of 1648 is also obscure;
but there are indications that he was trying to co-operate with
the English Presbyterians in Parliament, making common
cause with them against the threatened Scottish invasion.

Once the 1648 royalist rebellion broke out Vane's organizing
gifts were fully employed in taking steps to counter it, especially
in the Navy; whether after this he favoured coming to terms
with the king is doubtful. He certainly took part in the Newport
negotiations, but this does not prove that he sincerely wanted

peace. It is obvious that Pierrepont, Cromwell and Vane had
not concerted their policy on this. It seems that in the crucial
debate of 5 December 1648 on the Newport treaty, Vane
opposed continuing negotiations with the king, and one
royalist diurnal names him among those who were 'downright
for the army'. At his trial in 1662 Vane declared that he left
Parliament before Pride's Purge because he objected to Army
interference with Parliament; in the 1659 Parliament he spoke
as if he approved of bringing the king to trial, but not to
execution, and therefore absented himself from the House. The
latter version fits better what contemporary journalists and
letter-writers reported. It also accords better with the fact that
Vane returned to politics in early February 1649 (when after
all the Army still controlled Parliament) and with what he wrote
in his *Healing Question*.[1]

The years 1649–53 saw the apogee of Vane's political power.
He was one of the organizers of the union with Scotland, and a
frequent chairman of the important Irish and Scottish committee. He was also a major figure in foreign policy, and, during
the last months of this period, the man most responsible for the
brilliant record of the Navy, for which he worked indefatigably.
With his great power came the opportunity for Vane to put his
original and constructive ideas into practice—the projected
union with Holland had his warm support, and the new
administration of the Navy of December 1652 was his work. He
must however have been a politically isolated figure during the
latter part of this period. From August 1651 onwards there are
no more indications of the close co-operation that had certainly
existed between Vane and Cromwell at times during the
previous five years. St John was no longer taking an active part
in politics, and Hesilrige and Vane were now antagonists,
probably because of their differing attitudes to Roger Williams
and Rhode Island. Marten and the Levellers were almost
consistently Vane's opponents. His exclusion from the committee set up in September 1652 to consider the Army officers'

---

[1] *A Healing Question*, 8–9. 'These [the 'good Party'] . . . have stood by the
Army against all opposition whatever, as those that, by the growing light of these
times, have been taught . . . to look above and beyond the letter, forme and outward circumstances of government, into the inward reason and spirit thereof.'

petition for a new Parliament, may be due to nothing more than his absence from London at this time, though perhaps the Army officers were taking advantage of that. He could still have attended the committee under the 'All that come, to have voices' provision. At this period, the autumn of 1652 and early 1653, with the outcome of the Dutch War in the balance, his time was mainly spent on naval administration; friction between Vane and the Council of State over Navy policy may have contributed to Cromwell's decision to dissolve the Rump.

In the 1640s and the early 1650s party groupings in the Commons were very complex. The majority of the M.P.s were not in any way committed to a particular group in the House, and the very word 'party' was disliked by some contemporaries. There was a Presbyterian 'Whip' by 1646, and probably an Independent one also, but the Whips would have to rely even more than their modern counterparts on persuasion, and, where a party had a majority, on patronage. Whoever was working closely with Vane would sometimes be found at the same period voting against him, and this is equally true of Holles. Religious affiliations are not by any means invariably an indication of political attitude. Though Tate and Prideaux for instance were usually found on Vane's side in political matters, Baillie mentions the strong support they gave to the Scottish members of the Westminster Assembly in opposing religious toleration.[1]

Nevertheless there are numerous indications that individual M.P.s planned beforehand the policy they would follow in Parliament, and made use of procedural rules to secure a majority for their views. This was not a new parliamentary art, for it had of course been used by Elizabethan M.P.s, but Vane was an able and unscrupulous exponent of it. As early as May 1641 he was trying to secure the passing of a bill legalizing the impressment of sailors by introducing it in a thin house, and rushing the measure through, and in the same month he was one of those who persuaded Dering to introduce their Root and Branch Bill as his own. The two ordinances establishing the Committee of Both Kingdoms were Vane's work, and there is an indication in D'Ewes that Vane deliberately

[1] Baillie, ii, 237.

forbore to convene a committee one afternoon so that next morning early, probably when few Members were present, he could call the meeting and control the committee's findings. He could ignore parliamentary precedent on occasion; it was not usual for the names of committee members to be included in a bill when it was brought into the House, but this was done in the Committee of Both Kingdoms ordinance. Peregrine Pelham and Tate are both found more than once speaking in a way that gives a strong impression of prior arrangement with Vane. The London petitions which so opportunely expressed support for Vane's policy cannot have arrived by coincidence. He used the Independent majority in Parliament to secure control of peace negotiations for the Committee of Both Kingdoms in 1644, and of the Navy in 1647. His appointment as commissioner to the Army in 1647 was thought by Holles, and perhaps by Whitelocke also, to be the result of a previous arrangement among the Independent leaders, and there is evidence from Lilburne, Wildman and the royalist diurnals that there was an Independent 'Junto' at this period which concerted policy among themselves. Such Juntos naturally did not blazon their activities abroad, but the letters of Vane and Northern M.P.s such as Pelham and Widdrington show that often much preliminary work was necessary to secure action by the Commons.

Baillie asserted that Vane was Parliament's draftsman, and there is much evidence in the *Commons Journals* to support his statement. Replies to petitions, to messages from the king or to missives from foreign powers all fell to Vane's lot to frame, as did narratives of battles, letters of thanks to generals and instructions to officials. If there was difficulty in phrasing a document in such a way as to make it acceptable it was even more likely to be his responsibility. The latter part of the Grand Remonstrance seems to have been partly his work. His financial knowledge and acumen meant that he often had the responsibility for presenting long and intricate statements of sections of the nation's accounts to Parliament. In this sphere alone Parliament's dependence on his skill and clear-headedness is amply demonstrated.

Vane's relations with the City of London are important and

interesting, but in the nature of things, his contacts were likely to be clandestine. His attempt in 1643 to circumvent the Commons' refusal to accept the introduction of a punitive 'covenant' which the City wanted, is a case in point. It was Vane's friend, St John, with whom Vane was working closely, who 'rigged' the Common Council elections in December 1643. City petitions to Parliament were extraordinarily well-timed—for instance Alderman Fowke's petition in favour of re-establishing the Committee of Both Kingdoms, which was presented at the crucial moment in 1644. The same alderman's later petition, in October of that year, was used by Vane in an attempt to weaken the earl of Essex's forces. After 1645 these indications of his connexions with the City cease to appear, until 1659, when there are again hints of links between Vane and some City merchants.

Widely tolerant in religion, he was far from tolerant towards those who differed from him politically. The first victims of this ruthlessness (which has received little or no attention from his biographers) were the unfortunate Tomkins and Challenor, Edmund Waller's accomplices, who were tried by military law and very speedily executed. Vane argued in favour of their trial by court martial. His support for the City covenant of 1643 and for severe penalties to be imposed on those refusing the Solemn League and Covenant, are in keeping with his unwillingness to exempt royalists from stringent punishment, and with his assistance to Peregrine Pelham when that doughty puritan wished the bishops to be arraigned on a capital charge. Vane's vindictive attack on Christopher Love, which resulted in the loss of another life, is an illustration of the fact that to Vane politics were indeed a form of civilian war.

His equivocal attitude to that part of the Solemn League and Covenant which promised the establishment of Presbyterianism in England is only one instance of a certain lack of honesty which marks much of his political career. From the time he used specious arguments to prevent the French envoy from denouncing the vandalism of Marten and Gurdon at Somerset House, to December 1648, when he labelled as royalists those who wanted to continue peace negotiations with the king, one sees on many occasions his lack of scrupulous regard for truth.

This is of course a charge frequently levelled against politicians, and one supposes that M.P.s of the 1640s and 1650s were subject to the same temptations as others. Nevertheless Vane's 'juggling' seems to have no parallel among his contemporaries (unless Cromwell is admitted here), and goes far to justify the epithet 'Machiavellian' which Lilburne so frequently uses of Vane. To argue, as he did in 1644, that he did not owe his office of Navy Treasurer to Parliament, was disingenuous, even though he had originally probably bought the office from the king. The re-introduction in the Commons of an ordinance which the Lords had passed, and doubtless forgotten, establishing the Committee of Both Kingdoms, was dishonest, though legal. Whatever the purpose of his negotiations with Lord Lovelace, they are marked by deception. Contemporary allegations that Vane took part in peace negotiations which he intended to fail, are probably not far off the mark. Two of his missions, to York in 1644, and to De Retz at a later and uncertain date, are somewhat mysterious; this is in keeping with his devious political methods. His prolix but candid admission in 1656 shows that he was aware of the unorthodox nature of his expedients:

As to the capacity wherein these persons [the supporters of the 'good party'] . . . have acted, it hath been very variable, and subject to great changes . . . very seldome, if ever at all, so exactly, and in all points consonant to the rule of former Lawes and Constitutions of Government, as to be clearly and fully justified by them, any longer than the Law of Successe and Conquest did uphold them who had the inward warrant of Justice and Righteousness to encourage them in such their actings.[1]

From the beginning of the war until Pride's Purge, with the one exception of the vote of 'No Addresses' of August 1647, he appears as the determined opponent of negotiations with the king. Vane wanted Parliament to dictate the terms of peace. He was the spokesman in the Commons for the Committee of Both Kingdoms' very unencouraging response to peace 'feelers' in 1644, and probably drafted the chilly reply which was to be sent to the king. He certainly had a hand in the uncompromising answer to the Comte d'Harcourt's offer of mediation, and

[1] *A Healing Question*, 9.

was associated with the obstructive response to the Dutch offer. He was frequently found supporting peace terms which would be quite intolerable to the king. D'Ewes gives much evidence that Vane tried to divert the House from even discussing peace proposals. It is more difficult to determine the reason for his attitude. He probably feared the establishment of a national Presbyterian church, with its religious intolerance. Even in the king's extremity in 1648, at the Newport negotiations, Presbyterianism for three years was one of the conditions. No doubt another factor in his mind was the desire to keep all vital political control, such as that over the militia, in Parliament's hands.[1]

Was he a republican? He was certainly not a doctrinaire republican in the way that Marten was. His view is probably summed up in a phrase in his *Retired Man's Meditations*, when he speaks of: 'In whatever formes the government be administered (that in themselves, simply considered, are all lawful and Just)'.[2] He took the lead in giving Parliament control over the Navy, and in the making of a new Great Seal, he supported Parliament's assumption of authority over the militia, but there is no speech from Vane denouncing monarchy as such. The indications are that he wanted to transfer all political authority to Parliament, but he was prepared to vote for government by King, Lords and Commons if the realities of power were in Parliament's hands. He had supported war because only war would establish Parliament's control.[3] The removal of kingship, he asserted in 1659, had been 'the only happy way of returning to their [the people's] own freedom'.[4]

In the same way, the term 'radical' must be used of Vane only with caution and with precise definition. He certainly wanted to destroy the royal power, less certainly the monarchy or the king. He was however consistently hostile to the House of

[1] For Vane's perception of the importance of the militia see Burton, iii, 171. Also *A Healing Question*, 5 and 9–10. 'As not ignorant, that when once embodied in this their [the good party's] Military posture, insuch manner as they by common consent shall be found requisite for the safety of the body, they are most irresistible, absolute and comprehensive in their power; having that wherein the substance of all Government is continued.' See also above, p. 83.

[2] *Retired Man's Meditations*, 384–5. See also ibid., 388, and *A Healing Question*, 6.

[3] Burton, iii, 171.   [4] Ibid.

Lords. As early as February 1642 he was prepared to bargain with the Lords, suggesting a *quid pro quo* in amendments that shocked D'Ewes. In 1644 he prevented the Upper House from exercising their right to make nominations to the Committee of Both Kingdoms. In 1646 he resented the Lords framing an ordinance on matters already discussed in the Commons, and objected to asking the Lords' approval for the appointment of Batten as commander of the Fleet.

He was no democrat however. His republic was to be a republic of the 'good party'. 'Sovereignty', he wrote, 'ought to be in the whole body of the people *that have adhered to the cause.*'[1] He objected to an ordinance being submitted to the people for ratification. The Levellers found him one of their opponents, and in the conflict of interest between the Fen-men and the Undertakers, or entrepreneurs, for the draining of the fen known as the earl of Lindsey's Level, he was on the side of the Undertakers. He defended a prohibitively high property quali-fication for the franchise, as is well known, in 1653. In Vane's mind the natural right even of the godly was to 'enjoy the freedome (by way of dutifull compliance and condiscension from all the parts and members of this society) to set up meet persons in the place of Supreme Judicature and Authority amongst them, whereby they may have the use and benefit of the choicest light and wisdome of the Nation that they are capable to call forth, for the Rule and Government under which they will live'.[2] He did not advocate the right of the rank-and-file godly to govern themselves.

Vane's theoretical respect for Parliament is curiously at variance with the actual policy he followed on some occasions. Not only did he sometimes fail to wait for Parliament's instruc-tions, but it seems that when it suited him to do so, he ignored Parliament's orders. His delays in presenting his Navy accounts are an example of this (though when one sees the enormous amount of work that these involved, one has sympathy with Vane). His failure to pay half of his profits as Navy Treasurer to the committee of the revenue is a more flagrant example of the same attitude. By working closely with Ireton in the summer

---

[1] *A Healing Question*, 15. The italics are mine.
[2] Ibid., 3–4

of 1647 and almost certainly with Cromwell too, he was manifestly not defending Parliament against Army control.

Moreover there is evidence that when Vane's group were in a minority in Parliament or its committees he simply did not attend. Holles made this allegation concerning the Independent group's attendance at the Committee of Both Kingdoms in the latter part of 1646 and the early months of 1647, and it would certainly explain Vane's prolonged absence from the Admiralty committee and Parliament at that time. Similarly he absented himself from those bodies for about six weeks at the time of the king's trial. Failure to carry the House with him in his attitude to the vital negotiations with Holland in 1652 would explain his otherwise surprising absence from Parliament for two months at the beginning of the Dutch War. Similarly when Lambert expelled the Rump in October 1659 he withdrew from politics.

After his absence from Parliament in the summer of 1652 Vane returned, as after the king's execution, to put his outstanding organizing powers at the service of the State, and Britain's victory in the war was due to his administration of the Navy more than to any other factor except the genius of the British admirals. His maiden speech in Parliament had struck the keynote of his later work for the Navy. In this Vane's references to the British command of the sea showed that he was aware of the challenge of Richelieu's Navy, and that he saw the Navy as an important instrument of foreign policy. The Lord Admiral, the earl of Northumberland, had also shown much interest in the Navy, but Vane's speeches of this period had a force and urgency that Northumberland's lacked, and it was probably Vane who led the demand for an energetic policy. In November 1641 Parliament took an important step; it assumed control of the disposition of naval forces when it requested the Lord Admiral to assign four ships for the defence of Ireland; and Vane presented the ordinance which was to be Northumberland's warrant for carrying out Parliament's order. This action was consistent with his determination to wrest control of the militia from the Crown, and with his support for the making of a new Great Seal. The November ordinance was followed within a couple of weeks by his dismissal as

Navy Treasurer, and one wonders if the two events were connected.

When civil war had broken out in 1642, Parliament appointed six men to take over the duties of the Surveyor, Comptroller and Clerk of the Acts to the Navy; Vane was one of the six, and was re-appointed also as Navy Treasurer. But it was Giles Greene who dominated Navy administration until 1647; it was he who constantly reported from the important Navy and Customs committee, and who wrote the justification of that committee against its critics' ill-informed attacks. Vane was a member however of the many Navy committees of the period, and Greene paid tribute in his *Defence* to Vane's work as Navy Treasurer. During this period a new official, the deputy Treasurer, appears in the Navy Office. The committee of Navy and Customs sent for him when they needed details of Navy finance, and Vane himself admitted that he was unable to devote the personal attention to Navy finance that it required, because he was preoccupied with public affairs.

The last clause of the Self-Denying Ordinance protected Vane, if no-one else, from loss of office, and his tenure of the Navy Treasurership was further strengthened by an ordinance of Parliament of July 1645. This confirmed his appointment for the duration of the war, but stipulated that he should pay to the committee of the Revenue half the profits from his office. According to the accounts he belatedly presented to the Commons committee of Accounts, his profits for August 1642 to May 1645 were small, some £617 altogether. When he presented his accounts for May 1645 to May 1649 to the less public inspection of the Audit and Pipe Offices, a very different situation was revealed. He had derived a profit of some £4000 a year for the three years after May 1645, and well over £5000 a year for May 1649 to December 1650. He did not pay half to the committee of the Revenue, and the committee (of which his father was chairman) made no complaint. Nor did he surrender his office at the end of the war, as instructed, and the Commons raised no objection.

Vane probably did not attend very frequently the Admiralty committee set up in April 1645 but to which he was not appointed until October of that year; certainly he did not

attend from October 1646 to September 1647. But when the
Independents secured control of the committee in September
1647 he began to appear more regularly. Only for a month or
two however; in November 1647 he was rarely present, and in
December went off to the country for eight weeks, probably
on account of ill-health. Greene had returned to London in
that December after a three months' absence; it is very likely
that he was once more the directing spirit in naval administration, for even when Vane returned to Parliament he made
infrequent attendances at the committee. With the earl of
Warwick's appointment as Admiral in 1648, as a result of the
naval mutinies, the Admiralty committee lapsed. The Newport
negotiations and other vital political problems must have
occupied Vane in the late summer and autumn of 1648, and
he withdrew from public affairs early in December. The conclusion must be drawn that he was not a major figure in naval
administration from 1642 to 1648, except as Navy Treasurer.

In February 1649 he and two others were appointed as the
Admiralty committee of the Council of State. The very full
records of this committee, whose membership was soon
enlarged, give us an illuminating picture of Vane's astonishing
energy. His activity in naval administration at this time is his
true claim to be regarded as the creator of the Commonwealth
Navy. He was tireless in making plans for financing the Navy,
in devising inducements for officers, and in corresponding with
the generals-at-sea, whom he was at pains to consult on every
matter on which their experience would be valuable. His
mastery of Navy finance is shown in a hundred ways, and his
foresight on this and many other topics. Legislation on sailors'
pay, on impressment and on good conduct medals was passed,
and the care for the wounded at this period owes something to
Vane. One sees once more his administrative and political
methods. On occasion he would act first and seek authorization
from the Council of State afterwards, and he was aware of the
necessity for prior 'organization' if the Council was to be
moved to take action. The great shipbuilding programme of
November 1649 onwards was due to the initiative of the
Council's Admiralty committee, on which, it is clear from the
records of attendance at the committee, Vane was the main

figure, though the contribution of Valentine Walton and other
members must not be ignored. Parliament had built six ships
in 1647, none in 1648 and early 1649, in spite of the defection
in May 1648 of Batten and nearly half the Fleet. From the time
Vane became a member of the Admiralty committee, Parliament embarked on an ambitious shipbuilding programme—
six in 1649, ten each in each of the next three years, thirteen
in 1653. In September 1652, when the Dutch War had begun,
Parliament actually agreed to the building of thirty new
frigates, though this was probably beyond the country's
resources, and there seems to be no indication that this gran-
diose project was implemented.[1] The enormous programme
which actually was effected would have been impossible if
Vane had not devised the financial means for carrying it out,
and the lines in Milton's sonnet, sent to him in July 1652,

> Then to advise how war may best upheld
> Move by her two main nerves, iron and gold

were a reference to Vane's work in this sphere. Probably the
ships Parliament was building were of the new three-decker
type first built in the 1630s, and this explains the sale of many
royal ships at this time.

Proof of his diligent work in the Admiralty committee of
the Council of State is found in its minutes from February 1650
onwards, when fortunately the clerk began to record attendances conscientiously. By October 1651 there were thirteen
members of the committee, but the usual attendance was three
or four, of whom Vane was almost always one. The control by
the Council of State however and the delays which it entailed,
must have irked him, for in June 1651 he and Bond wanted the
Commons to set up Admiralty commissioners responsible
directly to Parliament; the Commons rejected the plan, and
vested control once more in the Council of State. Two further
attempts to persuade the Commons to appoint special
Admiralty commissioners failed, but in December 1652 the
British defeat at Dungeness convinced Parliament that Vane

---

[1] Bernard Pool (*Navy Board Contracts, 1660–1832* (London, 1966), 12) refers to
the 1677 plan to build 30 new ships as 'the first major ship-building programme',
but the Commonwealth project had preceded this by 25 years.

was right and nine Admiralty commissioners, including the three commanders of the fleet and two men who were not members of Parliament, were appointed. The balance of the committee was thus changed—a majority of the new men were Navy experts and not politicians. Hesilrige's tribute to Vane in 1659, 'When our affairs, as to the Navy, were such we could not turn ourselves unto them, did we not turn our eyes upon that gentleman, by whose providence it was so excellently managed?'[1] refers to this period in Vane's career. The new commissioners' letters have a religious tone absent from those of the previous Admiralty committee, and though Giles Greene had taken pride in his committee's consultation with the sailors and navy officials, this practice is much more marked in the December 1652 commissioners. Vane's prodigious activity during the next few months is beyond praise; his great administrative powers had full scope, and there is ample proof that the English victory in the Dutch War owed most to his efforts, though tribute should also be paid to his fellow-M.P.s, Carew, Salwey, and Thomson, and to Navy commissioner Langley. There was friction however with Cromwell and the Council of State; whether this was a cause or a result of his worsening relations with Cromwell there is no means of knowing.

In England Vane's 'republicanism' has overshadowed his contributions to the life of his time; in the *Catalogue of Seventeenth-Century Portraits in the National Portrait Gallery*, Vane, alone of all that galaxy of famous personages, is labelled 'Revolutionary',[2] though even Bradshaw and Cromwell are dignified with the appellation, 'Politician' or 'Statesman'. However, when the nineteenth-century struggles for religious equality and constitutional reform were agitating the educated section of the nation, it was natural that biographies of Vane should begin to appear, and that these should stress his role as religious reformer and radical politician, and omit the less admirable sides of his character and political strategy. In the United States, where republicanism was not a term of contumely, Vane was greatly

---

[1] Burton, iii, 442–3.

[2] D. Piper, *Catalogue of Seventeenth-Century Portraits in the National Portrait Gallery* (Cambridge, 1963), 360.

revered as a constructive statesman, and as one who had fore-shadowed many of the principles of the American constitution in his *Healing Question* of 1656.[1] He had suggested summoning a convention especially for the purpose of drafting a constitution; he had proposed that the government should be founded 'on certain fundamentals not to be dispensed with'; he had demanded religious and civil liberty as a prerequisite of the constitution. So significant was his book held to be that in a late nineteenth-century series of reprints at Boston of important documents that preceded the 1786 constitution, Vane's *Healing Question* was the sixth publication, following the Constitution itself, the articles of confederation, the Declaration of Independence, Washington's Farewell, and Magna Carta.[2] Academics spoke of Vane in extravagantly eulogistic terms as the 'noblest human being who ever walked the streets of yonder city [Boston]'.[3] Twentieth-century readers however may find Vane's ideal government far from democratic by modern standards, and consider not only his political theories, but his political practice.

It cannot be doubted however that Vane possessed a rare combination of great administrative ability and a mastery of political tactics. The Admiralty committee records of 1649–53, and much else, testify to his powers of administration, and his astuteness in managing Parliament is seen over and over again in the diaries of the 1640s and '50s. The Self-Denying Ordinance, for instance, was an exceedingly shrewd move. It not only rid the country of the ineffective leadership—as Vane and St John thought—of the earl of Essex, but it meant the suppression of a committee controlled by their rivals, led by Holles. It also countered allegations that the M.P.s were enriching themselves, and this last would make it very difficult for Holles, and the earls of Essex and Warwick, to oppose the measure in the country at large. Vane's original

---

[1] I am indebted to Professor Caroline Robbins for the information following in this paragraph.

[2] *Old South Leaflets*, n.d., no. 6.

[3] 'So you can find in Vane the pure gold of two hundred and fifty years of American civilisation, with no particle of its dross. He stands among English statesmen pre-eminently the representative of . . . trusting truth wholly to her own defence.' Wendell Phillips in his Harvard address on *The Scholar in the Republic* (ibid., 18–19).

mind often revealed itself; he wrote that no human ordinance must expect to be exempt from change and removal, if the spirit of Christ requires its alteration,[1] and his policy echoes this belief. In April 1653 he was at the pinnacle of power. Confident in the right of the godly to govern,[2] in the strength of his patriotism, in the victory which Blake had just won against the Dutch off Portland, confident also no doubt in his own abilities, he must have believed his position was unassailably secure. He was speaking when Cromwell and his troops entered the Commons, and in an hour Vane's power was destroyed. It was a blow far worse than his dismissal from the Navy Treasurership in 1642 and he had to wait until Cromwell's death to try to regain his old position. In 1659 he painstakingly tried to re-create the political situation which Cromwell had destroyed in 1653—only to find that it had gone for ever.

In the last nine years of his life Vane was a rather different person. He seems to have lost some of his self-control, and even on the scaffold he was roused to anger. His dreams of the coming triumph of the Saints over their enemies, as expressed in his writings, have an hysterical quality quite alien to what he spoke and wrote before 1653. One feels too that the earlier Vane would not have made the naïve judgements and political miscalculations that he made in 1659. He attempted to control Richard Cromwell's Parliament, but succeeded only in antagonizing it. He may well have been responsible, through his pamphlets, for the dissolution of that Parliament, and the recall of the Rump, but these were no solution to the country's difficulties. At the same time, taught by adversity, he showed a humanity which had not characterized him before. He spoke with real indignation of the unfortunates who had been deported to Barbados after Penruddock's rising in 1655, and of the soldiers whose lives Cromwell had sacrificed by embarking on the Jamaica expedition. He hounded none of his opponents in 1659.

---

[1] *Retired Man's Meditations*, 389.

[2] 'God . . . by the course he hath already taken to fit and prepare a selected number of the people unto this work of government that are tried and refined by their inward and outward experiences in this great quarrell.' (*A Healing Question*, 19.)

In some ways he did not change. His patriotism, always one of his impelling motives, was as strong as ever. Devious political skill came naturally to him, and he still used his sarcastic tongue with effect. His religious faith had deepened, enabling him to meet the cruel injustices inflicted on him by Oliver Cromwell and Charles II with dignity and courage. Those who were struggling to establish religious toleration found in Vane, as they had done since 1644, a steadfast champion. It is not surprising that his negative qualities should have made enemies, and perhaps some of his contemporaries were jealous of his quite exceptional administrative abilities. But in 1662 the enemies who struck him down saw in him the embodiment of the vigour, the astuteness and the achievements of the 'Good Old Cause'. He had played so large a part in the triumph of that cause that their fear and hostility are understandable.

APPENDIX A

The Independent Group in the Commons, 1645–46

The following M.P.s, one would judge from Whitelocke (printed and MS), Holles's *Memoirs*, the *Commons Journals*, and other sources, including the Press of the time, were 38 of the 50 M.P.s alleged by Holles to have been reliable members of the group. In the case of those marked * their political attitude admits of some uncertainty.

Sir William Armyn
Sir Nathaniel Barnardiston
Sir Thomas Barrington
Alexander Bence*
Squire Bence*
John Blakiston*
Samuel Browne
Sir William Constable*
Miles Corbet
Oliver Cromwell
Sir Thomas Dacres
Thomas Earle
Sir Walter Earle
Sir John Evelyn of Wilts.
Nathaniel Fiennes
John Glyn*
Giles Greene*
John Gurdon*
Sir Arthur Hesilrige

Cornelius Holland
John Lisle
Henry Marten
Sir William Masham
Sir Henry Mildmay
Antony Nichol*
Peregrine Pelham
William Pierrepont
Edmund Prideaux
Sir Benjamin Rudyerd*
Oliver St John
Robert Scawen
William Strode
Zouch Tate
Sir Henry Vane senior
Sir Henry Vane junior
Sir Peter Wentworth
Sir Thomas Widdrington
John Wyld

APPENDIX B

Division Numbers in the Commons,
5 December 1646 to 31 May 1647

(This list does not include divisions on personal or very minor matters, and it includes only those divisions where it is obvious from the identity of the tellers that Holles and his group were opposed to Hesilrige and his.)

CJ. v	1646	Subject
3	7 Dec.	The County Committee of Staffordshire to have £2000. Holles and Sir John Holland in favour, 60; Hesilrige and Westrow against, 56.
11	12 Dec.	To refer to a committee the book *Jus Divinum Regiminus Ecclesiastici* (in which Presbyterian church government was defended as most in accordance with Divine Will). Sir P. Wentworth and Sir Henry Mildmay in favour, 89; Earle and Lewes against, 72.
12	14 Dec.	To refer to a committee the Scots request for mutual assistance. Holles and Earle in favour, 80; Evelyn and Hesilrige against, 88.
25	22 Dec.	To consider a City petition requesting disbandment of the Army, and the suppression of heresy, prevalent in the Army. Hesilrige and Evelyn against, 99; Stapleton and Lewes in favour, 156.
27	24 Dec.	To make an addition to the thanks to be given the Scots Commissioners. Stapleton and North in favour, 105; Hesilrige and Evelyn against, 129.
28	25 Dec.	To add 'according to the Covenant' to a statement from the Lords, which was to be sent to the king informing him that Holmby House had been chosen as the place to which he was

CJ. v	1646	Subject
		to go. The additional words would follow a reference to the respect and safety of the king's person.
		Stapleton and Irby in favour, 133; Wentworth and Norton against, 91.
33	29 Dec.	To add to the statement about Holmby House a clause reaffirming the abolition of the Court of Wards.
		Heyman and Constable in favour, 71; Holles and Stapleton against, 133.
34	31 Dec.	The House to condemn not only those who preach without being ordained in the Reformed church, but also those who expound the scriptures without such ordination.
		Hesilrige and Cromwell against, 57; Earle and Irby in favour, 105.
	1647	
42	5 Jan.	Major-General Skippon (and not a committee of M.P.s) to receive the person of the king at Newcastle.
		Holles and Stapleton against, 130; Hesilrige and Hoyle in favour, 69.
73	3 Feb.	To have a report next day on the ordinance dealing with compounding with delinquents.
		Holles and Stapleton in favour, 83; Strickland and Hesilrige against, 74.
90	17 Feb.	To consider next day the garrisons and forces in each county. (The House decided instead to consider the number of cavalry to be kept in pay.)
		Hesilrige and Evelyn in favour, 145; Holles and Stapleton against, 147.
91	19 Feb.	To keep in pay more infantry than would be needed to maintain garrisons only.
		Hesilrige and Evelyn in favour, 148; Holles and Stapleton against, 158.
108	8 March	Officers who remain in the army must conform to the government of the church established by parliament.
		Holles and Stapleton in favour, 136; Hesilrige and Evelyn against, 108.

CJ. V	*1647*	*Subject*
127	27 March	(Both Divisions.) The House to consider two days later the government of Ireland, and the command of the forces there.
		Waller and Stapleton in favour, 49; Hesilrige and Morley against, 48.
		Stapleton and Lewes in favour, 45; Hesilrige and Morley against, 42.
131	31 March	The House to appoint commissioners to direct the war in Ireland.
		Holles and Tate in favour, 64; Hesilrige and Evelyn against, 56.
143	15 April	To allow the City of London to appoint militia commissioners not only for the City, but for all other places within the lines of communication and weekly bills of mortality.
		Stapleton and Glyn in favour, 81; Danvers and Hesilrige against, 61.
154	27 April	Capt. Robert Lilburne to be summoned to attend the House, to give account of his conduct in dissuading soldiers from going to Ireland.
		Lewes and Doyley in favour, 104; Evelyn and Livesey against, 81.
155	27 April	Soldiers disbanded from the army to have 6 weeks (only) of pay, when they are discharged.
		Stapleton and Glyn in favour, 114; Hesilrige and Livesey against, 7.
162	4 May	The House to inform those who had delivered a petition from 'divers well-affected persons' that the House dislikes it. [This was a radical petition, demanding religious toleration, the end of monopolistic trading companies, the use of English in legal proceedings, and other reforms.]
		Holles and Stapleton in favour, 80; Evelyn and Hesilrige against, 54.
179	20 May	To have this petition burned by the common hangman.
		Holles and Earle in favour, 94; Pierrepont and Evelyn against, 86.

CJ. V   *1647*   *Subject*

179   20 May   To burn the petition two days later, on
Saturday.
Holles and Massey in favour, 96; Armyn and
Evelyn against, 78.

The Manuscript Sources for the Committee of Navy and Customs and for the Admiralty Committees from 1642 to 1653

The committee of Navy and Customs (the financial committee) has left no records of its meetings, except Vane's own Order-Book, for the period November 1641 (when it was 'revived' after the recess) until March 1643. Vane's Order-Book was begun two days after the House appointed him as Navy Treasurer in 1642, and is now in the Bodleian, among the manuscripts collected by Pepys. (Rawl. A 220.) A minute-book of the committee was begun in March 1643, and reads as though one had not been kept before. (Rawl. A 221.) The membership of the Navy and Customs committee was almost identical with that of the Admiralty commissioners appointed in October 1642, and the work of both would be interrelated; perhaps therefore there would be no need for two minute-books at first—certainly there are no extant records of the October 1642 Admiralty commissioners. The Navy and Customs committee's minutes are continued in Rawl. A 222, and extend from March to August 1644; in the latter month seven new members were added to the committee, and probably the clerk began a new minute-book which has not survived. Giles Greene's printed *Apology* (see Chapter V) is a valuable source for both these committees.

With the establishment of the new Admiralty committee in April 1645 a remarkably complete series of minute-books for this committee begins, but they are scattered. Bodl. Rawl. C 416 is the minute-book for April to September 1645. The Admiralty MS in the P.R.O. (7/673) is the minute-book for October 1646 to February 1648, but the volume for March to May 1648 has found its way to the British Museum (Add.

9305). In May 1648, as a result of the mutinies, the earl of Warwick resumed the powers of lord high admiral, and the Admiralty committee lapsed. The Council of State set up its three-man committee of the Admiralty in February 1649, and this committee's first minute-book is in the P.R.O. (S.P. 25/123). The later minute-books, from October 1650 to August 1653, are all in the Bodleian (Rawl. A 225, 226, 227). The financial committee's minutes for 1645–8 have not survived but its minutes for January to October 1649 are in the Rawlinson MSS (A 224). Some of its papers, chiefly authorizations to make payments and receipts, are in the P.R.O. (S.P. 46/102 (1650–52), and S.P. 46/114 (1651–53)).

APPENDIX D

Sir Henry Vane's Profits from the Office of Navy Treasurer

Declared account	Dates covered by the account	Vane's poundage (3d in the £)	'Surplusage', i.e. sums due to Vane but not yet drawn by him	Date of account
C.J. vi, 14	8 Aug. 1642– 12 May 1645[1]	£9046 8s 8d[2]	£8428 17s 2¾d	9 Sept. 1648
A.O.I. 1706/90	13 May 1645– 31 Dec. 1646	£4909 17s 6d		
E 351/ 2286	1 Jan. 1647– 31 Dec. 1647	£2217 4s 10d	£352 12s 0¾d	2 Dec. 1650
E 351/ 2287	1 Jan. 1648– 12 May 1649	£4200 2s 6d		
E 351/ 2288	13 May 1649– 31 Dec. 1650	£8293 14s 6d	Nothing	26 June 1652
		TOTAL SUM DRAWN BY VANE £27,305 11s 9d[3]		

[1] Vane was appointed by Parliament to resume his post as Navy Treasurer (from which the king had dismissed him) on 8 August 1642. When the Commons confirmed his appointment in 1645, his re-appointment was to date from the day the Self-Denying Ordinance was passed, i.e. 12 May 1645.

[2] This sum includes Vane's Patent Fee (£551 13s 4d) and portage etc. (£910 2s 11d).

[3] Vane's Patent Fee of £220 13s 4d per year should be added to this, and also the considerable sums allowed him for portage, bags, wax and other charges for May 1645 onwards. Payments to Hutchinson, his Paymaster or deputy Treasurer, and to the clerks, are entered separately on the accounts, and were not deducted from the sums due to Vane. Hutchinson's salary as Navy Treasurer was finally raised to £2500, during the First Dutch War. Out of this Hutchinson, unlike Vane, had to pay his clerks.

APPENDIX E

Analysis of Attendances at Admiralty Committee, 23 February 1650 to 20 April 1653[1]

The period covered by the tables is that during which the clerk entered the attendances of the members. In most months however there were two or three days on which the clerk forgot to enter the names of those attending the committee's meeting, and it occasionally happens that no signatures for letters are given for that day either. The figures in brackets indicate the probable number of committee meetings during the month; where the Order-Book records only one warrant or an unimportant letter of a routine nature, it is assumed that the committee clerk, or a committee member calling at the office for a short time, despatched the business, and this has not been counted as a committee meeting. The 'possible attendances' figure indicates the number of meetings for which the names of those attending are available, usually through the clerk's record of attenders, but occasionally, where the clerk forgot this duty, through signatures to letters, as given in the Order-Book.

For 17 December 1652 onwards the record of all the eight Admiralty commissioners is given; for the previous period the attendances given are only those who appeared more frequently at the committee; there were many who attended occasionally.

[1] From S.P. 25/123, Bodl. Rawl. A 225, 226, 227.

Year 1650

Month	Feb.	Mar.	April	May	June	July	Aug.	Sept.	Oct.	Nov.	Dec.
Possible attendances	2 (2)	21 (21)	16 (18)	13 (16)	6 (10)	10 (17)	14 (16)	7 (15)	14 (21)	16 (19)	14 (17)
Vane	2	19	16	11	6	9	14	7	14	14	14
Bond		1	5[1]	5	3	5	11	5	11	12	13
Walton		20	16	1[2]	6	5	0	0	9[3]	8	2
Purefoy	2	10[4]	0	0	3	9	8	1	2	8	5
Challoner		9	8	5	4	5	7	4	8	5	4

[1] Added to the Committee. [2] Absent until 20th. [3] Absent until 30th. [4] Absent after 16th.

Year 1651

Month	Jan.	Feb.	Mar.	April	May	June	July	Aug.	Sept.	Oct.	Nov.	Dec.
Possible attendances	20 (21)	10 (10)	12 (13)	13 (19)	15 (18)	16 (20)	16 (22)	12 (14)	9 (9)	12 (13)	12 (13)	10 (11)
Vane	16	9	12	13	6[1]	14	10	8	9	12	9	6
Bond	9	7	12	9	15	15	14	9	8	9	6	9
Walton	6	4	9	7	3[3]	0	0	1	0	2[2]	8	8
Purefoy	9	6	0	0	11	0	0	4	5	9	1	7
Challoner	11	3	8	3	7	4	3	6	3	2	2	6
Trevor			2[4]	8	7	8	11	7	5	2	5	0[5]

[1] Absent after 17th. [2] Returns on 27th. [3] Returns on 27th. [4] Added to the Committee.
[5] Not re-nominated to the Committee.

Year 1652 to 26 November

Month	Jan.	Feb.	Mar.	April	May	June	July	Aug.	Sept.	Oct.	Nov.	Dec.
Porsible attendances	10 (10)	11 (12)	16 (17)	12 (15)	10 (11)	7 (7)	12 (14)	10 (10)	11 (11)	11 (12)	9 (9)	(0)
Vane	0[1]	0[1]	8[2]	6[3]	6	6	0	0	8	9	7	
Bond	8	11	12	10	6	2	11	3[4]	0	7[5]	6	
Blake	8	9	3	0	0	0	0	0	0	0	0	
Challoner	3	4	6	4	3	1	4	3	3	1	1	
Dixwell					1	5[6]	3	0	9	9	5	
Marten[7]	4	3	1	1	4	3	1	2	3	0	1	
Morley[7]	6	0	8	7	7	7	5	0	5	0	4	
Nevile[7]	6	4	6	5	5	3	8	5	4	5	1	
Purefoy	4	5	3	0	0	1	8	4	7	9	3	
Walton	0	8	10	5	0	0	0	0	0	4	4	

Dec.: No meetings recorded. Committee probably superseded.

[1] In Scotland.
[2] Returned on 15th.
[3] Absent after 14th.
[4] Absent after 11th.
[5] Returned on 11th.
[6] Added to Committee.
[7] Nominated to Committee in December 1651.

Year 1652. 17 December 1652 to 18 April 1653

Month	17–31 Dec.	Jan.	Feb.	Mar.	April
Possible attendances	6 (6)	18 (18)	22 (22)	19 (19)	11 (11)
Vane	6	18	22	17	10
Carew	6	15	22	18	11
Langley	2	15	15	9	8
Salwey	4	16	15	16	5
Thomson	5	18	22	14	9
Blake	0	3	1	0	0
Deane	0	4	1	2	0
Monck	5	0	0	1	0

(Cromwell attended once in February 1652, once in April, and once in November of that year)

APPENDIX F

'The Character of Sir Henry Vane
by Algernon Sidney'

(Hertfordshire Record Office D/EP F 45)

This undated MS is among the papers of the Cowper family of Panshanger, Hertford, which have been deposited at Hertford Record Office. The MS consists of 20 small quarto pages, which have been inserted between two blank leaves of a commonplace book which once belonged to Lady Sarah, wife of Sir William Cowper (1639–1706), the second baronet. The book's only other contents are a number of portraits, cut out from printed sources, of seventeenth- and early eighteenth-century personages, including James I, Queen Anne, Matthew Hale and Jeremy Taylor, and two poems, one an anti-Jacobite ballad published soon after the battle of Blenheim, and one a 1705 ballad attacking Dr Sacheverell. The Sidney MS is a copy, in a hand which probably belongs to the period 1680–1720, and may well be that of Sir William's eldest son, the future lord chancellor. The watermark is an unidentifiable coat of arms, encircled by the Garter, with the words 'Honi Soit Qui Mal Y Pense', surmounted by a crown.

Algernon Sidney was a nephew of the tenth earl of Northumberland, the lord admiral and friend of Sir Henry Vane the elder. Sidney's official duties as governor of Dover Castle brought him into contact with the younger Vane in 1649 (*CSPD. 1649, 1650*, 172, 412–13). He accompanied St John on the unsuccessful mission to form a union with the United Provinces in 1651 (A. C. Ewald, *The Life and Times of the Hon. Algernon Sidney*, London, 1873, 142). Sidney served with Vane on several Council of State and Commons committees in 1652 and 1653 (*CSPD. 1652–53*, 2, 9; *CJ*. vii, 222). Like Vane, he was especially interested in foreign affairs. Like Vane also, he withdrew from politics in April 1653, returned in 1659, and was appointed to the Council of State by the Army in May of that year. He was one of the delegation which included Vane's brother-in-law, Sir Robert Honeywood, and Vane's son, to negotiate peace in the Baltic in 1659.

Sidney was still in Scandinavia at the Restoration, and went into exile in Rome, whence he sent to his father 'characters' or descriptions, of several cardinals in that city (A. Collins, *Letters and Memorials of State*, London, 1746, ii, 711 *seq.*). He wrote to a friend in August 1660, 'Where Vane, Lambert, Haselrig cannot live in safety, I cannot live at all' (Sidney, *Works*, London, 1772, 25). At his own trial in 1683, he referred more than once to that of Vane (ibid., 5–6, 53). (The author of the Panshanger MS is incorrect in stating that Vane pleaded guilty, *Tryal*, 20). Sidney was executed in 1683 for his part in the Rye House, Hertfordshire, Plot. According to Sidney's father, Vane was in 1652 the 'great friend' of Philip, Lord Lisle, Sidney's elder brother (H.M.C. *MSS of Viscount Lisle, V.C.*, vi, 614).

Sir William Cowper, the second baronet, was a relation and close friend of the earl of Shaftesbury (letter in D/EP F 24, Hertfordshire Record Office; W. D. Christie, *Life of Antony Ashley Cooper, First Earl of Shaftesbury*, London, 1871, ii, 459). When Shaftesbury was in the Tower in 1681, Cowper stood bail for him in £1500 (ibid., 441). In one of his letters to Cowper Shaftesbury refers to his friend and himself as 'men of our Hethrodox opinions' (D/EP F 24, letter of 8 September 1678). When the duke of York was indicted before the Middlesex Grand Jury as a recusant in 1680 by Shaftesbury and others, Cowper was among the signatories (ibid., printed broadsheet). It is clear that Cowper was a member of the inner circle of Whigs. He was also a friend of William Penn, whose close association with Algernon Sidney lasted for several years (letter from Penn, ibid.). All in all, it is not surprising that a work by Sidney should be found in the Cowper MSS.

Sir William Cowper's eldest son, the future lord chancellor, was born in 1659 and sat for Hertford in Parliament from 1695 to 1700, his father being the senior member for the constituency.

* * *

Sʳ Harry Vane was descended from a noble Family, and tho his Father was too well vers'd in the intrigues of an infamous Court, yet he [the younger Vane] prov'd the Glory and support of a reviving State. In his youth he was not so careful of his conduct as he ought to have been, nor so wholly free from the vices incident to that age, but about eighteen years old returning to a better course, strenuously betook himself to piety and virtue, at which time the severity of his manners join'd to a great Genious, rendring him suspected and disagreeable to the Court he went to New England, a place that then flourisht by reason of its good order and discipline; he was there created Governor of those colonies and performed his Office with great vigilance and honesty. Having spent there about three years, he returned home with great reputation, and much improved in his knowledge of things, both human and divine. The general admiration he had gained, caused as I have heard, the Earl of Northumberland to make him Paymaster of the Navy, which he discharged with equal diligence and integrity. Being then elected a Member of Parliament he appeared a vehement Asserter of the rights and liberties of his Country; insomuch that he was soon reckon'd among the chief Oppossers of the Court Party, who notwithstanding they were all older than he, yet none of them were superiour to him either in Authority or Wisdom; but in sanctity of life and piety not one his Equal. During the War he lived with great frugality and gave his utmost assistance both by his industry and advice towards the carrying on the affairs of the Parliament. When after a vast effusion as well of money, as blood with little or no advantage to their present Circumstances; but on the contrary, the effect of their victories was defeated either by the disagreement of the Generals, or by their ignorance and perfidiousness; so that all their affairs stood in a wavering and uncertain condition He delivered thus boldly his opinion to all the Principal Officers both at Scotland, [sic] that the chief command of the Army should be made void, and the Army itself new modelled. Whereupon by his assistance out of four powerful armies and their Commanders one great Army was compos'd, of which the Lord Farfax was made a General. Thus being restor'd to good disciplin, fortune chang'd, and success attended their Arms. By this means having stir'd up the envy and hatred of a great many against him, who often endeavord to ensnare him, and tho dayly admonisht to take care of himself; nevertheless being fixt upon his design, and secure in his own mind, he did not at all alter his usual course of Life. A few months after, being in bed and asleep, he was awakt about midnight by a terrible knocking at the doors, which suden accident greivously frighted his Lady, the servants crying out that there were Theifs breaking open the doors, some try'd to get out of the House, others endeavor'd to hinder the Thiefs from breaking in; whereas H orderd his Servants to open the Doors, which was no sooner done but there enter'd an officer sent from the Army, and attended by abundance of Gentlemen to inform him of a Battle fought near Naseby, wherin Farfax had an intire Victory over the Kings forces, the Royal Army routed, and its Party ruin'd and destroy'd beyond all hopes of recovery. Having heard this joyful news by which he saw his Party was not only establisht, but himself likewise made secure, and an immortal glory obtain'd for him by that Success; Very well, says he, I'm glad to hear the News, so turning away, went again to bed, and always preserved the same steady resolution of mind, without being ever transported with joy or ruffled and disturbed with Anger; and fearless and unmov'd in danger, so that by obeying reason, he at once seem'd to renounce all kind of unbecoming passions and affections: nay, such was his Magnanimity, that if the frame of the whole world had been dissolv'd and gon to rack about his ears, he would have remained undaunted in the midst of its ruins.

He was a Man of a midle Stature, and rather inclining to fat: his Countenance was grave and serene, with an Air that was august and venerable: his Conversation was diverting and easie; with a good degree of Eloquence and Wit, full of facetious and innocent mirth. He had the mildest disposition imaginable, his Principles were honest and sincere, ready to do right to all Mankind, grateful and obliging to those he esteem'd good; of an inviolable Fidelity; One whom no body ever repented trusting with the most important affairs. Tho his Eloquence was great, his justice and prudence were much greater, as those who consulted him in matters of the highest consequence always acknowledg'd. He often used to bring over the Parliament to his

Single Opinion, when their own sentiments and debates, till his
were heard, had a different tendency and view. His very Enimies
being overcome by the force of his Arguments frequently yielded
to him. At length, to the detriment and misfortune of England
his Authority was rejected, and the Advice of others prefer'd to
his, which occasioned almost the destruction of the Nation. He
was not a little conversant in human Learning, but th'roly
vers'd and skill'd in the Sacred Writings. In the execution of
business he took the pains upon himself, and confer'd the reward due to his industry upon others; He was as sollicitous for
the public good, as he was negligent of his own private interest,
leaving the care of his domestic affairs intirely to his Wife. He
never endeavour'd to accumulate Riches, and when by the increase of the Naval Forces, the Revenue of his Place grew to an
immense Sum, he Presently vacated and abolisht the Office;
and tho the profit ceased his care and diligence still continued.

He was an absolute Master of the Naval affairs, he invented
and perfected that kind of vessel, they call, a Frigat, which at
this time is so famous all over the world. He zealously promoted
the peace with Holland, and helpt to carry on vigorously whatever War was begun by any other Nation. His industry and prudence did not less contribute to the obtaining of Victories than
the Valour of the Generals. There was a long and particular
Friendship contracted between Cromwell and him, which he
broke off as soon as he observ'd Cromwell to aim at the sole
power, and attempt it by force. He was never to be captivated
by fine words, and never to be chang'd by rewards or menaces,
but constantly adhear'd to what he thought just: and proposed
to Cromwell no other way of renewing their Friendship, but
that of quitting his Usurpation; and he alone unarm'd and
imprisoned us'd severely to condemn him for his illegal power,
for being puffd up and elevated with prosperity, and usurping
the Command of the Army, by which reflexions he often dis-
turbd and terrify'd him.

Now that Valor and wisdom and that Glory of unblemish'd
life, which were so long his defence and bulwark prov'd afterwards the cause of his untimely end; for when Cromwell had by
his artifice corrupted the Army, their regular discipline decayd

and vanish'd, and the Soldiers began to be turbulent and seditious, and subject to bribery, and in contempt of the Oath they had taken to the Parliament, rise up against it, and destroyed the public peace by their unnatural devisions. The Nation growing weary of its burthen, and almost sinking under it, did then respect their Exil'd King, as the final remedy of their Evils. The Friends of Sr Harry Vane urg'd him to provide for his safety, and that those who were accounted Guilty, ought to prepare for their Escape. He answerd that he was conscious of nothing that ought to create in him either shame or fear; and to those who insisted farther upon it, he said, that as he was far from despising or deserting the Public good, so he thought it base and unworthy to neglect that for his own private Security. For his part that he desir'd life no longer, than while he might be serviceable to his Country; but to ask it of his Enimies, who would be proud of the fame and reputation of so much Clemency, he disdain'd that as an ungrateful and unprofitable Office. Presently after a while, he was seiz'd by the Guards and put into Prison; from whence he was carried to the Island of Sylly, where he continued two years, refuseing several opportunities which were offer'd him of makeing his Escape. As soon as he was sent for to London, he was brought upon his Tryal and after the Indictment was read he pleaded guilty, confessing all that was laid to his Charge, and then provd them to be all agreeable to Equity, and that he had don nothing contrary to Law. And to some of his Friends who tryed a little to mollify his strict and steady virtue, he said, that hitherto he had shew'd himself the Leader and Conductor of Others, and if they in the day of temptation and tryal should appear with a wavering resolution and courage, they would inevitably suffer and be destroyed, and which if he should do, seeing he was the Author not only of his own but others Crimes he should ruin and blacken his own reputation, and also betray his Country by so base and inglorious a fear. The Judge too began to accuse him of being wilful and Stubbon, for which they declar'd he deserv'd to dye since he was inform'd of the Kings Clemency to him, in case he had yielded himself Guilty without defense or reply but thus arrogantly to defend himself was more criminal than all his other treasonable Practices: and that it was now to no purpose to consider what he might have done for his own preservation; since what he had done was by all confess'd and Universally known. But certainly an Action ought to be determin'd by Law before it can be adjudged and pronounced a Crime, and no body unless by an actual Violation of a Law, can be thought Guilty of breaking the Laws. If therefore Sr Harry Vane acted according to the Laws of his Country, and is notwithstanding accus'd and convicted of Crimes; tis surely absurd to say, that the defence of himself can be imputed as a Crime. For he was never a Man that considered what would most likely turn to his own advantage; he consider'd only what was in itself, equitable, true and just, and would probably contribute to the good of his Country. He was not sollicitous about obtaining or meriting the Kings favour by the Actions of his life; nor much concerned at his displeasure: his only aim being not to live long but well; and if he could not be secure of his life without forfeiting his innocence he was heartily willing to offer up his life for an everlasting memorial and testimony to truth and justice. So when they saw that his mind was infinitely exalted above all the Arts of flattery and never to be enervated by the severest inflictions of punishment; and altho they had slaughter'd a great many noble and brave Men to make way for the Subversion of our tottering liberty, and the Corruption of that virtue which was odious to the Restor'd Prince it was resolved to sacrifice him as a finishing Stroke. For none of the forementioned Gentlemen any more than himself were publicly condemn'd and sentenc'd to death by the Judges, but makeing a Shew as if they intended to be so, they left the Bench. After which he was carried back to Prison, where for a few days his Friends were permitted to visit him. He appear'd with the utmost tranquillity of mind, and recommended to them always to preserve a constant and steddy behaviour and resolution in the greatest adversity, and then they would not fail to assert the rights and Liberties of their Country against those wicked Ministers of whome a multitude should be found in all Ages, who would level their pernicious practices at the Subversion of the Government, and the utter extirpation of liberty and Property. And he had likewise observ'd that many under the specious pretence of defending the Protestant and established Religion, were endeavouring to undermine it, by the connivance and encouragment of licentious Principles in all those who would servilely and implicitly obey them, and be the tools and instruments of their Wickedness. Tho still he hop'd that if his Friends would in good earnest follow his advice, they might restore their Religion, Laws and Property, and settle them upon a durable and firm foundation.

Upon the very day he dy'd, he was well dress'd, haveing put on a new Suit of Cloaths, and appearing with a Chearfull countenance, went to the Place of execution, which was guarded and encompass'd with Soldiers, where as soon as he came, he began to make a Speech to the People, but the Officer fearing lest he should say anything reflecting upon the King, ordered the Trumpets to sound, and the Soldiers to Hussay that so he might not be heard; therefore finding that they would not suffer him to speak publicly, he turn'd to his Friends, and talkt a little with them, and then with great zeal and devotion pray'd to God: which some of the Magistrates who stood near him observing, askt him whether he did not pray for the King too, yes, says he, I do and implore of God that many and those the best and most Glorious things may be granted him; which are that he may withdraw himself from his most pestilential and flagitious intentions, and pursue at last a wise and just administration; and ever consult that which may be most for his own advantage and happiness, and the prosperity of the Nation. So turning again to his Friends, he repeated by exhortation to 'em of Constancy and fidelity, and tryumphing over his own and the Enimies of his Country by his invincible Spirit and magnanimity, he laid down his Head, which being Struck off at one blow, without the lest Sign of motion or any Convulsive Struglings; he calmly gave up his Spirit.

Thus dyed the Man, who for his Genious, his Eloquencies, his Virtue, his Wisdom and Piety was so eminent as even to be dreaded. Who was the greatest ornament of his Country; A faithful Witness to Truth which already lamented his loss, and to Justice for which he was so much envied. And as he was once the Defense of a reviving Liberty, so he was now the willing and happy Victim of its Decay. Nothing could have devided him from the public Service, except Death, which was to him pleasant, but to his Country intollerable greivous. Now whether this Kingdom after his punishment, can remain fixt and durable, or rather whether by the Spilling of innocent blood, being infected with the poyson and pestilence of the Authors of his Death, it will not wither and perish, time the discoverer of all Events will shew.

Finis

SELECT BIBLIOGRAPHY

PRIMARY SOURCES

A. MANUSCRIPT

I. PUBLIC RECORD OFFICE

(i) *Admiralty*

Minutes of the Committee of Admiralty, 8 October 1646–29 February 1648. Adm. 7/673.

(ii) *Chancery*

Close Roll C 54/3550, Grant of lands by the Commissioners for the sale of Dean and Chapters' lands to Sir Henry Vane, 26 October 1650.

Close Roll C 54/3568, Sir Henry Vane's surrender of his office as Treasurer of the Navy, 31 December 1650.

Close Roll C 54/3589, Grant by the earl of Lindsey of church property in Lincolnshire to Sir Henry Vane, 18 November 1650.

(iii) *Exchequer*

Pipe and Audit Office Declared Accounts: Treasurer of the Navy.
    A.O.I./1704/81   1 January–31 December 1638.
    A.O.I./1704/83   1 January–31 December 1639.
    A.O.I./1706/90   13 May 1645–31 December 1646.
    E 351/2286   1 January 1646–7–31 December 1647.
    E 351/2287   1 January 1647–8–12 May 1649.
    E 351/2288   13 May 1649–31 December 1650.

(iv) *State Papers Domestic*

S.P. 21/1–8, 10, 16–23, 27   1 June 1644–1 August 1648   Draft Day Books and other records of the Committee of Both Kingdoms.

S.P. 25/1–4, 21   17 February 1649–30 August 1651   Draft Order Books, Council of State.

II. BRITISH MUSEUM

D'Ewes, Sir Symonds, *A Journall of the Parliament begunne November 3 Tuesday Anno Domini 1640*. 3 November 1640–3 November 1645. Harl. 162–6.

Whittaker, Lawrence, *Diary of proceedings in the House of Commons 8 October 1642–8 July 1647*. Add. 31,116.

Yonge, Walter, *Journal of proceedings in the House of Commons 19 September 1642–10 December 1645*. Add. 18,777–80.

Harrington of Kelweston, John, *The Memorandum book of*, March 1646–November 1653 (various periods).

Whitelocke, Bulstrode, *Memorials*. Add. 37,343 and 37,344. November 1634–July 1649.

Despatches of French Envoys, 1644 and 1645. Add. 5,460 and 5,461.

Minutes . . . of the proceedings of the parliamentary commissioners of the Admiralty and Navy from 1645 to 1648. Add. 9,305.

Letters to Henry Cromwell, 1655–9. Lansdowne 823.

III. CORPORATION OF LONDON, GUILDHALL RECORD OFFICE

Journal of Common Council vol. 39   7 November 1639–29 October 1642.
Journal of Common Council vol. 40   24 March 1641–2–2 June 1649.
Common Hall Book, vol. 1   5 November 1642–20 October 1646.

IV. SOMERSET HOUSE

Prerogative Court of Canterbury Wills
    Sir Henry Vane senior 1655. Register Aylett 159.
    Sir Henry Vane junior's son, Henry. Register Laud 120.

V. BODLEIAN LIBRARY, OXFORD

Rawlinson A 220–4   March 1643–October 1649   Orders and Order Books of the Committee of Navy and Customs.

Rawlinson C 416   April–September 1645   Order Book of the Committee of the Admiralty.

Rawlinson A 225–7   October 1650–August 1653   Order Books of the Committee of the Admiralty.

Clarendon MSS 60, 61, 68, 69 *et al.*   News-letters.

Parliamentary Diary of Sir Thomas Peyton   6 November 1640–17 March 1642 (Microfilm no. 39).

Rawlinson C 179   Minute Book of the Proceedings of the Council of State from 19 May to 10 August 1659.

VI. CITY AND COUNTY OF KINGSTON UPON HULL, GUILDHALL

Corporation Bench Books
    vol. v   1609–50
    vol. vi   1650–64
Letters 1643–53.

VII. RABY CASTLE

Estate Deeds belonging to Lord Barnard.

VIII. HERTFORDSHIRE COUNTY RECORD OFFICE, HERTFORD

Panshanger MSS   D/EP F 24, 45.

B. PRINTED

(i) Letters

ABBOTT, W. C., *Writings and Speeches of Oliver Cromwell*, 2 vols. (Cambridge, Mass., 1937–9).

BAILLIE, R., *The Letters and Journals of*, ed. D. Laing, 3 vols. (Bannatyne Club, Edinburgh, 1841–2).

CARTE, T., ed., *A collection of Original Letters, 1641–68 . . .*, 2 vols. (London, 1739).

DYVE, SIR LEWIS, 'The Tower of London Letter-Book of, 1646–47', ed. H. G. Tibbutt, *Publications of the Bedfordshire Historical Records Soc.*, vol. xxxviii (1958), 49–97.

MONTEREUIL, JEAN DE, and the brothers DE BELLIÈVRE, French ambassadors in England and Scotland, 1645–8, *The diplomatic correspondence of*, ed. J. G. Fotheringham, 2 vols. (Edinburgh, 1898–9).

MORDAUNT, JOHN VISCOUNT, *The Letter-Book of, 1658–1660*, Camden Soc. (London, 1945).

NICHOLAS, SIR EDWARD, *Correspondence of*, ed. Sir G. F. Warner, Camden Soc., 4 vols. (London, 1886–1920).

NICKOLLS, J., *Original Letters and Papers of State . . . found among the political collections of Mr. John Milton* (London, 1743).

(ii) Diaries

BURTON, THOMAS, *Diary of . . .*, ed. J. T. Rutt, 4 vols. (London, 1828).

D'EWES, SIR SIMONDS, *The Journal of . . .*, ed. W. Notestein (New Haven, Connecticut, 1923).

D'EWES, SIR SIMONDS, *The Journal of . . .*, ed. W. H. Coates (New Haven, Connecticut, 1942).

NORTHCOTE, SIR JOHN, *Notebook of*, ed. A. H. A. Hamilton (London, 1877).

VERNEY, SIR RALPH, *Notes of proceedings in the Long Parliament, by*, ed. J. Bruce, Camden Soc. (London, 1845).

(iii) Calendars

Calendar of State Papers, Domestic series. The reign of Charles I, 1625–49. 22 vols., 1858–93. Addenda vol., 1629–49 (London, 1897).

Calendar of State Papers, Domestic series. Commonwealth and Protectorate, 1649–60. 13 vols., 1875–86.

Calendar of State Papers, Domestic series. Reign of Charles II, 1660–81, 22 vols., 1860–1921.

Calendar of State Papers and Manuscripts relating to English affairs . . . in the archives . . . of Venice . . ., vols. 25–32, 1924–31, ed. H. F. Brown and A. B. Hind (London, 1900–25).

Calendar of the Proceedings of the Committee for Compounding, 1643–60, ed. M. A. E. Green, 5 vols. (London, 1889–92).

(iv) *Pamphlets*

GREENE, GILES, *A Declaration of Vindication of the Honour of the Parliament; and of the Committee of the Navy and Customs against all Traducers.* 1 September 1647. E 405(8).

ST JOHN, O., *The Case of Oliver St John, Esq.* 30 July 1660. E 1035(5).

VANE, SIR HENRY, JUNIOR, *The Retired Man's Meditations* (London, 20 April 1655).

—, *A Healing Question Propounded* (London, 12 May 1656).

—, *Proceeds of the Protector* (London, 1656).

—, *A Needful Corrective* (London, 1659) (Bodl.)

(References to other pamphlets and all diurnals quoted are given in footnotes to the text. Those prefixed E are in the Thomason Collection, British Museum.)

(v) *Miscellaneous*

BAXTER, RICHARD, *Reliquiae Baxterianae*, ed. M. Sylvester (London, 1696).

—, *Holy Commonwealth* (London, 1659).

BERKELEY, SIR JOHN, *Memoirs of*, in *A Narrative by John Ashburnham of his attendance on King Charles the First* (London, 1830).

BURNET, G., *History of my Own Time*, ed. O. Airy, 2 vols. (Oxford, 1897).

CARY, H., ed., *Memorials of the Great Civil War, 1646–52*, 2 vols. (London, 1842).

CLARENDON, EDWARD EARL OF, *The History of the Rebellion and the Civil Wars in England*, ed. W. D. Macray, 6 vols. (Oxford, 1888).

—, *State Papers collected by*, ed. R. Scope and T. Monkhouse, 3 vols., fol. (Oxford, 1767–86).

Commons, Journals of the House of, vols. ii to vii, 1803–.

Durham and Northumberland Records of the Committees for Compounding with delinquent royalists in . . . 1643–60, ed. R. Welford, Surtees Soc. (1905).

FIRTH, C. H. and RAIT, C. S., *Acts and Ordinances of the Interregnum, 1642–1660* (Oxford, 1906).

FIRTH, C. H., ed., *Selections from the Papers of William Clarke*, Camden Soc., 4 vols. (London, 1891–1901).

GARDINER, S. R., ed., *The Constitutional Documents of the Puritan Revolution, 1625–60* (Oxford, 1906).

HALLER, W., *Liberty and Reformation in the Puritan Revolution* (New York, 1955).

Historical Manuscripts Commission.

  Report on the MSS of F. W. Leyborne-Popham, Norwich (1899).

  Report on the MSS of Sir Harry Verney, bart., Report vii, App. i, 433–509.

  Report on the Percy MSS, 10th Report, App., part iv.

  Report on the Marten-Loder MSS, 13th Report, App. iv, 378–404.

  Report on the MSS of the House of Lords, Report vi, part i, App.

HOLLES, DENZIL, LORD, *Memoirs of*, reprinted in *Select Tracts*, ed. F. Maseres, 2 vols. (London, 1815), 183–320.

HOLLOND, J., *Two Discourses of the Navy, 1638 and 1659*, ed. J. R. Tanner (Navy Records Soc., 1896).

Lords, Journals of the House of, vols. iv–vii.

LUDLOW, E., *Memoirs of*, ed. C. H. Firth, 2 vols. (Oxford, 1894).

The Rump, or an exact collection of the choycest poems and songs relating to the late times, reprinted London (1874).

RUSHWORTH, JOHN, *Historical Collections*, 7 vols. (London, 1659–1701).

Somers Tracts, *A collection of scarce and valuable tracts . . . selected from . . . public as well as private libraries, particularly that of the late Lord Somers*, ed. Sir W. Scott (London, 1809–15).

Statutes of the Realm, ed. A. Luders, T. E. Tomlins, J. Raithby, 1810–28 (London).

THURLOE, J., *A Collection of the State Papers of John Thurloe, Esq.*, ed. T. Birch, 7 vols. (London, 1742).

WHITELOCKE, BULSTRODE, *Memorials of English Affairs*, 4 vols. (Oxford, 1853).

WILLIAMS, ROGER, *The Bloody Tenent of persecution . . . discussed* (London, 1644). Reprinted by the Hansard Knollys Soc. in *Tracts on liberty of conscience and persecution, 1614–61*, ed. E. B. Underhill (London, 1848).

—, *The Bloody Tenent yet more Bloody . . .*, 28 April 1652 (London), E 661(6).

SECONDARY SOURCES

A. PRINTED

BROWN, L. F., *The Political Activities of the Baptists and Fifth Monarchy Men in England during the Interregnum* (Washington, 1912).

DALTON, C., *History of the Wrays of Glentworth*, 2 vols. (London, 1880–1).

DAVIES, GODFREY, 'Elections for Richard Cromwell's Parliament', *English Historical Review*, lxiii (1948), 493.

—, *The Restoration of Charles II* (San Marino, California, 1955).

FIRTH, C. H., 'Cromwell and Sir Henry Vane', *English Historical Review*, xxvi, (1911), 751–4.

—, 'Letters concerning the Dissolution of Cromwell's Last Parliament', *English Historical Review*, vii (1892), 102–10.

GAMMELL, W., *Life of Roger Williams*, Library of American Biography, vol. iv (Boston, 1846).

GARDINER, S. R., *History of England from the Accession of James I to the Outbreak of the Civil War*, 10 vols. (London, 1883–4).

—, *History of the Great Civil War, 1642–49*, 4 vols. (London, 1893).

—, *History of the Commonwealth and Protectorate, 1649–56*, 3 vols. (London, 1894–1901).

GUIZOT, F. P. G., *History of Richard Cromwell and the Restoration of Charles II*, trans. A. R. Scoble, 2 vols. (London, 1856).

HEXTER, J. F., *The Reign of King Pym* (Cambridge, Massachusetts, 1941).

HOSMER, J. K., *The Life of Young Sir Henry Vane* (Boston and London, 1888).

HUTCHINSON, T., *History of the Colony of Massachusetts Bay* (Boston, Massachusetts, 1765–8).

JUDSON, MARGARET, *The Political Thought of Sir Henry Vane the Younger* (Pennsylvania, 1969).

KEELER, M. F., *The Long Parliament 1640–41* (Philadelphia, 1954).

KNOWLES, J. D., *Memoir of Roger Williams* (Boston, 1834).

MASSON, D., *Life of Milton*, 7 vols. (Cambridge and London, 1859–94).

NOTESTEIN, W., 'The establishment of the Committee of Both Kingdoms', *American Historical Review*, xvii (1912), 477–95.

OPPENHEIM, M. A., *A History of the Administration of the Royal Navy . . . 1509–1660* (London, 1896).

—, 'The Navy of the Commonwealth, 1649–60', *English Historical Review*, xi (1896), 20–58.

PEARL, V., *London and the Outbreak of the Puritan Revolution, 1625–43* (London, 1961).

Return of the names of every . . . member in each parliament, 2 vols. s.l. (1878).

RETZ, J. F. P. DE GONDI, CARDINAL DE, *Mémoires*, ed. M. Allem (Paris, 1956).

SHAW, W. A., *History of the English Church during the Civil Wars and under the Commonwealth, 1640–1660*, 2 vols. (London, 1900).

WILLCOCK, J., *The Life of Sir Henry Vane the Younger* (London, 1913).

WOOD, A., *Athenae Oxonienses . . .*, ed. W. Bliss (Oxford, 1817).

—, *Fasti Oxonienses* (London, 1813).

WOOLRYCH, A. H., 'The Good Old Cause and the Fall of the Protectorate', *Cambridge Historical Journal*, xiii (1957), 2, 133–61.

YULE, G., *The Independents in the English Civil War* (Cambridge, 1958).

B. UNPRINTED THESIS

BROWN, G. H., *The Place of Sir Arthur Hesilrige in English Politics 1659–60* (Oxford B.Litt., 1949).

INDEX

Abbott, W. C., 158
Admiral, Lord High: *see* Northumberland, earl of; Warwick, earl of
Agostini, Venetian ambassador, 23 n. 4, 38, 48, 51, 53, 57, 65, 76, 233 n. 6
Aquidneck, Rhode Island, 199
Army, New Model: *see* New Model Army
—, Scottish: *see* Scotland, Army
Ashley Cooper, Antony, earl of Shaftesbury, 276
Atkins, Sir Robert, 68
Aylmer, G. E., 7
Ayscough, Sir Edward, 84
—, Sir George, Admiral, 147
—, Sir John, 12

Baillie, 25, 44, 63, 68, 195–7, 244, 249, 250, 286
Balmerino, Lord, 81
Baltic, 213, 214, 219, 221, 222, 276
Barbados, 155, 261
Barnard Castle, 2, 3 n. 4, 7
Barnardiston, Sir Nathaniel, 70, 263
Battles: *see* Cropredy, Dunbar, Dungeness, Kentish Knock, Marston Moor, Naseby, Newburn, Portland, Scariffhollis
Baxter, Richard, 215 n. 1, 218, 227, 228, 244, 287
Bedford, earl of (William Russell), 45
Belleau, Lincs., 172, 200, 202, 204, 205, 242
Bence, Alexander, 127, 263
Berkeley, Sir John, 99, 287

Biddle, John, 197–8
Bishop, George, 223
Blackborne, Robert, 180
Blake, Robert, 144, 147, 151, 175, 177–9, 181–3, 189, 261, 273, 274
Blakiston, John, 89, 263
Bland, John, 103, 136
Bond, Dennis, 151, 166, 167, 173–5, 258, 272
Booth, Sir George, 220, 225, 235
Bordeaux-Neufville, Antoine de, 222
Boston, Massachusetts, 4, 5
Boteler, Major General William, 214–15
Bourne, Nehemiah, 176, 188, 216
Bradshaw, John, 155, 205, 259
Brereton, Sir William, 90, 103
Brewster, Thomas, 210
Bridgwater, Som., 79
Brienne, Henri de Loménie, Comte de, 65
Bristol, 207, 208, 223
Brodrick, Alan, 215
Brooke, Sir Basil, 38, 42, 43, 45
Brooke, Lord (Robert Greville), 4, 29 n. 5
Browne, Samuel, 34, 42, 45, 59, 66, 71, 76, 89, 236, 246, 247
Buchanan, David, 69 n. 4, 74
Bures, M. de, 18
Burnet, Bishop Gilbert, 23, 109, 297
Burrell, Andrew, 93
Burrough, Edward, 223
Burton, Thomas, 211, 218, 286

Camden House MSS., 32 n. 4
Capel, Sir Arthur, 23

Monck, George, 179, 185, 189, 231, 274

Montereuil, Jean de, 81–4, 88, 100, 286

Mordaunt, Lord, 207, 286

Morland, Sir Samuel, 217–18 n. 5, 222, 231, 237 n. 2

Morley, Col. Herbert, 219, 225, 266, 273

Moyer, Samuel, 210

Naseby, battle of, 87 n. 1, 241, 278

Navy
impressment, 118, 119, 185
Treasurer of, 7, 8, 10, 22 n. 2, 46, 57, 58, 90, 91, 105, 116, 117, 120, 122–5, 128–31, 133–7, 140, 163, 169 n. 1, 170, 229, 238, 252, 254, 256, 257, 261, 268, 270, 279, 284
Deputy Treasurer of, 7, 137, 138, 164, 170, 171, 256
Treasurer's House, Deptford, 76, 85, 105, 130

Netherlands, Dutch, 3, 40, 41, 50, 81, 145–7, 151, 154, 180, 181, 182, 184–6, 199, 214, 221, 243, 248, 249, 255, 258, 259, 261, 275

Neville, Henry, 140, 227, 273

New Model Army, 66, 67, 77, 103, 125, 277

Newburn, battle of, 22 n. 2

Newcastle, 89
—, earl of, 26

Newport, Isle of Wight, peace negotiations at, 107, 109, 115, 247, 248, 253, 257

Newtown, Massachusetts, 5, 6

Nicholas, Sir Edward, 8, 80, 224, 233, 286

Northumberland, earl of (Algernon Percy), 3, 7, 9, 13, 67, 75, 84, 108, 117, 118, 120, 121, 232 n. 5, 255, 275

Oppenheim, M. A., 129, 136 n. 2, 168 n. 6

Ordinance, Self-Denying, 1, 55, 57–59, 125, 126, 128, 129, 135, 176, 256, 260

Osbaldeston, Lambert, 3, 71, 72

Oxford, peace negotiations at, 21, 29, 52, 64, 69, 72
—, university of, 3, 114

Palatine, Charles Lewis, Elector, 54, 55, 59

Palmer, Sir Geoffrey, 235

Parker, Henry, 35 n. 2

Pauw, Adrian, 146, 154

Pelham, Peregrine, 12, 80, 106, 127, 193, 250, 251, 263

Pelham, Sir Thomas, 12

Pembroke, earl of (Philip Herbert), 12, 73, 146

Penn, William, Admiral, 186, 187

Penn, William, 276

Pennington, Isaac, 28, 31 n. 1, 174 n. 3

Peters, Hugh, 4, 5, 72 n. 3

Pett, Peter, 164, 182

Peyton, Sir Thomas, 123, 285

Phillips, Wendell, 260 n. 3

Pierrepont, William, 51, 62, 64, 68, 73, 75, 78, 89, 99, 103, 110, 114, 248, 266

Popham, Edward, 158, 162, 163, 165, 167, 175

Portland, battle of, 151, 184, 261

Portsmouth, 181, 185, 186, 229, 230

Portugal, 145, 167–9, 222

'Pride's Purge', 113, 139, 248

Prideaux, Edmund, 26, 57, 64, 66, 89, 90, 112, 249, 263

Prynne, William, 136, 222, 223, 227

Pye, Sir Robert, 116

Pym, John, 4, 10, 11, 12, 15, 16, 19, 20, 21, 23, 25, 26, 27, 29, 32, 57, 58, 124, 143, 194, 245, 288

Pyne, John, 73, 74

Quakers, 219, 223, 224; see also Bishop, George; Burrough, Edward; Fox, George; Fry, John; Penn, William